THE FOOD INDUSTRIES OF EUROPE IN THE NINETEENTH AND TWENTIETH CENTURIES

The industrialization of food preservation and processing has been a dramatic development across Europe during modern times. This book sets out its story from the beginning of the nineteenth century when preservation of food from one harvest to another was essential to prevent hunger and even famine. Population growth and urbanization depended upon a break out from the 'biological *ancien régime*' in which hunger was an ever-present threat. The application of mass production techniques by the food industries was essential to the modernization of Europe.

From the mid-nineteenth century the development of food industries followed a marked regional pattern. After an initial growth in north-west Europe, the spread towards south-east Europe was slowed by social, cultural and political constraints. This was notable in the post-Second World War era. The picture of change in this volume is presented by case studies of countries ranging from the United Kingdom in the west to Romania in the east. All illustrate the role of food industries in creating new products that expanded the traditional cereal-based diet of pre-industrial Europe.

Industrially preserved and processed foods provided new flavours and appetizing novelties which led to brand names recognized by consumers everywhere. Product marketing and advertising became fundamental to modern food retailing so that Europe's largest food producers, Danone, Nestlé and Unilever, are numbered amongst the world's biggest companies.

T0300347

*Dedicated to the memory of Adel Peter den Hartog (1937–2012),
geographer and nutritionist.
Founder member and Past President of the International Commission
for European Research into European Food History.*

Adel den Hartog
Reproduced with permission from his son-in-law, Edward de Bock

The Food Industries of Europe in the Nineteenth and Twentieth Centuries

Edited by

DEREK J. ODDY

and

ALAIN DROUARD

Routledge
Taylor & Francis Group

LONDON AND NEW YORK

First published 2013 by Ashgate Publishing

Published 2016 by Routledge
2 Park Square, Milton Park, Abingdon, Oxfordshire OX14 4RN
711 Third Avenue, New York, NY 10017, USA

First issued in paperback 2016

Routledge is an imprint of the Taylor & Francis Group, an informa business

British Library Cataloguing in Publication Data
The food industries of Europe in the nineteenth and twentieth centuries.
   1. Food industry and trade–Europe–History–19th century. 2. Food industry and trade–Europe–History–20th century. 3. Processed foods–Europe–History–19th century.
   4. Processed foods–Europe–History–20th century. 5. Food–Preservation–Technological innovations–Social aspects–Europe–History–19th century. 6. Food–Preservation–Technological innovations–Social aspects–Europe–History–20th century. 7. Food habits–Europe–History–19th century. 8. Food habits–Europe–History–20th century.
   I. Oddy, Derek J. II. Drouard, Alain.
   338.4'7664'094–dc23

The Library of Congress has cataloged the printed edition as follows:
Oddy, Derek J.
   The food industries of Europe in the nineteenth and twentieth centuries / by Derek J. Oddy and Alain Drouard.
      pages cm
   Includes bibliographical references and index.
   ISBN 978-1-4094-5439-7 (hardback : alk. paper)
   1. Food industry and trade–Europe–History–19th century.
   2. Food industry and trade–Europe–History–20th century.
   I. Drouard, Alain. II. Title.
   HD9000.5.O33 2013
   338.1'94–dc23

2013000250

ISBN 13: 978-1-138-24898-4 (pbk)
ISBN 13: 978-1-4094-5439-7 (hbk)

Contents

List of Figures *vii*
List of Tables *ix*
Notes on Contributors *xi*
Preface *xiii*
Acknowledgements *xv*

1 Introduction 1
  Derek J. Oddy

PART I THE ORIGINS AND GROWTH OF INDUSTRIAL ORGANIZATION

2 Pioneering Spadework in the History of the German Food Industry
  during the Nineteenth and Early Twentieth Centuries: Beet Sugar,
  Wheat Starch and Health Foods 17
  Karl-Peter Ellerbrock and Hans-Jürgen Teuteberg

3 Vinegar and Sugar: The Early History of Factory-Made Jams,
  Pickles and Sauces in Britain 41
  Peter J. Atkins

4 Rural Capitalism: The *Société des Caves de Roquefort*, from c.1840
  to 1914 55
  Sylvie Vabre

5 Modernizing the Mediterranean Olive-Oil Industry, 1850s–1930s 71
  Ramon Ramon-Muñoz

PART II CREATING NEW FOODS

6 'The biggest chocolate factory in the world': The Menier Chocolate
  Factory in Noisiel 91
  Alain Drouard

7   'Czech chocolate is the best!' Nationalism in the Food Industry
     in the Czech Lands around the Year 1900   107
     Martin Franc

8   Margarine in Competition with Butter in Germany (1872–1933):
     The Example of Van den Bergh's Margarine Factory in Kleve   119
     Sabine Merta

9   The Nutritional Transformation of Danish Pork, 1887–1960   133
     Tenna Jensen

10   The Rise of the Frozen-Fish Industry in Iceland and Norway:
     The Case of Fish Fingers   147
     Guðmundur Jónsson and Örn D. Jónsson

PART III   THE EFFECT OF FOOD TECHNOLOGY ON
CONSUMPTION PATTERNS

11   Food Labelling and Packaging in the Dutch Food Industry:
     Persuading and Informing Consumers, 1870–1950s   165
     Adel P. den Hartog

12   Promoting Packaging and Selling Self-Service: The Rapid
     Modernization of the Swedish Food Retail Trade   181
     Jenny Lee and Ulrika Torell

13   Food Preservation in Flemish Women's Magazines, 1945–1960   199
     Anneke Geyzen

14   The Growth of Bread Consumption among Romanian Peasants,
     1950–1980   213
     Lucian Scrob

15   From Roast Beef to Chicken Nuggets: How Technology changed
     Meat Consumption in Britain in the Twentieth Century   231
     Derek J. Oddy

16   The European Food Industries in Perspective   247
     Derek J. Oddy

Index   *263*

List of Figures

2.1   Hoffmann's Starch was the market leader in nineteenth-century Germany   25
2.2   The Maggi company was the pioneer of the modern soup industry   28
2.3   Dr. Volkmar Klopfer's cereal-products factory, Dresden   30

4.1   Making Roquefort cheese mid-nineteenth century   58
4.2   Making Roquefort cheese in 1913   66

5.1   Olive crushers in the Mediterranean basin in the nineteenth and early twentieth centuries   73
5.2   Olive-oil presses in the Mediterranean basin in the nineteenth and early twentieth centuries   74
5.3   The regional mechanization of the olive-oil industry in Italy, 1903–1911 (firms using mechanical power, as a percentage of each region's total olive-oil firms)   77
5.4   The adoption of hydraulic presses in Spain by regions, 1857–1911 (1890 = 100)   78
5.5   The mechanization of the olive-oil mills and factories in Italy and Spain, 1903–c.1935 (olive-oil firms or factories using mechanical power, as a percentage of each country's total olive-oil firms or factories)   79

6.1   General view of the Menier works at Noisiel   94
6.2   View of the grinding shed at Noisiel   98
6.3   The Valle Menier plantation near Lake Nicaragua   101

7.1   Slavic chocolate advertisement   113

9.1   Differences in the proportions of Landrace, Yorkshire, Crossbred, and the Ideal export pig, 1890   135

11.1   A grocery shop in 1841   167
11.2   An advertisement for tinned sterilized full-cream milk, 1930   168
11.3   Government certified butter label, 1905 model   172

12.1   Propaganda from the Swedish packaging industry: brand-new flour
        packages and the modern equipment for the milling industry as
        presented in the trade journal *Svenska förpackningar*   184
12.2   Peepholes for the consumer   189
12.3   Mrs Consumer shopping for more than she ever intended to buy   191

13.1   Articles on food preservation types in *De Boerin/Bij de Haard*
        and *Het Rijk der Vrouw* (1945–1960)   203
13.2   Evolution of food preservation types in *De Boerin/Bij de Haard*
        (1945–1960)   204
13.3   Evolution of food preservation types in *Het Rijk der Vrouw*
        (1945–1960)   205

14.1   Percentage share of bread varieties in total bread production in
        Romania, 1950–1976   219
14.2   Total output of bread varieties in Romania (tons/year), 1950–1975   220
14.3   Quantity of industrially-produced bread per rural resident in
        Romania (kgs/head/year), 1948–1980   223
14.4   Growth indexes for urban and rural populations, urban levels of
        consumption and quantities of industrially-produced bread in
        Romania, 1948–1980   225

15.1   Steamship *Elderslie* (1884); refrigerated meat carrier   233
15.2   Steamship *Ayrshire* (1903); refrigerated meat carrier   234

16.1   The value of convenience foods: you can always invite a colleague
        home for a meal   258

List of Tables

2.1   Sugar consumption in Germany, 1800–1910   22

3.1   The origins of successful brands in pickling, potting, jams, sauces
      and essences   42

5.1   The olive-oil industry in Italy and Spain around 1935: production
      and refining   82
5.2   The modernization of the olive-oil industry in Spain and Italy by
      regions around 1935   84

9.1   The nutritional composition of Danish pork per 100 grams, 1888
      and 1914   139
9.2   The nutritional composition of Danish pork per 100 grams in the
      1950s from Groth Petersen, 1953   141
9.3   The nutritional composition of Danish pork per 100 grams in the
      1950s from Ege, 1959   142
9.4   The nutritional composition of Danish pork per 100 grams in the
      1950s from McCance and Widdowson, 1960   142

10.1 The frozen-fish industry in Iceland, 1939–1970   154

12.1 Total number of self-service shops in Western European countries
      in 1960   187

14.1 Changes in bread production, value of fixed funds, number of
      directly productive workers and average capacity of production
      per unit in Romania, 1950–1975   215
14.2 Changes in the consumption of *mămăligă* and bread in Romania,
      1906–1983   225

15.1 Numbers and size of British refrigerated vessels, 1896–1939   234
15.2 Imports of frozen meat into the United Kingdom, 1884–1926   235
15.3 Weekly household food consumption of meat in Great Britain,
      1950–2000   241

15.4   The nutritional analysis of meat and meat products in Britain in
        the 1990s   244

16.1   World trade in major perishable commodities, 1980–2000
        (million tons)   256

Notes on Contributors

Peter J. Atkins, Professor of Geography, Durham University, Durham DH1 3LE, UK. E-mail: p.j.atkins@durham.ac.uk

Alain Drouard, Director of Research (Honorary), National Centre for Scientific Research, Mail: 16 rue Parrot, 75012 Paris, France. E-mail: adrouard01@noos.fr

Karl-Peter Ellerbrock, Direktor der Stiftung Westfälisches Wirtschaftsarchiv (Head of the Westphalian Economic Archives Foundation), Dortmund, Germany. E-mail: k.ellerbrock@dortmund.ihk.de

Martin Franc, Ph.D., Researcher at the Masaryk Institute and Archives of the Academy of Sciences of the Czech Republic, Gabcikova 2362/10, 182 00 Praha 8, Czech Republic. E-mail: franc@mua.cas.cz

Anneke Geyzen, Researcher, Department of History, Social and Cultural Food Studies, Vrije Universiteit Brussel, Belgium. E-mail:Anneke.Geyzen@vub.ac.be

Adel P. den Hartog, Ph.D., formerly of the Division of Human Nutrition, Wageningen University, Postbox 8129 6700 EV Wageningen, The Netherlands. E-mail: apdenhartog@planet.nl

Tenna Jensen, Ph.D., Postdoctoral researcher, University of Copenhagen SAXO-Institute, Department of History University of Copenhagen. E-mail: tennaje@hum.ku.dk

Guðmundur Jónsson, Professor of History at the University of Iceland, School of Humanities, University of Iceland, Arnagardur, 101 Reykjaviki, Iceland. E-mail: gudmjons@hi.is

Örn D. Jónsson, School of Business, University of Iceland, Oddi, 101 Reykjavik, Iceland, E-mail: odj@hi.is

Jenny Lee, Ph.D, Researcher in the Department of Economic History, Uppsala University, Sweden. E-mail: jenny@atlanten.se

Sabine Merta, Ph.D., Kleve, Germany. E-mail: sabine.merta@web.de

Derek J. Oddy, Emeritus Professor of Economic and Social History, University of Westminster, London, UK. Mail: 51 Christchurch Avenue, London N12 0DG, UK. E-mail: DerekJOddy@aol.com

Ramon Ramon-Muñoz, Ph.D., Lecturer, Department of Economic History and Institutions, Faculty of Economics and Business, University of Barcelona, and Research Centre in Economics and Economic History 'Antoni de Capmany' (CEAC), University of Barcelona, Spain. E-mail: ramon@ub.edu

Lucian Scrob, Central European University, Budapest. E-mail: scrob_lucian@ yahoo.com

Hans-Jürgen Teuteberg, Ph.D., Emeritus Professor, Westfälische Wilhelms-Universität, Münster, Domplatz 20-22, 48143 Münster, Germany. E-mail: teuteberg-uni-muenster@gmx.de

Ulrika Torell, Ph.D., Institute for Ethnology, Nordic Museum, Stockholm, Sweden. E-mail: ulrika.torell@nordiskamuseet.se

Sylvie Vabre, Associate Professor, Department of History, Toulouse University/ Framespa-CNRS, France. E-mail: svabre@club-internet.fr

Preface

This volume arose from the discussions at the Twelfth Symposium of the International Commission for Research into European Food History (ICREFH) which took place at the University of Bologna, Italy, in September 2011. ICREFH's symposia have been held every two years since May 1989, which has been a remarkable achievement by the series of local organizers who have raised the necessary funds for them to take place. From the first meeting held in Münster, Westphalia, the established pattern has been for discussions to be held over several days and focused on various aspects of an agreed theme. Food history can be very diverse and may even appear to lack coherence, so the philosophy of ICREFH has been to examine changes in the production and consumption of food in European countries during the last two hundred or so years. This means that the emphasis has always been on social and economic development in Europe; industrialization has been the major factor affecting the lives of its people and with industrialization has come urbanization. Although the rate of change has varied in different parts of Europe from being faster and more complete in the west to slower and less pervasive in the east of the continent, over the past two centuries Europe has developed a complex industrialized food supply system which has transformed food consumption. Food processing and food manufacturing have become major industries in Europe since the late nineteenth century so there is a good case for examining how these developments occurred.

The city of Bologna, situated in the Po Valley of Northern Italy, is the capital of the administrative region Emilia-Romagna. It has preserved much of its mediaeval city centre which is characterized by towers and long stretches of arcades. It was a great privilege to hold the Symposium at Europe's oldest University and in a city which is a major centre of the food industry in Italy with a longstanding culinary tradition with typical dishes like tortellini, tortelloni and tagliatelle al ragù (bolognese sauce). The University's Department of History, Anthropology and Geography together with the Department of Paleography and Medieval Studies hosted the Symposium at the Villa Gandolfi Pallavicini on the outskirts of Bologna. The Villa Gandolfi Pallavicini is a fine example of Palladian architecture built in the first half of the seventeenth century by the Bolognese family Alamandini. The suffix Pallavicini refers to its purchase in 1773 by Gian Luca Pallavicini, a Genoese field marshal in the service of the Austrian Empire. Its eighteenth-century residents included a young Wolfgang Amadeus Mozart.

Acknowledgements

The participants in this Symposium were extremely grateful to Professor Alberto De Bernardi, Professor of Contemporary History and Director of the Department of History in the University of Bologna, and Professor Massimo Montenari, Professor of Medieval History in the University of Bologna and Director of the journal *Food and History*, for hosting this meeting in such elegant surroundings. Members of the Symposium were fully appreciative of the generous hospitality provided by the Local Organizers, Professor De Bernardi, and Professor Montenari.

The editors acknowledge with gratitude the collaboration of the contributors in keeping to the editorial timetable. They feel particular admiration for Adel den Hartog who bravely completed his chapter whilst seriously ill.

They are also grateful to Judy Oddy for her contribution to the correction and proof-reading process.

The editors, authors and publishers gratefully acknowledge permission to reproduce [material] from the Stiftung Westfälisches Wirtschaftsarchiv, Dortmund [Westphalian Business Archives, Dortmund].

Figures 12.1, 12.2 and 12.3 are reproduced by permission of the *Svenska förpackningar* (1937–1958) Malom, Akerlund & Rausing.

Figure 15.1 is reproduced by permission of the Curator of Archives, North Otago Museum, Oamaru, Aotearoa, New Zealand.

Figure 15.2 is reproduced from the photograph collection of Ian J. Farquhar by kind permission of John Clarkson and Dr Roy Fenton, Editors, *Ships in Focus Record 40*, 2008, 241.

Figure 16.1 is reproduced by kind permission of PRIVATE EYE / S.J. Russell, issue 1285, 23.

Every effort has been made to trace any copyright holders not herewith acknowledged. If there is any inadvertent omission, every endeavour will be made to rectify the error in any future editions.

ICREFH Symposia

The Current State of European Food History Research (Münster, Germany, 1989).
The Origins and Development of Food Policies in Europe (London, United Kingdom, 1991).
Food Technology, Science and Marketing (Wageningen, The Netherlands, 1993).
Food and Material Culture (Vevey, Switzerland, 1995).

Order and Disorder: the Health Implication of Eating and Drinking (Aberdeen, Scotland, 1997).
The Landscape of Food: Town, Countryside and Food Relationships (Tampere, Finland, 1999).
Eating and Drinking Out in Europe since the late Eighteenth Century (Alden Biesen, Belgium, 2001).
The Diffusion of Food Culture: Cookery and Food Education during the last 200 years (Prague, Czech Republic, 2003).
Food and the City (Berlin, Germany, 2005).
From Undernutrition to Obesity: Changes in Food Consumption in Twentieth-Century Europe (Oslo; Norway, 2007).
Food and War in Europe in the Nineteenth and Twentieth Centuries (Paris, France, 2009).
History of the European Food Industries in the Nineteenth and Twentieth Centuries (Bologna, Italy, 2011).

Publications

ICREFH I – Teuteberg, H.J. (ed.), *European Food History. A Research Overview*, Leicester, Leicester University Press, 1992 (ISBN 0718513835).
ICREFH II – Burnett, J. and Oddy, D.J. (eds), *The Origins and Development of Food Policies in Europe*, London, Leicester University Press, 1994 (ISBN 0718514742 (hb) and 0718511694 (pb).
ICREFH III – Hartog A.P. den (ed.), *Food Technology, Science and Marketing: European Diet in the Twentieth Century*, East Linton, Scotland, Tuckwell, 1995 (ISBN 1 898410 71 2).
ICREFH IV – Schärer, M.R. and Fenton, A. (eds), *Food and Material Culture*, East Linton, Scotland, Tuckwell, 1998 (ISBN 1 86232 002 0).
ICREFH V – Fenton, A. (ed.), *Order and Disorder: The Health Implications of Eating and Drinking in the Nineteenth and Twentieth Centuries*, East Linton, Scotland, Tuckwell, 2000 (ISBN 1 86232 117 5).
ICREFH VI – Hietala, M. and Vahtikari, T. (eds), *The Landscape of Food: The Food Relationship of Town and Country in Modern Times*, Helsinki, Finnish Literature Society, 2003 (ISBN 951 746 478 9 and ISSN 1458 526 x).
ICREFH VII – Jacobs, M. and Scholliers, P. (eds), *Eating Out in Europe. Picnics, gourmet dining and snacks since the late eighteenth century*, Oxford and New York, Berg, 2003 (ISBN 1 86973 658 0 and 1 85973 653 x).
ICREFH VIII – Oddy, D.J. and Petráňová, L. (eds), *The Diffusion of Food Culture in Europe from the late eighteenth century to the present day*, Prague, Academia, 2005 (ISBN 8020013253).
ICREFH IX – Atkins, P.J., Lummel, P. and Oddy, D.J. (eds), *Food and the City in Europe since 1800*, Aldershot, Ashgate, 2007 (ISBN 075464989X).

ICREFH X – Oddy, D.J., Atkins, P.J. and Amilien, V. (eds), *The Rise of Obesity in Europe. A Twentieth Century Food History*, Farnham, Ashgate, 2009 (ISBN 9780754676966).

ICREFH XI – Zweiniger-Bargielowska, I., Duffett, R. and Drouard, A. (eds), *Food and War in Twentieth Century Europe*, Farnham, Ashgate, 2011 (ISBN 978-1-4094-1770-5).

Chapter 1
Introduction

Derek J. Oddy

Prior to the nineteenth century, food supplies everywhere were unpredictable and Europe suffered from a succession of subsistence crises. In the words of Fernand Braudel 'cereal yields were poor; two consecutive bad harvests spelt disaster.' Such uncertainties of existence were marks of 'the biological *ancien régime*'.[1] Braudel's idea was taken up by Professor J.D. Post who called the European-wide dearth of the 1740s the 'last great subsistence crisis'[2] even though Europe experienced a widespread shortage of food in 1766, as did Britain in the 1790s (especially 1795–1796), and 1801. Yet Post discounted the acute food shortages in post-Napoleonic Europe during 1816–1817, because he assumed that new techniques being developed in agriculture would lead to increases in the output of crops and numbers of animals. An increased food supply, including imported foodstuffs during the nineteenth century, would result in Europe becoming capable of sustaining population growth. Post's assessment was broadly correct: continent-wide subsistence crises did not appear in Western Europe or North America later than the eighteenth century. After the immediate post-Napoleonic War crisis, famine in nineteenth-century Europe was much more localized, though it was extensive in the northern provinces of European Russia in 1891.[3]

From the 1790s, Europe underwent a protracted period of warfare which lasted until the battle of Waterloo in 1815. Assembling armies and navies and keeping them in the field or at sea was a major stimulus to the expansion of the food industries. Armies and navies required immense supplies to feed the thousands of men assembled for the campaigns of the Napoleonic Wars. Much was achieved by depredations practised on the civilian populations by army commissariats but weather conditions around the turn of the eighteenth century also meant local food crises. One constant element in the conflict was Great Britain's Royal Navy which blockaded ports on the Atlantic and Mediterranean coasts of mainland Europe for months on end regardless of season or weather. At the height of the wars, the Royal Navy's Victualling Board had the task of supplying 800 ships and feeding over 140,000 men, many of whom were widely dispersed. In addition, the Victualling Board was responsible for sending supplies to the British army in its overseas garrisons and at times provided food for other allied armies and for more than

---

1 Braudel, 1981, 70.
2 Post, 1976, 1977.
3 See Figure 10.1, in Wheatcroft, 1993, 156.

70 thousand prisoners-of-war.[4] The Navy's demand for suitable foodstuffs created numbers of agents in England's home ports to supply preserved (salted) meat in barrels and ships' biscuits known as 'hard tack' for use when fresh bread was not available.[5] The baking of ships' biscuits was the first modern industrialized food process recognizably operating on mass-production lines and perhaps matched in scale only by the larger breweries.

Food Preservation in Pre-Industrial Europe

There was a marked contrast between the food needs of the combatants and people in those parts of Europe unaffected by the campaigns of Napoleon Bonaparte or the alliances formed against him. Away from the conflict, people remained dependent upon local agriculture for their foodstuffs, either from their own crops and animals or supplies from local markets. The rationale of the food 'industries' prior to the onset of industrialization was to preserve crops and animal produce and extend the availability of foodstuffs from one season to the next in order to avoid any shortfall or 'hungry gap' in the months before the following harvest. The universal problem affecting every population's food supply was storage in a manner that would limit any deterioration which made food inedible later. The storage of the grain harvest and its conversion into flour was the principal requirement of townspeople and those in rural areas who could not produce their own food. Granaries and mills therefore performed an important economic activity across Europe since bread was the universal food in northern and western lowland areas where suitable bread-grains – wheat or barley – were cultivated. However there were regions, notably in the south and south-east – where maize-growing predominated – in which grain needed little processing. Maize required simple cracking in hand-mills since it was used for maize porridge known as *mămăligă* in the Danube Basin, Romania and Moldavia, or *polenta* in Italy; it formed the staple food of the poorer people over wide areas of southern and south-eastern Europe.[6] Similarly, in colder northern countries and highland zones where only oats or rye could be grown, porridge was also a staple food.

Millers and bakers generally functioned on a small scale in the late eighteenth and early nineteenth centuries using technology that had changed little over the centuries: millers relied on wind or water to power the rotating mill stones that ground grain into flour while bakers employed a long process of dough-making which might take up to a day before the dough went into wood-fired ovens. Keeping

---

4   The Board worked to a ration scale of 1lb (450g) of bread a day and 6lbs (2.7kg) of meat a week together with peas, oatmeal, cheese and butter.

5   See MacDonald, 2010.

6   In areas of Europe which relied mainly on cornmeal (maize) diets, people were liable to pellagra, a deficiency disease resulting from the malabsorption of niacin. Pellagra was said to be widespread in Europe until the twentieth century.

flour could be difficult, so when grain surpluses occurred in the eighteenth and early nineteenth centuries, it was common practice to convert them to alcoholic beverages by brewing or distilling.

Storing food for later use depended heavily upon the availability of salt, not just to preserve meat but also to salt green vegetables such as beans, cucumbers, and the almost universal cabbage which became the *sauerkraut* eaten widely in northern Europe. Since salt drew out the liquid from food, much food appeared to be preserved in brine and could be washed, cooked and eaten throughout the winter and until the next harvest season made fresh vegetables available again. This cottage industry required no equipment beyond an earthenware crock but a trade in salt was important to link areas where salt was mined or where evaporation pans provided an alternative source. Salting was often linked to smoking as a means of preserving fish and meat, especially meat from pigs as ham or bacon. Smoke houses could also operate on a domestic scale if sufficient fuel was available; where it was not, food could be dried by wind as cod (stockfish) in Norway or by sun like grapes, fish and meat (Serbia) in southern Europe.[7] Ice was available in colder parts of the continent where it could be harvested from flooded fields in winter for storage in icehouses, though for most of the nineteenth century the use of ice was limited to rich families for dinner-table decoration and ice cream rather than used widely for long-term food preservation. Icehouses were often found on the estates of wealthy people, frequently half-buried in the ground for insulation. Indeed, perhaps the most residual storage technique of all was to bury food in the ground for storage, as potatoes frequently were, or else to keep it in cellars.

Self-sufficiency was declining by the early nineteenth century as fewer people lived in very isolated circumstances except on islands, or in forests or highland regions of Europe. In general, Europe was a fertile region, able to supply its people with food. From the Pyrenees to Russia a coastal plain of broad-leaved deciduous woods and grasslands spread north and east across Europe, intersected by rivers flowing westwards into the Atlantic and North Sea or north into the Baltic. The land supported temperate grain crops, with pastures yielding meat and dairy products, so that the food supplies of the countries of the northern regions – France, Belgium, the Netherlands, Denmark, northern Germany and the British Isles – were similar. Further south and to the south-east highland areas were more pastoral economies, while the Mediterranean regions were noted for arboreal crops (olives, figs, citrus and stone fruits) and viticulture.

Demographic Change in Europe

It is difficult to know how big the population of Europe was in 1800, as few countries took censuses, but one estimate suggests that Europe (excluding Russia)

---

7   United Nations, Food and Agriculture Organization, *South East Europe Technical Seminar*, 2008, 6.

contained just over 190 million people, a figure which had risen to about 420 million by 1900. Thereafter it did not increase significantly in the first half of the twentieth century as population limitation, war, and emigration occurred.[8] The pattern of growth was clear: birth rates commonly exceeded 30 per thousand during the nineteenth century, while death rates were some 20 per thousand or more. Regional variation developed from the 1880s. In western and north-western Europe death rates declined to around 15 per thousand in the 1930s, though they remained close to 20 per thousand in eastern and south-eastern Europe. Between c.1875 and 1950, life expectancy at birth rose from under 40 years to the mid-60s for males and nearly 70 for females.[9] Industrialization and urbanization was stimulated by rapid population growth rates: by 1880, Germany's population after unification had reached 40m, France 39m, with the United Kingdom and Italy around 30m each.

The expanding population meant increasing numbers of people were no longer self-sufficient in foodstuffs, however simple their diet was. Home-brewing also declined. Reliance on markets as the source of foodstuffs grew, while numbers of traders such as dry-salters and 'Italian oilmen'[10] increasingly became food retailers in towns and industrial districts. The nineteenth century was therefore a period of sustained and increasing demand for foodstuffs, especially in the core of European economic development comprising France, Britain and the Low Countries. As urban centres expanded they relied on the growth of railways in the second half of the nineteenth century to transport food from distant sources while the larger cities became ringed with market gardens to supply more perishable foodstuffs. In some instances where the spatial concentration of industry became pronounced as when industry came to rely on mineral fuel, separate built-up areas began to merge together into city-regions, and the term 'conurbation' was coined to describe this phenomenon.[11] In the last quarter of the nineteenth century urban food outlets proliferated, some of which became retail 'chains' of shops, that were able to introduce trademarks and own-brand names for their goods. Rural areas of central, eastern and south-eastern Europe shared minimally in these developments and their food supplies changed little during the nineteenth century, though some urban centres contained 'colonial-goods shops' in the first half of the twentieth century.[12] Although some predominantly rural areas appeared backward by the standards of development experienced in north-west Europe, the rural economies of Europe did develop specialist lines of production as cash crops, such as tomatoes, olives and citrus fruits, which could be exported to the colder north. By the early twentieth century, European emigration to North

---

8   *Cambridge Economic History*, VI, 1965, Table 6, 58.

9   *Camb. Econ. Hist.*, 1965, 62.

10   Oil shops or warehouses sold whale and seal oil for lighting and various vegetable oils for lubrication, soap-making and paint-making before branching into imported foods. See ch.3.

11   See Geddes, 1915. This was most evident in Britain between the 1880s and 1930s.

12   Godina-Golija, 2009, in ICREFH X, 46–7.

and South America even created an international demand for emigrants' 'home' produce. Nevertheless, subsistence agriculture remained significant in central and eastern Europe throughout the twentieth century and its demise was delayed by state policies from the 1940s onwards.[13]

The location of industrial facilities for food processing and manufacture was problematic and, for crops, might depend on the density of the yield. If the raw material was bulky, as with some cereals or vegetables, processing on a rural site as near to the source of production as possible might be favoured, but animals and geese were usually expected to walk considerable distances to slaughtering facilities adjacent to markets. As the scale of cereal marketing grew beyond local needs, crops were transported by cart to large mills closer to urban centres though a rural site was often preferred for processing food materials, particularly if perishability was an issue, as cheap seasonal labour was usually available. In central and eastern Europe, the rural population made up some 70–80 per cent of the total, and these proportions did not fall until the early twentieth century.[14] In general, as urban areas expanded, transport became more important. The processing of milk in the countryside was common if it was done close to railway or road transport facilities. Where waterways allowed cheap transport, surprisingly little value was added near the point of production for commodities such as grain. Even perishable soft fruit was often brought to urban factories because their economies of scale and other advantages of market-orientation outweighed any losses in quality there might be en route. By the twentieth century, it was the 'necessity to market a homogeneous product that prompted concentration of processing'.[15] In short, the relationship between the locational factors was complex and changed through time and across space to such an extent that food factories frequently went out of business or were moved in order to optimize their advantages.

The Industrialization of the Food Supply

The origins of most modern food industries in Europe date from the 1860s. Until then, food trades were local, dispersed and used traditional processes. New sources of raw materials brought changes to production methods, food qualities and flavours. North American 'hard' wheat yielding 'strong' flour entered European markets through west-facing ports and began to replace traditional flours made from 'soft' wheat. Wind or water mills using rotating millstones were gradually replaced by mills driven by mechanical power and using roller technology. Introduced in Hungary in 1865 for the more effective milling of locally-grown 'hard' wheat, roller mills began to be operated in Britain at Glasgow and Liverpool in the 1870s

---

13 Abele and Frohberg, 2003.
14 *Camb. Econ. Hist.*, 1965, ch.6, 608–9.
15 *Camb. Econ. Hist.*, 1965, 667.

to deal with hard-wheat from the mid-west of the United States of America.[16] By 1914, milling in Britain was a large-scale operation in the hands of a few very big firms producing millions of sacks of flour a year.[17] They produced white flour of low extraction (using just over 70 per cent of the grain) which stored better and yielded more loaves of bread per sack of flour. From the 1880s making bread on an industrial scale employed dough-kneading machines and continuous ovens in large factory bakeries. The result was that bread became a more standardized product and even an ordinary loaf could be given a brand name if speciality flours like Hovis or Allinson's were used. Firms owning chains of bread shops existed before the First World War in Britain, though small cellar bakeries still operated in poor working-class areas of towns. However, by the later nineteenth century, bread alone was not enough: even the poorest people were eager for something to stimulate their palates by the addition of either some fat or sugar.

Dairy products, like other foods of animal origin, were too expensive for most working-class households to consume with any regularity or in any significant quantity, but one of the most intriguing developments was an industrially produced substitute for butter. In 1869, Hippolyte Mège, a chemist in Paris generally known as Mège-Mouriès, obtained French and British patents to manufacture what was called 'New Animal Fatty Butter' or margarine. It was based on melting down beef fat, which was then churned with cream. The process was rapidly adopted in Denmark and the Netherlands, and exported to the United Kingdom in the 1870s as 'butterine', though agricultural interests soon made that name illegal in England. From the beginning margarine was a branded factory product with protected trademarks, yet advertised its 'dairy' connexions everywhere. The dairy product which was rapidly taken up for industrial production was milk. Evaporated milk, a product from which some water was removed was developed in the 1850s followed by condensed milk which was partially evaporated but had a large amount of sugar added. That increased its energy content and acted as a preservative after the milk was canned. Processed milk was an immediate target for branding and Henri Nestlé (1844–1890) established a factory at Vevey in Switzerland from which he sold '*Farine Lactée*' (powdered milk) as an infant food. Its popularity led Nestlé to merge with another Swiss firm, the Anglo-Swiss Milk Company, in 1905 and begin production in Rotterdam in 1912 to compete with Dutch proprietary milk foods.[18] Processing milk together with imported cocoa beans led to other proprietary foods such as 'Dairy Milk Chocolate' produced by Cadbury Brothers at Bournville, near Birmingham, and drinks based on cocoa powder such as 'drinking chocolate'.

16   See Perren 1990. *Econ. Hist. Rev.* XLIII, 3, 420–37. English varieties of wheat yielded 'soft' flour.
17   Burnett, 1989, 121.
18   The Anglo-Swiss Milk Company was founded at Cham, Switzerland, in 1866. See Knechte-van Eckelen, 1995, in ICREFH III, 41–4 and Valenze, 2011, 190–96.

Sweetness gave palatability to the carbohydrate staples of the limited diets eaten by poor people across Europe. Sugar, expensive when taxed, as it frequently was, came initially from tropical sugar cane. Refineries to crush, clarify and crystallize sugar developed in the ports of countries which traded with the West Indies but it was sugar beet which, after similar processing, provided much of continental Europe's supplies.[19] Sugar could be processed further to reach the table cheaply as factory-made syrup, treacle, and jams from the middle of the nineteenth century onwards. Syrup, or 'Golden Syrup', as manufacturers labelled it, was one of the first foods to be successfully sold in cans as the high sugar content rendered sterilization unnecessary.[20]

The development of industrial processes meant that the scale of operations in the food industries expanded significantly in the twentieth century. Production became increasingly capital-intensive as machine-usage increased; continuous operation rather than batch production was introduced in baking and freezing. Pasteurizers and spray-driers were used to modify milk; blenders and packing machines standardized dairy products; emulsifiers were required to produce margarine and spreads; and centrifuges separated sugars and syrups. The concentration of the labour force into production facilities or factories, the use of motive power and the growth of capital equipment consequent to technical innovations, meant food processing became increasingly industrialized and reliant on capital and entrepreneurial skills, which contrasted sharply with the local, domestic scale of production in the nineteenth century.

Advances in Preservation Techniques

Preserving food in cans is traditionally associated with the name of the Frenchman Nicolas Appert (1749–1841), though his process was initially designed to keep food in glass jars. Appert built a bottling factory during the Napoleonic Wars but it burnt down in 1814. Although it has been said that Dutch ships had taken food to sea in heavy metal containers since the 1770s, Peter Durand patented a method of preserving food in metal cans in England in 1810. Some examples were taken to sea and on return tested by scientists of the Royal Society and Royal Institution. Durand then sold his patent to Bryan Donkin (1768–1855) who together with John Hall built a canning factory in Bermondsey, London, in 1813. Although canned meats were tested in 1814 by the Admiralty, it was not general issue to the Royal Navy until much later. Nevertheless, bottled or tinned food was available from the 1820s onwards but users faced problems of opening metal containers without the use of a hammer and chisel until can openers were patented in the 1850s. The early use of tin cans led to some problems with sterilization; when cans were soldered

---

19   Sugar cane yielded around 15 per cent sugar, while sugar beet contained some 18 per cent sugar when similarly treated.

20   See Pyke, 1970, Plate 102.

to seal them, any holes in the seal meant food would deteriorate and air would cause the can to 'blow'. Manufacturing tin cans by hand expanded in the late nineteenth century but modern canning plants using open-top production lines in Europe depended upon leasing American technology in the late 1920s.[21]

The other major development in food technology was the use of low-temperature storage to preserve perishable foods like meat, fish and fruit. Bulk freezing of meat cargoes from the Southern Hemisphere to Europe developed during the 1880s as well as the use of low-temperature storage to chill beef imported by shorter voyages from North America. Early voyages from South America and Australasia carried cargoes of 500–1,500 tons of frozen meat, particularly mutton and lamb, but as larger ships were built, 2,500 tons became common in the 1890s and 3,500 tons after 1900. Cargoes on this scale delivered to Britain, France and Italy during the First World War were used to feed their armies.[22] Refrigeration of meat therefore operated at the wholesale level before the Second World War, including the building of vast refrigerated stores in major ports and urban areas in Western Europe.[23] Major importing firms soon developed chains of retail butchers' shops as outlets for chilled and frozen meat. Only after the Second World War did American fast-freezing technology spread to Europe so that all meat, even fresh-killed meat, was presented to retail customers as chilled meat. This remarkable change, which facilitated the growth of meat products by the food industries, was fostered by the increasing standardization of retailing through the new supermarket chains.

The production of artificial ice also aided the French, Belgian and British fishing industries to concentrate on the North Sea, as the growth of trawling from the 1870s meant fishing vessels putting to sea carried supplies of ice in which to pack their catch after each haul of their nets. Ice also meant the catching area expanded as fishing vessels could remain at sea longer. By the First World War, fishing vessels sailing to 'distant waters' from North Sea ports counted the Barents Sea, the Murmansk coast, northern Norway, Bear Island, Spitzbergen and Iceland amongst their fishing grounds. Their catches were sold as 'fresh' fish but from

---

21   Reader, 1976, chs 4–7. Metal Box arranged exclusive rights in Britain with the American firm, Continental Can. This covered canning machinery, technical advice, training, and patent licenses for open-top cans for foods. By the mid-1930s, Metal Box had taken over Thomassen and Drijver (Netherlands) and had links with Sobemi and Boites Métalliques (Belgium) and J.J. Carnaud (France). In 1937, Metal Box was selling 335 million cans a year. By the 1960s, Metal Box was the leading packaging supplier to some of the largest companies in the world, including Unilever, Nestlé, Heinz, Imperial Tobacco, BAT, ICI, Hoechst, and Shell.

22   'The Long, Long Trail'. By November 1918, 3 m men on the Western Front received 4.5 m lbs (2 m kg) bread and 90 m lbs (41m kg) meat per month. See Dentoni, 2003, in ICREFH VI, 157–70; Duffett, 2011 in ICREFH XI, 27–39; also Murphy and Oddy, 2011, 12–36.

23   See Dentoni, 2003, in ICREFH VI, 157–70, for cold storage expansion at Genoa and Naples during the First World War. Refrigeration stores were also built to support the Salonika campaign.

the 1920s canning of fish – mainly surface-swimming 'oily' fish such as herrings, sardines and especially 'tinned salmon' – based on imported Canadian fish – quickly became popular. American fast-freezing technology became important for the development of fish products, such as the fish finger, but these were post Second World War developments.

These new methods of treating freshly killed animals and creating new food products were the outcome of the adaption of scientific methods to industrial procedures and to the increasing number of scientists working in the food industries. To begin with, standardizing procedures, timing processes and using instruments such as thermometers were simple but effective methods of quality control. Furthermore, research became possible as scientific knowledge grew during the nineteenth and twentieth centuries though, until the First World War, nutritional policies were based on the analyses of protein content and energy value of food carried out between the 1880s and 1914. The dominant opinions were those of Max Rubner (1854–1932), who had studied under Carl Voit (1831–1908) in Munich, and W.O. Atwater (1844–1907) in the United States. Both advocated a high protein diet especially for men in the armed forces.[24] The research by Frederick Gowland Hopkins (1861–1947) at Cambridge on the 'accessory food factors' which later became known as vitamins, had no impact before the 1920s when the 'new knowledge of nutrition', as it was then called, was eagerly taken up by firms in the food and pharmaceutical industries, the leaders of which began to equip laboratories, appoint research staff and to develop foods containing vitamin supplements. Margarine enhanced by vitamins A and D went on sale in Britain from 1927 and baby milk with added vitamin D followed.[25]

The interwar years saw the food industries begin to adopt standard weights and package sizes for many foods: tea and coffee, chocolate and cocoa, sugar, salt, biscuits, cakes, butter, margarine, and milk, as well as novelties like potato crisps, or pickles and chutneys. Tinned goods with brand names such as Heinz or Nestlé were all sold by fixed weights or volumes. This practice was more general in urban areas, even if small shops in villages and those in country districts continued to sell much food 'loose' and measured out the individual amounts requested by customers. Some foods like processed or ready-cooked meats such as bacon, ham, polony or salami, were still generally cut by hand to the customer's requirements as was cheese, and eggs were also sold loose. By whatever means the retail trade was making progress, it was evident that in the advanced industrial regions of Europe food was available in much greater variety and of a much more standard quality than it had been before 1900 and customers were increasingly asking for items by brand names.

Once the growth of food processing and manufacturing began, markets for food began to change from local and immediate ones, where food was sold as soon as it

---

24 Voit had suggested 145 g of protein as a suitable daily allowance for adult males as early as 1881.

25 See Horrocks, 1995, in ICREFH III, 7–18.

was available, to larger scale markets or permanent outlets for which transport and storage became important. As the scale of trading in food increased, handling raw and part-processed food materials became industrialized in the hands of commodity traders and even developed on an international scale. Commodity brokers arose as grain began to be sold in distant markets such as Chicago or London. The success of such ventures depended upon the speed of communications between growers and brokers. Initially in the late 1850s, but permanently from 1868, a British transatlantic telegraph cable linked Europe to the United States. When additional cables were laid from the 1870s onwards, Europe and North America became joined by French, German, and American cables as well as the original British link. Early in the twentieth century telegraph messages could be sent rapidly and cheaply. The impact of this technology was to create futures markets in grain and animal products such as beef and pork.

The Thematic Structure of the Book

The programme of the Bologna symposium centred on three themes: the development of industrial organization in the food industries, the creation of new foods and the effect of food technology on consumption patterns. These themes illustrate the breakout from 'the biological *ancien régime*' achieved by the food industries in Europe since the mid-nineteenth century. Although progress has been uneven, the eleven countries discussed in the following chapters typify changes in which food has become increasingly processed. As a result, Europeans have developed the taste for a great variety of more complex foodstuffs which provide 'added value' for producers.

In Part I, *The Origins and Growth of Industrial Organization*, Chapters 2 to 5 on Germany, Britain, France and Spain discuss sugar, starch, sweet preserves, cheese and olive oil during the nineteenth and first half of the twentieth century. They show that improvements in technology led to business organization developing from individual entrepreneurship to joint stock companies eager to market their products as branded goods.

These characteristics can also be found in some aspects of the five chapters in Part II, *Creating New Foods*. This is particularly true for Chapter 6, which is a case study of the chocolate industry in France. It examines the development of business organization, including the vertical integration of the Menier enterprise, and also the firm's concern for the social welfare of its workforce – a feature of other chocolate firms like Cadbury and Rowntree. A different dimension of the same industry in the Czech lands in Chapter 7 emphasizes how the divided nationalities in Central Europe resorted to politics to market their products and promote nationalist ambitions. However, Chapter 8 explains that the most distinctive new food in Europe was not a luxury or 'treat' food but margarine, the economist's archetypal 'inferior good', which from the 1880s to the 1930s grew into a mainstay of working-class diets during periods of economic hardship, yet provided an element of variety to limited and monotonous consumption patterns – as did the cheap preserves discussed in Chapter 3.

Chapters 9 and 10 are more concerned with the presentation of well-known foods in new forms rather than new foods as such. Pig meat may well be one of the world's oldest foods of animal origin but Chapter 9 shows that in Denmark its composition was transformed between the late nineteenth century and the mid-twentieth century. Selective breeding made a dramatic reduction in the fat content of the meat so that former cuts of pork and bacon were unrecognizable to consumers in the second half of the twentieth century. The proof of this occurred in Britain during the Second World War when old-fashioned fat bacon arrived from the United States. It was regarded as almost inedible even by a population living on a diet rigorously constrained by rationing. Chapter 10 deals with changes to fish products made possible by new freezing technology licensed by the American Clarence Birdseye. By the 1950s quick-frozen fish replaced the traditional dried-fish markets for the Icelandic and Norwegian fisheries.

Part III, *The Effect of Food Technology on Consumption Patterns*, consists of five chapters presenting various aspects of industrially produced foods to the consumer by packaging, labelling and marketing. Chapter 11 considers the introduction of food labelling in the Netherlands, the effective branding of packaged foods and the early difficulties of quality control. The introduction of self-service retailing after the Second World War intensified the use of labels and packaging but little nutritional information appeared on them before the 1980s. That provides a link to Chapter 12, which examines the transformation of food retailing in Sweden. Although its introduction was delayed by rationing during the Second World War, Sweden began to adopt the American retail self-service system extensively. Its rapid growth gave Sweden the highest rate of self-service food retailing in Europe by 1960. Adopting self-service in shops changed the use of floor space and shelf space, and required new packaging technology. Retailers accepted the self-service shop as fostering impulse buying and unplanned purchases. The essence of this success was that shelving arrangements, store layout and fitments, if standardized and attractively designed, promoted customer familiarity and confidence.

Chapter 13 on attitudes of Belgian consumers shows remarkable conservatism towards commercial products in Flemish women's magazines, so that it was the end of the twentieth century before refrigerators and freezers were seen as domestic necessities. Flemish women's magazines for the rural population retained a preference for seasonal availability of foods rather than commercially canned foods. Articles in the press designed for urban women ignored seasonal patterns but approval for frozen foods focused on food hygiene and labour saving for women working outside the home.

The penultimate case-study in Chapter 14 on Romania shows that maize (cornmeal) was the principal cereal consumed. Publicly-funded bakeries were established after 1905, a move which was expanded once pellagra began to be better understood as a deficiency disease. The bread consumption programme received a setback during the Second World War and by the Nationalization Act,

1948, but was encouraged by the Five Year Plans. State marketing facilitated bread consumption by increasing the numbers of rural shops and pellagra was brought under control by the 1970s.

The final study in Chapter 15 examines how low-temperature technology brought perishable foods from the Southern Hemisphere to Britain. Meat was central to this trade in view of national demands for manpower. The Second World War food policy severely restricted the output of poultry as unnecessary 'festive foods'. Postwar delays in restoring choice of meat led consumers to turn to the newly industrialized poultry farming which began to supply oven-ready birds cheaply through supermarkets. Poultry consumption rose dramatically as traditional meat meals declined from about 1960 onwards.

Chapter 16 attempts to unify the disparate case studies which precede it. The evidence suggests an emerging pattern of development of the food industries. The industrialization of the European food supply and consumption is fundamental to modern European culture: advanced economies have complex food chains in which raw materials are extensively modified by food processors, refiners and retailers. In the period under discussion in this volume the west-to-east gradient from advanced economies to less industrialized ones was pronounced and there were marked dietary differences in consumption. Chapter 16 also provides a broader view of the nature of industrialized food production by examining the political economy of the food industries from the Second World War to the end of the twentieth century.

References

Abele, S. and Frohberg, K., eds, 2003, *Subsistence Agriculture in Central and Eastern Europe: How to Break the Vicious Circle?* Institut für Agrarentwicklung in Mittel und OstEuropa (IAMO), 22, Halle.

Braudel, F., 1981, *Civilization and Capitalism, 15th–18th Century: volume I The Structures of Everyday Life*, 3 vols, London: Collins.

Burnett, J., 1989, *Plenty and Want*, 3rd edn, London: Routledge.

The Cambridge Economic History of Europe, vol. VI, Parts I and II, 1965, edited by M.M. Postan and H.J. Habakkuk, Cambridge: Cambridge University Press.

Dentoni, M.C., 2003, 'Refrigeration and the Italian meat crisis during the First World War' in ICREFH VI: Hietala, M. and Vahtikari, T., eds, *The Landscape of Food*, Helsinki: Finnish Literature Society.

Duffett, R. 2011, 'British Army provisioning on the Western Front, 1914–1918' in ICREFH XI: Zweiniger-Bargielowska, I., Duffett, R. and Drouard, A., eds, *Food and War in Twentieth Century Europe*, Farnham: Ashgate.

Geddes, P., 1915, *Cities in Evolution: an introduction to the town planning movement and to the study of civics*, London: Williams and Norgate.

Godina-Golija, M., 2009, 'Slovenian Food Consumption in the Twentieth Century – From Self-Sufficiency to Mass Consumption', in ICREFH X: Oddy, D.J.,

Atkins, P.J. and Amilien, V., eds, *The Rise of Obesity in Europe: A Twentieth Century Food History*, Farnham: Ashgate.

Horrocks, S.M., 1995, 'Nutrition Science and the Food Industry in Britain, 1920–1990', in ICREFH III: Hartog, A.P. den, ed., *Food Technology, Science and Marketing; European Diet in the Twentieth Century*, East Linton, Scotland: Tuckwell.

Knechte-van Eckelen, A. de, 1995, 'The best substitute for mother's milk: proprietary preparations between the rise of paediatrics and the science of nutrition in the Netherlands during the twentieth century', in ICREFH III: Hartog, A.P. den, ed., *Food Technology, Science and Marketing; European Diet in the Twentieth Century*, East Linton, Scotland: Tuckwell.

Long, Long Trail, The: The British Army in the Great War, www.1914-1918.net/asc.htm.

MacDonald, J., 2010, *The British Navy's Victualling Board, 1793–1815*, Woodbridge: Boydell.

Murphy, H. and Oddy, D.J., 2011, 'The Business Interests of Sir James Caird of Glenfarquhar, Bt (1864–1954)', *The Mariner's Mirror*, 97:1.

Perren, R., 1990, 'Structural change and market growth in the food industry: flour milling in Britain, Europe, and America, 1850–1914', *Economic History Review,* 2nd series, XLIII, 3.

Post, J.D., 1976, 'Famine, Mortality, and Epidemic Disease in the Process of Modernization, *Econ. Hist. Rev.*, 2nd series, XXIX, 1.

Post, J.D., 1977, *The Last Great Subsistence Crisis in the Western World*, Baltimore and London: Johns Hopkins.

Pyke, M., 1970, *Food Science and Technology*, 3rd edn, London: John Murray.

Reader, W.J., 1976, *Metal Box, a History*, London: Heinemann.

United Nations, Food and Agriculture Organization, South East Europe Technical Seminar, 2008, www.foodqualityorigin.org/serbia/Rapport.pdf

Valenze, D., 2011, *Milk A Local and Global History*, New Haven: Yale.

Wheatcroft, S.G., 1993, 'Famine and food consumption records in early Soviet history, 1917–25', in Geissler, C. and Oddy, D.J., eds, *Food, Diet and Economic Change Past and Present*, Leicester: Leicester University Press.

PART I
The Origins and Growth of Industrial Organization

Chapter 2

Pioneering Spadework in the History of the German Food Industry during the Nineteenth and Early Twentieth Centuries: Beet Sugar, Wheat Starch and Health Foods

Karl-Peter Ellerbrock and Hans-Jürgen Teuteberg[1]

Historical research has so far failed to recognize the fact that the food industry in Germany has to be counted among the leading sectors of industrialization in the 'long nineteenth century'. The blast furnaces of the mighty iron and steel corporations, for example, did not only dominate the outer appearance of the 'industrial revolution', but they also held historians' attention. Thus, Walther G. Hoffmann of Münster, whose thesis claiming that the food industries had initially played a leading role but then fell behind the overall economic growth rate during the period of high industrialization, remained valid up to the 1990s.[2] This misjudgement can be put down to the fact that the exclusive consideration of highly aggregated statistical averages obscured important specific developments. Since the mid-nineteenth century, the food and luxury food industries had been developing an exceptional dynamic of growth which initiated the 'take-off' of the whole sector.[3] Thus, by 1895, every fifth employee in the food industry worked in a factory with more than 200 employees. According to the results of the trade census of 1907, the average company size amounted to 6.4 employees. However, the mass of small and very small businesses, such as butcheries and bakeries, was offset by big mechanized industrial companies with high technological standards, such as those in the sugar and brewing industries. By 1846, horsepower (h.p.) per employee in the food industry was the second highest, and only surpassed by the heavy iron and steel industry. This position was consolidated up to the First World War, which meant the food industry attained the leading position in terms of increments in production.[4] The high technical efficiency also explains

---

1 Hans-Jürgen Teuteberg wrote the section on beet sugar and Karl-Peter Ellerbrock has provided the study of Dr Klopfer's health-food enterprise and the rise of convenience foods.

2 Hoffmann, 1931.

3 Rostow, 1956, 26–48.

4 Ellerbrock, 1993, 244–69.

the tremendous capital needs of the sector. The food industry not only counted among the pioneers of modern joint-stock trading in Germany, but was ahead of other branches of the economy and industry up to the turn of the twentieth century; it also accounted for most of the companies in this modern and innovative form of business before the First World War. Moreover, most companies in the food industry were outstandingly successful, as the balance-sheet analysis of selected sectors shows.[5] What was long true of the food industry as a whole, is still valid today for some of its sectors: mechanically produced and packed flour, canned vegetables and fruits, ready-for-use sugar obtained from sugar beets, bottled beer or mineral water and, not forgetting the production of starch in factories, were new but they were soon considered 'mundane'. However, from today's perspective, their contribution to the late nineteenth and twentieth-century 'nutrition revolution' cannot be overestimated.

A large number of pioneering efforts contributed to these changes. The following examples consider two little regarded branches of the food industry: in particular, the collapse of one pioneering enterprise of the whole-food and health-food sector – today one of the most important growth points of the food industry – offers new insights into the complicated mixture of economic and cultural determinants which were relevant for the establishment of health foodstuffs.

Beet-Sugar Production as the Precursor of the Modern German Food Industry 1780–1914

There is much literature about the sugar industry in Germany. An examination of library catalogues and bibliographies shows nearly 150 titles dealing primarily with cane sugar in earlier centuries, but understandably German books are much more concerned with the German invention of beet sugar and its development since the nineteenth century.[6] A general survey is not possible here: this study is an account of the German beet-sugar industry in the period of industrialization, especially with regard to its effect on consumption and changes in food culture. This should show how the production of beet-sugar was the foundation of the German food industry

The Pre-History of Sugar

Cane sugar arrived in Germany directly from Venice. Cookery books and recipes show that it was well-known in high-ranking households in Germany during the fifteenth and sixteenth centuries, where it was used mainly for sugar

---

5   Ellerbrock, 1993, 270–326.

6   Compare Lippmann, 1929; Axa, 1967; Wiegelmann, 1986, 135–52; Hengartner 2001, 259–88.

bakery.[7] It remained rare and expensive and played no role in general nutrition. In ordinary households honey was used to sweeten dishes or to preserve fruits. The consumption of sugar remained very low for a long time, because coffee and tea, which needed sweeteners, played only a very small part in consumption. After the Spanish invasion of the Netherlands in the sixteenth century, many sugar bakers from Amsterdam emigrated to Hamburg where the first German sugar refineries sprang up. These enterprises grew from 365 in the year 1750 to 428 in 1807; their growth depended on easy access to imported raw material, a lack of labour regulations by contrast to other German towns, and the immigration of first-class workers. The much better Hamburg white sugar, like that of the Netherlands, could therefore be exported to parts of Middle and Eastern Europe.[8] The banker-merchant Splittgerber (later Delbrück & Co) in Berlin tried to break the Hamburg monopoly. He could refine West-Indian cane sugar from England and the Netherlands which arrived at Hamburg and Stettin on the Baltic Sea. The sales of his refineries tripled between 1752 and 1756. By 1785 he obtained a yearly turnover of 2 m. Taler and had engaged 2,000 workers. Other Prussian towns and German territorial states founded refineries based on his model. In 1790, Prussia produced some 100,000 quintals (Zentner) of cane sugar and 20,000 quintals of cane-sugar syrup.[9]

The Conversion to Beet Sugar

Around 1800 there were 32 surrogates for cane sugar in use for eating, drinking or medical purposes. Beetroot (*Beta vulgaris*), with its several subspecies, was already well known but no beet-sugar production existed.[10] The break-through came when the Berlin chemist, Andreas Sigismund Marggraf (1683–1764), showed that sugar from beets was identical with cane sugar.[11] From 100 parts of fresh beets Marggraf extracted 16 parts of sugar for the first time. He recommended that peasants should extract sugar solutione from this sort of root. His work remained forgotten until 1763 when, after the Seven Years War, he presented to the Prussian King, Frederick the Great, a sample of his new sugar. Marggraf's pupil and successor, Franz Carl Achard (1753–1821), son of a French Huguenot pastor, continued the fundamental research. Achard, like Marggraf before him, received orders from the king to look for cheap substitutes to replace the expensive cane sugar, because the Prussian state had to pay for imported goods. The rising prices for colonial cane sugar due to the Anglo-French Wars now provided a reason to put in motion the new beet-sugar production. Achard found a turnip with the highest sugar content after experiments on an estate near Berlin. He convinced the new Prussian king,

---

7   Langstedt, 1800, 198–267. See also Baxa, 1937.

8   Peterson, 1998.

9   One quintal is equivalent to two hundredweights avoirdupois or 53kg.

10   The term 'beet' is used in this chapter for all varieties of root vegetables processed in sugar production.

11   Marggraf, 1768, 70ff. Compare with Meyer, 1799; Achard, 1800.

Friedrich Wilhelm II, of the importance of the new sugar but not of the profitability of producing it. An increased tillage of the sugar beet was assisted by the state in view of its connexion to spirit distilleries, which could use much of the waste from beet-sugar production. Finally in 1802 Achard erected his first beet sugar factory in Silesia, but shortly after it burned down and ruined the inventor. Nevertheless, in 1812 Achard published three volumes about the production of beet sugar.[12] Further support for the production of beet sugar occurred during Napoleon's Continental Blockade and the British blockade of Europe which followed. Prices of cane sugar quickly rose threefold and by 1813 some 150–200 beet-sugar factories were founded in Germany. Although the output and the quality remained rather poor, the new production made high profits immediately, while peasants could use the waste for cattle feed. Following Achard, they also began to use the waste to produce spirits, vinegar, beer and tobacco.

The first urban beet sugar enterprise in the Prussian town of Magdeburg in 1812 became the largest European establishment. It produced 70–80,000 quintals (Zentner) of beet sugar in one year. Johann Gottlieb Nathusius, the owner of another small firm, brought an inspector from a Dutch sugar plantation in Surinam to assist him in developing his own sugar factory. Then, together with the Prussian agrarian pioneer Albrecht Daniel Thaer and the leading chemist Hermstaedt, Nathusius set up the first scientific sugar laboratory. The beet sugar seemed so good that Nathusius aroused suspicion that he was in fact refining cane sugar and defrauding customs and taxes.

German Beet-Sugar Enterprises between 1820 and 1840

When the Napoleonic Wars ended in 1815 there was a sudden fall in sugar prices. The lifting of the Continental Blockade meant large quantities of cheap English cane sugar were pouring into Germany. This caused a nearly total destruction of German beet-sugar production. The brown colour of the beet sugar, which was now more expensive than the white cane sugar, contributed to this ruin. Because the older 'sugar bakeries' recovered very quickly and grew in numbers only cane sugar was used. However, sugar consumption did not exceed the level before the Continental Blockade. Because of mass poverty during the economic crisis in Germany in 1816–17, demand for beet sugar again decreased.[13]

However, high prices of cane sugar between 1820 und 1840 brought a final recovery for German beet-sugar production. The output of 25,238 quintals of raw sugar from 21 factories in 1816–17 rose to 236,504 quintals in 1840–41. The building-up of the German beet-sugar industry coincided with the beginnings of liberal reforms and the revolutionizing of agrarian tillage methods. The English crop rotation economy which Albrecht von Thaer proposed as a model for

12   Achard, 1812.
13   Tannenberg, 1944, 260.

Germany, and the artificial manure invented by Justus Liebig, became standard. From the 1830s German beet-sugar production became so profitable that it could compete with cane sugar. But Prussia was interested, like other European nations, in keeping cane-sugar enterprises alive because they were a good source for taxation. In order to protect the German beet-sugar industry, a treaty was made in 1839 with the Netherlands as the largest sugar importer and Prussian customs duties for raw and unfinished sugar were decreased. Between 1840 and the founding of the German Empire in 1870 the number of German beet-sugar establishments rose from 54 to 304, a fivefold increase. The amount of beets utilized rose from 26,080 tons to 3 million tons, and the output of raw sugar from 1,304 tons to 186,418 tons.

Falling domestic production costs through the use of steam-engines and railways meant that colonial cane sugar was more and more excluded from German markets. In 1840 506,000 decitons cane sugar was still imported, in 1870 this had fallen to 43,000 decitons. At the end of the 1850s, beet-sugar production was already larger than home demand and the first export of the beet sugar to foreign countries began. In the next ten years Germany changed from being a sugar importer to a sugar-exporting country. Prices fell between 1836 and 1870 from about 174 marks to 92 marks per deciton,[14] though these developments were interrupted by crop failures, the German revolution in 1848 and the war between Prussia and Austria in 1866.

This great expansion of German beet-sugar production also brought the imposition of a tax. A special beet-sugar tax was introduced in 1837 during the competition with France which was intended to protect domestic agriculture. In the beginning it was directed at the manufactured product and assessed on the weight of beet sugar produced. Later it was levied by the weight of German beets used for sugar production. As techniques progressed more and more sugar could be obtained from the same quantity of roots so that for the beet-sugar industry there was a hidden tax reduction. In addition, the state paid subsidies on the export of German beet sugar. The sugar tax was raised from from 10 pfennigs (pence) in 1844 to 1.6 marks per deciton in 1859 because the state wished to eliminate small establishments and to increase industrial concentration in the sugar industry. The Prussian state retained this collection principle on roots until 1890 even though sugar output rose. This tax policy led in the long run to the over-production of beet sugar and to regional delivery percentages and dumping prices. There was also a threat of a British duty on imports because the colonial cane-sugar production could not meet rising demand. In order to overcome this international crisis of the sugar trade, a Sugar Convention in Brussels of leading European producers agreed to a general reduction of customs and taxes in 1902. This achieved some success before the First World War.

---

14   A deciton = one-tenth of a ton = one quintal = two hundredweights avoirdupois or 53kg.

Beet Sugar as a Foodstuff for the People

Cookery books show that rising sugar consumption in Germany during the early nineteenth century resulted from the growing pleasure of drinking coffee, tea and chocolate by the upper middle classes. These new luxuries came to urban households as transport costs fell. It made sour wine sweeter and was also drunk as 'sugar water'; it sweetened meat, fish and egg dishes, and there were also new sweetmeats, sweet-and-sour sauces, candied fruits and sweet cream. Sugar was profoundly changing the diet, though this was limited to the monied upper classes.

As price lists show, the masses of ordinary people in Germany, especially in the countryside, were mostly excluded from sugar consumption until the middle of the nineteenth century. Although sugar prices varied regionally, the lower classes bought the relative cheap syrup, a beet sugar by-product, for sweetening. In the Rhineland where turnip cultivation was already widespread before the beginning of sugar-beet production, turnip tops played a role as a sugar surrogate. In a report of the Chamber of Commerce in Cologne in 1863, 'bread with syrup' was still designated as the chief foodstuff of the poor people of the town. At this time there were in the Rhine province 303 beet-sugar establishments. Between 1865 and 1880 about 7,500 to 11,000 barrels (= two quintals) of syrup were produced, the greater part of which was transported to the near Netherlands, the Upper Rhine area bordering France and Switzerland, as well to the more distant kingdom of Saxony. Only after 1870 did this flourishing trade decline. Cologne became increasingly the location for the beet-sugar industry. Other regional centres of beet-sugar production existed in the territories of Saxony, Silesia, Hanover and Brunswick, but not in Southern Germany.[15]

Table 2.1   Sugar consumption in Germany, 1800–1910

Date	Consumption per head per year (kg)	Date	Consumption per head per year (kg)
1800	0.5–0.7	1860	4.1
1825	1.4	1870	5.4
1836	2.0	1880	6.8
1840	2.3	1900	13.8
1850	3.0	1910	19.0

Source: Teuteberg, 1979, 34–46; Teuteberg, 1986.

---

15   Korn, 1936; Kellenbenz, 1966, 54ff, 203–27. Compare with Joerissen and Wagner; 1998; Grafschafter Krautfabrik, 1909; Döring and Heizmann, 1981–1982, 58–78; Loebner, 2005; Pohl, 1987. For syrup production, see Bloc, 1920.

Without syrup, which is very difficult to calculate, these data would be slightly lower. By comparison with the second half of the twentieth century, in 1965 the Federal Republic of Germany had an annual sugar consumption per head of 32.2 kg, in 1970 of 35 kg and in 1982 of 37 kg. These more modern household statistics include processed sugar (sucrose), sweets (cacao, chocolate, sugar products and pastry as well as sweet cream and honey. These data demonstrate that consumption not only of household sugar but also the industrially processed sugar was rising.[16] Sugar consumption rose in the second half of the nineteenth century six times. Between 1840 and 1930 sugar consumption had on average doubled every twenty years. The long-term decrease in sugar prices was an important determinant of this growth. Sugar would have been much cheaper still if the international sugar cartel had not supported a standard price for sugar in 1902.[17] Sugar was one of the few foodstuffs in Germany in the nineteenth century for which the linear trend of prices continuously fell by contrast with prices for corn, barley and beef. In retrospect, during the boom in the economy after the foundation of the German Empire, rising sugar consumption was clearly observable. Between 1870 and 1913 the quantity of processed sugar-beet went up from 3.0 to 16 million tons and the raw sugar from 18 tons in 1864 to 2,715.67 tons in 1913. Scientific improvements in agriculture using new fertilizers and an expanded area under beet more than doubled output, while mechanization and rationalization of factories made further progress, aided by improvements in the rail transport system which facilitated the movement of raw materials.[18] Falling grain prices caused farmers to switch to sugar-beet cultivation especially since it attracted state subsidies. Decreasing production costs, falling sugar prices and greater urbanization contributed to the rising sugar consumption in Germany. In 1871 some 36 per cent of the population lived in towns; by 1900, this had risen to 54 per cent. As people were drawn from the traditional country way of life, they began to consume more sugar and the associated products of the chocolate and sweet industries. Sugar was, in other words, a typical product of industrialization and urbanization.

After the mid-nineteenth century sugar was consumed daily, not only by families of the upper classes but also by the middle classes. During the last two decades of the nineteenth century sugar became important to more and more households of the urban labouring classes. This had a double significance: since satisfaction from consuming meat and fats was limited by high prices, attractive cheap sugar was a welcome substitute that could make up energy deficits. Although consumers at that time could not see the connexion, there is no doubt that sugar had a substitution value. It was very important that sugar and sweetmeats belonged to the luxury stimulants which brought welcome breaks during a long

---

16   Deutsche Gesellschaft für Ernährung, 1984, 169–70.

17   Kaufmann, 1950.

18   See Verein der Deutschen Zuckerindustrie, 1950, for agrarian, technical and managerial improvements in the beet-sugar industry during the late nineteenth and early twentieth centuries.

working day. The official Industrial Inspection Board reports often mentioned the anger of workmen and especially women workers if they were denied a cup of coffee during working hours. Sugar helped 'passing the time' as well as being the medium for companionship in all social classes.[19] Sugar was no longer a luxury item because the sugar consumption of a working-class family of four persons corresponded to the average for the German nation.

Wheat Starch instead of Wholegrain. The Failure of the Health-Food Factory 'Dr. Klopfer' and the Rise of the Convenience-Food Industry 1900–1939

This study focuses on the development of the starch industry as an important basis for the growth of the convenience-food industry, which research has so far ignored.[20] Using the example of the cereal-products factory of Dr. Volkmar Klopfer in Dresden, this inquiry also examines reasons for the contemporaneous failure of the early standardized mass production of health food in Germany. The latter, an early ecological reaction to convenience foods, was based on the new values of nutrition and health as they had been developed in the context of the life reform movement since the late nineteenth century.

The Development of Industrial Starch Production since the Late-Nineteenth Century

The production of starch dates back to antiquity. During the Middle Ages Holland dominated the production of starch and traded it extensively. After Saxony, the Prussian province of Westphalia became the centre of German wheat-starch production in the late nineteenth century, whereas the production of potato starch was concentrated in Brandenburg and the agrarian Eastern provinces of Pomerania, Posen, East and West Prussia and Silesia. The beginning of commercial starch production in Germany is difficult to understand on the basis of statistics alone. According to the sparse sources available, it emerged around the seventeenth century as a branch of the baking industry. The oldest known record is from Halle an der Saale and dates back to the year 1620. This is where a preindustrial centre of German starch production comprising full-time as well as part-time workers developed. They not only supplied the local textile industry, but they also opened up supra-regional markets, profiting from the transport connexions across the Saale with Berlin, Magdeburg, Leipzig, Braunschweig, Kassel and Nürnberg. Along with the shift to factory production, which was accompanied by the introduction of steam power and new technology, the production of starch broke away from the bakery

---

19   For this special liking for sweetness, compare Teuteberg, 1996, and Mintz, 1985. The sweet coffee of Swiss textile workers is discussed by Braun, 1965, 92; for the physiological problems, see Kluthe and Kasper, 1999.

20   See Ellerbrock, 2008.

Source: Westphalian Business Archive, Dortmund.

Figure 2.1   Hoffmann's Starch was the market leader in nineteenth-century Germany

craft and established itself as an independent sector in the 1840s. According to expert judgements, Germany already played a leading role in the European starch industry around the mid-nineteenth century, alongside Belgium, France and Britain.[21]

The German starch industry changed structurally as early as the nineteenth century. Firstly, these changes concerned the types of starch. Until 1816, when potato starch was first produced in France, production had been limited to wheat starch. Around the mid-nineteenth century, the production of rice starch emerged in England, with Norwich as its centre. It could not develop in Germany before the abolition of the import duties in 1870.[22] German starch production gradually shifted from wheat starch to potato starch in the course of the nineteenth century. According to a reliable expert estimation, about 3 million decitons of potato starch, 250,000 decitons of rice starch, 100,000 decitons of wheat starch and 50,000 decitons of maize starch were produced in 1896.[23]

The demand for starch changed as well. Traditionally, the textile and shoe industries (shoemaker's glue) had bought starch. The rise of rice starch (around 1900 the factory for Hoffmann's Cat-brand starch in Bad Salzuflen was the market leader with about 1,200 employees and a yearly production of 6,000 tonnes) was slowed down after a vigorous collaboration between the wheat-starch makers and

---

21   Wágner, 1876, preface, emphasizes that Germany had already been playing this role 'for decades'.

22   See van der Borght, 1899.

23   See Saare, 1896, 5–7.

the agrarian lobby, which was very powerful in the German Empire. However, the sector ultimately overtook the traditional wheat-starch production. Rice starch was mainly used 'in very high quantities for laundry, and almost exclusively by housewives in housekeeping'.[24]

The well-known manual of starch production by Ladislaus von Wágner from 1876 shows that the food and luxury-food industries demanded starch products very early:

> It is used for the stiffening of laundry, the gluing of paper, for dressing and sizing in the linen and cotton industries, for the representation of starch rubber, of starch syrup and sugar, for the fabrication of pasta (noodles, macaroni), for the production of artificial sago. Moreover, wheat starch is eaten in every household in great quantities in the form of our staple food, i.e. bread, as well as in different pastries, which we usually produce with wheat flour.[25]

The restructuring and rise of the wheat-starch industry and the emergence of the convenience-food industry before the First World War were closely correlated. This development was abruptly interrupted by the economic control measures during the First World War. The consequences of the ensuing plight of the food industry and the industrial production of substitutes will be considered in more detail below. The development of the German starch industry in the interwar period is only sparsely documented. Concrete figures are only given in an older account from the postwar years.[26] According to this, the prewar production rate was reached, on average, in the years between 1924–1925 and 1938–1939, despite the cession of land stipulated in the Treaty of Versailles (most notably Alsace-Lorraine, Western Prussia and Posen which were important production locations). With an average of 282,000 tons, the former rate of production was even exceeded by 2,000 tons. Again, the sector underwent conspicuous structural changes. Thus, the share of potato starch fell from 82 per cent to 63 per cent of overall production. This was mainly a consequence of the loss of territory east of the Elbe. The share of rice starch also decreased, from about 9 per cent to 2.9 per cent, while the share of maize starch rocketed from 3.2 per cent to 28.8 per cent. Wheat-starch production, which amounted to 5.7 per cent, was unchanged from before the war. According to Gustav Deiters, head of the German wheat-starch association, only about one-fifth of the 44 wheat-starch producers which had existed before the First World War survived the war and the years of crisis. He noted that ten factories were active 'and, according to our exact measuring from early October 1926', process '360 sacks of 100 kilogrammes of wheat flour each every day'. The resulting outputcomprised '52 per cent Prima starch, 15 per cent Secunda starch and 10 per cent wheat glue'.[27]

---

24   Cited Saare, 1896, 67–8.
25   Wágner, 1876, 190.
26   Götze, 1950, 17–21.
27   Ellerbrock, 2008, 107.

The quantities of raw materials used by the German starch industry (potatoes, wheat, rice and maize) differed in the 1920s.[28] Maize and wheat showed only narrow fluctuations but rice and potatoes declined throughout the decade. When the world economic crisis broke in 1929, the use of wheat and maize declined to a low point in 1932. By contrast, the use of rice and potatoes rose. After the crisis, the use of rice was limited by the National Socialists' attempt to restrict the currency drain. Thus, the economic circumstances concerning the supply of raw materials meant that maize and wheat-starch production was maintained rather than rice and potato starch.

The operational structure of the German starch industry also changed noticeably. The trade census of 1907 documented 406 companies with 6,302 employees, including 362 'Motorenbetriebe' motor-powered companies totalling 14,299 h.p. Steam engines, which yielded a total power of 13,191 h.p. in 322 factories, still dominated, whereas only 32 companies were electrified.[29] A strong consolidation process took place after the First World War.[30] Up to the mid-1920s the number of factories had decreased to 204 and the number of employees to 4,776. By contrast, the mechanization of production had developed significantly with a total power of 19,000 h.p. Electrification, especially, had substantially increased. Expressed in operating numbers, the average company size increased from 15.5 to 23.5 employees and the average technical performance from 35.2 h.p. to 92.6 h.p. Up to the mid-1930s, when the food industry and commercial starch production gained special government attention in view of the future war economy, this process of consolidation continued. It was clearly envisaged by the Four Year Plan promulgated in 1936. According to an official production survey of German industry for 1936, only 103 starch factories were left on the market with, however, 6,838 employees. This meant a further increase in the average company size to 66.4 employees. The production volume of the sector was stated to be about 100 million marks.[31]

The Beginnings of the Convenience-Food Industry in Germany

Convenience food, that is, foods which shorten or facilitate the preparation of meals, emerged in the late nineteenth century, contemporaneously with the standardized industrial mass-production of food. Soup products like the 'Erbswurst' (pea sausage), soup tablets, meat extract, bouillon and condiment products began this development. Jakob Tanner talks about an 'alliance of science and shortage' as

---

28   See Hoffmann. 1965, 624–5.

29   Statistik des Deutschen Reichs, vol. 218, 382 and vol. 214, issue 1, 19.

30   See trade census results, 16 June1925; *Statistisches Jahrbuch für das Deutsche Reich* 1928, 106.

31   Die Deutsche Industrie, 1939, 55 (Schriftenreihe des Reichsamts für wehrwirtschaftliche Planung, 1).

Source: Westphalian Business Archive, Dortmund.

Figure 2.2   The Maggi company was the pioneer of the modern soup industry

well as about a 'rationalization of nutrition' which reached its climax in Germany during the first surge of Americanization in the early twentieth century.[32]

An examination of contemporary trade statistics shows that the early companies are hard to classify and to identify. Knorr AG, which in 1899 had emerged from the family business founded by Carl Knorr in Heidelberg in 1838, is listed among the canning factories, while Maggi and Dr. Oetker in Bielefeld were counted among the cereal-products factories. Finally, the Bahlsen company, founded in 1889, a pioneer of the modern baking industry, was listed among the bakeries. All these companies underwent considerable growth. In the canning industry, for example, the number of employees increased fivefold to over 16,000 between 1875 and 1907 and financially the companies of this sector were as extraordinarily profitable as the starch factories.[33]

In 1925 the German food industry already counted 52 factories producing bouillon cubes, 105 baking and custard powder factories and 94 cereal-products factories, which together amounted to 7,740 employees. The further development of this sector, which underwent a considerable process of consolidation after the

---

32   Tanner, 1997, 583–613, especially 593–4.
33   Ellerbrock, 1993, 318–26.

world economic crisis of 1929, shows how profitable this market was. Without counting the small businesses employing less than six persons, 92 factories of the cereal products industry employing 10,908 workers were counted in 1936 – a growth of 41 per cent. The turnover reached 167.5 million marks.[34]

The modern soup industry became one of the main customers for wheat starch. Everything started with meat extract, the invention of which is inseparably connected with Justus Liebig, professor of chemistry and pharmacy in Gießen, who had invented meat extract as a food for invalids in 1852.[35] Its development finally came from Julius Maggi, a mill owner and corn merchant in the Swiss Kempttal with subsidiaries in Zürich and Schaaffhausen, and the social policy maker, Friedrich Schuler, a physician and judge who also worked 'hands-on' as a factory inspector. The latter recommended producing easily digestible legume-flour from the protein-containing pulses, that is, peas and beans, as a substitute for expensive meat to prevent malnutrition and high infant mortality. Julius Maggi then started to experiment in this field and finally achieved his entrepreneurial breakthrough with Maggi condiments in 1887. Before the First World War, Maggi had become an international food manufacturer with a capital of 18 million Swiss francs, which brought 17 different soup cubes as well as 33 different soup rolls to the market. The demand for high quality wheat starch and protein products was insatiable. Besides Maggi, Carl Knorr also became prominent in the highly competitive soup market. Maggi's attempt to oust Knorr from the market by forming a 'soup trust' with the American Liebig company failed, as well as his strategy 'to buy stock from C.H. Knorr on every possible occasion.'[36] Knorr finally found a strong partner with the Deutsche Maizena GmbH, which bought a considerable share in Knorr in 1922. The Deutsche Maizena had been founded in Hamburg in 1916 by the American concern Corn Products Company (CPC), which had already run a sales bureau in the city since 1905. Maizena produced food containing starch in Barby on the Elbe-Saale estuary, in Hamburg and in Krefeld, most notably the eponymous product Maizena, entered as a trademark in 1916, and starch flour produced from maize, free of protein, fat and fibres, which was used to bind and thicken soups, sauces and desserts. Knorr and Maizena merged at the end of the 1950s and later formed part of the Unilever concern together with CPC.

In spite of some slumps as a consequence of economic vicissitudes during and after the First World War and during the world economic crisis in 1929, the convenience-food industry established itself firmly within the German food industry. However, the development of a cereal-products factory by Dr. Volkmar Klopfer in Dresden, a pioneer company of standardized health-food mass production in Germany ran completely differently: it failed.

---

34 Die Deutsche Industrie, 55.
35 See Teuteberg with Ellerbrock et al., 1990.
36 Speech by Julius Maggi before the board of directors on 22 April, 1909; cited in Ellerbrock, 1993, 367.

Source: Source: Westphalian Business Archive, Dortmund.

Figure 2.3   Dr. Volkmar Klopfer's cereal-products factory, Dresden

The Foundation and Failure of the Cereal-Products Factory Dr. Volkmar Klopfer in Dresden

The company was founded in 1900 by the student of chemistry, Volkmar Klopfer (1874–1943), and had become a flagship company of the so-called life-reform movement which developed in the late nineteenth century. In terms of architecture, the factory building set new design principles by its *Art Nouveau* style. The life-reform movement in the second half of the nineteenth century – also known as 'reform of the way of life', 'hygienic reform movement' or 'diet reform' – is generally interpreted as a bourgeois cultural movement with anti-modern ideals. Neither economic nor social interests motivated the value-based behaviour of its disciples but the implementation of a new 'cultural identity'. The 'loosening of religious ties' created an ideological vacuum filled by the life-reform ideas, which were invested with the character of a reformist ersatz religion.[37]

The life-reformers' criticism was 'aroused by the increasing process of scientification and rationalization of society, which [is felt as] a lack and deprivation of individual existence'.[38] Serious 'ravages of civilization' (ecocide caused by progressing urbanization, the question of habitation, grave air pollution, changed

---

37 Frecot et al., 1972, 18.
38 Krabbe, 1974, 14; Barlösius, 1997.

eating habits and health problems caused by factory work) had 'already lead to an extensive physical and psychological degeneration of the peoples in the European cultural sphere'.[39] The vegetarian and naturopath Adolf Just put the new self-conception in a nutshell in his famous appeal from 1896: 'City life ruins body, spirit and soul because more and more it leads away from nature and everything natural.'[40]

Recent research has shown that the life-reform movement was above all looking for alternatives to the industrial mass production of food which would take up the 'reactionary idea of natural agriculture' and 'natural keeping of animals' and question the pioneering scientific progress of agronomy: 'They were fighting agitatingly and demonstratively against the devaluation of food quality by chemical conservation, refining, additives and colourings which, in their opinion, went at the expense of the consumer's health.'[41] However, it overlooked the fact that it was precisely standardized industrial mass production based on continual scientific exploration which had produced a lasting improvement in the quality of life. The short-sighted call 'back to nature' uttered by the consumer on the basis of a subjective perception often failed to see that the image of a pre-industrial idyll did not have much in common with modern nutritional and hygienic standards.[42]

Klopfer, who had obtained a PhD in chemistry at the University of Rostock in 1913, produced food made from bread-grains in his factory. He employed special procedures based on extensive studies of the ingredients, namely of minerals and protein content. The first technique patented by Klopfer was based on the separation of wheat flour into starch and protein. He used the protein and mineral extracts gained by this process to increase the nutritional value of bread and noodles.[43] Contemporary advertisements said: 'Dr. Klopfer noodles – as nutritious as meat'. For his innovation in the production of lecithin, Klopfer won the Grand Prize at the first international hygiene exhibition in Dresden in 1911.[44] At about the same time, he developed the purely plant-based protein concentrate Glidine. This product, which is still on the market, 'contains all essential amino acids and is therefore suitable for vegetarians and senior citizens who often eat too little protein-containing food'.[45] The contemporary poster advertisements said: 'Dr. Klopfer-Glidine gives blood and nerves'.

In 1913 Klopfer started to produce whole-grain flour from rye which, by contrast to wheat, had hitherto been used mainly as animal feed. Klopfer obtained

---

39   Krabbe, 14.
40   Just, 1896.
41   Merta, 2003, 82.
42   Ellerbrock, 1987, 127–88. On the question of food quality see 'Consumer Protection in International Pespective', *Economic History Yearbook* 1, 2006; and Hierholzer, 2010.
43   See his 1917 essay *'Über den Eiweißgehalt der Stärke und eine Methode der Herstellung eiweißfreier Stärkepräparate'*.
44   Klopfer obtained lecithin from wheat flour by use of a centrifuge he had developed. He then sold the product to be processed into tonic foods for invalids.
45   Protina Pharma GmbH: Firmen- und Produktgeschichte, 4.

yet another patent for a procedure aimed at the production of the so-called 'Klopfer bread', which made coarse whole-grain bread from whole-grain flour easily digestible while at the same time considerably improving its nutritional value.[46] His inventive genius was unlimited: when after the First World War the railway freight charges rose to a point that it was no longer economic to transport flour farther than 100 kilometres, Dr. Klopfer developed rye bran. Bran is much lighter than flour and could be sent all over Germany. The consumers could mix the patented Klopfer bran with white flour and obtain a full whole-grain flour.[47]

The company was not an economic success and fell under the control of the banks, probably as early as 1921.[48] The Mitteldeutsche Grundstücks-Aktiengesellschaft and the Sächische Aktiengesellschaft in Leipzig became the new owners. Dr. Klopfer stayed on as a director at first, but then left the company in 1928. He had already founded a second company, the Chemisches Werk Dr. Klopfer, with his life companion Martha Hadlich (1881–1961) in 1924. This company exists to this day in Ismaning, Bavaria, and trades under the name of 'Protina Pharma GmbH und Klopfer-Nährmittel Vertriebs GmbH'. It focused its production on drugs with mineral active ingredients like glidine, Basica, Diasporal and the sulphur bath Dr. Klopfer. The old Klopfer factory was eventually continued as the Dr. Volkmar Klopfers Nahrungsmittel-Aktiengesellschaft founded by the financiers Paul Agust Hoppe from Hamburg, the Kommerzialrat (councillor of commerce) Karl Taussig from Prague and Friedrich Karl Freiherr von Wechmar, Willy Schmidt and Willy Fritzsch from Dresden on 5 January 1928. The company was endowed with a share capital of 400,000 marks with the aim of 'renting the properties hitherto owned by Dr. August Volkmar Klopfer in Dresden in order to restart and continue the food factory as well as to utilize the procedures of food production patented by Dr. Klopfer'.[49]

Balances from this economically unpleasant period document a poor profit situation. In 1929, only shortly before the spectacular stock market crash in New York, the share capital was doubled to 800,000 marks. After the 'Black Friday', the company plummeted and made a loss of 506,849 marks in the financial year 1929. The refinancing used up 560,000 marks so that the share capital sank to 240,000 marks. Then it was raised to 390,000 marks by a share issue. Despite a surplus from the reconstruction amounting to about 50,000 marks the following financial year was again clearly negative with a loss of 160,601 marks. The shares were merged in the ratio of five to one in a second attempt at refinancing which diminished the capital to 78,000 marks. The capital was again raised to 200,000

46   Klopfer, 1930.
47   Klopfer, 1918.
48   The company archives of Crespel & Deiters contains the detailed estimation by a 'sworn' expert of the 'mechanical equipment' of the Klopfer factory. The document is dated 29 January 1921 and lists the factory's equipment down to the last screw. It is probable that this inventory was arranged by the creditor banks; WWA F 196, Nr. 17, vol. 1.
49   *Handbuch der Deutschen Aktiengesellschaften* 1928, vol. 1, 1619.

marks by another share issue. After a further bad result and a loss of 377,929 marks the company became insolvent on 18 October 1935. The insolvency proceedings which had initially been agreed upon by a majority in order to avoid bankruptcy were cancelled in December and a liquidation procedure was initiated. The company expired in January 1936.[50]

Convenience Food instead of Wholegrain Food: Four Theses

The economy of scarcity and ersatz – the First World War and the 'nostrum market' (for quack or patent medicines), which had already emerged at the end of the nineteenth century, permanently discredited whole-grain bread and dietetic products like those produced by the Klopfer factory in the eyes of the customers and influenced consumer behaviour in the 1920s.

Dietetic preparations, which were often traded as '*Geheimmittel*' had already begun to flood the market under fantasy names in the late nineteenth century, but could only rarely do justice to the promises of quality given by their producers. The failed attempts to introduce Tropon and Siris to the market are a case in point.[51] Financial means of over a million marks were provided for advertisement purposes – a gigantic sum by the standard of the times. These problems of acceptance among the customers increased as a result of the economic control during the First World War.

After the failure of the food economy the double motto of the war economy was dilution and ersatz.[52] The tense supply situation brought an increasing number of unscrupulous producers of surrogates and downright fraudulent companies into the arena and consequently the entire substitute industry was discredited: 'a whole new market was created where coffee tablets, tea pills, punch and grog cubes, meat juice pastilles and other products were extolled under names with the greatest possible advertising appeal. The imagination was boundless and patriotism proved to be excellently suited to advertising purposes.'[53] Dr. Klopfer's advertising slogan 'As nutritious as meat' was bound to trigger increasingly negative associations among customers.

On the other hand, the experience of penury and shortages gave an important impetus to the consumption of convenience-food products, namely instant soup. American market analyses in the 1950s found that consumers associated soup with deep cultural and psychological concepts such as 'mother', 'family' or 'warmth'.

The structures of distribution and sale – were not suitable for the sale of large quantities of health foods. Compared to the distribution system of industrially

---

50 .See *Handbuch der Deutschen Aktiengesellschaften* (4) 1930, (IV) 1931, (IV) 1931, (V) 1933, (II) 1934 and (VI) 1935.

51 Redlich, 1935, 162 et seq.

52 Roerkohl, 1991, 216–29.

53 Roerkohl, 1991, 218.

produced food and adjusted to the different market potentials, they were inefficient and backward. Infrastructure provisions (the triumph of lorry traffic started in the 1920s), advertising campaigns and branded products further advanced the principle of chain stores in the food-retailing industry after the First World War. Moreover, department stores with food halls and co-operative societies (*Genossenschaften*) in food retailing (most notably Co-op, Rewe, Edeka) were booming. This sophisticated organization of distribution and sale of standardized mass products of the food industry was opposed by the '*Reformhaus*' (health store), where products for natural cures, vegetarian food and for personal hygiene were offered. The first store, the '*Gesundheits-Zentrale*', was opened by Carl Braun in Berlin in 1887. The notion '*Reformhaus*' was coined by Karl August Heynen for his health store '*Jungbrunnen*' in Wuppertal in 1900. There were no more than 200 health-food stores when the '*Vereinigung Deutscher Reformhäuser*' (Union of German health-food stores) was founded in 1925; from 1927 it became the '*neuform Vereinigung Deutscher Reformhäuser e.G.*'. This co-operative union was to strengthen the position of health-food retailers by centrally organized purchasing, advertisements in common and a uniform design for the stores.

The small number of health-food stores is due to the fact that the market potential was limited. The *Deutsche Verein für Naturheilkunde und für volksverständliche Gesundheitspflege* (German Association of Naturopathy and Health Care Intelligible to the People) was founded in 1883. In 1900 it changed its name to *Deutscher Bund der Vereine für naturgemäße Lebens- und Heilweise* (German Association of Societies for Natural Life and Healing). In 1889 this umbrella organization united 142 local branches with 19,000 members and in 1913, 885 local branches with 148,000 members. After several national vegetarian associations had been founded in the nineteenth century, the *Deutscher Vegetarierbund* (German Association of Vegetarians) was founded as an umbrella organization with headquarters in Leipzig. In 1912, there were 25 German vegetarian associations with about 5,000 members. However, the number of members declined considerably at the time of the Weimar Republic.[54] Even though about 150,000 people were organized in associations of the life reform movement before the First World War, their share of the total population of about 64.6 million people was exceedingly small.

A recent study has shown that the idea of self-reliance was widespread among the members of the life-reform movement.[55] Thus, the life-reform movement does not seem to have had a great impact on per capita consumption. According to Hans J. Teuteberg's research, there even was a decline in the consumption of rye bread in the late nineteenth century,[56] whereas the consumption of wheat-flour bread as

---

54   See Fritzen, 2006, Krebs and Reulecke, 1998.
55   Gundermann, 2003, 375–411, especially 386–90.
56   Teuteberg, 1986, 225–79, especially 236 et seq.

a status symbol of the upper classes who had a 'more refined system of nutrition' was constantly growing.[57]

The influencing of consumption failed – in the case of whole-grain bread; on the contrary, the starch industry and convenience-food production expanded after the failure of the planned economy of National Socialism.

The National Socialists took up some of the ideas of the life-reform movement such as the concepts of allotments and settlements. They propagated the consumption of whole-grain bread and Adolf Hitler, who ate very little meat but was not a complete vegetarian, was presented as an ascetically living vegetarian, animal lover and non-smoker in National Socialist propaganda. Recent studies even talk about the 'whole-grain bread policy' of National Socialism.[58] This was supported by Richard Wagner's treatise '*Religion und Kunst*' (Religion and Art), stylized as an iconic document of National Socialism, where the consumption of meat was denounced as a Semitic, non-Aryan heritage.[59] However, to impute the anticipation of National Socialist thought to the life-reform movement would go too far since the reactions within the movement were mixed. While, for example, the German Vegetarian Association dissolved in 1935 to evade the *Gleichschaltung* (forcible co-ordination), the *Genossenschaft Eden*, on the other hand, turned to racial nationalistic thought.

After the seizure of power, the National Socialist economic policy created new regulatory conditions and vast employment-creation programmes as well as beginning to rearm, which triggered a strong economic recovery that even exceeded the years of the 'economic miracle of the Federal Republic' with an average rise in the national income of 8.2 per cent per year. The starch-processing industries, especially the food industry, also profited from this economic boost and registered a more-or-less steep upswing. At the same time, the ideologically motivated influencing of the consumers failed, the consumption of rye bread stagnated and fell behind the level of 1913.[60] On the one hand, the starch industry won importance due to the National Socialists' striving for autarky within the food economy, which was supposed to help fill the gaping supply gaps caused by the failed policy of the '*Reichsnährstand*' (State agriculture). On the other hand, the convenience-food production for military purposes, that is, food supply for the front, boomed.

New styles of consumption – with slight exaggeration, one could say that the rise of the convenience-food industry was caused by new style of consumption after the American model that was already emerging in the 1920s, but which had initially been impeded by non-economic political factors. They eventually became apparent during the economic miracle of the Federal Republic.

---

57   Thoms, 2005, 443 et seq.
58   Spiekermann, 2001, 91; also see Melzer, 2003.
59   Fest, 1973, 74 et seq.
60   Teuteberg, 1986, 236–7.

A mixture of economic and cultural phenomena was thus responsible for the rise of the convenience-food industry on the one hand and for the failure of the first health-food factory. The early entrepreneurial failure of the Dr. Klopfer cereal-products factory should, however, not be interpreted solely as the failure of the nutrition reform movement as it introduced lasting innovations not only in terms of the history of ideas. Breads like *Schrotbrot, Grahambrot, Simonsbrot* or *Steinmetzbrot* were product innovations similar to Klopfer's inventions and developments for which the market was not yet ready in the late nineteenth century or in the interwar period.[61] This did not change with the whole-grain bread policy of National Socialism. Neither was the *Fresswelle* (wave of gluttony) of the Federal Republic affected by the ideas of the nutrition reform movement. It was only with the change of values of the whole society which began in the late 1960s that the origins of the mega trend 'healthy food' can be found. 'Healthy food' is today the most important growth driver of the food market.[62] Its sale is no longer confined to health-food stores, which made their first milliard turnover in the early 1980s,[63] but has already conquered the supermarket shelves. Dr. Volkmar Klopfer certainly was one of its pioneers, but he failed in the 1920s because he was ahead of his time and only reached a small elitist group of consumers with his products.

References

Achard, F.C., 1800, *Kurze Geschichte der Beweise von der Ausführbarkeit im Großen und von den vielen Vortheilen der Zuckerfabrikation aus Runkelrüben*, Berlin.

Achard, F.C., 1812, *Die europäische Zuckerproduktion aus Runkelrüben (...) 3 Theile*, Leipzig.

Axa, J. and Bruhus, G., 1967, *Zucker im Leben der Völker. Eine Kultur- und Wirtschaftsgeschichte*, Berlin.

Barlösius, E., 1997, *Naturgemäße Lebensführung. Zur Geschichte der Lebensreform um die Jahrhundertwende*, Frankfurt, New York.

Baxa, J., 1937, *Die Zuckererzeugung 1600–1850*, Jena.

Bloc, B., 1920, *Rübensirup. Seine Herstellung, Beurteilung und Verwendung*, Leipzig.

Borght, R. van der, 1899, *Beiträge zur Geschichte der Deutschen Reisstärkeindustrie*, Berlin.

---

61 Merta, 2003, 93–208, especially 107–9.

62 Bundesvereinigung der Deutschen Ernährungsindustrie, Gesellschaft für Konsumforschung, *Report Consumer's Choice*, published on the occasion of the 2007 Allgemeine Nahrungs- und Genussmittel-Ausstellung in Cologne [the world's biggest Food and Beverage Fair].

63 Fritzen, 2006, 122.

Braun, R., 1965, *Sozialer und kultureller Wandel in einem ländlichen Industriegebiet im 19. und 20. Jahrhundert*, Erlenbach, Zürich and Stuttgart.

Deutsche Gesellschaft für Ernährung, 1984, *Erährungsbericht*.

Deutsche Industrie, Die, 1939, *Gesamtergebnisse der amtlichen Produktionsstatistik*, Berlin.

Döring, A. and Heizmann, B., 1981–1982, Krautkochen im Rheinland, in *Rheinisch-Westfälische Zeitschrift für Volkskunde*, vols 27–8.

Economic History Yearbook 1, 2006, 'Consumer Protection in International Perspective'.

Ellerbrock, K.P., 1987, 'Lebensmittelqualität vor dem Ersten Weltkrieg: Industrielle Produktion und staatliche Gesundheitspolitik', in Teuteberg, H.J., ed., *Durchbruch zum modernen Massenkonsum. Lebensmittelmärkte und Lebensmittelqualität im Städtewachstum des Industriezeitalters*, Münster.

Ellerbrock, K.P., 1993, *Geschichte der deutschen Nahrungs- und Genußmittelindustrie 1750–1914*, Stuttgart.

Ellerbrock, K.P., 2008, *Auf Stärke gebaut. Geschichte der Fa. Crespel & Deiters 1858–2008. Ein unternehmensgeschichtlicher Beitrag zur Geschichte der deutschen Weizenstärkeindustrie im 19. und 20. Jahrhundert*, Münster.

Fest, J.C., 1973, *Hitler. Eine Biographie*, Frankfurt.

Frecot, J. et al., 1972, *Fidus 1868–1948. Zur ästhetischen Praxis bürgerlicher Fluchtbewegungen*, München.

Fritzen, F., 2006, *'Gesünder Leben'. Die Lebensreformbewegung im 20. Jahrhundert*, Stuttgart.

Götze, W., 1950, 'Die westdeutsche Stärkewirtschaft in Vergangenheit und Gegenwart', in *Die Stärke*, no. 1, 2.

Grafschafter Krautfabrik Josef Schmitz KG., 1909, Meckenheim.

Gundermann, R., 2003, '"Bereitschaft zur totalen Verantwortung" – Zur Ideengeschichte der Selbstversorgung', in Prinz, M., ed., *Der lange Weg in den Überfluss. Anfänge und Entwicklung der Konsumgesellschaft seit der Vormoderne*, Paderborn, München, Wien and Zürich.

Handbuch der Deutschen Aktiengesellschaften, 1928, vol. I (4), 1930, (IV) 1931, (IV) 1931, (V) 1933, (II) 1934 and (VI) 1935.

Hengartner, T. and Merki, C.M., eds, 2001, *Genussmittel. Eine Kulturgeschichte*, 2nd edn, Frankfurt a. M. and Leipzig.

Hierholzer, V., 2010, *Regulierung von Nahrungsmittelqualität in der Industrialisierung 1871–1914*, Göttingen.

Hoffmann, W.G., 1931, *Stadien und Typen der Industrialisierung. Ein Beitrag zur quantitativen Analyse historischer Wirtschaftsprozesse*, Jena.

Hoffmann, W.G., 1965, *Das Wachstum der deutschen Wirtschaft seit der Mitte des 19. Jahrhunderts*, Berlin, Heidelberg and New York.

Joerissen, P. and Wagner, R., 1998, *Süßes Rheinland. Zur Kulturgeschichte des Zuckers,* Bonn.

Just, A., 1896, *Kehrt zur Natur zurück! Die naturgemäße Lebensweise als einziges Mittel zur Heilung aller Krankheiten und Leiden des Leibes, des Geistes und der Seele*, Braunschweig.

Kaufmann, W., 1950, *Weltzuckerindustrie. Fiskalische Vorzugsbehandlung, Kartelle, internationales und koloniales Recht*, Berlin.

Kellenbenz, H., 1966, *Die Zuckerwirtschaft im Kölner Raum von der napoleonischen Zeit bis zur Reichsgründung*, Köln.

Klopfer, V., 1917, 'Über den Eiweißgehalt der Stärke und eine Methode der Herstellung eiweißfreier Stärkepräparate', in *Medical Microbiology and Immunology*, vol. 83, issue 21.

Klopfer, V., 1918, *Die Verbesserung des Brotes durch Ausschießung der Kleie und Vervollkommnung des Backverfahrens*, Dresden and Leipzig.

Klopfer, V., 1930, *Brot*, Dresden.

Kluthe, R. and Kasper, K., 1999, *Süßwaren in der modernen Ernährung*, Stuttgart and New York.

Korn, W., 1936, *Untersuchungen zur Standortfrage des deutschen Zuckerrübenbaus*, Würzburg.

Krabbe, W.R., 1974, *Gesellschaftsveränderung durch Lebensreform. Strukturmerkmale einer sozialreformerischen Bewegung im Deutschland der Industrialisierungsperiode*, Göttingen.

Krebs, D., and Reulecke, J., eds, 1998, *Handbuch der deutschen Reformbewegungen 1880–1933*, Wuppertal.

Langstedt, F.L., 1800, 'Thee, Kaffee und Zucker' in *Historischer, chemischer, diätetischer, ökonomischer und botanischer Hinsicht*, Nürnberg.

Lippmann, O., 1929, *Geschichte des Zuckers von den ältesten Zeiten bis zum Beginn der Rübenzuckerproduktion*, 2nd edn, Berlin.

Loebner, H.D., 2005, *Die schlesische Rübenzuckerproduktion*, St. Katharinen.

Marggraf, A.S., 1768, *Chymische Schriften* vol. 2, Berlin.

Melzer, J., 2003, *Vollwerternährung. Diätetik, Natrheilkunde, Nationalsozialismus, sozialer Anspruch*, Stuttgart.

Merta, S., 2003, *Wege und Irrwege zum modernen Schlankheitskult. Diätkost und Körperkultur als Suche nach neuen Lebensstilformen 1880–1930*, Stuttgart.

Mintz, S., 1985, *Die süße Macht. Kulturgeschichte des Zuckers*, Frankfurt a. M. and New York.

Peterson, A., 1998, *Zuckersiedegewerbe und Zuckerhandel in Hamburg von 1814–1834*, Stuttgart.

Pohl, M., 1987, *Südzucker 1887–1987. 150 Jahre Süddeutsche Zucker-Aktiengesellschaft*, Mainz.

Redlich, F., 1935, *Reklame. Begriff – Geschichte – Theorie*, Stuttgart.

Roerkohl, A., 1991, 'Hungerblockade und Heimatfront. Die kommunale Lebensmittelversorgung' in *Westfalen während des Ersten Weltkriegs*, Stuttgart.

Rostow, W.W., 1956, 'The Take-Off into Self-Sustained Growth', in *Economic Journal* LXVI.

Saare, O., 1896, *Die Industrie der Stärke und der Stärkefabrikate in den Vereinigten Staaten von Amerika und ihr Einfluss auf den englischen Markt*, Berlin.

Spiekermann, U., 2001, 'Vollkorn für den Führer. Zur Geschichte der Vollkornbrotpolitik im Dritten Reich', in *Zeitschrift für Sozialgeschichte des 20. und 21. Jahrhunderts* 16.

Tannenberg, G., 1944, *Der Kampf um den Zucker*, Leipzig.

Tanner, J., 1997, 'Industrialisierung, Rationalisierung und Wandel des Konsum- und Geschmacksverhaltens im europäisch-amerikanischen Vergleich', in Siegrist, H., Kelble, H. and Kocka, J., eds, *Europäische Konsumgeschichte*, Frankfurt and New York.

Teuteberg, H.J., 1986, 'Der Verzehr von Lebensmitteln in Deutschland pro Kopf und Jahr seit Beginn der Industrialisierung (1850–1975). Versuch einer quantitativen Langzeitanalyse', in Teuteberg, H.J. and Wiegelmann, G., *Unsere tägliche Kost. Geschichte und regionale Prägung*, Münster.

Teuteberg, H.J., with the assistance of Ellerbrock, K.P., et al., 1990, *Die Rolle des Fleischextrakts für die Ernährungswissenschaften und den Aufstieg der Suppenindustrie*, Stuttgart.

Teuteberg, H.J., 1996, Kulturwissenschaftliche Betrachtungen über das Schmecken, in Südzucker, A.G., ed., *De gustibus (non) est disputandum – Geschmack als Erfolgsgarant für Lebensmittel*, 22. Südzucker-Symposium, Mannheim and Ochsenfurt.

Thoms, U., 2005, *Anstaltskost im Rationalisierungsprozess. Die Ernährung in Krankenhäusern und Gefängnissen im 18. und 19. Jahrhundert*, Stuttgart.

Verein der deutschen Zuckerindustrie, 1950, *Hundert Jahre deutsche Zuckerindustrie 1850–1950*, Berlin.

Wágner, L., von, 1876, *Handbuch der Stärkefabrikation. Mit besonderer Berücksichtigung der mit der Stärkefabrikation verwandten Industriezweige namentlich der Dextrin-, Stärkesyrup- und Stärkezuckerfabrikation*, Weimar.

Wiegelmann, G., 1986, 'Zucker und Süßwaren im Zivilisationsprozess' in Teuteberg, H.J. and Wiegelmann, G., *Unsere tägliche Kost. Geschichte und regionale Prägung*, 2nd edn, Münster.

Chapter 3
Vinegar and Sugar: The Early History of Factory-Made Jams, Pickles and Sauces in Britain

Peter J. Atkins

Packaged goods preserved in sugar or vinegar appeared on an industrial scale in Britain in the eighteenth and early nineteenth centuries, yet they are rarely accorded any significance in food histories or histories of the retail grocery trade. Their extended shelf life was a very welcome feature in an era before refrigeration; in this they resembled hams and cheeses but they had the additional advantage that they were often in hermetically sealed bottles and so could be carried to the other side of world without deterioration. Where the bottles bore a label they were also standard bearers of the brand revolution to come. Customers learned to trust the brands and the implicit quality-guarantee they bore. In several ways, therefore, these goods prefigured the globalization of foodstuffs that is commonplace today.

When did these particular British tastes begin (see Table 3.1)? The scaling up of preserved fruits and vegetables from domestic to industrial products started in the 1760s but there was a long, drawn-out period from about 1830 onwards when factory methods, including mechanization and production lines, were adopted. This chapter will only be about those foods (mainly fruits and vegetables) that were preserved in vinegar or sugar. Unfortunately there is not space here to look at alternative preservation methods, such as drying, salting, smoking, fermenting, canning and freezing.

The Early Years: 1760–1830

Vinegar is a strong preservative because of the acidic environment it creates. It was expensive but readily available from the increasing number of vinegar breweries. One unfortunate side-effect is that acetic acid causes a chemical reaction with lead in the glaze of some earthenware, so, to avoid poisoning, pickles had to be stored in stoneware jars or in glass.[1] As a result, a pottery industry grew that was dedicated to producing 1lb and 2lb (454 g and 908 g) jars for pickles, jams and

---

1 Stoneware is a specialized type of pottery that is vitrified by firing at high temperatures, thereby becoming non-porous. Brears, 1991, 32–65.

Table 3.1   The origins of successful brands in pickling, potting, jams, sauces and essences

Origin	Company name	Factory location	Principal products
1750	Shippams	Chichester	Potted meat paste
1760	John Burgess and Son	London	Anchovy Essence
1793	E. Lazenby	London	Sauces and pickles
1797	James Keiller and Son	Dundee	Marmalade
1802	Cocks and Co.	Reading	Reading Sauce
1824	Batty and Co.	London	Nabob Pickles
1824	H.W. Brand	London	Essence of Chicken; A1 Sauce
1828	John Osborn	Not known	Gentlemen's Relish
1830	Crosse and Blackwell	London	Pickles, sauces, jam
1837	Lea and Perrins	Worcester	Worcestershire Sauce
1837	Goodall, Backhouse and Co.	Leeds	Yorkshire Relish
1853	Kenyon, Son and Craven	Rotherham	Jam, pickles, sauce, confectionery
1857	Barnes and Co.	London	Nile Sauce, Scarlet Strawberry Jam
1859	James Robertson and Sons	Paisley, Manchester	Marmalade
1867	T.W. Beach	Brentford	Jam
1869	Margetts and Co.	London	Preserves
1869	Hayward Bros	London	Pickles and sauces
1868	W.A. Baxter and Sons	Fochabers	Soup, jam
1870	Holbrooks	Birmingham	Sauce
1871	William Hartley and Sons	Liverpool, London	Jam
1872	Clarke, Nickolls and Coombs	Hackney	Confectionery (Clarnico), jam
1873	Chivers and Sons	Histon	Jam
1873	Maconochie Brothers	London	Pan Yan Pickle, sauces, jam
1874	Frank Cooper	Oxford	Marmalade
1875	F.G. Garton	Birmingham	HP Sauce
1880	T.J. Brewer	Plymouth	Colonial Fruit Sauce
1881	Duerr's	Manchester	Jam
1882	Allen Jeeves and Sons	Sandy	Pickles and sauces
1885	Wilkin	Tiptree, Essex	Jam
1885	George Mason and Co.	London	OK sauce
1880s	E. and T. Pink	Bermondsey	Jam
1889	Sharwoods	London	Chutney, pickles, curry powder
1892	Lipton	Bermondsey	Groceries, tea, jam
1893	Elsenham Quality Foods	Elsenham, Essex	Jam

Sources: Jeremy, 1984–1986; Slaven and Checkland, 1986–1989; Harrison, 2004; and various others.

marmalades. Glass was reserved for bottled sauces, at least until technological developments in sheet glass made it possible to mass produce cheap jam jars from the 1920s onwards.

It is sometimes said that packaged goods, especially those recognizably branded, were an innovation of the second half of the nineteenth century, growing in parallel with the grocery trade and with the expansion of disposable incomes.[2] While this is true of jam, branded table sauces and pickles operated to a different chronology. In the last forty years of the eighteenth century some of the larger Italian warehousemen in London began advertising in newspapers. John Burgess, for instance, offered West India Pickles, Cayenne Pepper, Bengal Currie Powder, Japan Soy, Lemon Pickle, Oyster Ketchup, Shallot Ketchup and Devonshire Sauce.[3] Other grocers listed a variety of other proprietary keeping sauces, along with generic ketchups and pickles and items such as capers, oils and mustard.[4] The evidence suggests that consumption of all of these items was restricted to those with middling to upper levels of disposable income.[5]

It is unclear how many Italian warehousemen were also manufacturers. A few claimed to be the originators of particular table sauces but their main function was as wholesalers to the grocery trade and retailers in their own right. Whenever a particular pickle or sauce became popular, demand was met by a gradual scaling up from a domestic to a workshop context. Lazenby's is a good example of this. In 1793 Elizabeth Lazenby was given the recipe of a fish sauce by her innkeeper brother, Peter Harvey, as a means of supporting her family. She manufactured it herself and sold it from Edward [now Wigmore] Street, Portman Square. It was advertised in the newspapers as Harvey's Sauce and sales over the years were sufficiently buoyant for her to receive an annuity in retirement of £300 a year.[6] Harvey's Sauce became well known and was frequently mentioned in the popular media but it was only one of a stable of products that in the early nineteenth century became known as Lazenby's Pickles. Steady growth meant moving to a factory in Southwark in 1808, where they remained until 1926, right in the centre of London's south bank cluster of food and leather industries.[7]

Two factors were important in this early period. First, most table sauces were described as being for use either with fish or meat and they were consumed by the kind of relatively prosperous urban middle-class households whose intake of animal protein was increasing. Sauces and other condiments may have been ways of improving the palatability of foods that were often of low quality, given the problems in building efficient food-supply systems in these early decades of rapid

2 Winstanley, 1983.

3 From about 1760 onwards, John Burgess was based in The Strand. His business flourished and his emphasis gradually shifted towards manufacturing.

4 Cox and Dannehl, 2007.

5 Burgess's Fish Sauce retailed at 3s. and 1s.6d a bottle. *The Times*, 19 March 1853, 7C.

6 *The Times*, 14 January 1819, 3B; 29 July 1829, 3C.

7 Darlington, 1955.

urbanization, and pickles gave access to vegetables in seasons when fresh greens were expensive. Eating out was also a part of the changes taking place, and bottled sauces and pickles were used in the chop houses, taverns and dining rooms that abounded in the larger towns and cities.[8]

The second factor was that the increasingly global projection of British political power from the mid-eighteenth century onwards required preserved foods that could reliably be transported to different climates. Table sauces and pickles, for instance, were frequently part-cargoes on ships sailing to India and Australasia. Ideas travelled in the reverse direction via returning imperial servants, including the former governor of Bengal, Lord Marcus Sandys, who gave the chemists Lea and Perrins a recipe and asked them to make up a sauce that he had enjoyed in India. After a false start, they produced a spicy Worcestershire Sauce that was released in 1837 and was a great success. In less than three decades they were selling 300,000 bottles a year.

The Mid-Nineteenth Century: 1830–1870

One of the earliest, largest and most successful manufacturing and wholesaling firms was Crosse and Blackwell. In 1830 Edmund Crosse and Thomas Blackwell purchased the business of West and Wyatt, oilmen of King Street, Soho, whose stock was mainly whale and seal oil and some casks of pickles. By moving into packaged groceries and receiving a Royal Warrant (for 'oilery in ordinary') from the newly crowned Queen Victoria in 1837, they placed themselves firmly up-market. Located in the cosmopolitan and culinary heart of London, they were well placed to benefit from the expertise of exiles, such as the Italian chef, Qualliotti.[9] He brought with him a number of recipes, for potted meat, piccalilli and table sauces. In 1849 another celebrity chef, Alexis Soyer of the Reform Club, signed a contract that allowed the firm to sell Soyer's Relish, Soyer's Sauce and Soyer's Nectar under their brand, with his face on the label.[10]

The 1840s were a threshold decade for Crosse and Blackwell. In 1840 they dispatched their first consignment to Calcutta: 80 cases of pickles, 20 of bottled fruits, 9 of sauce, and also lesser amounts of mustard, vinegar and capers. This was the beginning of an export trade that was ultimately very profitable for them and within a few decades made them into a multinational company and a global brand. But India was not just a market; it also provided the inspiration for a number of products, including Captain White's Oriental Pickle, Col. Skinner's Mango Relish, and Crosse and Blackwell's Unsurpassed Currie Powder. Also in 1840 jam was added to their manufacturing portfolio.

---

8   Pickles were a common accompaniment to cold meat, and table sauces with hot meat or fish. Malden, 1890, 710–32.
9   London Metropolitan Archives/4467/A/03/001.
10   *The Times*, 13 March 1849, 11A.

A low point in the firm's history came in 1851 when they were named by Dr. Hassall in the *Lancet*.[11] He was conducting a high profile survey of adulterated foods and published the results, along with lists of offenders. Crosse and Blackwell were accused of producing pickles that were contaminated with copper sulphate. This was the result of boiling vinegar in the copper vessels. When called before the Select Committee on Adulteration of Food in July 1855, Thomas Blackwell confirmed that the company had immediately stopped this practice when they encountered the negative publicity and that they now used enamelled iron vessels for small batches of 12–15 gallons.[12] New vessels with a capacity of 325 gallons were purchased soon after, and these were heated by steam through a 32 foot platinum-coated coil.[13]

Crosse and Blackwell's pickle business dipped for a short period after the copper sulphate scandal but they received some credit for their openness and honesty. With growth resuming, in 1857 they added a second Soho Square property to one occupied in 1840. Together, these became the focus of an expansion into adjacent streets (Dean Street, Denmark Street, Stacey Street, and Sutton Street) and by 1865 they controlled 38,000 square feet of factory and warehouse space in the locality.[14] The economies of scale this brought and the use of technology reduced their costs per unit of output and a pot of jam that had cost 2s. in 1840 was retailing at 9d twenty-five years later.

By 1860 the firm was using contracts to tie in their suppliers. At this point they were sourcing onions from East Ham, cauliflowers and beans from Deptford, Greenwich, Kent and Bedfordshire, soft fruit from Fulham, cabbages from Essex, and mushrooms from Leicestershire.[15] Unusually for manufacturers at this date, they bypassed the wholesale markets such as Covent Garden. Instead agents were sent out to check the produce in the fields and make arrangements for transport direct to the factory in central London. As a result, Crosse and Blackwell were able to establish a system of farm-to-factory quality control, a major advantage over their competitors at a time when the adulteration of foodstuffs was at an all-time peak and the deterioration of fruits and vegetables was common before they reached market.[16]

In 1845 the number employed by the firm in manufacturing was only fifteen but this had grown to 386 by 1865, with 300 more in the summer when fresh vegetables and fruits were arriving daily by the ton.[17] In 1864 they used 140,000 gallons of vinegar, 225 tons of sugar and 18,000 gallons of olive oil, 16 tons

---

11 Hassall, 1855.
12 Select Committee on Adulteration, 1854–1855, Qq.1567–72.
13 Mayhew, 1865, 174–88.
14 Mayhew, 1865, 174–88.
15 Whitehead, 1878, 455–94.
16 Atkins, 1985. 102–33.
17 By 1881 there were 1,200 employees.

of capers, 80 tons of anchovies, 5,000 gallons of shrimps, 20 tons of Labrador salmon, 14,000 bushels of pickling onions, and 450 tons of fruit for jam.[18]

What may have been workshop output in 1840 had certainly become industrial in scale twenty years later. In 1864 Crosse and Blackwell were producing 27,000 gallons of ketchup annually, along with one million bottles of pickled walnuts, 160,000 bottles of anchovy sauce, 250,000 bottles of table jelly, 17,000 one-pound tins of peas, 420,000 bottles of preserved fruit, 200,000 gallons of pickles (equivalent to 1.6 million bottles), 338,000 tins of sardines, and 200,000 one-pound tins of Nova Scotia lobster. In all, nine million Crosse and Blackwell labels were used in 1864 on bottles and pots.[19] This astonishing throughput – among the largest in the world at this time – was matched by a vast storage capacity. The Soho warehouses at any one time held in barrels and tanks on average 20,000 gallons of ketchup, 6,400 gallons of olive oil, and 2,300 gallons of soy sauce.

It is difficult to estimate Crosse and Blackwell's market share. In 1868 they were said to supply one-quarter of the jam and marmalade consumed in London and this represented about 25 per cent of their total output of sweet spreads.[20] Their main export markets were in India, Australia and China.[21] Throughout the nineteenth century Crosse and Blackwell advertised extensively in newspapers and magazines. Although no doubt an expensive strategy, this reached their target middle-class readers and helped to make them into a household name. In 1835 they started with national titles, such as the *Morning Post*, and by the early 1840s they had extended to the provincial press. By the 1850s grocers were giving quality products free publicity in the local press by listing the luxury items they had in stock, such as Crosse and Blackwell sauces and Huntley and Palmer's biscuits. The products named in Crosse and Blackwell's own advertisements came and went in a rapid cycle of innovation. In the 1830s it was Soho Sauce and Dinmore's Essence of Shrimps. In the early 1840s Oriental Sauce was on offer 'to late residents of India and other hot climates', along with Sir Robert Peel's Sauce, Essence of Anchovies, Strasbourg potted meats and Imperial Pickle. By 1845 Abdool Fygo's Chutney and Fyzool Kurreem's Currie and Mulligatawny Pastes had been added to the list. Royal Table Sauce was new in 1846 and Soyer's New Sauce arrived in 1849. This was a company that did not stand still; they were constantly seeking new opportunities.

It is difficult to say what proportion of British exports of pickles and table sauces was represented by Crosse and Blackwell but it was probably a substantial one. In terms of declared value, this category in the *Annual Statement of Trade* rose from £146,380 in 1852 to £435,194 in 1870. The majority of goods at both dates went to British possessions around the world, notably to the settler colonies in Australia, New Zealand, Southern Africa and Canada. The Empire took 69

---

18   Mayhew, 1865, 174–88.
19   Mayhew, 1865, 174–88.
20   Routledge, 1868, 502–18.
21   Mayhew, 1865, 174–88.

per cent in 1860, 60 per cent in 1870, 67 per cent in 1880, and 62 per cent in 1890.[22] In 1875 pickles and sauces outshone the value of several other major food exports, notably butter, cheese, biscuits, cereals and flour, and they were bettered only by refined sugar and fish. There was genuine marketing skill here by several companies in carving out new markets, assisted no doubt by the need of colonists, the armed forces and imperial civil servants for a taste of home. The problem with this type of market, though, was that it had an upper limit. Products had to appeal to more than Britishness to be a long-term global success equivalent to the later achievements of Heinz.

The period 1830–1870 was so dominated by Crosse and Blackwell that it is easy to forget that other enterprises were producing preserved goods on an industrial scale. One of the most intriguing was James Keiller and Son of Dundee. Their beginnings were small. Keiller was a grocer and in 1797 he experimented with some overripe bitter Seville oranges and produced a variant of the already well-known sweet marmalade. There were other marmalade manufacturers but Keiller's masterstroke was in recognizing that the duties on sugar were holding down a potentially large market. In 1857 the firm opened a factory in Guernsey, where the duty was lower and for twenty years this accounted for one-third of their 1,000 ton a year output.[23] In 1879 they moved this operation to Silvertown, near London but continued production in Dundee and still sold their marmalade in stoneware jars made in Newcastle at the Maling pottery.[24]

Another famous marmalade manufacturer was James Robertson, who in 1856 was apprenticed to a grocer in Paisley. Three years later he had his own shop and was producing marmalade in a back room. This was scaled up to factory production in 1864 and in 1890 he moved to Droylesden, Manchester, to be closer to the market and later had another factory at Ledbury near to the fruit growers. The main products were Golden Shred (orange) and Silver Shred (lemon) marmalades, along with jam and mincemeat.[25]

The Late-Nineteenth Century: 1870–1914

The significance of the date 1870 is that this was the year that the sugar duty was halved, followed in 1874 by its abolition. A major factor in the subsequent growth in jam and marmalade manufacture, the reduced retail price also attracted more low-income consumers than had participated in the preserved goods market

---

22   In 1900 the percentages were 64 for pickles and sauces and 63 for confectionery and jam.

23   Bremner, 1869; Mathew, 1998a, 1998b.

24   These white ware jars were Maling's stock in trade for decades and in the 1860s represented 90 per cent of the jam and marmalade jars made in Britain. At one point they claimed to be the biggest pottery in the world.

25   The company trademarks are now owned by Premier Foods.

hitherto. The upward trend in the real wages of artisans at this time made it possible for them to pay more visits to their local corner shop or to the High Street grocer, and they were now able to choose from a number of jams. But a substantial portion of working families continued to live in or close to a state of chronic undernourishment and, for them, even the cheapest of jams (6d per pound in 1900) would have been unaffordable unless as part of a strategy of making palatable a diet mainly of bread. Butter was too expensive and margarine only just appearing.[26] According to Drummond and Wilbraham, 'bread and jam became the chief food of poor children for two meals out of three'.[27] Many of the household budgetary surveys from the 1870s and 1880s onwards mention tea, white bread and jam as an increasingly well-established combination, and consumption amongst this social group was a major factor in the doubling of the sugar intake that took place between 1863 and the 1890s.[28] Pickles and table sauces were rarely mentioned in these surveys.

The story of jam-making is more complex than a simple model of increasing demand and reduced prices suggests. There were, for instance, several hundred small jam factories serving their local areas, with concentrations particularly in the large cities and industrial districts. Because this was a highly competitive sector, profit margins were tight and there were many company failures in the forty years before the First World War.[29] Very few of this type of jam-maker made it through to national exposure, exceptions being E. and T. Pink and Wood Brothers, the latter producing 3,500 tons a year.[30] Where they did grow, this type of firm did so using imported fruit pulp and industrial glucose.[31] The pulp came from Australia, New Zealand and Canada during the off season and so kept the factories working throughout the year.[32] At this cheap end of the market various colorants were added, and salicylic acid and boric acid were also widely used as preservatives until banned in 1927. By contrast, at the top end there were two categories of jam-makers. First, there were the high volume manufacturers, who could keep costs low and who had extensive distribution networks. Lipton's were one example and Crosse and Blackwell another, although the true metier of both was in other food sectors.[33] Second, there was also a small group of elite producers of jam, whose clientèle was amongst those for whom changes in sugar duty meant little.

---

26 Johnston, 1977, 49.

27 Drummond and Wilbraham, 1959, 332.

28 Torode, 1966, 115–34; Oddy, 1970, 314–32.

29 Haggard, 1902, vol. 2, 52.

30 A 3lb (1.36kg) jar of Pink's jam cost only 6½d. Dept. Cttee on Fruit Culture, 1906, Q.11,849.

31 Dept. Cttee on Fruit Culture, 1906, Q.5249.

32 Dept. Cttee on Fruit Culture, 1906, Qq.8,008-8,185. Evidence of T.F. Blackwell.

33 From 1892 Lipton produced about 8,000 tons of jam a year but the factory in Bermondsey was closed in a phase of rationalization. Haggard, 1902; Mathias, 1967.

In addition to these considerations of market niches, there were also several routes into jam-making. The first was through agriculture. It is sometimes asserted that the depression in cereal prices from the 1870s was a push factor in persuading arable farmers to convert to fruit.[34] This seems unlikely, not least because of the change in mind-set that was required. Rider Haggard made this point clearly: 'A good fruit farmer is in his way something of an artist and, although the skills were plentiful in specialist districts such as the Vale of Evesham, they were absent in many wheat-growing counties'.[35] Also the uncertainty of tenant rights in some districts discouraged investment in tree, cane and bush fruits, which had to be spread over a number of years. Farmers who were habituated to rotational cropping were better off growing vegetables.[36] It is much more likely that the rapid increase in fruit growing from the 1870s was the result of demand from jam and bottling factories, met especially by smallholders in their immediate locality and by the expansion of production in the traditional fruit-growing regions.[37] Examples include Chivers of Histon, near Cambridge, and Wilkin of Tiptree Heath in Essex.[38]

The second route into jam-making was the grocery trade. Typically it was grocers in the industrial districts who saw a growing demand and sought to meet it. William Hartley of Pendle, Lancashire, is an example. He began in 1871 when a supplier failed to meet a contract and his own home-made substitute sold well.[39] Within three years he had moved to a factory at Bootle, near Liverpool, and then in 1886 to larger premises at Aintree, nearer to the railway. Hartley sold mainly to working-class consumers in industrial Lancashire and a tithe of his profits was always devoted to local philanthropy, including the so-called Hartley Village near the factory. As business expanded into the Midlands and south of England, he opened another factory, in Southwark, in 1901 and was soon producing a total of 1,000 tons of jam a week in season. Other grocers who went into jam-making include Margetts, Duerr's and Baxter's (later of soup fame).

As a result of these two types of jam-makers, it is not surprising that their factories were differentiated by location strategy into the rural, raw-material orientation and urban, market orientation.[40] The former had the advantage of fresher fruit but the latter, although generally taking second or third-rate raw material, had

---

34 Fruits and vegetables increased from nine to thirteen per cent of total value of crop output between 1875–1879 and 1895–1899. For fruit, one estimate has increases from 1890–1896 to 1911–1914 of 38 per cent by tonnage and 46 per cent by value. Perren, 2000, 215, 591–2.

35 Haggard, 1902, vol.1, 339.

36 Perren, 1995.

37 Jam-makers took 90 per cent of the country's raspberries, 60 per cent of the strawberries, and 40 per cent of the plums. Dept. Cttee on Distribution and Prices 1923.

38 Horridge, [1988]; Bear, 1899; Benham, 1985.

39 Peake, 1926; Beable, 1926.

40 For comments on the London and Scottish industries, see Board of Trade Report 'Progress of the sugar trade', 1884; and Sugar trade, Return, 1888.

a ready pool of casual labour to hand and reduced transport costs for the final product.[41] In 1906 there were 200–300 jam-makers, the five largest between them using 20,000 tons of fruit a year.[42] The Census of Production the following year recorded an output of £3.8 million in marmalade, jams and fruit jellies, which was significantly ahead of the £0.6 million for sauces and condiments, £0.4 million for pickles and preserved vegetables, and £0.3 million for other preserved fruits.[43]

Throughout the nineteenth century much continued to be done by hand, for instance the sorting and grading of fruit, and the podding, skinning, washing, trimming and dicing of vegetables.[44] For pickling there was soaking in brine to be done and boiling in vinegar. This was labour-intensive work and, as a result, manufacturers often employed the cheapest hands – women and girls – particularly as casual help in the high season. Hours of work were long and working conditions were notoriously bad, leading occasionally to strikes, such as the 1911 walk out at Pink's jam factory in Bermondsey.[45]

Although, as we have seen, some factories were mechanized in the second half of the nineteenth century, this was not implemented on the basis of any knowledge of organic chemistry.[46] There is no evidence of companies employing full-time chemists; any analytical input came through consultancy. Even as late as 1900 there was a reliance upon hand stirring in jam factories and 'customary means of knowing how long to boil and how to get the jam to set'; there was also some reluctance in adopting the jam-boiling thermometer.

The period 1870–1914 was undoubtedly the era of jam but sauces and pickles also continued to prosper as middle-class demand consolidated and some popular products reached the market, for instance various 'brown' sauces, such as HP (1875), OK (1885) and Daddies' Sauce (1904).[47] Crosse and Blackwell continued to plan: in the spirit of backward and forward integration, they owned a vinegar brewery and transported their own products on the River Thames, first from Victoria Wharf, Puddle Dock, until this was swept away by the Victoria Embankment in the late 1860s and later from Soho Wharf at the eastern end of Westminster Bridge. When this in turn became the site for County Hall, the company occupied Imperial Wharf at Battersea (1907), whence they barged 46,000 tons of products to the docks in just one year (1899).[48] At the beginning of the twentieth century Crosse and

---

41   Whitehead, 1878, 455–94.

42   Pratt, 1906.

43   The figures in the 1924 Census of Production were £11.0 million for marmalade, jams and fruit jellies, £3.1 million for pickles and sauces, and ££0.2 million for other preserved fruit.

44   Samuel, 1977, 6–7.

45   An. Rpt of the Chief Inspector of Factories and Workshops, 1900, 181–96; De la Mare 2008, 62–80.

46   'Makers of excellent jams had probably never heard of pectin, the substance in fruits that causes jams and jellies to set'. Morris, 1958, 38.

47   Landen and Daniel, 1988.

48   Royal Commission on the Port of London, 1902, Q.9,119.

Blackwell became increasingly acquisitive. In 1919 they took controlling interests in Keiller (marmalade) and Lazenby (pickles),[49] and the following year in Batger and Co. (preserves and confectionery) and Alexander Cairns (glass jars and patent lids). Their capital value at this time was £10 million.[50] In 1920 a parliamentary inquiry on the fruit industry was alerted to concerns about the firm's power nearing that of a 'combine' but the charge was rejected by the committee and instead they reported that Crosse and Blackwell had been operating responsibly during a period of high soft-fruit prices. We can see why the company's competitors were worried if we consider their declaration to the committee that they were by then in control of between 17 and 20 per cent of the nation's jam output.[51]

Crosse and Blackwell had already opened manufacturing capacity in Hamburg, before the First World War, and in the 1920s they added factories in Baltimore, Brussels, Buenos Aires, Paris and Toronto, and moved their London factory from Soho to Crimscott Street, Bermondsey. In 1929 Sarsons together with Champion and Slee, both vinegar brewers, were acquired, with obvious further benefits of integration for pickle and sauce manufacture. One of their most famous investments after the war was in 1922, when they purchased a redundant arms factory at Branston, near Burton-on-Trent and started making their iconic Branston Pickle, still a market leader today.[52] Despite their growth and outward-looking strategy, Crosse and Blackwell, along with other contemporary British food companies, are seen as conservative by historians of capitalism and brands.[53]

Conclusion

My argument in this chapter has been that the better-off members of the middle classes were influenced by table sauces and pickles in the period 1760 to 1870 and the lower income groups by jam from 1870 to 1914. These time periods and food groups were not mutually exclusive though; there is evidence of small scale domestic production of sweet spreads throughout the period under discussion and working people eventually participated with gusto in the application of mustard and sauces to their food from the end of the nineteenth century.

---

49   *Economist* 13 March 1920, 612.The issued capital of the three companies at the time of merger was Crosse and Blackwell £568,000, Keiller £344,000, Lazenby £249,000.

50   *Economist* 29 May 1920, 1222.

51   Findings and decisions of a sub-committee appointed by the Standing Committee on Trusts, 1920.

52   The original recipe included sugar, beetroot, carrot, malt vinegar, onions, white vinegar, cauliflower, water, dates, salt, courgette, apple purée, cornstarch, tomato paste, gherkins, caramel, lemon concentrate, and spices. Because of inefficiencies, in 1924 production moved to London.

53   Chandler, 1980, 401; Collins, 2009, 153–76.

There is some scope for arguing that the use of sauces, pickles and jams was one of the facilitating mechanisms behind the modernization of the food system in as much as they lubricated the difficult transition from traditional rural to modern urban diets. Britain's was the earliest and most rapid such change in Europe. It happened in the face of an ideological commitment to free trade that undermined several sectors of British agriculture and at a time when the integration of the British economy was so powerful that many distinctive regional foods were overpowered by cheap ingredients such as the potato, and imported cereals, frozen meat and dairy produce.

Some writers seem to argue that the rise of preserved foods coincided with a 'deterioration' of the quality and variety of the British diet in the nineteenth century.[54] Jam most closely fits this description for low-income families since the cheap versions contained very little fruit and they did facilitate the consumption of items generally frowned upon in our own age, notably sugar and poor quality white bread made out of roller-milled flour. Yet, on the other hand, jam did at least offer a small nutritional bridge for poor families who had little choice but to go for the cheapest options.[55]

References

Official Publications

First Report from the Select Committee on Adulteration of Food, *British Parliamentary Papers* 1854–1855 (432).
Board of Trade, 'Progress of the sugar trade', *BPP*, 1884 (325) lxxiv. 426.
Board of Trade, Sugar trade, Return, *BPP*, 1888 (353) xciii. 554.
Annual Report of the Chief Inspector of Factories and Workshops for the year 1898. Part II: Reports, *BPP*, 1900 (Cd.27) xi.181–96.
Royal Commission on the Port of London. Minutes of evidence taken before the Royal Commission on the Port of London, *BPP*, 1902 (Cd.1152) xliii.
Departmental Committee on Fruit Culture in Great Britain, *BPP*, 1906 (Cd.2719) xxiv.
Standing Committee on Trusts to inquire into the price of fruit in the United Kingdom, *BPP*, 1920 (Cmd.878) xxiii. 491.
Departmental Committee on Distribution and Prices of Agricultural Produce. Interim report on fruit and vegetables, *BPP*, 1923 (Cmd. 1892) ix. 231.

---

54 An example is Spencer, 2002, 288–92. The eight factors he mentions are not unique to Britain and so the argument overall is unconvincing.
55 One 20 g serving of jam contains 55 kcal (230 kj).

Books

Atkins, P.J., 1985, 'The production and marketing of fruit and vegetables 1850–1950', in Oddy, D.J. and Miller, D.S., eds, *Diet and Health in Modern Britain*, London: Croom Helm.

Beable, W.H., 1926, *Romance of Great Business*, London: Heath Cranton.

Bear, W.E., 1899, 'Flower and fruit farming in England, III: fruit growing in the open', *Journal of the Royal Agricultural Society of England*, 3rd series, 10.

Benham, M., 1985, *The Story of Tiptree Jam 1885–1985*, Tiptree: Wilkin and Sons Ltd.

Brears, P., 1991, 'Pots for Potting: English pottery and its role in food preservation in the post-mediaeval period', in Wilson, C.A., ed., *Waste not, want not: food preservation from early times to the present* day, Edinburgh: Edinburgh University Press.

Bremner, D., 1869, *The Industries of Scotland*, Edinburgh: Black.

Chandler, A.D., 1980, 'The growth of the transnational industrial firm in the United States and the United Kingdom: a comparative analysis', *Economic History Review*, XXXIII, 3.

Collins, E.J.T., 2009, 'The North American influence on food manufacturing in Britain, 1880–1939', in Segers, Y., Bieleman, J. and Buyst, E., eds, *Exploring the food chain: food production and food processing in western Europe, 1850–1990*, Turnhout: Brepols.

Cox, N. and Dannehl, K., 2007, *Dictionary of traded goods and commodities, 1550–1820*, University of Wolverhampton.

Darlington, I., 1955, 'Trinity House Estate' in Darlington, I. ed., *Survey of London: Volume 25: St George's Fields The Parishes of St George The Martyr, Southwark and St Mary, Newington*, London: London County Council.

De la Mare, U., 2008, 'Necessity and rage: the factory women's strikes in Bermondsey, 1911', *History Workshop Journal*, 66.

Haggard, R., 1902, *Rural England*, London: Longmans, Green.

Harrison, B., ed., 2004, *Oxford dictionary of national biography*, Oxford: Oxford University Press.

Hassall, A.H., 1855, *Food and its adulterations: comprising reports of the Analytical Sanitary Commission of 'The Lancet' for the years 1851–1854*, London: Longmans.

Horridge, G.K., [1988], *The growth and development of a family firm: Chivers of Histon, 1873–1939*, [Godalming]: Ammonite Books.

Jefferys, J.B., 1954, *Retail trading in Britain, 1850–1950*, Cambridge: Cambridge University Press.

Jeremy, D.J., ed., 1984–1986, *Dictionary of business biography*, London: Butterworths.

Johnston, J.P., 1977, *A hundred years of eating: food, drink and the daily diet in Britain since the late nineteenth century*, Dublin: Gill and Macmillan.

Landen, D. and Daniel, J., 1988, *The true story of HP Sauce*, London: Methuen.

Malden, W.J., 1890, 'Crops for pickling and conserving', *Journal of the Royal Agricultural Society of England*, 3rd series, 1.

Mathew, W.M., 1998a, *Keiller's of Dundee: the rise of the marmalade dynasty 1800–1879*, Dundee: Abertay Historical Society.

Mathew, W.M., 1998b, *The secret history of Guernsey Marmalade. James Keiller and Son Offshore 1857–1879*, St. Peter Port, Guernsey: La Société Guernesiaise.

Mathias, P., 1967, *Retailing revolution*, London: Longmans.

Mayhew, H., 1865, 'The establishment of Messrs Crosse and Blackwell, sauce and pickle manufacturers', in Mayhew, H., ed., *The shops and companies of London*, vol. 1, London: Strand Printing and Publishing Co.

Morris, T.N., 1958, 'Management and preservation of food', in Singer, C.J., Holmyard, E.J., Hall, A.R. and Williams, T.I., eds, *A history of technology*, vol. 5, Oxford: Clarendon.

Oddy, D.J., 1970, 'Working-class diets in late nineteenth-century Britain', *Econ. Hist. Rev.* XXIII, 2.

Peake, A.S., 1926, *The life of Sir William Hartley*, London: Routledge.

Perren, R., 1995, *Agriculture in depression, 1870–1940*, Cambridge: Cambridge University Press.

Pratt, E.A., 1906. *The transition in agriculture*, London: Murray.

Routledge, J., 1868, 'The food supply of London (No. II)', *Contemporary Review*, 9.

Samuel, R., 1977, 'Steam power and hand technology in mid-Victorian Britain', *History Workshop* 3.

Slaven, A. and Checkland, S. 1986–1990, *Dictionary of Scottish business biography, 1860–1960* Aberdeen: Aberdeen University Press.

Spencer, C., 2002, *British food*, London: Grub Street.

Torode, A., 1966, 'Trends in fruit consumption', in Barker, T.C., McKenzie, J.C., and Yudkin, J., eds, *Our changing fare*, London: MacGibbon and Kee.

Whitehead, C., 1878, 'The cultivation of hops, fruit and vegetables', *Journal of the Royal Agricultural Society of England*, 14.

Winstanley, M.J., 1983, *The shopkeeper's world 1830–1914*, Manchester: Manchester University Press.

Chapter 4

Rural Capitalism: The *Société des Caves de Roquefort*, from c.1840 to 1914

Sylvie Vabre

The territorial identification of food products is not an obvious route into industrial capitalism, yet, in the latter half of the nineteenth century, a capitalist food industry developed in a village in south-west France. Roquefort, a village in the south of the department of Aveyron, which was located along the edges of a limestone plateau, the Larzac, approximately 200 kilometres from Montpellier and 800 kilometres from Paris, went through a capitalist and industrial revolution. In just a few decades, this poorly accessible village, built on a scree, became **the** factory town for the *affineurs* (refiners) of Roquefort cheese. Was this a far cry from the rationality that is normally attributed to capitalism and industry? The prosperity that *affinage* (refining) brought to the village could have provided the input for Alfred Marshall's observations on the concentration of industries.[1] How, then, may we explain the establishment of the Roquefort *affinage* territory in the nineteenth century? Its commercial success was based on a sheep's milk cheese that had acquired a reputation well before the birth of the company that developed to control its production.

The story began in the 1840s, when a boom in consumption brought to light the extremely favourable location of the village of Roquefort. Its territory was home to a unique set of qualities. 'Aptitude' and 'natural gifts' could be turned into profits. From 1851 onwards some *affineurs* recognized the need for a large company to exploit the emerging market. A homeowners' association accounted for 50 to 75 per cent of total production. The large company, known today as the Roquefort *Société*, was the oldest of all the small *affinage* businesses.[2]

Three distinct chronological periods nurtured the progressive development of a Roquefort industry that was tied to the territory of the village. From 1840 to 1860, the village's situation was perceived as a source of guaranteed earnings, but it was not easy to find the ideal legal status for a large company in such a situation. Once this difficulty was overcome, industrialization and capitalism triumphed;

---

1   Marshall, 1898.

2   The company archives are housed at the Departmental Archives of Aveyron, with inventory 54J accounting for about two hundred metres of shelving. This chapter takes up the conclusions of my thesis, *Roquefort Société: histoire d'une entreprise agroalimentaire en Aveyron (vers 1840–1914)*.

from 1860 to 1890 machines and steam power were accepted into the organization of the *Société des Caves*. The third stage was characterized by the company's renewed attachment to the territory of the village while it asserted its capitalist power and its desire to mould the market for its own benefit.

A Large Company in the Country: Exploiting the 'Vocations' of the Territory (1840–1860)

The Roquefort market of the 1840s was tiny but extremely promising – or so it seemed from the analysis made by a few investors seeking to make a fortune in the cheese industry. However, the idea of a large company being essential to the Roquefort trade did not meet with unanimous support.

A Cheese that was increasingly sought after in Parisian Circles

Production had risen continuously from 250 tonnes in 1810 to 850 tonnes in 1854. These numbers are corroborated by the statistics provided by Armand Husson on consumption levels in Paris: that of Roquefort experienced a remarkable increase compared to other types of cheese.[3] In fact, this success had been preceded by the popularity of Roquefort, which dated back to the late eighteenth century. Voltaire and Diderot are said to have enjoyed it, Casanova praised its virtues, and the people of the Enlightenment found it very much to their liking. Its blue-veined aspect was the result of a certain know-how that was dear to the *Encyclopédistes*, and its distinctive tangy flavour catered to the mature palate. Roquefort was the only blue cheese derived from ewe's milk, which gave it a unique taste. It stood out plainly from the other cheeses on Parisian tables, such as the English Stilton made from cow's milk, the Mont-Cenis or the Sassenage, both of which came from a blend of different types of milk.[4] Later on, its reputation was praised by gourmets and it rapidly gained popularity among the new bourgeoisie: after all, did not Monteil declare it the King of Cheeses in his History of France?[5] This Parisian taste for Roquefort prompted and encouraged transformations in the production and *affinage* sites.

Cellars and Know-how on the Larzac Plateau

The limestone plateau of Larzac housed many natural hollows and caverns that were exploited from very early on. Pliny did indeed report in his writings the existence of a blue cheese made beyond the Gévaudan that was much enjoyed by the Romans. The cold draughts required for the maturation process were a

3   Husson, 1875.
4   Husson, 1856 edition.
5   Monteil, 1846.

common feature of the vast Rock of Combalou on the edges of the Larzac, which effectively possessed the greatest number of cellars built and developed within the Rock. This is where the village of Roquefort was built, based on the model of a naturally ventilated cellar with a domestic business right above it. Meanwhile, expertise in *affinage* was evolving constantly and by the middle of the nineteenth century, a third of the '*surchoix*' (top-quality) cheese was being produced in the coldest cellars in the village. Indeed, this particular grade of Roquefort was so named that its maturation grade enabled it to be dispatched to Paris with minimal deterioration. It was then sold at higher prices than anywhere else, thereby guaranteeing the village wholesaler a large share of the profits. Thus, the presence of natural elements compensated for the major disadvantage of being located far away from the largest consumer markets, though that became less of a problem with the development of rail transport from the middle of the century.

These 'natural' elements were accompanied by a marked development of dairy sheep farming on the Larzac plateau. In the nineteenth century, sheep farming was carried out in practically all French departments; indeed, it would be quicker to name the departments where no sheep could be found than make a comprehensive list of all sheep-farming areas.[6] However, a unique phenomenon was observed on the limestone plateau of Larzac. Here, unlike everywhere else where sheep were being bred for their wool and meat, flocks of dairy ewes occupied the lands. The 1852 farm survey confirmed this specialization in sheep farming and highlighted its orientation towards dairy production. Out of the 30,073 sheep recorded in the communes of Cornus, Viala-du-Pas-de-Jaux, La Couvertoirade, L'hospitalet and La Cavalerie, all of which are close to Roquefort, more than 50 per cent were ewes, which was unique in France. This trend had been in place since the early nineteenth century. Sheep farming developed in conjunction with the nearby textile industry of Lodève. The early introduction of forage crops by some landowners, coupled with the construction of a North–South trunk road in the early nineteenth century, which encouraged the use of Languedoc-produced salt in sheep farming, were some factors behind an increase in flock numbers. The success of Roquefort cheese was directly related to sheep farming and the falling demand for wool, resulting from the crisis in the textile industry. Expertise in sheep farming, on which the production of Roquefort relied, was complemented by expertise in cheese-making. It was the women of the farms who were responsible for transforming milk into curds, which they then placed into moulds to form 'loaves'.[7] After draining for several days, the curd loaves were sold to wholesalers who then took charge of the *affinage* and commercialization processes.

---

6   Toutain, 1992, 111.

7   The name given to curds that have been shaped by a mould. Some words in italics are 'Roquefort terms'. For an overview of the Roquefort vocabulary, see: Aussibal, 1984, 156 .

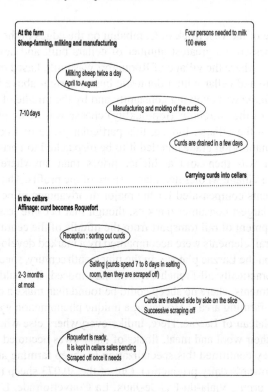

At the farm | Four persons needed to milk
Sheep-farming, milking and manufacturing | 100 ewes

Milking sheep twice a day
April to August

7-10 days

Manufacturing and molding of the curds

Curds are drained in a few days

Carrying curds into cellars

In the cellars
Affinage: curd becomes Roquefort

Reception : sorting out curds

2-3 months
at most

Salting (curds spend 7 to 8 days in salting
room, then they are scraped off)

Curds are installed side by side on the slice
Successive scraping off

Roquefort is ready.
It is kept in cellars sales pending
Scraped off once it needs

Source: Vabre, 2010.

Figure 4.1   Making Roquefort cheese mid-nineteenth century

A Large Company for Acquiring Revenue from the Land?

The proposed development and optimization of these natural and human assets divided the community of village wholesalers. To some, a large company represented the most efficient means of controlling the inherent risks in the *affinage* and commercialization processes, and would therefore ensure profits. Such was the sentiment of the Durand-Fajon bank in Montpellier. The fortune that it had acquired since the beginning of the nineteenth century, most notably in trade with Spain, its experience in dealing with a wide range of businesses and its ownership of several excellent Roquefort cellars since the 1820s led it to team up with a businessman who had made a fortune in the Languedoc salt marshes to create a monopoly of all the village cellars in 1839.

This concentration of assets met with opposition from the major landowners who were very much attached to the existence of the many *affineurs* in the village. Their vast estates had been formed during the revolutionary era, thanks to the sale of National Assets originating from the many monastic orders on the limestone plateau. The competition between *affineurs* to obtain supplies from sharecroppers suited the landowners very well. An arrangement between *affineurs*, or worse still the establishment of a monopoly, was seen by the landowners as an interference aimed at seizing a portion of the revenue that was their due. The landowners managed to break the monopoly by funding the excavation of new cellars in partnership with the owners of several small plots on the scree. These were local artisans who worked for the cellars: carpenters or cafe owners whose shops were located at one end of the row of cellars. With the help of several investors who were against the idea of a large company, they held their own by converting their shops into an *affinage* business.

This resistance ended in a consensus that materialized through the birth of the *Société Civile des Caves* in 1851. This civil-law association brought together 16 cellars and an extremely diverse set of owners. From the very day it was created, it displayed several unusual characteristics. First of all, it had sufficient weight to hold a majority stake in the Roquefort trade, but was not so dominant as to be able to claim a 'monopoly'. Additionally, the association's statutes attested to its wariness about restrictive frameworks. The business project was, first and foremost, designed to be ephemeral and could be dissolved at the end of each production year. Indeed, article 6 of the agreement mentioned that 'there is no solidarity between partners'; the fear of bankruptcy was thus present. One last point to note is that the association was cleverly managed by Etienne Coupiac from 1858 and subsequently grew strong and sustainable at the turn of the 1860s.

The Parisian demand triggered a huge momentum in the village of Roquefort and its neighbouring countryside. Each group tried to capture a portion of the expected profits. The three subsequent decades contributed to the obliteration of these difficult beginnings. The organization of the Roquefort industry and the emergence of true capitalism in the countryside were the singular characteristics of this period.

Industrialization and Capitalism in the Village (1860–1890)

In 1850, the term 'cheese industry' was used for the very first time. It was coined by Lubin Roche, a veterinary surgeon at Saint-Affrique, who used it to describe the growing quantities of ripened cheeses.[8] Alain Faure has pointed out that the word was used in the 1861 survey to refer to the use of steam power and machines or a business whose production was not directly intended for the local consumer market.[9] Compared with the previous national survey – the 1840–1845 one that characterized industries according to company size and preferred the term 'manufacturer' to that of 'factory' – this was an important semantic evolution. This is how the cellars became factories: 'Our factories are by far the best', Etienne

---

8   Roche, 1850, 153–73.
9   Faure, 1983, 199–215.

Coupiac assured buyers from 1863 onwards.[10] Emphasis was placed on the production process and the concentration of affinage and staff at Roquefort. A few years later, the introduction of steam-powered machines, the firm's conversion into a '*société anonyme*' and the organization of company-controlled dairies upstream of the *affinage* stage all ensured the whole enterprise of Roquefort kept to the path of the industrial revolution. Between 1860 and 1890, production went from 855 to 1,886 tonnes and sales figures increased from 1.3 million to 3.23 million francs![11]

The Industrialization of Affinage

The *affinage* stage had always been perceived by wholesalers as a real bottleneck. The danger lay in the transformation of curd loaves into Roquefort, which took several months – 3 to 4 in 1840 – and generated significant amounts of waste. Women workers known as *cabanières* would scrape the loaves with a knife to remove any surface vegetation, thereby enabling blue veins to develop within the cheese. In the 1840s, the amount of waste generated was in the order of 30 per cent. Such losses added on to raw material costs that accounted for 60 per cent of the final price of Roquefort, which was nothing unusual in many food industries at the time.[12]

In the first half of the nineteenth century, two methods of accelerating the maturation of cheeses in the cellars were developed. The first method consisted of introducing powdered mouldy bread while curds were being placed into moulds at the farm. In doing so, the farm women shortened the *affinage* process by two to three months, thereby reducing the number of visits to the cellars by half. The adoption of this process is most certainly related to Chaptal's research work on the acceleration of vinification. The analogy between the addition of sugar to wine and that of mouldy bread to cheese curds is all the more evident given the fact that Chaptal, the chemist from Montpellier, had made several observations about Roquefort in the *Annales de Chimie* in 1787.[13] Does this mean that this innovation was introduced by Chaptal himself during one of his visits to Roquefort? Evidence may be lacking, but it must be acknowledged that Roquefort did indeed benefit from the fundamental contributions of research conducted by chemists in the early nineteenth century on methods of accelerating the natural maturation processes. Other dry cheeses such as Cheshire, Dutch and Gruyère, which were the Roquefort's main competitors, only had food colour additives,

---

10   Departmental Archives of Aveyron, 54J 3355, f.181, 20 July 1863, Etienne Coupiac, director at Estachon, representative of the Société des Caves in Marseilles.

11   Departmental Archives of Aveyron, Grand livre 54 J 2500 – 54 J 2692. Meanwhile, total production in the village went from 2,700 to 5,200 tonnes; the sales figures of other companies are unknown.

12   Verley, 1997b, 38–72.

13   Chaptal, 1787.

at the very most.[14] In this respect, the mouldy bread technique used at Roquefort was the most similar to that used in vinification.[15] In the middle of the nineteenth century, yet another milestone was achieved in the mastery of the *affinage* process. It was then that the entrepreneurs started to observe that the shape of the loaves influenced the ripening process. This led them to identify the shape that would yield the most consistent results in meeting client expectations. They then supplied cheese moulds to farmers and the shape of Roquefort became 'standardized'. These contributions of the first half of the nineteenth century formed the basis of the industrialization phase that started in the 1870s.

Two machines, the *piqueuse* ('piercer') and the *brosseuse* ('brusher'), made their appearance in cellars in the late 1870s.[16] The former was used to pierce loaves. Developed by Etienne Coupiac, the head of the Société des Caves, it was designed to poke 100 holes in each curd loaf that arrived at a cellar. The acceleration of the maturation process was coupled with a reduction in waste that was amplified by the use of the *brosseuse*. By 1882, both waste and maturation time had been reduced by half: from 30 to 15 per cent, and from three to one-and-a-half months, respectively. While wholesalers in other French cheese-making regions only saw production growth in terms of skills and knowledge transfer – at this time Swiss cheese-makers were being hired in the Jura – the wholesalers at Roquefort tried to adapt the *affinage* process to the techniques developed in other food or industrial sectors, as in the case of introducing mouldy bread at the start of the century.

Roquefort became more easily identifiable at stalls and in shop displays: its shape and the blue patterns in its white base became its distinguishing features. However, the introduction of steam power revealed certain flaws in the factories. Indeed, the running of unconnected, nested, multi-level cellars belonging to different owners soon became a real problem. Steam-powered machines could be used for several cellars, but this required a common machine room. Industrialization led to the creation of a company that was more than a mere partnership between owners: a *société anonyme*.

1882: Creation of the Original Société Anonyme

The previous '*société civile*' status allowed the owners of cellars to unite around a common ambition, but it prevented the establishment of a large industrial project requiring significant financial investments to combine the various cellars into a single unit: from this stemmed the idea of creating a *société anonyme*, a public limited company. At the time, this type of company was still relatively new in France. Although the Act of July 24th, 1867 had abolished the administrative approval instituted by the French Commercial Code in 1807, the development

14 *Art de faire du beurre et les meilleurs fromages* [Art of making butter and the best cheeses], 1833, 332.
15 These observations agree with those made by Jean-Robert Pitte, 1987, 201–14.
16 Archives INPI [National Institute of Industrial Property], 1874, and 1875.

of *sociétés anonyme* remained modest: 'the average number of '*sociétés*' created between 1866 and 1870 was 126, 202 between 1871 and 1875, and 419 from 1876 to 1880'.[17] Therefore, the creation of a *société anonyme* at Roquefort was the product of a form of voluntarism. The new entity's share capital amounted to 5,100,000 francs divided into 10,200 shares worth 500 francs each, which immediately ranked the *Société Anonyme des Caves et des Producteurs Réunis de Roquefort* among the biggest companies in France. Indeed, from 1889 to 1913, the average nominal capital of the *sociétés anonyme* that were created was 870,000 francs, and only 200 of them had a capital exceeding 10 million. The *société anonyme* would allow the commencement of important work to group the cellars into *affinage* clusters.

Organization of the Supply Chain: An ever-increasing Radius

Increased production was ensured by the organization of the supply chain, of which the company had taken charge. The collection *radius* was no longer limited to the Larzac plateau and was progressively extended towards the west, the Camarès, the Tarn Valley and the Monts de Lacaune. The transport of cheese and its safe delivery to Roquefort was of paramount importance within this expanding territory. The extension of this *radius* would not have been possible without a dynamic network of collectors, or *ramasseurs*, who worked for the *Société des Caves*. These were the people who went from farm to farm, gathering the cheese for the company and delivering it to Roquefort on a regular basis. Therefore, they played a fundamental role in the provision of supplies and consequently in the growth of the *Société*. Despite the development of the collection process, the extension of the *radius* was still constrained by the limitations of road travel. Indeed, beyond 80 km, it was difficult to transport safely a consignment of very fragile curd loaves on the poor roads of southern Rouergue – thereby making night travel necessary in summer to protect them from the intense heat. The railway line from the south did not reach Roquefort until 1874, when the Tournemire station was opened some 3 kilometres away. Meanwhile, in 1877, some cheese production trials were being carried out at distant sites such as Aubais close to Sommières in the Gard. However, these examples remained rather limited as they were faced with a poor understanding of the art of producing loaves that would readily undergo ripening in the village cellars. Although all types of ewe's milk could be used to produce curds, the skills of dairy production could not be acquired overnight, and even visits from the farm women of Roquefort to explain the secrets of curd production did not suffice to obtain good results. The problem of milk blends added to these difficulties: indeed, large amounts of cows' milk were often added to ewes' milk. This was done for economic reasons: while a ewe in 1904 produced an average of 63.19 litres of

---

17   Lefebvre-Taillard, 1985, 449.

milk, since 1874 a cow was capable of producing 3,000 litres.[18] This problem did not occur on the Larzac plateau where cows were something of a rarity, but it was becoming increasingly prevalent in other areas as the *radius* was being widened. As ewe's milk curds were becoming highly sought after, farmers were tempted to mix different types of milk, especially since such a fraud was virtually impossible to detect: the taste of the ripened cheese was the only real indicator of the difference. Between 1870 and 1880, the limits to the growth of Roquefort became apparent. The widening of the *radius* helped to increase production but also brought changes to the cheese.

During the period 1860 to 1890, the *affinage* of Roquefort was radically transformed. The arrival of machines, the formation of a *société anonyme* and the extension of its *radius* were the three characteristic features of the industrialization and capitalist foothold of this cheese industry. Meanwhile, the company expanded commercially: its Roquefort cheese was now available in places such as Guingamp and New York, and indeed, exports continued to rise from the late 1860s, accounting for almost 15 per cent of sales figures in 1892.[19] However, owing to the Great Depression in the last quarter of the century, this model was subsequently forced to undergo radical changes.

Capitalist Power, Innovation and a Sense of Attachment to the Territory of the Cellars (1890–1914)

The Roquefort industry was not spared from the effects of the Great Depression, even though the results indicated that their difficulties were relatively slight. Until 1892, the five-year averages revealed a stagnation in sales figures while production increased only slightly. However, the *Société* itself felt that the Great Depression had stretched it to breaking point. The crisis revealed that Roquefort was no longer popular. A solution to this was finally found thanks to scientific research, which was the technical characteristic of the second industrial revolution. Specific issues relating to the cellars, supplies and *affinage* techniques were raised, and several parties that were previously on the side-lines became involved in the company's activities. As such, the company's production went from 1,886 to 4,134 tonnes between 1890 and 1914, while that of the village increased from 5,200 to 9,250 tonnes.

---

18 Marre, 1906 ; National Archives, F11 2847, *Enquêtes sur la production des beurres et des fromages (1873–1874)* [Investigations on the production of butter and cheese (1873–1874)], *for the arrondissement of Fontainebleau.* The production of ewes was expressed in kilograms of cheese throughout the nineteenth century.

19 Departmental Archives of Aveyron, 54 J 2611.

New Collaborations with Scientists

In the 1880s, the focus of a development strategy around the '*surchoix*' line revealed difficulties in selling the secondary qualities. The profits made with the superior line no longer compensated for the lower takings brought in by the other qualities, and the environment gradually underwent changes. Thanks to industrialization and urbanization, the consumption of Roquefort had become accessible to a significant portion of the population. The gourmet had given way to the consumer who had less of a trained eye and palate but nevertheless wished to savour famous cheeses of reasonable quality and price. This change had swept across many different markets. Patrick Verley highlighted the decline in the quality of silverware as well as that of silk fabrics, which essentially evolved into fabric blends during the nineteenth century.[20] But the rise of a market favouring average quality and low prices was not confined to France: indeed, the English-speaking countries were the earliest to experience this phenomenon. Between 1874 and 1879, the amounts of cheese imported by the United States increased by 70 per cent while prices decreased by 66 per cent! In the end, after a decade of indecision, the *Société des Caves* began a programme of radical transformation.

The creation of dairies – initially planned in the 1880s – truly took off in the 1890s and enabled the control of milk quality while ensuring high-volume outputs.[21] In 1895, there were 29 dairies in operation; this number went up to 215 in 1909, to which one may add another ten or so establishments in Corsica and the Basses Pyrénées. It was the development of railway lines that made it possible to set up dairies in such distant places, which supplied high-quality milk at lower prices than those in the traditional area around Roquefort. The manufacture of cheese 'loaves' complied with industrial principles: tanks contained 400 litres of milk from which 40 'loaves' were manufactured. Both facilities and premises were designed to meet these needs. The milk was weighed before being mixed in order to detect the presence of cow's milk, and the rennet, from industrial origin, was accurately measured. These precautions allowed a good regular quality of cheese to be obtained. In distant territories such as Corsica, staff and material came from Roquefort, as making Roquefort cheese was an industrial secret. In order to thwart fraudulent schemes, a contract was signed with Auguste Trillat, a professor at the Institut Pasteur, and Forestier, his assistant, to carry out studies on ewe's milk. They provided the necessary knowledge for checking the milk that arrived at the cheese factories. This collaboration was in line with a long tradition established by Chaptal in the early nineteenth century, while the engagement of Paul Lebrou – a young engineer and graduate of the Arts et Métiers – in 1889 institutionalized industrial research.

---

20   Verley, 1997a, 713.

21   These were purely dairies and not cheese factories. Only milk, and nothing more, was processed in these dairies. Loaves only became Roquefort cheese upon leaving the cellars.

The setting up of laboratories was part of a major trend in the industrial world from which food companies were not immune. The German chocolate maker Stollwerck created its research laboratory in 1884.[22] In France, it is not easy to establish the exact figures due to the lack of sources.[23] But the fact remains that the laboratory lay at the heart of factories and no distinction was made between research and manufacturing activities. In his modest laboratory, Paul Lebrou adapted the *affinage* process to the refrigerating machines invented by Charles Tellier in just a matter of years, thereby opening the door to a new era in cheesemaking. The *affinage* process was transformed: from then on, the maturation of loaves could be arrested and Roquefort could be stored, so that in 1911, after twenty years of studies and experiments, waste levels fell to just 5 per cent. The possibility of storing cheeses from one production year to the next meant that Roquefort became available all year round. This innovation bore the seeds of a complete transformation of the company and raised the question of the usefulness of the naturally ventilated cellars now that the control of temperature and humidity could be ensured by refrigerating machines.

The Incorporation of Refrigerating Devices within Village Cellars

While the engineer Paul Lebrou envisaged company growth without the village cellars, the board of directors preferred to 'incorporate' them into the existing industrial system. However, the choice of keeping the cellars and fitting them out with refrigerating devices meant having to convert them completely. The discussions on this subject were not recorded in any board meeting minutes, but the investments made indicate the solution that was picked: each cellar or group of cellars was to be equipped with one or more refrigerating devices, but there was not to be any refrigerating device without a cellar. The cellars remained a key issue in the affinage process that had to group all related activities. There was a certain reluctance to incorporate refrigerating devices within the much-treasured street cellars, for this was the centre of *affinage*, the theatre – and indeed, the starting and end point – of all activities. Did the installation of refrigeration in natural cellars not amount to renouncing their qualities? It was only in 1903 that work on the street cellars finally began. Close to a million francs were ultimately invested to convert them into one big unit, where the machine room and refrigerating devices were a central feature. In the village, the total shelf area occupied by wheels of cheese doubled from three to six hectares between 1890 and 1906.[24]

From 1892 to 1914, the *Société des Caves*' capital assets increased by more than 3.3 million francs, or 71 per cent. The sums came from reserve funds that had

---

22 Chandler, 1990, 860.

23 The large dairy survey conducted by the Ministry of Agriculture in 1903 contained no inventories. Ministère de l'agriculture, *Enquête sur l'industrie laitière*, 1903.

24 Marre, 1906; Tellier, 1926.

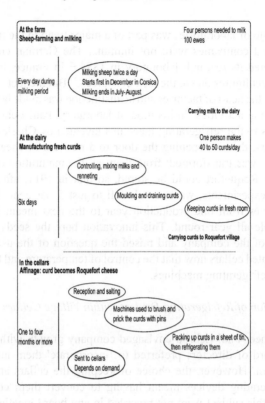

| At the farm | Four persons needed to milk |
| Sheep-farming and milking | 100 ewes |

Every day during milking period — Milking sheep twice a day / Starts first in December in Corsica / Milking ends in July-August

Carrying milk to the dairy

| At the dairy | One person makes |
| Manufacturing fresh curds | 40 to 50 curds/day |

Controlling, mixing milks and renneting

Moulding and draining curds

Six days — Keeping curds in fresh room

Carrying curds to Roquefort village

In the cellars
Affinage: curd becomes Roquefort cheese

Reception and salting

Machines used to brush and prick the curds with pins

One to four months or more — Packing up curds in a sheet of tin, then refrigerating them

Sent to cellars / Depends on demand

Source: Vabre, 2010.

Figure 4.2   Making Roquefort cheese in 1913

been accumulated since the *société anonyme*'s creation, for at Roquefort, just like anywhere else, self-financing was the hallmark of a healthy business.

Everything and Nothing Changes

These industrial changes made it possible to retain what seemed to be vital for the company: Roquefort cheese continued to be ripened in its namesake village, deep within the bowels of the scree. Its success since 1851 was borne by a commercial strategy based on the distinctiveness of a cheese that was ripened in special cellars. These natural assets that were once portrayed as a mystery of Nature were now known, but were not called into question. Better still, in 1892 the law used these historical roots as an argument for charging some manufacturers of fake Roquefort. For the village *affineurs* gathered as the *Société des Caves*, it was the first time that the court of Aix had recognized, in the name of history, the 'intellectual property' of the cellars and the Roquefort name. This important consideration was mainly based on the age-old tradition of ripening the cheese in natural cellars, the historical evidence of which was produced by wholesalers during the trial. The affair reflected the industrial concerns of that period. Indeed, faced with a proliferation of copycat productions, manufacturers in various sectors sought the recognition of patents and products by international authorities that had been established for this very purpose.[25] However, a court decision does not change the law. A decade later, this particular decision was challenged at Roquefort itself when the affinage process was adapted to refrigerating devices. Having discovered that no patent had been filed for this process, some competitors started building large refrigerated factories in the commune of Roquefort, far away from the scree, just beside roads to enable easy access to the factories. In 1904, the village *affineurs* gathered together under the leadership of the *Société des Caves* to take action against one 'imposter'.

Charged in 1904, the 'imposter' was accused of fraud but subsequently made an appeal, which led the court to appoint several expert chemists and bacteriologists to get to the bottom of the matter.[26] Their arrival in the village led to the union of all the *affineurs*. An agreement that put an end to the proceedings was eventually signed on April 27th, 1907. The manufacturer who used artificial refrigeration was allowed to carry on with production on one condition: all cheese loaves were required to spend several hours in the village cellars in order to earn the right to carry the Roquefort name. The Société provided this manufacturer with a cellar for this very purpose and also paid compensation. This was the price for ensuring that the cellars remained the heart of Roquefort.

On top of the colossal investments in industrial equipment, there was the price of maintaining a monopoly on the Roquefort brand. The cost argument, which quite often determines choices in the name of 'economic rationality', was well and truly undermined in this case. Indeed, this was a logical choice in which cost did not represent the greatest risk. New developments were to blend into the overall structure to help mark the business's continuity in spite of the upheavals experienced.

The development of the refrigerating device enabled the *Société* and other *affineurs* to get ahead of their competitors while remaining rooted in a renowned tradition. From then on, the cellars became modern factories and sanctuaries, with the *Société* as guardian of the temple.

Conclusion

From the middle of the nineteenth century, large company status became necessary to establish a foothold in markets. The rise of the *Société des Caves* to handle the Roquefort industry was one factor and another was the incorporation of scientific research into the production process. These were common features of many sectors of industry from the 1890s onwards. The times were significant for the

---

25   Bonin, 2006, 776–89.
26   Vabre, 2010, 201–14.

growth of capitalist industry but the characteristics of Roquefort were secured by the *affinage* being anchored in the natural cellars in the village. Therein lay the originality of the *Société des Caves*. No matter what the situation it faced, it managed to adapt itself and make use of the power it had acquired to ensure that the village of Roquefort was the only recognized centre of *affinage* for the cheese.

Thus, in the nineteenth century, Roquefort was the only type of cheese to be identified by its territory of production. This constituted a means of distinguishing itself, an invisible boundary for ensuring a dominant position. Comparable examples of success can only be found in the vine-growing and wine-producing industry. Around the same period, champagne manufacturers were also striving to create territorial identity markers that new consumers both in France and abroad would be able to appreciate. Thus, at the turn of the century, champagne became a French wine that was produced in its namesake region.[27] By 1914, both Roquefort and champagne were export goods: the overseas market accounted for more than 25 per cent of the *Société des Caves'* sales, and between 60 and 70 per cent of those of Moët & Chandon.[28] The distinguishing of territories therefore proved to be an asset in economic globalization in cases where the companies of a particular industry were powerful enough to impose their modes of production.

References

Archives INPI [National Institute of Industrial Property], no.107595, 18 September 1874 and no.105023, 10 April 1875.

Art de faire du beurre et les meilleurs fromages [Art of making butter and the best cheese], 1833, Paris: Huzard, imprimeur-Libraire.

Aussibal, R., 1984, *Les caves de Roquefort. Inventaire des mots, des instruments et des procédés traditionnels de l'affinage* [The Roquefort caves. Inventory of glossary, instruments and traditional methods of affinage], Musée du Rouergue.

Bonin, H., 2006, 'la contrefaçon et les guerres industrielles – L'union des Fabricants et l'INPI acteurs de la lutte contre la contrefaçon', in Béaur, G., Bonin, H., and Lemercier, C., eds, *Fraudes, contrefaçon et contrebande*, Geneva: Droz.

Chandler, A., 1990, *The dynamics of Industrial Capitalism*, Cambridge, Mass: Harvard University Press.

Chaptal, L., 1787, 'Etude sur le fromage de Roquefort', *Annales de chimie*, Paris.

Departmental Archives of Aveyron, 54 J 2611: copies of business letters, 54J 3355, f.181, July 20th, 1863, Etienne Coupiac, director at Estachon, representative of the *Société des Caves* in Marseilles; 54 J 2500 – 54 J 2692. Grand livre.

Desbois-Thibault, C., 2003, *L'extraordinaire aventure du champagne, Moët & Chandon, une affaire de famille* [The extraordinary adventure of champagne, Moet & Chandon, a family affair], Paris: PUF.

---

27   Guy, 2003, 250.
28   Desbois-Thibault, 2003, 230.

Faure, A., 1983, 'Note sur la petite entreprise en France au XIXe siècle. Représentation d'Etat et réalités', in Caron, F. (ed.), *Entreprises et entrepreneurs XIXe siècle-XXe siècle*, Paris: Presses Universitaires de la Sorbonne.

Guy, K.M., 2003, *When Champagne became French: Wine and the Making of a National Identity*, Baltimore: Johns Hopkins University Press.

Husson, A., 1875, *Les consommations de Paris* [Consumption of Paris], Paris: Guillaumin et Cie, 1856, and 2nd edn, Paris: Hachette.

Lefebvre-Taillard, A., 1985, *La société anonyme au XIXe siècle* [The company in the nineteenth century], Paris: Presses Universitaire de France.

Marre E., 1906, *Le Roquefort* [Roquefort cheese], Rodez, Carrière.

Marshall, A., 1898, *Principles of economics*, London: Macmillan.

Ministère de l'agriculture [Ministry of Agriculture], 1903, *Enquête sur l'industrie laitière* [Inquiry into the dairy industry].

Monteil, A., 1846, *Histoire des Français des divers états, ou histoire de France aux cinq derniers siècles* [French history of the various states, or history of France in the last five centuries]*, vol. 1, Paris: Coquebert.

National Archives, F11 2847, *Enquêtes sur la production des beurres et des fromages (1873–1874)* [Investigations on the production of butter and cheese (1873–1874)], for the arrondissement of Fontainebleau.

Pitte, J.R., 1987, 'Une lecture ordonnée de la carte des fromages traditionnels de France', in Brunet, R., ed., *Histoire et géographie des fromages*, Caen: Publication de l'université de Caen.

Roche, L., 1850, 'Nouvelle instruction sur l'industrie fromagère du Roquefort', *Bulletin de la Société centrale d'agriculture de l'Aveyron*, Rodez.

Tellier G., 1926, *L'industrie fromagère de Roquefort* [Roquefort cheese industry], law thesis, Montpellier.

Toutain, J., 1992, 'La production agricole de la France de 1810 à 1990: départements et régions – Croissance, productivité, structure', *Economie et Société*, no.11–12.

Vabre, S., 2010, '1900: Une étape dans la construction du Roquefort comme produit de terroir au XIXe siècle', in Marache, C., ed., 'Les produits des terroirs Aquitains', *Revue de l'Agenais*, no. 2.

Vabre, S., *Roquefort Société: histoire d'une entreprise agroalimentaire en Aveyron (vers 1840–1914)*, thesis defended on 13 November 2010 at the University of Toulouse.

Verley P., 1997a, *L'échelle du monde – Essai sur l'industrialisation de l'Occident* [The scale of the world – Essay on the industrialization of the West], Paris: Gallimard Essais.

Verley, P., 1997b, 'Les industries alimentaires au XIXe siècle: croissance industrielle et consommation', in J. Marseille, ed., *Les industries agroalimentaires en France – Histoire et performances,* Paris: Le Monde Editions.

Chapter 5
Modernizing the Mediterranean Olive-Oil Industry, 1850s–1930s[1]

Ramon Ramon-Muñoz

During the century before the Second World War, the food industry was fundamentally transformed. New and better machinery was adopted; factories were progressively driven by steam and later by electrical power; commercial methods were modified, and large capitalist firms emerged. This chapter focuses on olive oil, an important food industry in countries bordering on the Mediterranean Sea. It shows that this industry experienced extensive modernization but one which differed across countries and regions. This chapter briefly examines the main technological innovations, as well as their diffusion and effects. Technical progress is compared by focusing on Spain and Italy, the world's two largest olive-oil producers and exporters during the period under consideration.

Technical Change in Crushing, Pressing and Refining

The period between the 1850s and the 1930s represents a crucial phase in the modernization process of the Mediterranean olive-oil industry. This is not to say that in previous years olive-oil technology had remained stagnant. On the contrary, some of the innovations that spread after the mid-nineteenth century were already known and, in some cases, had begun to be adopted in the course of the century after about 1750.[2] Nevertheless, it was only from the second half of the nineteenth century that the diffusion of better industrial practices and new technology accelerated and became more general. As a result, by the early 1920s the number

1   I should like to thank the participants at the Twelfth Symposium of ICREFH, the editors of this volume, as well as Jaime Reis for their comments and suggestions on a previous draft of this chapter. This research has benefited from the financial support of the Spanish Ministry of Science and Innovation through the project HAR2009-07571, the Spanish Ministry of Economy and Competitiveness through the project HAR2012-33298, the Network in Economics and Public Policies (XREPP), launched by the Generalitat de Catalunya, and the Research Centre in Economics and Economic History 'Antoni de Capmany', University of Barcelona. All remaining errors are mine.

2   See, for example, Mazzoti, 2004, 277–304.

of olive-oil mills and factories driven by mechanical power had already overtaken those driven by animal power in several areas of the Mediterranean littoral.[3]

The decisive fact driving change was the collapse of traditional markets for non-edible olive oil. In the mid-nineteenth century, industrial markets for olive oil were enormous since it was in demand to lubricate machinery, for oiling wool after scouring by the textile industry, as a raw material for soap making, and as a fuel for lighting. However, cheaper and more efficient seed oils, animal fats and mineral oils started to replace olive oil's industrial applications. In response, producers and traders accelerated technical change in order to improve the product quality and, therefore, to enlarge markets for edible olive oil.

Modernization spread throughout the whole production process, beginning with the storage of the olives and ending with the storage of olive oil itself.[4] Of all the changes experienced by this industry, those that took place in crushing and pressing need to be stressed since they represented a very remarkable step towards quality improvement. The olive is a perishable fruit that easily ferments when it is stored for long periods or in bad conditions before being crushed and pressed, something that in the nineteenth century occurred generally in the largest areas of production.[5] The oil from fermented fruit yields a rancid taste, as well as an objectionable odour. Thus, the long storage of the olives was a serious problem for the industry as it hindered the production of a higher quality product.

To reduce the storage period more powerful equipment was required. By the mid-nineteenth century, many olive crushers still consisted of a single wheel edge runner revolving in a pan where the olives were placed. The wheel and the pan were made of stone and the crusher was driven by a horse, a mule or an ox. Most of the olive-oil presses working in the Mediterranean basin were traditional wooden beam or screw types (Figure 5.1). These were generally driven by human or animal power, worked slowly, and were not very powerful. So the long storage of the olives could hardly be reduced. Nevertheless, the collapse of markets for industrial olive oils accelerated the farmers' and manufacturers' efforts to increase the crushing capacity of millstones and reduce the period of storage. The new crushing equipment differed across countries and regions, but it attempted to overcome problems related to the speed and capacity of crushing. The number of millstones was increased, their area of contact with the pan expanded and the

---

3   For example, the cases of Liguria and Tuscany in Italy, Lesvos in Greece, and the province of Lleida in Spain. Istituto Centrale di Statistica, 1929, vol. VII; Sifneos, 2004, 267; Ramon-Muñoz, 1999, 168.

4   The production of bulk olive oil was not a complex activity. Once the olives were in the mill, the process consisted mainly of crushing the fruit which was reduced to a uniform paste by means of millstones, in pressing this olive paste and, finally, in collecting the resulting olive oil in tanks.

5   Manjarrés, 1896, 84.

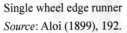
Single wheel edge runner
Source: Aloi (1899), 192.

Edge runner with three conical rolls
Source: Manjarrés (1896), 115.

Figure 5.1   Olive crushers in the Mediterranean basin in the nineteenth and early twentieth centuries

crushing velocity grew as a result of the mechanization of the process by steam power and, later, electricity. This made crushing more efficient and speedier.[6]

The storage period of the fruit could only be reduced if the crushing capacity of the mills grew in parallel to their pressing capacity.[7] From the mid-nineteenth century wooden presses were replaced by modern iron hydraulic presses as shown in Figure 5.2.[8] Used initially in the oilseed industry, hydraulic presses were introduced in the production of olive oil after the Napoleonic Wars. They were much more powerful and worked faster, especially with mechanical power. This made them more cost effective by reducing the time the olives were stored.[9]

In spite of these advantages, the diffusion of the new hydraulic presses was initially slow due to a number of technical problems that hampered their adoption. This fits well with Rosenberg's analysis on technological diffusion, as before the new machinery was widely accepted post-invention and post-innovation processes were required.[10] The drawbacks that prevented hydraulic presses from being more widely adopted were progressively overcome by the first third of the twentieth century.

---

6   See, for example, Aloi, 1899, 191–216; and Manjarrés, 1896, 107 and 114.

7   For technical imbalance (or technical disequilibria) as a cause of innovation, see Rosenberg, 1976, 111–17.

8   Hydraulic presses had been first introduced by Joseph Bramah (1748–1814), a British mechanical engineer and inventor, who applied the principle of Pascal's law which states that fluids transmit pressure equally in all directions, in the development of the first hydraulic press patented in 1795.

9   See Parejo and Zambrana, 1994, 32–4; Simpson, 1995, 168–71; and Zambrana, 1987, 145–51.

10   See Rosenberg, 1976, 75–7; and, for the drawbacks of the first hydraulic presses in Italy, Carrino and Salvemini, 2003, 524–5.

 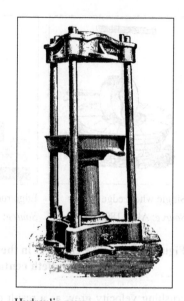

Calabrese wooden press   Hydraulic press
Source: Aloi (1899), 218.   *Source*: Aloi (1899), 229.

Figure 5.2   Olive-oil presses in the Mediterranean basin in the nineteenth and early twentieth centuries

Another major technological breakthrough was the spread of industrial refining plants. Refining is the process of removing impurities and free and solid fatty acids which tend to cause objectionable tastes, odours and colour. Traditional refining methods consisted mainly of removing impurities by manual techniques of clarification and filtration. Chemical, physical and mechanical processes were already known, and successfully applied to inedible oils, but were not always satisfactory in the production of edible olive oils. Clarification was achieved simply by resting the olive oil in storage tanks so that impurities and injurious substances sank to the bottom of the tank, allowing the oil to be drawn off from the sediment. Filtration, was generally practised by means of boxes containing filters of cotton fibres or other substances that removed solid substances from the olive oil in order to increase its transparency. Filtration was generally carried out in factories belonging to traders and exporters. Occasionally, olive oil was also washed by means of a chemical solution of water and tannic or citric acids in order to accelerate clarification and filtration. These techniques presented three main limitations: they were very slow, labour intensive and not always satisfactory, since the original deficiencies in taste, odour or colour were almost impossible to eliminate.[11] The end of the nineteenth century witnessed important improvements in refining vegetable oils and fats. By 1900, David Wesson had introduced an improved system of refining cotton oil.[12] This system was soon applied to other oleaginous products; and in the period 1912–1914 industrial refining plants for olive oil were set up in the Mediterranean basin. The amount of capital these plants required was relatively high, which in many cases led to the formation of joint stock companies. Also, refining factories tended to be relatively large, in part because of the economies of scale existing in this industry.[13] The introduction of industrial refining processes allowed large scale production of edible and neutral olive oils, being tasteless, odourless, colourless and lacking in acidity, which thus improved product homogeneity. Although processes and equipment varied between factories, refining usually consisted of three different operations: neutralizing the acid with a sodium hydroxide solution; de-coloration with fuller's earth; and deodorization by treatment with superheated steam in a vacuum.[14]

Unsurprisingly, in the largest producing countries the introduction of industrial refining plants was generally activated by olive-oil exporting firms, especially those dealing with bottled, canned and trademarked olive oil. They produced regular supplies of good quality oil of uniform type which could be adjusted to a foreign market's taste. All this was essential to produce branded olive oil and maintain it in the market.

To sum up, crushing, pressing and refining operations were modernized by the use of better machinery, improved methods of production, and widespread mechanization, which gave better product quality. In fact, the sector as a whole experienced an important transformation in both the agricultural and commercial phases. Modern marketing techniques, including branding, packaging and advertising, were introduced by traders and exporters during the last decades of the nineteenth century.[15] Since the 1850s, the industry had also been able to produce successfully a new by-product thanks to the application of chemical processes. This was olive-kernel oil (or sulphur oil), obtained from an after-pressing residue called olive foot cake (or olive pomace) and used initially for industrial purposes such as soap making and some large firms emerged in this industry too. Olive-oil production was certainly an activity that continued in small-scale mills located near areas of olive production, and belonging to peasants or local manufacturers. However, there were several examples of important companies in the production, export and refining of olive oil. Some of these large firms were vertically integrated

---

11   For traditional techniques of clarification and filtration, see, Aloi, 1899, 322–40; Manjarrés, 1896, 255–300; and Mingioli, 1901, 89–99 and 135–47.

12   The major developments in oil refining are summarized in Weber and Alsberg, 1934, 251–9.

13   Ramon-Muñoz, 2000, 184.

14   For further details of both processes and equipment used in olive-oil refining, see Morini, 1930, 65–117.

15   Ramon-Muñoz, 2010, 402–3.

and combined two or more phases of the supply chain.[16] In some cases, they added the extraction of olive-kernel oil (and even soap making) to the production of olive- oil. In other cases, production and foreign trade were integrated, while it was not uncommon to find the largest exporters owning an olive-kernel establishment, a refining factory and an olive-oil packaging plant.

Italy and Spain during the Second Half of the Nineteenth Century

Between the 1850s and 1930s the improvements that modernized the olive-oil industry did not spread homogeneously in the case of the world's largest olive-oil producing and exporting countries at the time, namely Italy and Spain. By the mid-nineteenth century, according to the available evidence, the Italian olive-oil industry was making greater use of modern technology and industrial practices than Spain but had a regional rather than a national dimension. The industry of the northern and central regions of Liguria and Tuscany had already initiated important changes. These included careful harvesting methods, concern for fruit selection; a rapid crushing and pressing of the olives through better machinery; the differentiation of the product by pressings; the introduction of clarification and refining methods as well as a more intensive use of blending and packaging operations. The consequence was an increase in the quality of the olive oil produced in Liguria and, particularly, in Tuscany.[17]

The southern Italian regions continued to be attached to older crushing and pressing machinery as well as traditional methods of production. An exception to this general rule was the province of Bari (Apulia), where the average quality of the product was improved due to a process of technological change initiated by Pierre Ravanas in the 1820s.[18] Thus, two-wheel edge runners were progressively adopted; better screw presses began to be used; and hydraulic presses were introduced in the province of Bari. In spite of this, southern Italy remained relatively backward.[19] By around 1900, the mechanization of southern factories and mills was still below the country's average and continued so until the First World War, despite remarkable improvements in the use of mechanical power shown in Figure 5.3.

16   See for Italy, Cerisola, 1973, 128–89; for Greece, Sifneos, 2004, 259–67; also, for Spain, Castejón, 1977, 185–205; Nadal, 1987, 23; Sierra, 1992, 94–6; Zambrana, 1993, 78; Ramon-Muñoz, 1999, 156–64; Díaz Morlán, 2002, 139–40; or Pérez Moral, 2010, 41–5.

17   In 1857, a French consular report stated that 'the olive oils from Tuscany rank among the best ever known'. Ministère de l'Agriculture, 1863, 25 (my translation). For Liguria, see Boulanger, 1996, 51–5, who explains that quality improvement began before the nineteenth century.

18   Ricchioni, 1938, 32–7; Carrino and Salvemini, 2003, 509–38; and Mazzoti, 2004, 302–3.

19   Some old *Calabrese* wooden presses were still operating in Sicily and Calabria at the end of the nineteenth century. However, Flaminio Bracci argued that in the latter region *Calabrese* presses had been almost totally replaced by the more efficient *Genovese* presses from around the middle of the nineteenth century. Aloi, 1899, 219; Bracci, 1916, 167.

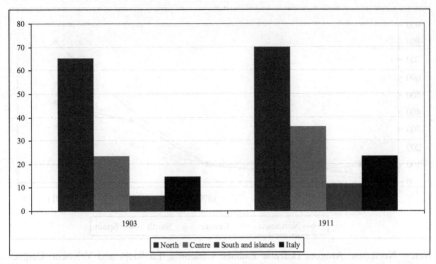

Notes: North: Emilia-Romagna, Liguria, Lombardy, Piedmont and Veneto. Centre: Lazio, Marche, Tuscany and Umbria. South and islands: Abruzzo, Basilicata, Calabria, Campania, Molise, Apulia, Sardinia and Sicily. For 1903, mills and factories, including also those working for oil seeds.

Sources: Ministero di Agricoltura, Industria e Commercio, *Statistica Industriale*; and Ministero di Agricoltura, Industria e Commercio, *Censimento degli opifici*.

Figure 5.3   The regional mechanization of the olive-oil industry in Italy, 1903–1911 (firms using mechanical power, as a percentage of each region's total olive-oil firms)

Modernization of the olive-oil industry also started relatively early in Spain. In 1833, the first Spanish hydraulic press was installed in the southern region of Andalusia; and by 1856 this region already had 198, that is, 85 per cent of all the Spanish hydraulic presses. Although in the 1870s the number seems to have fallen during the years of the agrarian crisis, they tended to increase again in the last decade of the nineteenth century. By 1903, the available data show that in Andalusia the number of presses amounted to 475, of which 266 were driven by mechanical power. Nevertheless, it was in the north-east of the country, particularly in Aragon, Catalonia and Valencia, that the speed of technological change proved to be more intense. Between 1856 and 1903, the number of hydraulic presses increased from 25 to 230 in north-eastern Spain (or by a factor of 9) whereas it only tripled in the rest of the country (see Figure 5.4).[20] By 1900–1904, they already accounted for 12 per cent of the total presses installed in Aragon, Catalonia and Valencia and represented almost 23 per cent of the total pressing capacity of these three regions. These percentages are in line with the Spanish average and, sometimes,

20   See Nadal, 1987, 30–31. Parejo and Zambrana (1994) 24, argue that the gap between the south and the north-east was lower than the available statistics suggest.

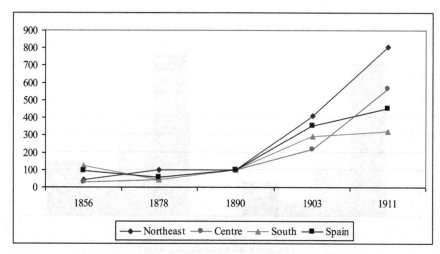

Notes: Northeast: Aragon, Balearic Islands, Catalonia, La Rioja and Valencia; Centre: Castile-La Mancha, Madrid, and Extremadura; South: Andalusia and Murcia.

Sources: *Estadística administrativa*, various issues.

Figure 5.4   The adoption of hydraulic presses in Spain by regions, 1857–1911 (1890 = 100)

they are even lower than other regions. However, north-eastern producers made a more intensive use of mechanical power than those of the rest of Spain, either per hectare of olive grove or per quantity of olives harvested.

From the end of the nineteenth century, agricultural operations such as ploughing, pruning and harvesting were improved, while modern marketing techniques for selling abroad were also adopted.[21] As in northern Italy and the province of Bari, these changes helped to make a remarkable improvement in the quality of the product. Olive oil from the north-eastern regions of Spain started to gain credit in the major international markets for edible olive oil but probably still fell behind Italy. Ramon de Manjarrés, one of the most reputed Spanish experts, was clear in this respect. In his book on the Spanish olive-oil sector published in 1896, Manjarrés argued that throughout the second half of the nineteenth century an increasing number of olive-oil millers followed modern production practices which were already well known in the main olive-growing areas. He also pointed out the marked improvement reached by local industry in the development of olive-oil machinery, which suggests that modern crushers or presses were at the disposal of Iberian millers. In fact, according to Manjarrés, the olive-oil machinery developed by most of the Spanish engineering firms was at least as modern as that constructed in the French and Italian factories. Yet he also recognized that the modernization process had been more intense in Italy than in Spain, which

---

21   Giralt, 1990, 249–52; Ramon-Muñoz, 2010, 393–4.

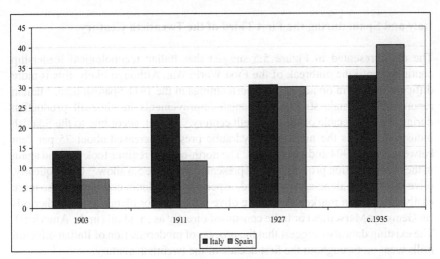

Notes: Firms or factories using water, steam, gas, oil or electricity power. Italy: data for 1903, 1927 and 1937 refer to mills or factories, while all figures exclude those firms or factories working for oil seeds. Spain: the source only considers those firms using mechanical power driving hydraulic presses; firms are identified as taxpayers in the source; firms working exclusively for oil seeds are excluded, although include those partially devoted to press peanut seeds. For potential shortcoming in the data, see text and footnotes.

Sources: Italy: Figure 5.3 and Istituto Centrale di Statistica, *Censimento industriale e commerciale*; and Istituto Centrale di Statistica, *Censimento industriale, 1937*. Spain: Figure 5.4.

Figure 5.5   The mechanization of the olive-oil mills and factories in Italy and Spain, 1903–c.1935 (olive-oil firms or factories using mechanical power, as a percentage of each country's total olive-oil firms or factories)

allowed the Italian olive-oil sector to open up new foreign markets for edible olive oil faster and more intensively than the Spaniards did.[22]

Figure 5.5 compares levels of mechanization in the olive-oil mills (as a proxy for modernization) in Italy and Spain throughout the first third of the twentieth century. Unfortunately, Spanish sources only specify the type of power driving the hydraulic presses. No information is provided regarding the power driving other presses, although around 1900 the use of mechanical power in Spain was the exception rather than the rule for non-hydraulic presses.[23] Despite this and other limitations, such as the fiscal nature of the data, the picture emerging from this figure seems to confirm Manjarrés' views: around 1900 the modernization of the olive-oil mills was still greater in Italy than in Spain.

---

22   Manjarrés, 1896, 137, 190, 285, 300 and 376.
23   Zambrana, 1987, 146.

Italy and Spain during the First Third of the Twentieth Century

The data presented in Figure 5.5 suggest that Italian technological leadership continued until the outbreak of the First World War. Although likely, this is more difficult to confirm on account of shortcomings in the 1911 Spanish data.[24] Italian reports and journals stress the Spanish improvements in olive-oil production during the first decade of the twentieth century.[25] In fact, according to the Spanish industrial sources the number of hydraulic presses increased about 75 per cent between 1900–1904 and 1910–1914. The north-eastern regions took the lead again in the modernization process, as data presented in Figure 5.4 show.[26] Consequently, olive oils from Valencia, Aragon and, especially, Catalonia continued to be more easily accepted in markets for edible olive oil, either for blending with other oils (in Genoa or Marseilles) or to be consumed directly as salad oil (in the Americas). The existing data also suggest that the process of modernization of Italian olive-oil mills went on throughout the first decade of the twentieth century.

As far as refining is concerned, the number and capacity of Spanish refineries seems also to have increased, though existing sources do not give precise data. In any case, around 1914, two important industrial plants were set up in Andalusia (southern Spain): the first belonged to Ybarra, an important Spanish olive-oil exporter from Seville; the second was owned by Carbonell, another outstanding export firm from Córdoba.[27] It is also well documented that between 1912 and 1914, two industrial refineries were established in the northern region of Liguria. The first one, called SAIRO (*Società Anonima Italiana Raffinazione Olii*), was founded in 1912, and two years later, in 1914, the RIO (*Raffineria Italiana Olii*) was set up, both in the coastal city of Porto Maurizio.[28]

Might it therefore be concluded that Italian technological leadership continued until the outbreak of the First World War? American reports suggest this was so. E.W. Thompson, an agent of the Department of Commerce, recognized the Spanish improvements in milling technology and product quality prior to the First World War, although he limited them to the northern regions.[29] According to him,

> ...in the north of Spain [as well as in Italy or France] there have been many
> improvements made in the manufacture of olive oil and very little of the low
> grades is manufactured [...]. It is only in the south of Spain and in the Levant,

---

24   The quantitative sources for 1911 probably underestimate the Spanish level of mechanization because joint stock companies were not included. The contrary might be true for Italy. Franciosa, 1940, 65.

25   See Gianolio, 1913, 77.

26   By 1911 the number of hydraulic presses as a percentage of all olive-oil presses was already slightly higher in the northeast than in any other Spanish region.

27   Zambrana, 1987, 155; Sierra, 1992, 45; Arenas, 1995, 167–9.

28   Cerisola, 1973, 37–8.

29   Thompson, 1913, 9 and 22.

where primitive methods are employed, that low grades of olive oils are produced that need to be deodorized. [In fact,] Italy has made more progress than other nations in [cultivation, fertilization, grafting, and pruning], as well as in improved methods of making oil'.

Judging from this American report, before the First World War Italian technological leadership was not only in milling and pressing but also in refining, blending and packaging. In 1907, for example, a report from the Manufactures Bureau concluded that in Spain 'refining is also done on a large scale, but the results are not comparable with those obtained by Italian and French refineries'.[30] In 1924, a documented study from the University of California argued that Italy and France had made in the past 'more rapid progress [...] in the refining, blending, packaging, and foreign marketing of olive oil'.[31] Although the existing evidence is far from conclusive, these were probably the areas in which Spain remained significantly backward relative to Italy prior to the First World War. This picture, however, changed throughout the interwar period. If during the decade prior to 1913 Spain had been falling behind Italy, by the mid-1920s it had already caught up; and around 1935 had probably overtaken Italy in both the mechanization of its mills and the capacity of its refineries. The existing data clearly show the dynamism of the Spanish olive-oil industry during the interwar period.[32] Between 1911 and 1927 the percentage of mechanized mills in Spain grew by 2.6 times (increasing from 12 to 30 per cent), whereas in Italy it had only increased by 1.3 times (from 23 to 31 per cent). Thus, by the mid-1920s the level of mechanization of the Spanish mills was already similar to that of Italy, and Spanish 'fine oils rank with the best of Italy and France'. In the course of the next decade, Spanish mechanization continued; consequently, around 1935 the percentage of mechanized mills was higher in Spain (40 per cent) than in Italy (33 per cent), as Table 5.1 shows.[33]

The Spanish process of catching-up and probably overtaking Italy was not limited to milling and pressing technology. It spread over other areas of the sector, such as refining, blending, packaging and foreign marketing. By the mid-1930s, for example, Spain appears to have been producing more refined olive oil than Italy.[34] In addition, the knowledge acquired by the Spanish exporting firms in blending

---

30   Manufactures Bureau, 1907, 110.

31   Cruess, 1924, 3.

32   For Spain, the given percentages are probably a lower limit of the true levels of mechanization of mills and factories. This seems particularly true during the interwar period since trading companies are not included in the source, that is, the *Estadística administrativa de la contribución industral y de comercio*.

33   Cruess, 1924, 3.

34   The data shown in Table 5.1 suggest that Italy had more refining factories than Spain. However, the opposite would be true if only those Italian establishments exclusively devoted to oil refining were taken into account. According to the Italian industrial census of 1937 they amounted to less than 40. Istituto Centrale di Statistica, 1940, 108.

Table 5.1   The olive-oil industry in Italy and Spain around 1935: production and refining

	Italy	Spain
Panel 1: Olive-oil firms, mills or factories[a]		
1. Mechanized, as a percentage of each country's total olive-oil firms or factories	33	40
2. Hydraulic presses, as a percentage of each country's total olive-oil presses	48	55
3. Olive-oil production, in thousands of metric tons[b]	209	357
4. Industrial yields, kilograms of olive oil per 100 kilograms of olives[b]	16	19
Panel 2: Olive-oil refining establishments[c]		
1. Number of establishments	63	57
2. Production of refined oil, in thousands of metric tons	53	74
3. Output per establishment, in metric tons of refined oil	837	1,317

Notes: [a] For Italy, mills and factories in 1937; for Spain, firms, which in the source are identified as taxpayers, using mechanical power driving hydraulic presses in 1933. [b] 1931/1935, yearly average. [c] For Spain, establishments operating the first semester of 1936 and production for the 1935 year. For Italy, all figures refer to 1937. The number of establishments also includes factories devoted to other activities apart from refining. For both Italy and Spain total production includes refined oil obtained from both olive oil and olive kernel oil (or sulphur oil). See also text and footnotes.

Sources: Figure 5.5; Federación de Fabricantes de Aceite de Orujo de España, *La Federación*, 275; and, for panels 1.3 and 1.4, Franciosa, *L'olivo*, table 5; *Bollettino mensile*, various issues; and Zambrana, *Crisis y modernización*, appendices.

operations had become similar to the Italian ones, as suggested by *El Aceite de Oliva de España*, the official bulletin of Spanish olive-oil exporters. Articles in this bulletin also point out another interesting point: the commercialization of the product, that is, foreign marketing did not hold any secrets for the Spanish exporters, while packaging techniques did not differ substantially from the Italian ones either.[35]

Spanish technological dynamism was coincident with important changes in regional patterns of modernization. Contrary to the prewar period, between 1913 and 1935 technical change both in pressing and refining proved to be more intense in the south than in the north-east of the country. Thus, by 1933, the percentage of hydraulic presses driven by mechanical power as well as the percentage of hydraulic presses relative to total presses was much higher in the south (57 and 78 per cent, respectively) than in the north-east (35 and 42 per cent, respectively). Nevertheless, the ratio of hydraulic presses to olive production was still lower in

---

35   See, for example, *El aceite de oliva de España*, 1931, no. 28, 2.

the south than in north-east, which suggests that the problem of long-term olive storage had not been totally solved in the south of the country. Olive storage had become a less serious shortcoming during the interwar period simply because of the expansion of industrial refining processes. Andalusia also took the lead in this area: on the eve of the Spanish Civil War, this region contained about 60 per cent of the Spanish refining establishments and almost 70 per cent of the total productive capacity of refined olive oil. As a partial result of all of these changes, between 1909–1913 and 1931–1935 production and exports of edible olive oil (including pressed and refined olive oil) increased more rapidly in southern Spain than in the rest of the country. Total production of olive oil expanded too, accounting for 60 per cent of the total Spanish output in the period 1931–1935. Conversely, north-eastern olive-oil exports and production remained stagnant relative to the rest of the country, partially because of competition from the refined oils produced in Andalusia.[36]

Patterns of regional modernization also changed in Italy in the interwar years, although the intensity of these changes was moderate relative to Spain. As shown in Table 5.2, by the eve of the Second World War, southern Italian olive-oil mills were still less mechanized than in the north, although it is true that between 1903 and 1937 the percentage of firms using mechanical power increased fourfold in southern Italy, while it only multiplied by 1.2 in northern Italy. In addition, southern olive-oil mills, which had a higher percentage of hydraulic presses, were also equipped with a higher proportion of wooden presses. Finally, physical productivity in both Italian olive-oil mills and refining plants appears to have been lower in the south than in the north.

A rapid comparison with southern Spain provides further evidence of the slower intensity of the southern Italian modernization. To start with, the southern regions of Italy did not reach the levels of modernization that had been achieved in southern Spain. By the mid-1930s, three-fourths of the presses installed in Andalusia were hydraulic, whereas only one-half were hydraulic in southern Italy. The mechanization of the firms or factories was also higher in the former than in the latter. Olive-oil refining also developed on a larger scale in southern Spain than in southern Italy, where only one-half of the Italian refining establishments were located and less than one-third of the Italian total of refined-oil production.

Conclusions

As was the case in many other industries, between the 1850s and the 1930s the olive-oil industry experienced a fundamental phase of modernization through innovations in equipment, processes and energy. An important stimulus was the collapse of markets demanding olive oil for industrial purposes. The replacement

36 See Zambrana, 1987, 71 and 264; Pinilla, 1995, 365–72; and Ramon-Muñoz, 1999, 142–6.

Table 5.2   The modernization of the olive-oil industry in Spain and Italy by regions around 1935

	Spain		Italy	
	North-East	South	North-Centre	South
Panel 1: Olive-oil firms, mills or factories				
1. Olive-oil production (%)[a]	18	59	27	73
2. Size and structure (Spain or Italy =100)				
2.1. Average pressing capacity per firm or factory	92	119	88	106
2.2. Presses per firm or factory	98	103	81	109
3. Mechanization and modernization (%)[a]				
3.1. Firms or factories driven by mechanical power	35	57	45	27
3.2. Hydraulic presses	42	78	43	50
4. Industrial yields, kilograms of olive oil per 100 kilograms of olives (Spain or Italy =100)[b]	104	98	109	97
Panel 2: Olive-oil refining establishments				
1. Establishments (%)[a]	32	58	52	48
2. Productive capacity (%)[a c]	26	67	69	31
3. Productive capacity per establishment (Spain or Italy =100)[c]	82	117	132	65

Notes: [a] As a percentage of each region's total; [b] For Spain, average for 1926/1935, and for Italy average for 1931/1935; [c] For Italy, production instead of productive capacity. See also text and footnotes.
Sources: Figures 5.3, 5.4 and Table 5.1.

of wooden presses with the new hydraulic ones, especially when they employed mechanical power, was probably one of the major events in the modernization of olive-oil production prior to the Second World War. Another important step was the expansion of industrial refining plants from about 1912 onwards. This modernization process made product innovations possible which was crucial to enlarge markets for edible olive oil.

The speed in the adoption of new technologies and techniques differed across countries, however. Focussing on the cases of Italy and Spain, this chapter has shown that modernization began earlier and spread more rapidly in the former than in the latter country. Thus, the modernization of the Spanish olive-oil industry fell behind the Italian one in the second half of the nineteenth century and, perhaps, during the first decade of the twentieth century. The adoption of new machinery and better methods of production accelerated more rapidly in Spain than in Italy from the years around the First World War to the mid-1930s. Consequently, by the first half of the 1920s Spain had caught-up with their Italian competitors in milling, pressing and refining, as well as in blending and packaging, and in the early 1930s Spain had probably surpassed Italy in some of these areas. Interestingly, the previous sections of the present work have also made clear that for both Italy and Spain technological progress had a strong regional dimension. What this chapter has not discussed are the reasons why the speed of technical change in the olive-oil industry and therefore of modernization differed between Italy and Spain and across their regions, an issue that awaits further research.

References

Aceite de oliva de España, El [The Spanish olive oil], Madrid: 1929–1935.

Aloi, A., 1899, *El olivo y el aceite: cultivo del olivo, extracción, purificación y conservación del aceite* [The olive tree and olive oil: olive tree cultivation, extraction, purification and conservation of the oil] (Spanish translation from the fourth Italian edition), Valencia: Pascual Aguilar.

Arenas, C., 1995, *Sevilla y el Estado, 1892–1923. Una perspectiva local de la formación del capitalismo en España* [Seville and the State, 1892–1923. A local perspective on the formation of capitalism in Spain], Sevilla: Universidad de Sevilla.

Bollettino mensile di statistica agraria e forestale [Monthly bulletin of agricultural and forest statistics], various issues, Roma: 1931–1935.

Boulanger, P., 1996, *Marseille, marché international del'huile d'olive: un produit et des hommes de 1725 à 1825* [Marseilles, the international market of olive oil], Marseille: Institut Historique de Provence.

Bracci, F., 1916, *Manuale di olivicoltura ed oleificio* [Handbook of olive growing and olive-oil making] (Third edition), Milano: Casa Editrice Dottor Francesco Vallardi.

Carrino, A. and Salvemini, B., 2003, '*Trasferimento tecnologico e innovazione sociale: Pierre Ravanas e l'olio del Mezzogiorno d'Italia fra Sette e Ottocento*' [echnology transfer and social innovation: Pierre Ravanas and olive-oil production in the South of Italy between the eighteenth and nineteenth century], *Quaderni Storici*, vol. 38, no. 2, 499–550.

Castejón, R., 1977, *La Casa Carbonell de Córdoba, 1866–1918. Génesis y desarrollo de una sociedad mercantil* [The Carbonell House from Cordoba, 1866–1918. Origins and development of a trading company], Córdoba: Monte de Piedad y Cajas de Ahorros de Córdoba.

Cerisola, N., 1973, *Storia delle industrie imperiesi* [History of the Imperial industries], Savona: Casa Editrice Liguria.

Cruess, W.V., 1924, 'The preparation and refining of olive oil in Southern Europe', *University of California. College of Agriculture. Agricultural Experiment Station*, Circular no. 279.

Díaz Morlán, P., 2002. *Los Ybarra. Una dinastía de empresarios, 1801–2001* [The Ybarra. A dynasty of entrepreneurs], Madrid: Marcial Pons.

Estadística administrativa de la contribución industrial y de comercio [Administrative statistics for taxes on industry and commerce], Madrid: 1857, 1879, 1890–1891, 1900–1933.

Federación de Fabricantes de Aceite de Orujo de España, 1937, *La Federación de Fabricantes de Aceite de Orujo de España* [The Federation of manufacturers of olive-pomace oil of Spain], Madrid: Gráfica Administrativa.

Franciosa, L., 1940, *L'olivo nella economia italiana* [The olive tree in the Italian economy], Roma: Tipografia Failli.

Gianolio, E., 1913, '*Notizie sul mercato di esportazione e su prezzi degli olii di oliva*' [News of the olive-oil export market and the prices of olive oil], *Bollettino de la Società Nazionale degli Olivicoltori*, no. 5, 76–9.

Giralt, E., 1990, '*L'agricultura*' [Agriculture], in Nadal, J., Maluquer de Motes, J., Sudrià, C., Cabana, F., eds, *Història econòmica de la Catalunya contemporània. Volum II: Segle XIX. Població i agricultura*, Barcelona: Enciclopèdia Catalana, 121–305.

Istituto Centrale di Statistica, 1929, *Censimento industriale e commerciale al 15 ottobre 1927* [Industrial and commercial census of 15 October 1927], vols VI and VII. Roma: Istituto Poligrafico dello Stato.

Istituto Centrale di Statistica, 1940, *Censimento industriale, 1937. Industria degli Olii Vegetali. Censimento al 30 novembre 1937* [Industrial census, 1937. The vegetable oils industry. Census of 30 November 1937], Roma: Tipografia Faili.

Manjarrés, R. de, 1896, *El aceite de oliva. Su extracción, clarificación y refinación* [Olive oil. Its extraction, clarification and refining], Madrid: Hijos de D.J. Cuesta Editores. Manufactures Bureau, 1907, 'Olive culture' [in France, Spain and Italy], *Monthly Consular and Trade Reports*, no. 327, 104–13.

Mazzoti, M., 2004, 'Enlightened Mills. Mechanizing Olive-Oil Production in Mediterranean Europe', *Technology and Culture*, vol. 45, Baltimore, MD: Johns Hopkins University Press.

Mingioli, E., 1901, *Oleificio moderno* [Modern olive-oil making], Torino: Unione Tipografico-Editrice.

Ministère de l'Agriculture, du Commerce et des Travaux Publics, 1863, *Annales du commerce extérieur. Italie (Faits commerciaux), 1844 à 1862* [Annals of foreign trade. Italy (Commercial facts), 1844 to 1862], Paris: Imprimerie et Librairie Administratives de Paul Dupont.

Ministero di Agricoltura, Industria e Commercio, 1906, *Statistica Industriale. Riassunto delle notizie sulle condizioni industriali del Regno (1903)* [Industrial statistics. Summary of the news on the industrial conditions of the Kingdom (1903)], Roma: Tipografia Nazionale di G. Bertero.

Ministero di Agricoltura, Industria e Commercio, 1914, *Censimento degli opifici e delle imprese industriali al 10 giugno 1911* [Census of factories and industrial firms on 10 June 1911], vol. II–IV. Roma: Tipografia Nazionale di G. Bertero.

Morini, U., 1930, *L'industria olearia. Manuale Pratico sugli impianti d'estrazione dell'olio dalle sanse di oliva con solventi, raffinazione, ecc.* [The oil industry. Practical handbook on the establishments devoted to the extraction of oil from the olive pomace through solvents, refining, etc.], Torino: Lavagnolo.

Nadal, J., 1987, '*La industria fabril española en 1900. Una aproximación*' [Spanish manufacturing industry in 1900: an approach], in Nadal, J., Carreras, A. and Sudrià, C., eds, *La economía española en el siglo XX. Una perspectiva histórica*, Barcelona: Ariel, 23–61.

Parejo, A. and Zambrana, J.F., 1994, '*La modernización de la industria del aceite en España en los siglos XIX y XX*' [The modernization of the olive-oil industry in Spain in the nineteenth and twentieth centuries], in Nadal, J. and Catalan, J., eds, *La cara oculta de la industrialización española*. Madrid: Alianza, 13–42.

Pérez Moral, L., 2010, *La Casa Pallarés. Familia y negocio* [The Pallarés House. Family and business], Cabra: Lourdes Pérez Moral.

Pinilla, V., 1995, *Entre la inercia y el cambio. El sector agrario aragonés, 1850–1935* [Betweeen inertia and change. The agrarian sector in Aragon, 1850–1935], Madrid: Ministerio de Agricultura, Pesca y Alimentación.

Ramon-Muñoz, R., 1999, '*Estructura empresarial, empreses i canvi tècnic en la indústria de l'oli d'oliva de les comarques de Lleida, 1890–1936*' [Business structure, firms and technical change in the olive-oil industry of the counties of Lleida, 1890–1936], in Vicedo, E., ed., *Empreses i institucions econòmiques contemporànies a les Terres de Lleida, 1850–1990*. LLeida: Institut d'Estudis Ilerdencs, 141–87.

Ramon-Muñoz, R., 2000, 'Specialization in the international market for olive oil before World War II', in Pamuk, Ş. and Williamson, J.G., eds, *The Mediterranean response to globalization before 1950*, London and New York: Routledge, 159–98.

Ramon-Muñoz, R., 2010, 'Product differentiation and entry barriers: Mediterranean export firms in the American markets for olive oil prior to World War II', *Business History*, vol. 52, no. 3, 390–416.

Ricchioni, V., 1938, *L'olivicoltura meridionale e l'opera di Pietro Ravanas* [The southern olive growing and the work of Pietro Ravanas], Bari: Alfredo Cressati.

Rosenberg, N., 1976, *Perspectives on technology*, Cambridge: Cambridge University Press.

Sierra, M., 1992, *La familia Ybarra, empresarios y políticos* [The Ybarra family, entrepreneurs and politicians], Sevilla: Muñoz Moya y Montraveta.

Sifneos, E., 2004, 'On entrepreneurs and entrepreneurship in the olive-oil economy in the Aegean: the case of Lesvos island', *The Historical Review*, vol. 1, 245–73.

Simpson, J., 1995, *Spanish agriculture. The long siesta, 1765–1965*, Cambridge: Cambridge University Press.

Thompson, E.W., 1913, 'Edible Oils in the Mediterranean District', *Special Agents Series*, no. 75.

Weber, G.M. and Alsberg, C.L., 1934, *The American vegetable-shortening industry, its origin and development*, Stanford: Stanford University Food Research Institute.

Zambrana, J.F., 1987, *Crisis y modernización del olivar español, 1870–1930* [Crisis and modernization of the Spanish olive grove, 1870–1930], Madrid: Ministerio de Agricultura, Pesca y Alimentación.

Zambrana, J.F., 1993, '*Las industrias de los aceites y las grasas vegetales en España: un desarrollo limitado, 1850–1950*' [The industries of vegetable oils and fats in Spain: a limited development, 1850–1950], in *Revista de Historia Industrial*, no. 4, 57–89.

PART II
Creating New Foods

Chapter 6

'The biggest chocolate factory in the world': The Menier Chocolate Factory in Noisiel

Alain Drouard

Introduction

France played an important role in the development of the food industry in the nineteenth century. Major technical innovations such as the process of extracting sugar from beets, heat sterilization and industrial refrigeration resulted in some large canning, biscuit and chocolate companies.[1] In the second half of the nineteenth century, the Menier chocolate factory to the east of Paris at Noisiel (Seine and Marne) became 'the biggest chocolate factory in the world'.[2] In 1900, about 2,000 factory workers produced more than 15,000 tons of chocolate each year. This factory was not only typical of the large capitalist company based on rationalization of production and the organization of labour, but it was also an exceptional example of industrial architecture and its name is inseparable from that of the working-class neighbourhood built by Menier to accommodate their staff.

It was the heart of what was called 'the Menier empire'. This powerful conglomerate of factories, cocoa plantations, merchant ships, sugar refineries and rural buildings, was at that time a successful example of vertical integration. Beyond the exceptional success of a dynasty of contractors, the Noisiel example testifies as much to the modernity and power of the food industry in France[3] as to the originality of 'ideal' capitalism, because it managed to combine efficiency and social progress.[4]

A Dynasty of Entrepreneurs

The creation of a large capitalist company – the Noisiel factory – and the construction of an industrial empire were the work of an employers' dynasty whose story starts at the beginning of the nineteenth century.

---

1 Chaptal, 1818, 347–88; Appert, 1810; Tellier, 1910.
2 This expression was used during the 1893 World Fair in Chicago.
3 Marseille, 1997.
4 Marrey, 1984.

Jean-Antoine-Brutus Menier (1795–1853)

The founder of the dynasty, Jean-Antoine-Brutus, was born on 17 May 1795 in Bourgueil (Indre and Loire) in a family of tradesmen. After studying pharmacy, he founded a commercial firm – a hardware store – with 16,000 francs in Paris in 1816. Jean-Antoine-Brutus conceived it like a central establishment for pharmacists. One idea became a success: spraying pharmaceutical substances to produce powders. After starting with a simple man-powered mill, which he later converted to be operated with horses, he rented a mill in Noisiel in 1825, for fifteen years.[5] At that time, chocolate was still considered as a drug for pharmaceutical purposes and as a luxury item.

The surplus of energy delivered by the mill made it possible for Jean-Antoine-Brutus Menier to improve the spraying of vegetable or mineral drugs and to develop his production quickly. An individual entrepreneur, he gathered capital from backers and could therefore acquire modern materials necessary for the production of perfect medicinal substances. To produce his drugs on a commercial scale, Jean-Antoine-Brutus's associates provided him with buildings located at 41 rue des Lombards in Paris.

The pharmaceutical profession quickly recognized the high qualities of the powders manufactured by Menier. In 1832, a commission of the Société d'encouragement pour l'industrie nationale [Society for the Encouragement of National Industry] went to Noisiel to visit M. Menier and M. Adrien's establishment.[6] It underlines the company's achievement:

> The art of spraying was not yet considered as a special branch of industry, each industrialist prepared the powders he needed, himself. An establishment in which all these well made preparations could be found was missing in France.[7]

That year, the Society gave a gold medal to the hydraulic factory of Noisiel. In 1834, Menier set up a new *commandite* [a private limited joint stock company] whose object was:

> the manufacture of powders and flours for pharmacists, general storekeepers and herbalists, the grinding of the grains, the manufacture of chocolate, the spraying and the preparation of the medicinal products and the trade of all that relates to the hardware store.[8]

---

5   This old mill had a hanging wheel which, with the help of jacks, could go up or down as the water level rose or fell. At the end of the fifteen-year lease, the mill was sold for 117,950 francs to the Menier Company.

6   M.Adrien was Menier's partner in Noisiel.

7   Amédée-Durand, 1832, 248.

8   Piganiol, 1983.

By 1841, there were 21 workers in Noisiel, 75 workers in Paris and seven to eight sales representatives. Faced with criticism from pharmacists who complained about competition from him, Menier went back to pharmacy school, and successfully passed his examinations. After receiving his diploma, he solicited his admission to the Pharmacy Company in 1842.

Until the 1840s, chocolate was not an essential product for the company. It became essential because Jean-Antoine-Brutus developed its production to decrease its price and therefore to support its consumption. From this time on, he implemented a sales strategy based on the brand and the use of publicity. The Menier brand of chocolate was created as early as 1849: the chocolate bar was divided into six semi-cylindrical divisions, the paper was of a different colour depending on the quality and the price of the chocolate; the label, with black lines on a white background, included facsimiles of the head and tail of the 1832 and 1834 coins.[9] Jean-Brutus Menier played the publicity card. As Turgan (1870) puts it:

> In our country, Mr. Menier Senior was one of the rare French manufacturers who had foreseen the power of advertisement, this powerful instrument of success for those who understand it. Facing the still powerful prejudices of the time, he made a broad publicity around his product and as he was one of the few people in the newspapers then, this publicity had an immense repercussion.[10]

From 1832, the company started winning awards. Its turnover increased from 2,000,000 francs in 1844 to 3,000,000 francs in 1849. It won the gold medal at the 1849 exhibition and a Prize Medal in London in 1851. By then, 8,000 pharmacists had accounts with the company. On 1 January 1853, the award of the *Légion d'honneur* validated the professional success of Jean-Antoine-Brutus.

Emile-Justin Menier (1826–1881): 'The Cocoa Baron'

Emile-Justin Menier, the son of Jean-Antoin-Brutus built 'the Menier empire'. His success led him to be nicknamed 'the cocoa baron' by his neighbour, the Duchess Ernestine of Guermantes (1800–1884). After pharmacy studies and residence abroad, especially in England and the United-States, he worked in the family business. When his father died in 1853,[11] he inherited a business worth 1,500,000

---

9 The decrees of 23 June 1837 and 27 June 1857 on trademarks and trade provided the Menier business with the legal base for the many court actions which they brought against counterfeiters.

10 Turgan, 1870, 112.

11 During its development, the Menier company changed its structure and legal status several times. From 1834 onwards, with a few changes in 1845 and 1849, it became a *société de commandite* [private limited joint stock company] during Jean-Antoine-Brutus's leadership, then a *société commerciale en nom collectif* [a business firm in collective name] with Emile-Justin in 1879. It became a *société anonyme à responsabilité limitée* [public

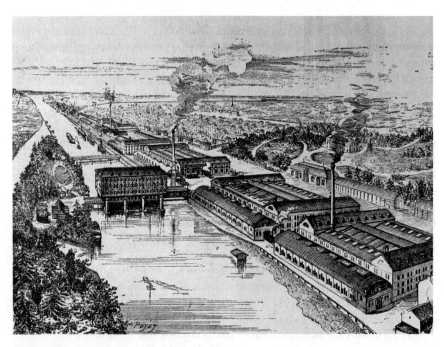

Source: Nansouty, M. de, 1889–1890, 12–20.

Figure 6.1   General view of the Menier works at Noisiel

francs and took over the role of manager. His first concern was to expand and modernize his establishment on the edge of the Marne. In 1854, he expanded the existing mill by building a third arch which allowed the engineer, Louis-Dominique Girard, to install two water turbines. This innovation was noticed during the 1855 World Fair which took place in the capital. The jury noted that the Menier establishments provided supplies to four-fifths of the French pharmacists as well as very many others abroad. The jury remarked that more than 200 people worked for the Menier House, both in Paris and in Noisiel and awarded Emile-Justin Menier a medal of honour.

Emile-Justin Menier was also interested in the spatial organization of his site. He called upon Jules Saulnier, a student of Jules Bonneau at the School of Fine Arts to create in Saint-Denis what was going to be the biggest chemical and

---

company with limited liability] only in 1948, then a *société anonyme* [a public joint stock company] in 1960, that is, shortly before disappearing. As co-manager from 1 July 1851, Emile-Justin was to receive full management of the Company in the event of his father's death. The management granted him two-thirds of the profits from 1 July 1851, with the silent partners dividing the remaining one-third, in addition to the interests on their funds.

pharmaceutical factory in France.[12] The year 1867 was an important date in the history of the company: Menier gave up pharmacy to devote himself mainly to the production of chocolate and François Dorvault, director of the Central Pharmacy business firm, bought the Menier factory in Saint-Denis.[13]

Gaston-Emile-Henri (1855–1934): The Chocolate Empire

When Emile-Justin Menier's widow died in 1895, her three sons, Henri, Gaston and Albert, became the exclusive owners of the Menier establishments. After the death of his brothers (Albert in 1899 then Henri in September 1913), Gaston took over as the leader of the Menier empire, then at its apex, at the turn of the twentieth century. From 1881 Gaston was President of the Union of Chocolate-sellers and Confectioners in France. Gaston continued his father's philanthropic policy.

The company began a diversification of production to maintain its positions vis-a-vis its foreign competitors (Van Houten, Kohler, Lindt, Nestlé). After plain chocolate, which had allowed him to dominate the market until 1900, Gaston Menier started producing fancy and luxury confectionery, as well as milk chocolate and chocolate powder.

Georges Gaston (1880–1933) and Jacques Menier (1892–1953): The Belle Époque and the Factory

Gaston Menier's children, Georges and Jacques, were more interested in leisure – yachting and hunting in particular – than in the Noisiel factory and the group's businesses.

Power and glory   At the end of the nineteenth century, the Meniers had become one of the ten richest families in France. They had acquired an immense estate of land as well as property in France and abroad. The Noisiel estate located in the village of Noisiel and the surrounding villages, representing 3,700 acres included cultivated land, beet fields, natural meadows, parks and stud farms. It was organized around a model farm known as the Farm of the Saint-Antoine Bush, which accommodated the agricultural competition of the World Fair in 1889 and for this reason was visited by the President, Sadi Carnot. But there were

---

12   Later Saulnier's major accomplishment was the mill which was to carry his name at Noisiel. Many well-known chemists worked in Saint-Denis and Noisiel. The most famous of them was Marcellin Berthelot, before he became professor at the Collège de France. Paul Jean Rigollot, manager of the Saint-Denis factory, invented the sinapism (mustard plaster) which carries his name.

13   From 1867 onwards the Central Pharmacy became the first French pharmacy company.

also especially the private mansions,[14] the castles and parks in the Ile de France (Noisiel, Emerainville, Rentilly) and in the country (Chenonceaux), the villas in Neuilly sur Seine, in Lamorlay, in Provence in Cannes, Houlgate and abroad. Emile-Justin Menier's first son, Henri, acquired the island of Anticosti in the province of Quebec at the mouth of the St. Lawrence in 1895; it was comparable in size to Corsica. There he created a village, introduced wild animals, and developed fishing. Enjoying hunting, yachting, racing and receptions, the Meniers were not unaware of the practices and customs of the high society of their time.

More than the exceptional success and fortune of a family dynasty, it is necessary to stress that the Meniers were all very involved in the society of their time. Indeed, from generation to generation they accumulated parliamentary seats, municipal magistratures, press and publishing positions, as well as participating in innumerable associations and learned or philanthropic societies. The Meniers were mayors of Noisiel without interruption from 1870 to 1959. Emile-Justin was its mayor between 1870 and 1881, and represented it in the Chamber of Deputies between 1876 and 1881. His son Gaston was mayor of Noisiel, deputy for Meaux between 1898 and 1909 and a senator between 1909 and 1934. With only one exception, all the Meniers received the *Légion d'honneur*.

Contrary to his father Jean-Antoine-Brutus, who was Bonapartist, Emile-Justin Menier was for the Republic. A defender of the freedom of the press, he founded a bi-monthly review called *Economic reform*, and a daily newspaper of radical tendencies called *Public property* which became the *Voltaire*. He published many economic and political works and was in favour of income tax.[15]

A Multinational Corporation: The Menier Empire

At the end of the nineteenth century, the Menier empire was characterized by the constant search for innovation and by its vertical integration.

Science, Technology and Innovations

Emile-Justin Menier was indeed a curious spirit, a friend of many scientists, member of several learned societies, a rationalist and a convinced positivist. In his eyes, science was the key to technical innovation which ordered economic and social progress. The scientific method was to clarify actions and rationalize

---

14   In Paris, there were private mansions by the Monceau park: 5 avenue Van Dyck, 4 avenue Ruysdael and 8 rue Alfred de Vigny competed in their luxury and the sumptuousness of their decoration.

15   Menier, 1872.

the organization of industrial work. He defended his project of income tax to the Chamber of Deputies by saying:[16]

> I noticed, as a manufacturer as well as a farmer, that it was always necessary to seek to obtain a maximum effect with a minimum effort in a minimum time.
> Here is my starting point.
> To achieve this result, what should be done? It is necessary to apply examination and reasoning to any question; to use the method of observation, induction, that is, the scientific method; to break up the facts, then to synthesize them; to see well what one sees and to seek to see what one does not see; to realize consequently the questions of incidence and repercussion; to make in a word what caused the great discoveries of modern science.

He applied these principles to the Noisiel factory as well as in the management of the other factories of the company. Specialists and engineers, several of whom were former students of the Central School of Arts and Manufactures took part in the creation as well as in the management of the Noisiel factory.[17] Innovation and mechanization were at the heart of the policy of modernization and rationalization led by Emile-Justin Menier, as the testimonies of many observers – journalists, engineers and specialist technicians – attested after visiting the factory.[18]

The construction of the new factory entrusted to Jules Saulnier (1817–1881)[19] lasted more than a dozen years from the beginning of the 1860s. It was carried out without interruption of production and led to a single unit where the rational organization of work, the aesthetic concerns and the search for social peace were based.The investments resulted in an adjustment of space and a recasting of the production process. From the sorting out of beans to the folding of the wrapping of the chocolate bars, the production cycle was organized in a series of operations conducted in specialized workshops whose distribution aimed at controlling and limiting the movement of men. The flow of goods was improved by creating a

---

16   Menier, E-J., 1876, *Annales du Sénat et de la Chambre des Députés, Séance du 9 décembre 1876*: 144–9.

17   See, among others, Charles Callon, specialist in hydraulic factories, Emile Müller, Louis Sautter, Armand Moisant who built the mill, Emile Baudet and Alfred Donon.

18   Turgan, 1870, 97–128. Turgan devoted a volume to Noisiel in his series: *The Big Factories of France*. Tresca and Duchêne, 1869, 321–31, visited Noisiel on behalf of the Society for the Encouragement of National Industry. Finally, Armengaud Senior, 1856, devoted a major part to Noisiel in its review *Industrial Publication*.

19   Providing the workshops for crushing the cocoa beans and for mixing the chocolate, the Mill was Jules Saulnier's main work. The architect designed a metal framework, and a simple glazed hollow-brick filling for the walls. This process made it possible to create an artistic decoration where a series of glazed, polychrome ceramic tiles represented the monogram 'M' of the Menier house and the cacao-tree flowers. The Noisiel mill was the first building in the world to have been conceived on a metal structure and inspired many French and foreign architects.

Source: Nansouty, M. de, 1889–1890, 12–20.

Figure 6.2   View of the grinding shed at Noisiel

private railway network. In 1879, Emile-Justin Menier had approached a private railway company, the Eastern Railway, in order to connect his mills to the rail network. He was granted permission in April 1881 by the General Council of the Seine and Marne. With a length of 10 km, these rails replaced the horse-drawn carriages which had been in use since the creation of the factory. They made it possible to dispatch the finished products and to receive the raw materials like sugar and cocoa unloaded in Le Havre.

The inside of the factory was designed to address the preoccupation with rationalization. Laid out around a central court and connected to each other by passages in the basement, the buildings were divided into three sub-units corresponding to the principal phases of the product's development : first, the reception, storage and preparation of raw materials (sorting and roasting of beans, drying and spraying of sugars in the part known as 'upstream' located to the right of the entrance; second, the crushing and mixing of the cocoa paste and sugar, working up on the three levels of the 'building on water'; and third, the raising, cooling, releasing from the mould, packing and shipping in the downstream part. The standardized production resulted in productivity gains while increased mechanization made it possible to limit handling. In addition to hygiene, the benefits consisted in the possibility of using a less qualified, rural and increasingly female labour force.[20] The increase in the energy needs related to mechanization led the factory to set up steam engines developing 70 horsepower each in 1866, and to increase the power of the mill by installing two Girard siphon turbines. The water restraint system was improved by the construction of a mobile dam on the Marne from 1869 to 1872. The electrical production of the Hydraulic Factory of Noisiel[21] was increased. Mechanical refrigeration was another major innovation at Noisiel.[22] Charles Tellier (1828–1913), who was called 'the father of the cold' installed his first refrigerating machines in 1868.[23]

A report of the Society for the Encouragement of National Industry (1869) described the important expansion of the Noisiel factory and the rebuilding of the mill which made it possible for the Menier House to increase the production of chocolate and cause a drop in its price. In 1889, the World Fair published a booklet describing the performance of the factory. It mentioned that the turbines' driving force of 400 horsepower, in addition to the identical power of the steam engines transmitting the movement to the machinery, ensured the manufacture of chocolate in the Saulnier mill. Since the arrival of cocoa, the various manipulations were carried out in large workshops connected by railways with tip trucks and elevators. Eighteen ovens roasted the beans; and twenty grinding-stone mills crushed roasted almonds. After making a homogeneous mixture of sugar and cocoa paste, twenty-eight automatic machines cast the chocolate. In the last workshop, 450 workers took care of the wrapping and packing the bars. A workshop making wood cases was annexed to the main factory. The Noisiel establishment was connected to the head office 'for the prompt execution of orders by a direct and particular telephone and telegraph'. In 1889, annual production had already reached 15,000 tons and the labour force numbered 1,500 workers. The development of the factory benefited greatly from the initiative of Jules Logre, engineer and principal collaborator of the company since 1869, and his son Louis, architect of many buildings built at Noisiel in the last two decades of the nineteenth century. However, one original feature of the Meniers' work was to have combined economic progress and social progress by

---

20 In 1867, the report of the international jury of the Paris World Fair, published under the direction of Michel Chevalier, concluded: 'It is in France that the improvement of the (chocolate) industry made the most progress, thanks to the machines invented by French mechanics'.

21 'Hydraulic Noisiel Factory' is a half-erased inscription currently located on the southern gable of the mill.

22 The more quickly the chocolate drawn up in the moulds was cooled down, the more rapidly the solidification of the cocoa butter occured thus determining a clean break. Before the use of mechanical refrigeration, there was a difference between summer chocolate and a winter chocolate of higher quality.

23 It was a machine that liquefied ammonia by mechanical compression.

creating an area of workers' housing called 'Menier Ville'. While Noisiel only had 119 inhabitants in 1836, its population reached 1,248 inhabitants in 1906.

A Factory Housing Estate

At the beginning of the nineteenth century, within a rural framework like Noisiel, it was important to attract and keep the labour supply necessary for the functioning of the factory. But the project of a workers' model village, like the one Emile-Justin Menier was thinking of, cannot be reduced to strict economic imperatives. It was also a social utopia following the example of other contemporary utopias whether Godin's 'Phalanstery' in Guise or the model housing in Mulhouse.[24] After having tried to stabilize the working population by a policy of advantages and collective services (cafeterias for outside workers; catering within the framework of a lodging house for workers; lodging of unmarried workers in dormitories where they received an elementary education), Emile-Justin Menier provided 50 acres of land to found a model community composed of houses laid out in patterns of five with individual gardens whose rent in 1874 was fixed at 150 francs per year. Convenient shops were opened in 1876. Emile-Justin Menier organized a co-operative society for his workers which provided various supplies. Cereals, dairy products, and eggs came from Menier's farms. Purchases were made in cash or credit, or taken from workers' salaries. A school complex was built from 1874 to 1876 and expanded in 1892. Cafeterias for the workers from the surrounding villages were built between 1884 and 1885, an old people's home called Claire Menier, from the name of Emile-Justin's widow, was founded in 1898. Two hotel-restaurants, the Navy hotel and the fisherman's hotel, were erected on the village's plaza and were intended for the single people of the factory.

The houses had toilets and a boiler for clothes washing though Noisiel, like all French villages, did not have running water, which was then only the privilege of big cities. This is why the factory community seemed a model of hygiene since fountains, baths and conveniences were at the inhabitants' disposal. The cleaning of streets was ensured by a body of street sweepers and part of the household rubbish was placed in a special pit to be used as manure in the gardens. Two doctors and a pharmacist provided medical treatment. Medicines were free. Noisiel also had a private company of firemen taking charge of the safety of the factory and model community. Construction was completed in 1900. The factory housing estate which had cost a million francs, included 138 houses and 312 other dwellings but could not accommodate all the workers. The Meniers had 53 additional houses and five shops built in the neighbouring village of Champs sur Marne.

---

24   Emile Müller, architect of the working city of Mulhouse, collaborated with Jules Saulnier during the construction of the mill in 1871. Even though he influenced the plans of the Noisiel workers' community, there were other influences, like Saltaire, the factory model village near Bradford, England, created by the initiative of the industrialist Titus Salt.

Source: Turgan, 1870, 104.

Figure 6.3   The Valle Menier plantation near Lake Nicaragua

Vertical Integration

To develop chocolate consumption, it was necessary to reduce its production cost. In order to reduce costs, it was important to control the factors of production. Emile-Justin Menier decided to cultivate his own cacao-trees, to produce his own beets and to refine his own sugar. In 1862, he bought an immense property of a surface area of 3,700 acres called Valle Menier, located about twenty kilometres from the south-western part of Lake Nicaragua and about sixty from the Pacific Ocean, where he built his first cacao-tree plantations. In 1865, Emile-Justin Menier created another plantation of approximately 15,000 acres, San Emilio, by Lake Nicaragua. In the 1880s, more than 300 workers were employed on both plantations. The transportation of cocoa to France was carried out from Nicaragua via Rio San Juan and Greytown and San Juan del Norte harbours, but also from Trinidad and Venezuela. The Menier house had its own merchant fleet. All its ships, the *Cruzeiro*, the *Brazileiro*, the *Claire-Menier*, the *Emile-Menier*, the *Noisiel* and the *Denis-Crouan*, have since disappeared, except the *Belem*, a three-masted steel ship of 546 tons, built in 1896 by the Dubigeon shipyard. Today, a sail-training vessel, the *Belem* made many voyages across the Atlantic, transporting cane sugar and cocoa.

The Meniers also produced beet sugar. The central sugar refinery of Roye and its two additional refineries located in the Somme were acquired in 1866, a few years before the acquisition of other sugar refineries in the Seine et Marne at Villenoy in 1869 and Lizy sur Ourcq in 1873. In the 1880s, nearly 500 workers made sugar for the Noisiel chocolate factory.

The Menier empire based its power on technical innovations and the new industrial production which they generated. In 1850, Emile-Justin Menier married Claire Henriette Clémence Gérard. Emile-Justin thus joined the family of the Aubert and Gérard company which specialized in rubber and held the Goodyear licence for vulcanization.[25] The Menier enterprise therefore invested in the rubber and gutta percha industry by creating the Grenelle factory in 1870 as well as a new factory in Prussia at Harburg. Following the example of the Noisiel chocolate factory, the Grenelle factory was a modern establishment equipped at the end of the nineteenth century with the latest inventions – Gramme machines, electric lamps, Decauville tip trucks and telephones. It produced industrial rubber which was used in the manufacture of equipment and machines, belts, pipes, springs, and tyres. In addition to the use of rubber, Menier transformed another type of latex: gutta percha, which had exceptional insulating qualities. It was immediately used in the manufacture of electric cables for underground and underwater telegraphy. In 1873, the first French underwater cable between Le Havre and Pennedepie close to Honfleur was produced by the Menier establishments.

Sales Strategy and Publicity

The Menier factory implemented a sales strategy to attract consumers and soon invested in publicity to make their product known. Menier first praised in the press the medicinal virtues of the product and insisted on its exotic origin. Then, thanks to chromolithography, the commercial poster became a vector for advertisement at a time when, with the progress in education during the second half of the nineteenth century, children became the privileged target and the preferred advertising target of chocolate sellers.[26] A communication strategy was then elaborated with poster artists, in particular the illustrator Firmin Bouisset (1859–1925). His advertising poster created in 1892 showed his oldest daughter, Yvonne.[27] This little girl with long braids, writing neatly on a Menier Chocolate wall, and 'Avoid the counterfeits' was going to become the emblem of Menier chocolate. The poster was extremely simplified, there was little text, and the poster's background used the "canary" yellow of the packages. It was about to cover, little by little, all the walls of French villages.[28] Beside the poster, other forms of publicity were developed in the first half of the twentieth century: the painted wall, the portable advertisement panels,

25   With vulcanization, rubber became an everyday product which was about to revolutionize transportation with Goodyear's, Hancock's and Goodrich's discoveries.

26   In 1884, the Poulain house launched its breakfast chocolate with vanilla flavoured cream that came with a toy and a chromolithograph picture. The collection of these chromolithographies either composed a story or each treated a different subject.

27   As Gérard Messence and Bernard Logre, 2005, remark, Firmin Bouisset designed three posters for the Menier house between 1892 and 1893. Two are nearly identical with a little girl, facing backward, and writing on walls the words 'Chocolat Menier'. A third poster shows a little girl facing forward, tracing the advertisement message on a grocery-shop window.

28   The little girl does not disappear along with the artist. Her image evolved with other designers: Auguste Rödel, Jacob, Roumy, Vic.

the press and the radio. The Menier's delivery and freight vehicles were also used as an advertising medium.[29]

Menier made most publicity efforts at World Fairs. At the 1889 World Fair in Paris, they built a block of 250,000 bars in the shape of the Arc de Triomphe, which represented the production of one single day, that is to say a weight of 50 tons and a value of 200,000 francs. The company, which produced half of the chocolate consumed in France, received three Grands Prix and five Gold medals. The 1900 World Fair in Paris accommodated a gigantic, life-size reproduction of the prow of the vessel *Le Triomphant* which transported the first cocoa cargo produced in the French West Indies under Louis XIV. Inside the vessel, the company's history and the description of the chocolate production were told. This exhibition represented the triumph of the Menier House.

Finally, the Meniers were pioneers in industrial tourism conceived as a communications tool. With the railway development in 1881, Emile-Justin Menier opened the doors of his chocolate factory to the members of scientific, technical and hygiene commissions; then to a variety of groups: grocers, industrialists, heads of state, and monarchs. The visitors could witness all the operations necessary for chocolate manufacture.

Conclusion

At the end of the nineteenth century, the 'largest chocolate factory in the world' had contributed a remarkable increase to chocolate consumption in France, since France had become the largest chocolate consumer per head in 1904.[30] Even if we do not know precisely by what proportions, the dominant position on the market went hand-in-hand with the 'democratization' of a product which until then was a luxury item.[31] But at the beginning of the twentieth century, French production was faced with foreign competition – mainly American and English – which was

---

29 In 1939, the Menier obtained the exclusive rights to adapt Walt Disney's movie, *Snow White and the Seven Dwarfs* (1937). A two-part album recounting the movie was edited. The images were made available in the Menier's chocolate bars. Once the collection of images was completed, children received presents from the Menier House.

30 According to Catherine Jarrige, 1993, consumption was as follows: France: 0.880 kg; England: 0. 746 kg; Germany: 0.708 kg. United States: 0.586 kg.

31 According to the report of the 1900 International World Fair, Class 59 (Sugars and confectionery products): 'From a luxury product, chocolate became a popular product thanks to its decrease in prices, and its consumption greatly increases year after year'. This 'democratization', which started in the 1880s, could have progressed even more, but the high customs duties on cocoa and sugar facilitated the competition from British, German and American chocolate manufacturers.

less expensive and offered new products: powdered cocoa, milk chocolate, and filled chocolate-bars, such as Mars and Rowntree's Kit-Kat.[32]

From the turn of the century, foreign competition shook Menier's dominant position, but the decline of the company truly started with the economic crisis of the 1930s. In 1936, Noisiel witnessed its first strikes during the introduction of workers' delegates and the paid vacations set up by the Popular Front. The decline continued until the Second World War and after when Gaston's nephews – Hubert (1910–1959) and Antoine (1904–1967) – became managers of the company. Deterioration accelerated after the departure of the Menier family from Noisiel in 1960. The first lay-offs took place in the 1960s. In 1965 the Menier company was purchased by Perrier and later, in 1971, passed into foreign ownership, when bought by Rowntree Mackintosh. The symbol of Menier's decline became clear in 1986 when thirteen of Noisiel's buildings were added to the inventory of France's historic buildings. By then Noisiel was mainly significant as a symbol of France's industrial heritage. With the purchase of Rowntree Mackintosh by Nestlé in 1988, chocolate production ended in 1992 and by 1995 the head office of Nestlé France was installed in Noisiel.

References

Amedée-Durand, 1832, *Rapport fait par M. Amédée-Durand au nom d'une Commission spéciale tirée des arts mécaniques, chimiques et économiques sur l'établissement de MM. Menier et Adrien situé à Noisiel-sur-Marne près Paris et destiné à la pulvérisation en général ainsi qu'à la fabrication en grand des chocolats, gruaux d'avoine et orges perlés*, [Report by M. Amedée-Durand in the name of the committee of mechanical, chemical and economic arts on the factory of MM. Menier and Adrien located in Noisiel (Seine et Marne), near Paris and devoted to spraying and production of chocolate, oatmeal and pearl barley] *Bulletin de la Société d'encouragement pour l'industrie nationale* [Bulletin of the Society for encouragement of national industry] 339, August 1832.

Appert, N., 1810, *Le livre de tous les ménages ou l'art de conserver pendant plusieurs années toutes les substances animales et végétales* [The Art of Preserving all kinds of Animal and Vegetable Substances for several years], Paris: Patris et Cie.

Armengaud, J.E., 1856, '*Fabrication du chocolat*' in *Publication industrielle des machines, outils et appareils les plus perfectionnés et les plus récents, employés dans les différentes branches de l'industrie française et étrangère* [Industrial publication of the most sophisticated and most recent machines,

---

32   In spite of its 88 chocolate manufacturers, France was no longer the dominant country in 1913. Germany had 191 chocolate confectioners, the United States 107, and Great Britain 90.

tools and apparatuses used in the various branches of French and foreign industry], vols 7 and 8.

Chaptal, J.A., 1818, '*Mémoire sur le sucre de betterave*'[Memoir on sugar beet], *Mémoires de l'Académie des sciences* [Memoirs of the Academy of Sciences], vol. 1.

Exposition Universelle Internationale de 1900, Classe 59, Groupe X, Aliments, Première Partie, Sucres et produits de la confiserie: Condiments et stimulants, [1900 International World Fair, Class 59, Group X, Food, First Part, Sugars and confectionery products: Condiments and stimulants] Paris: Imprimerie Nationale, 1902.

Jarrige, C., 1993, *L'industrie chocolatière française (1810–1939)* [French Chocolate Industry (1810–1939)] *Mémoire de Diplôme d'études approfondies d'histoire des techniques sous la direction de François Caron*, Université de Paris IV, Sorbonne.

Les industries agro-alimentaires en France, Histoire et performances, [Agribusiness Industries in France, History and Performance], Le Monde-Editions, Paris, 1997.

Logre, B. and Messence, G., 2005, *Chocolat Menier, Evitez les contrefaçons!* [Menier Chocolate, Avoid the Counterfeits!], Boulogne-Billancourt: Du May.

Marrey, B., 1984, *Un capitalisme idéal* [An Ideal Capitalism], Paris: Editions Clancier Guénaud.

Marseille, J., ed., 1997, *Les industries agro-alimentaires en France: histoire et performances* [Food Industries in France: history and performances], Paris: Le Monde Editions.

Menier, E.-J., 1872, *L'impôt sur le capital, son application, ses avantages, ses conséquences,* [Income Tax, Its Application, Its Advantages, Its Consequences], Paris: Guillaumin.

Menier, E.-J., 1876, '*L'impôt sur le capital devant la Chambre des Députés, discours de M. Menier, réponse de MM. Rouvier et Léon Say*', [The Income tax in front of the Chamber of Deputies, speech by Mr. Menier, answered by Messrs Rouvier and Leon Say], *Annales du Sénat et de la Chambre des Députés, Séance du 9 décembre* 1876.

Menier, E.-J., 1877, *Manuel de pulvérisation* [Spraying manual], Paris: Plon.

Nansouty, M. de, 1889–1890, '*Exposition universelle de 1889, Etablissements Menier'* in *Le Génie civil*, 10th year, vol. XVI, no.1, Paris.

Piganiol, J.-M., 1983, *Emile-Justin Menier (1826–1881) capitaliste éclairé, positiviste et républicain radical,* [Emile-Justin Menier (1826–1881) Enlightened Capitalist, Positivist and Radical Republican], *Université de Paris 1: Mémoire de maîtrise d'histoire contemporaine.*

Tellier, C., 1910, *Histoire d'une invention moderne Le frigorifique* [History of a modern invention: refrigeration], Paris: Delagrave.

Tresca and Duchesne, 1869. *Rapport fait par MM. Tresca et Duchesne, au nom du comité des arts mécaniques et économiques sur la fabrique de chocolat de M. Menier sise à Noisiel (Seine et Marne), Bulletin de la Société d'encouragement pour l'industrie nationale* [A report by MM. Tresca and Duchesne, in the name of the committee of mechanical and economic arts on the chocolate factory of M. Menier located in Noisiel (Seine et Marne), Bulletin of the Society for encouragement of national industry], vol. XVI, 68 (2nd series), June 1869.

Turgan, J. 1870, '*Usine de Noisiel, Fabrique du chocolat Menier*' ['The Noisiel factory making Menier chocolate'] in *Les grandes usines de France Tableau de l'industrie française au XIXe siècle* [The Big Factories of France, A Portrait of French industry in the nineteenth century], vol. 7, Paris: Michel Lévy Frères.

Chapter 7

'Czech chocolate is the best!' Nationalism in the Food Industry in the Czech Lands around the Year 1900

Martin Franc

Nationalism, aimed particularly against the competitive German ethnic group living in the Czech lands, was a fundamental factor in the life of Czech society at the turn of the nineteenth and twentieth centuries. This influence was also strongly visible in the food-processing industry and in advertising relating to this sector. Many key figures of the National Revival movement had a background in the emerging environment of processing agricultural products (such as the millers, brewers and butchers); for example, the composer Bedřich Smetana whose father was a brewer, while the father of another distinguished musician, Antonín Dvořák, was a butcher and innkeeper. The emerging Czech self-awareness also had a profound impact on the establishment of modern food-processing plants. The significance of national aspects in food processing can be illustrated by the strategy of one of the most dynamic food-processing factories in the Czech lands at that time: A. Maršner's *První česká továrna na orientálské cukrovinky a čokoládu na Královských Vinohradech* (First Czech Factory for Oriental Sweets and Chocolate in Královské Vinohrady),[1] whose extensive advertising campaign was based on extreme patriotism. There were many others to follow suit which was evident from the presentation of the Czech food-processing sector at one of the most representative economic events at the end of the nineteenth century – the Anniversary Land Exhibition, organized in Prague in 1891. This anniversary exhibition was a milestone event in the second half of the nineteenth century; symbolically it should have followed up a similar exhibition organized a hundred years before, in 1791. Even though the exhibition ought to have presented exhibitors from the Czech lands regardless of nationality, German-speaking entrepreneurs withdrew from the project and the exhibition thus turned into a monumental demonstration of the emerging power of Czech business. In terms of food production, it was important that the exhibition was not ignored by representatives of the nationally neutral aristocracy whose food-processing

---

1 For the history of the business and its patriotically oriented promotional campaigns see, in particular, Novák, 2003, 16–27. This text has also been used in other sections dealing with this company.

operations (for example dairy shops) still played a major role in food production. The modified balance of the exhibitors strengthened the national aspect of the event, which was obvious from the promotional presentation of many participants. Those who neglected the national aspect or even predominantly identified themselves with the German-speaking environment were under heavy pressure from the strongly nationalistic media including the official exhibition daily *Praha*, edited by Jan Herben.[2] Today, this periodical remains the most prominent source of information on the presentation of food production at the exhibition.

In terms of proportion, huge attention was paid to the production of sugar, a typical agricultural product in the Czech lands in the late nineteenth century. Quite understandably, increased attention was also given to beer,[3] even though at that time the Czech lands still lagged significantly behind Germany in its consumption. However, the greatest national conflict concerning beer in the Czech lands was yet to come several years after the Anniversary Land Exhibition. It had to do with beer production in České Budějovice. At the turn of the nineteenth and twentieth centuries, this city was to a large degree an anomaly. Although its surroundings were dominated by Czechs whose number was growing even in the city itself, the city hall managed to maintain a German majority until 1918, though with the help of certain election tampering. Just as in Plzeň in the past, Budějovice's brewery *Měšťanský pivovar* (Citizen's Brewery), owned by the so-called 'brewing-righters', was predominantly a German firm. In 1894, however, one of the 'brewing-righters'[4] and, at the same time, the leader of Budějovice's Czechs – the lawyer Augustin Zátka – founded, with the help of other investors, the *Český akciový pivovar* (Czech Joint-Stock Brewery),[5] which immediately started competing against the *Měšťanský pivovar*. As the name implies, this competition was associated with nationalist aspects which were also reflected in the distribution areas.[6] The surrounding municipalities with a mainly German population were mostly supplied with beer from *Měšťanský pivovar*, but the Czech villages, which clearly predominated in the region, were serviced almost exclusively by *Český akciový pivovar*. In light of the Czech dominance, it came as no surprise that the much younger competitor managed to overtake *Měšťanský*

---

2   Unless specified otherwise, information on the food-processing industry at the Anniversary Land Exhibition is taken from this gazette.

3   The exhibition presented many Czech breweries, including the most famous ones, such as those in Plzeň, Smíchov in Prague and the Třeboň brewery owned by the Schwarzenbergs.

4   This was a group of citizens who each owned a house with a brewing right.

5   Pavel Jákl characterizes its programme as 'Czech beer for Czech consumers'. Jákl, 2010, 128.

6   The machinery was supplied to the brewery by companies from the vicinity of Prague – except for Novák and Jahn. However, most of it came from the principally German firm Emil Ringhoffer from Prague-Smíchov.

pivovar in terms of beer sales as early as the 1904–1905 season.[7] Quite obviously, the nationalist clash also reverberated in advertising – for example, in the shape of *Český akciový pivovar*'s logo, displaying a girl wearing a Blata[8] folk costume and holding a glass of beer in each hand. The nationality-driven competition between the two firms continued even after 1918 and the founding of Czechoslovakia. Just after the end of the First World War, the whole dispute flared up once again. As Pavel Jákl, a contemporary Czech historian, commented, Budějovice beer became a truly 'nationalist beverage'.[9]

Apart from sugar mills and breweries, there were obviously other food-processing sectors represented at the Anniversary Land Exhibition. Virtually in all significant exhibition areas the pressure mounted by the media forced at least bilingual texts, with a dominance of Czech where possible.[10] The only exceptions were rare German firms which for various reasons did not join the exhibition boycott (for example, the sweets producer Augustin Tschinkel Söhne).[11] This went in parallel with the pattern of visitors, where the Czechs were clearly a majority. Visiting the Anniversary Land Exhibition was presented as a patriotic duty; local authorities sponsored school visits (especially from areas subject to nationalist struggles) and Czech businessmen organized trips for workers from their factories. In addition to Czech, however, the boards and labels promoting the presented food products often displayed French, as the language of the country of gourmets and a suitable counterbalance to the German competition. The individual producers emphasized their worldliness, for example, by showing medals awarded at different exhibitions throughout Europe, on the products themselves or on other advertising materials. Even the nationalist-minded press took pride in the export success of individual products including successful exports to Germany.[12] The exhibitors proudly presented comparisons with the rest of the world, yet appealed to the nationalist mood among the Czech population, trying to take advantage of it to promote their products. In some cases this showed directly in the product names – there were biscuits named after the famous Czech journalist and poet Jan Neruda and others called after another major living Czech poet, Jaroslav Vrchlický, offered at the event.[13] What is more, the

---

7   The beginnings of *Měšťanský pivovar* in České Budějovice dated back to the end of the eighteenth century, specifically to 1795.

8   Blata was a South Bohemian region with a dominantly Czech population.

9   For these issues, see Jákl, 2010.

10   Strong criticism was also aimed against restaurants where waiters addressed their guests in German and firms whose texts and other documents were written in poor Czech – for example. the Viennese firm Manner.

11   However, even this company used Czech advertising, for example in the exhibition gazette *Praha*. And to make it even, the gazette wrote that 'the company's owners …are Germans, but we have to admit that they are absolutely just to the Czech nationality and take a great care to provide language equality in the factory…'

12   This also applied to František Maršner's firm.

13   Biscuits were offered by Ladislav Jiránek's factory from Lužec u Jenšovic. It also supplied Slávie biscuits and the packages of some other biscuits showed figures in national

exhibition also presented some specifically Czech food specialties, such as the *Hořické trubičky* wafers, Lomnice crackers and Prague ham,[14] and even Czech bread, produced using specifically Czech technology (mainly Prague-based), and made exclusively from flour produced from Czech grains. Other Czech products were promoted as the perfect substitutes for foreign food specialities. By preferring them, Czech consumers would help the country's economy.[15] In certain cases, Czech products were claimed to have special extra features that elevated them from the position of a mere substitute to a somewhat higher status. The *Praha* exhibition gazette reported, for example, that Czech wine from Mělník was much healthier than Tokaji and Malaga wine or sherry thanks to an exceptionally high content of phosphoric acid. And beer from Beřkovice was said to have similarly healing effects. The contribution of Czech machinery to food processing was not neglected, either – the exhibition featured four factories that offered machines for the production of bonbons, including Adolf Řezníček's biggest enterprise. But it seems that the 'Czech sweets only on Czech machines' motto did not quite apply – large companies did not in any way reject purchasing new machines abroad or from nationally indifferent domestic firms. Only when the offers were comparable, were companies from a non-German-speaking environment preferred.

Curiously enough, even Oriental sweets, namely Turkish Delight, were presented as a Czech specialty. At the beginning of its article on the exhibits by *První výroba orientálských cukrovinek na Královských Vinohradech*, Balbínova ulice (First Production of Oriental Sweets in Královské Vinohrady, Balbínova Street),[16] the

costumes. A liquor factory in Golčův Jeníkov, owned by Th. Kornfeld and sons (probably a Jewish firm), advertised not only an Anniversary Liquor of the Land Exhibition, but also the Libuša liquor (Libuše was a legendary duchess of Bohemia). Otherwise in spite of their rather radical nationalism the Czechs were quite limited in giving patriotic names of great Czechs to food products and certainly no more than the Hungarians did. In this respect, there was a lively comparison of a version of the most popular Czech cookery book of those times – *Domácí kuchařka* (Home Cookery book) by M.D. Rettigová (edited by Antonie Dušánková) with a version of the *Pesther Kochbuch* by Josephine von Saint-Hilaire from the end of the nineteenth century.

14   The history of Prague ham dates back to the second half of the 1850s, when it came to prominence especially because of its production by Antonín Chmel's Czech factory. Antonín Chmel was also present at the exhibition, its presentation decorated with red-and-white curtains.

15   Popular types of salami – Krakow and Hungarian salami – were often criticized. Czech sellers allegedly imported them in bulk from their countries of origin, while equal products of Czech firms went abroad. There were also huge clashes over Hungarian salami, specifically its brand, in the decades to follow – a big conflict in Budapest at the beginning of the 1930s ended up in a compromise – Czech firms should refrain from identifying their products as Hungarian salami, while Hungarian producers were supposed to stop using the brand 'Prague ham' for their products.

16   In 1897, the company's name changed to '*První česká továrna na orientálské cukrovinky a čokoládovnu na Královských Vinohradech*, A. Maršner'. The explicit word

exhibition gazette praised the company for breaking the previous monopoly of wandering Turkish confectioners who had offered this sweet in the Czech lands since the mid-nineteenth century, by switching to factory production. According to the author, the company managed to do even more, penetrating markets in Vienna, Budapest and big German cities with its products, even with Czech-language packages. In addition to Turkish Delight, the company also offered Sultan bread with *succade* (candied fruits) and a dessert called *sujuk*. Other specialties sold by this firm included effervescent bonbons[17] and one new, original product – chocolate figures for Christmas trees.[18] They were all products without any tradition in the Czech environment. However, this did not prevent the company from playing the nationalistic tune in its promotion. The manufacturer remained loyal to the paradoxical connexion of exotic goods with nationalist Czech propaganda[19] for twenty years to come, while it was managed by its founder František Maršner.[20]

During Maršner's rule, however, this was not the only aspect, even though it drew the biggest attention to the company in the Czech context. For its products intended

---

'Czech' was used, as it was quite customary among Czech businesses at that time (František Maršner himself published the economic magazine *Český Lloyd* and the periodical *Obchodní listy*). Interestingly, the factory owner (and wife of František Maršner) Albína Maršnerová was mentioned in the German version of the company name without the Czech ending '-ová'.

17   The package of effervescent bonbons was not designed as nationalist, but the bilingual (Czech and German) text used by the firm in a purely German environment was a major element.

18   The figures were introduced by the company in 1896, laying the grounds for an incredibly strong tradition, maintained until the present day in the Czech (and Slovak) cultural environment. The so-called Christmas collections were almost a mandatory gift given by trade unions to their members until 1989 (the number of collections was based on the number of children in the family). For collections cf. Koura, 2010, 278–9. Interestingly, Maršner was not using nationalist appeals for Christmas collections, either, although they constituted a new domestic product.

19   On the other hand, some other big chocolate factories in the Czech lands were perceived as the strongholds of Germanism at that time. This applied to the Prague-based firm Kluge and to Fürth, of České Budějovice. However, these enterprises did not accentuate nationalist issues in their promotional activities over much. They were even willing to use Czech in their advertising, as illustrated e.g. by a Kluge poster. See Krámský and Feitl, 2008, 23, 36–7 and 59.

20   František Maršner (29 April 1857–1828 July 1917), owner of a grocery shop in Kladno from 1879. Later, from 1881, he published the periodical *Český Lloyd*. In 1891 he joined his wife's sweets production business. He contributed to the modernization and enlargement of production, *inter alia*, with a proprietary international method of production of cocoa butter. He published articles on the national economy in *Obchodní listy* and in nationally-minded periodicals, such as the most influential nationalist daily *Národní listy*. He converted the firm into a joint-stock company in 1901 but withdrew from the company's management in 1912, due to financial problems. Toward the end of his life, he owned a large country estate in Svatý Jan pod Skalou. Cf. Šimek 2005.

for sale outside the Czech-speaking society in the Czech lands,[21] the company flexibly used another promotional device by emphasizing the top quality of its products, their health benefits,[22] and their foreign awards (for example, its effervescent bonbons were promoted not only on the grounds of an award given in Brussels in 1893, but also by a medal the firm received in the stronghold of German nationalism in the Czech lands – Cheb – a mere one year after the Anniversary Land Exhibition). The packages also bore notes that the technology used for chocolate production conformed to Swiss technology, that is, that it was chocolate '*á la suisse*'.[23] In the Czech environment, nevertheless, this element was used for nationalist propaganda – the Czech surrogate was to be preferred by Czech patriots to German, Dutch and Swiss originals, preventing the drainage of Czech money abroad and helping the nation build its economic strength. It should also be noted that another of František Maršner's activities – the magazine *Český Lloyd* – echoed the first trademark of his wife's factory in the shape of the Czech land symbol with a silver, two-tailed lion supplemented with an anchor, taken over from the United Kingdom.[24]

In spite of all this, Maršner used themes that had nothing to do with nationalist appeals even in the Czech society – its ginger beer was recommended by an *Art Nouveau* poster of a lady holding a cup flirtatiously and its Bacao banana cocoa was promoted with a poster showing well-built African-Americans carrying a cluster of bananas.[25]

The nationalist aspect in advertising was, however, hard to miss and played a major role in the firm's expansion. It resonated in the names of certain products (Slavic Chocolate, Crown Chocolate,[26] *Sokol* Chocolate)[27] as well as on their packages, trademarks and periodic promotional campaigns.[28] The trademark used

---

21   The key export markets for the factory were eastern and south-eastern Europe (Serbia, Montenegro. Bulgaria, Albania, Greece, Russia), and also Turkey, Egypt and Japan. These were all non-German-speaking countries and in many of them it was possible to use pan-Slavic propaganda (Serbia, Montenegro, Russia), so popular in the Czech lands, especially among more conservative circles. However, it has to be noted that the firm often exported goods sold without any packaging (Turkish Delight). On the other hand, its effervescent bonbons built a very good market in Austria and Hungary.

22   This was especially true of the so-called Reform Chocolate, where a lot of stress was given to its high content of calcium, iron, theobromine and sugar.

23   French was often used on packages instead of German and Czech.

24   Krušoftová, 2009, 18.

25   Krušoftová, 2009, 42–3.

26   The requirement to have Franz Joseph I officially crowned as Czech King strongly resonated in the Czech lands, even though it never happened. The package of '*Korunní čokoláda*' – Crown Chocolate – was decorated by the most important Czech coronation jewel – St. Wenceslas' Crown.

27   *Rodinné stříbro: Tajemství výroby čokolády*, 2009. '*Sokol*' was the name of a strongly nationalistically oriented Czech sporting association.

28   Ibid. On the package of Slavic Chocolate there are silhouettes of Prague and Moscow, coats of arms of Slavic territories in Austria-Hungary, Slavic tricolours and an

Figure 7.1   Slavic chocolate advertisement

for Maršner's cocoa, registered in 1900, became extremely famous. It was the picture of a child holding a cup of cocoa, accompanied with the tell-tale sentence 'Czech cocoa and chocolate are the best'. Just as in other cases, it was a very simple message that did not require any of the arguments that had to be used to prop up statements on the health benefits of Reform Chocolate. Quite clearly, Czech cocoa and chocolate were the best because they were simply the best. In 1905, the glossy pictorial magazine *Český svět* portrayed Maršner as a Czech genius. At any rate, his massive promotional campaign proved very successful – in 1902–1903, the firm processed a full one-tenth of all cocoa beans imported to the whole of Austria-Hungary; in 1910, the processed volume was 350 tonnes of beans. However, the atmosphere within the company started changing and the abuse of superficial nationalist appeals for commercial goals started to be

---

allegorical figure of Slávie. The chocolate was also accompanied by cards with the portraits of famous Slavic personalities. The first series was dominated by Czechs such as the historian Palacký, the poet Svatopluk Čech and Antonín Dvořák and Bedřich Smetana, but there were also portraits of the Polish revolutionary Kościuszko, the Russian tsar Nicholas II and the Russian painter Vereshchagin.

somewhat laughable, especially for the generation of young Czechs.[29] In relation to the promotional campaigns employed by Maršner and other producers, this was well illustrated by the scorching irony of Jaroslav Hašek, a leading Czech writer and observer of the national life, who described, in his book *The History of the Party of Mild Progress within the Bounds of Law*, a promotional campaign organized under the name 'Prague – for Viennese Czechs', aimed at raising funds to support the Czech minority in the Austrian capital:

> Maršner's sweets factory in Vinohrady will dispatch several factory workers in impossible national costumes, embellish a truck with red-and-white draperies, fix a flag on top of the vehicle, saying 'Banana Cocoa, Maršner's Cocoa's the Best!' Fairies in bizarre national costumes toss promotional slips to the audience reading 'Drink Maršner's chocolate and Maršner's sweets', whilst cheering 'Hello to Czech Vienna!'. This highly applauded truck, as it is also likely to be in some way related to Czech Vienna, is followed by eight minions, dressed as medieval freelance warriors, although had these men appeared in their costumes in the Middle Ages, they would have been hanged immediately without pardon at the nearest tree, marked as the hyenas of the battlefield. And these eight young men wear posters with the text 'Holoubek's Soap is the Best', hanging on their necks. You cannot see it because the youths are dirty, but people welcome them with a roar: 'Cheers to Czech Vienna!' ... Then follows a bandwagon of the Vinohrady brewery. Eight men in medieval costumes are sitting around a huge barrel, waving pitchers and shouting: 'Try Vinohrady beer.' They pretend to be drunk, and they are... This bandwagon attracts the greatest following and is cheered the most.[30]

Even though the volume of the company's production was still growing at the beginning of the twentieth century, it ran into economic trouble before the First World War. It is hard to guess the extent to which this was caused by obsolete promotional methods, but obsolete technology was likely to have played a vital role here, as it prevented any sign of success in more competitive markets. At any rate, František Maršner was succeeded by someone coming from the younger generation, one that despised flag-waving and continuous emphasis on nationalist themes. This man was Milan Čapek, aged 27 at that time, who principally influenced the Czech chocolate-making industry for decades to come. The company was renamed and a brand was established that has accompanied it until today – a four-pointed star called Orion. Initially, however, the First World War brought a revival

---

29   The Manifesto of Czech modernism was published in 1896; it voiced the concerns of a generation 'disgusted with "Where is my home"-ism and "Hey, Slav"-ism'. (www. ceskaliteratura.cz/dok/mmoderny.htm; searched on 13 June 2011)

'Where Is My Home' is the name of the Czech anthem and the song Hey, Slavs, is a type of a pan-Slavonic anthem – both songs were performed at every patriotic demonstration.

30   Hašek, Jaroslav 1982: 153–4.

of nationalist themes. In this case, most of the activity came from the German side, appealing to military patriotism. This was once again interestingly described by Jaroslav Hašek in his famous novel *The Fateful Adventures of the Good Soldier Švejk During the World War*, where he described all kinds of gifts that a patriotic German noblewoman brought to the main character during his hospitalization:

> A dozen roasted chickens packaged in pink satin paper and wrapped in a black-and-yellow silk ribbon,[31] two bottles of a military liquor with the label '*Gott strafe England*' (God Will Punish England); on the other side of the label there was a picture of Franz Joseph with William[32] holding each other's hands, as if about to play the famous children's game 'Little rabbit sitting alone, what happened to you, my poor one, that you cannot jump…' Then there were packs of chocolate with the same '*Gott strafe England*!' text, once again with pictures of the Austrian and German emperors. This time they were not holding hands and each was separate, with their backs against each other. A nice gift was a two-line toothbrush with the text '*Viribus unitis*',[33] making sure that everyone brushing his teeth thinks about Austria. A set for cleaning fingernails was another elegant gift, so good for use at the front of the battle as well as in trenches. There was a picture on the box, showing bursting shrapnel and a man with a basinet charging forward with a bayonet. And underneath: '*Für Gott, Kaiser und Vaterland*!'[34] A pack of biscuits was without any picture, but contained a rhyme: '*Österreich, du edles Haus,/steck deine Fahne aus,/lass sie im Winde wehn,/Österreich muss ewig stehn*' and with a translation on the other side: 'Austria, a noble house,/put your flag up,/let it flow in coming winds,/and Austria shall stand firm.'[35]

On the other hand, the promotion of Slavism was censured in many ways. This also affected Czech chocolate works, even though the blow was not aimed against Orion, but against another important patriotic enterprise – *Akciová továrna na čokoládu a cukrovinky* (Joint-Stock Chocolate and Sweets Factory), formerly known as the First Joint Moravian Sweets and Chocolate Factory in Olomouc, Ltd), founded in 1898.[36] From 1908, this company offered some of its products under the brand Zora, which turned into the firm's unofficial name. For the first

---

31 Black and yellow were the colours of the Austrian Empire.
32 The Austrian and German emperors.
33 Latin for 'With United Force' – the emperor's motto.
34 German for 'For God, Emperor and Fatherland!'
35 Hašek 1922: 84–6.
36 The company was established by a group of Czech merchants and the founding general meeting took place symbolically in the centre of Czech national life in Olomouc – in the National House. The Moravian sweets factory was driven by the idea of 'freeing Czech merchants and confectioners from the bondage of Austrian factories'. Like Maršner's company, it vocally supported various Czech cultural institutions. Its advertising motto, however, was less radical: 'Competes with Every Foreign Brand.' Cf. Viktořík, 2008, 83–5.

time, this name was entered in the Companies Register in January 1915. A year later, the company was confidentially recommended to change its name – because the word 'Zora' could conceal the name of the morning star of Greater Serbia. However, the factory retorted that it would never even dream about this connexion, pointing at the fact that Zora was a diminutive for Mary Theresa, used commonly in the Czech language for a hundred years. The company therefore wanted to wait for an official ban – which did not come in the end.[37] The war brought many other problems, and speculation over the names of individual products was meaningless in the light of massive supply shortages.

The nationalistic brawls between the Czechs and the Germans, which can be considered one of the fundamental features of social life in the Czech lands in the second half of the nineteenth century and at the beginning of the twentieth century, significantly affected the economy as well. Around the year 1900, nationalistic aspects of food production were brought forward especially by the strengthening Czech producers, who could find support among a growing number of patriotic and financially strong consumers. This was clearly demonstrated at the Anniversary Land Exhibition in 1891, where many food products were presented in very patriotic settings. A major aspect certainly was that the Czechs had quite a strong position in the food processing industry, because of their agricultural background. Many producers, such as the chocolate and sweets producer *První česká továrna na orientálské cukrovinky a čokoládu na Královských Vinohradech*, of A. Maršner and the brewery *Český akciový pivovar* in the nationalistically divided České Budějovice, tried more or less successfully to present the preference for their products as a type of national obligation, against the backdrop of their German-speaking competitors. The success of the Czech brewery against its German municipal competitor was even perceived as a certain compensation for the Czechs' failure in the previous municipal elections. In the case of Maršner, however, advertising had to do with the exotic origin of the main input material, which could be hardly associated with the Czech nation. Milk chocolate at least, accentuated an association between the Czech agricultural background and milk. At the same time, a certain level of exoticism of cocoa and the use of French words on packages made it possible to implant the image of F. Maršner as a Czech who succeeded globally, which further boosted the national pride surrounding the products coming out of his factory. The main export regions were located especially in the south-east of Europe, that is, regions populated by Slavic nations, which supported the associations of nationalistic propaganda and popular pan-Slavic aspects. However, Maršner's company, and its German competitors in the Czech lands, did not want to lose customers from the other nation, which resulted in parallel advertising campaigns shorn of any nationalistic aspects and even with certain concessions (e.g. use of Czech on posters by Kluge). Direct nationalistic aspects in the promotion of certain food products seemed to be archaic to the younger generation before the First World War and were instead replaced by

---

37   Viktořík, 2008, 91–2.

emphasis on the modernity and worldliness of the products. The First World War brought a new wave of patriotic movies, but this involved state-sponsored Austrian patriotism, while patriotic Czech feature films, especially if they hinted at the pan-Slavic idea, were strictly censured. When the Czechoslovak Republic was founded in 1918, nationalism once again came to life in the promotion of food products, but had only a short duration. In the 1920s, most promotion was conversely based on worldliness and modern lifestyle. This was fully visible on the Orion brand packaging which completely changed the image of its products. It hired the leading avant-garde painter, who created a new corporate image and designed several packages that are used until today. But that is another story.

References

Hašek, J., 1922, *Osudy dobrého vojáka Švejka za světové války* [The Fateful Adventures of the Good Soldier Švejk During the World War], Prague.

Hašek, J., 1982, *Dějiny strany mírného pokroku v mezích zákona* [The History of the Party of Mild Progress within the Bounds of Law], Prague.ákl, P., 2010, *Encyklopedie pivovarů Čech, Moravy a Slezska II. Díl Jižní Čechy* [Encyclopaedia of Breweries in Bohemia, Moravia and Silesia, Part II South Bohemia], Prague.

Jákl, P., 2010, *Encyklopedie pivovarů Čech, Moravy a Slezska II. Díl Jižní Čechy* [Encyclopaedia of Breweries in Bohemia, Moravia and Silesia, Part II South Bohemia], Prague.

Koura, P., 2010, *Kourová, Pavlína: České vánoce od vzniku republiky do Sametové revoluce* [Czech Christmas from the Foundation of the Republic to the Velvet Revolution], Prague.

Krámský, S. and Feitl, J., 2008, *Kniha o čokoládě* [Book on Chocolate], Prague.

Krušoftová, E., 2009, '*Vizuální styl, design a propagace značky Orion do roku 1989*' [Visual Style, Design and Promotion of the Brand Orion until 1989], Bachelor's thesis, Brno.

Novák, P., 2003, '*Čtyři zastavení na cestě české čokolád*' [Four Stops on the Path of Czech Chocolate] in Nikrmajer, L. and Petráš, J., *Dobrou chuť* [Bon Appetit], České Budějovice.

Praha, exhibition gazette, 1891.

Rodinné stříbro: Tajemství výroby čokolády [Family Silver: The Secret of Chocolate Production], Czech TV2, broadcast on 14 May 2009 (www.ceskatelevize.cz/ivysilani/10216430730-rodinne-stribro/209572232240001-tajemstvi-vyroby-cokolady/titulky/; searched on 26 February 2012).

Šimek, R. '*Čokoládový hrdina*' [The Chocolate Hero], Profit.cz, 18 December 2005 (www.profit.cz/clanek/cokoladovy-hrdina.aspx; searched on 26 February 2012).

Viktořík, M., 2008, *Čokoládovnický a cukrovinkářský průmysl v Olomouci* [Chocolate and Confectionary Industry in Olomouc], Olomouc.

Chapter 8

Margarine in Competition with Butter in Germany (1872–1933): The Example of Van den Bergh's Margarine Factory in Kleve

Sabine Merta

The general socio-economic background of the 'new' margarine industry was expressed clearly by the industry's historian:

> In the second half of the nineteenth century various social and economic factors combined to create the margarine industry. These were population increase, urban development, industrialization, the general rise in purchasing power, and the need for sufficient and above all better nutrition. This development had its starting point in Europe.[1]

Increasing mechanization meant the development of new production equipment and the factory as workplace. Investments of huge dimensions were made: streets, railways and factories were built; the infrastructure was improved. Thousands of new workplaces were created in industrial production. At the same time, the way of life changed, especially for people's eating habits. Apart from traditional food, the use of fat in the diet ranged from fresh butter in the upper classes, to so-called 'mixed butter' produced from cheap butcher's fat like lard, suet and mutton fat amongst the poorer people. The population explosion during the era of industrialization made the fat supply inadequate. The demand for easy-to-spread fat rose enormously because more people worked in industry where there were no canteens, so that taking one's own food to work was imperative. Fat played an important role in the diet, yet for most people there was a shortage of dairy fat – butter was too expensive for many families.[2] The working classes could only buy adulterated fats, known as 'mixed butter' or later in the nineteenth century margarine, which cost half as much as fresh butter. The demand for margarine increased so much that German production could not meet demand and the import of margarine from the Netherlands became increasingly necessary.

---

1 Stuyvenberg, 1969, 9.
2 Blank, o.J., 232.

What was Margarine in the Nineteenth Century?

According to E.H. Burckhardt, a member of the association of farmers [*Bund der Landwirte*], margarine was quite different in 1895 from what it had been in 1870. In his pamphlet about unfair competition in the butter trade, he explained that it had become an easy-to-spread substance which was produced from an emulsion of fat and oil and skimmed fresh milk.[3]

By the end of the 1860s, '*graisse de ménage*' [kitchen fat] or '*graisse de conserve*' was for sale in Paris. Acting on behalf of Napoleon III, Hypolite Mège-Mouriès, a food chemist and former pharmaceutical assistant at a Parisian hospital, invented a new food fat – an artificial butter – produced from beef tallow and milk, which he registered as 'margarine' on 15 July 1869 at the patent office in Paris. He called the product 'margarites' or 'margarin' (pearl) because of its pearly glimmer. The word became modified into 'margarine'. It was to become one of the most important new industrial products of the nineteenth century. On 12 April 1872, the public health department of the Seine granted M. Mège-Mouriès permission to produce and sell margarine to the public and he began production in a little factory at Poissy, near Paris. It was a cheap and perishable substitute for butter intended for the military as well as the new urban working class. The process discovered by Mège-Mouriès was also patented in England in 1869 and in America in 1873.

The exact recipe for margarine at that time was as follows: beef tallow and suet had to be washed and cut into pieces. The mass was then heated at a temperature of 45°C and mixed with water, ash, potassium carbonate and small pieces of sheep or pork stomach (pepsin) in an emulsifying churn. At the end of this process, a clear yellow fat rose to the surface, while the residue remained in the water. The oily mass was fed through a tube into a hot boiler containing a 2 per cent salt solution. It was then poured into 20 litre oil pans in a crystallizing room where it remained for twenty-four hours at a temperature of 24°C until only a stable mass was left which was pressed through a cloth in order to separate stearin and fluid oleomargarine from the rest of the mass. When it had cooled down the oleomargarine produced in this way was a tasty, yellow and neutral food fat.

In June 1871, Jan Jurgens of Oss visited Mège-Mouriès in Paris. He bought Mège-Mouriès's patent for 60,000 francs and began producing margarine. A Jewish butter dealer, Simon Van den Bergh (1819–1907), read about the invention of margarine in the newspaper *London Reader*. He travelled to Paris with Henry, one of his seven sons, to have a look at the production process for making margarine which he subsequently imitated in his own factory in Oss, near Nijmegen. Jurgens informed Simon Van den Bergh what he was doing and showed him the new margarine. Jurgens and Van den Bergh started to produce margarine in the Netherlands for the industrialized urban working-class trade in England.

---

3   Bösmann, 1969, 10–11. Nowadays, plant oils are mainly used for the production of margarine.

The Production of Margarine in the Netherlands

In 1880, the Van den Bergh factory employed 120 workers and supplied the Netherlands, the Niederrhein (Lower Rhine region) and the industrial area of the Ruhrgebiet (Ruhr district) with margarine. The location of the margarine factory was later moved to Rotterdam where plant oils from overseas were unloaded. Simon Van den Bergh also opened up a new factory in Brussels to supply Belgium with margarine.

The German Chancellor, Otto von Bismarck, objected to Dutch margarine being imported and in 1887 introduced a margarine law imposing a duty of two hundred Reichsmarks on each tonne of margarine. Due to this expensive customs charge, Van den Bergh transferred a part of his Dutch production facilities across the border to Kleve in western Germany. In the autumn of 1887, he acquired an area of 67.5 Are[4] in the community of Kellen because the city fathers of Kleve did not want to ruin the city's image as a tourist spa. They were to regret this later because they thus lost a great deal of income from taxes. They had to fight for ten years to incorporate the community of Kellen.[5] The Van den Berghschen Margarinewerke was built under the direction of Van den Bergh's son Isaak, while his son Arnold managed the production. Another son, Henry, was responsible for buying the raw material. Large amounts of beef fat were imported from Chicago via New York to Rotterdam in the Netherlands.[6] In August 1888, Van den Bergh started production in Kleve with 14 workers. The community of Kellen was perfect because it was located next to the railway station and close to the Rhine, which led into the North Sea. There were cheap workers, who even spoke a local dialect intelligible to Dutch speakers. Moreover, there were many dairy farmers as well as those willing to grow plants for oil production (sunflower oil or rapeseed oil). The management stayed in the Netherlands. Van den Bergh's enterprise was followed by Jurgens. In 1888, in partnership with the Prinzen family from s'Hertogenbosch, Hendricus Jurgens opened the Margarinewerke Jurgens und Prinzen GmbH in Goch. [7]

The first German margarine factory was built in 1870 at Frankfurt am Main, the most important trading centre in Germany. Many other factories followed. The rise of margarine factories coincided with a period of crisis in the agricultural economy. There were already 45 margarine factories in Germany by 1886 and ten years later, in 1895, the number of margarine producers had risen to 73. By 1907 there were 125 on the official register. The yearly consumption of margarine per head in Germany rose from 2.4 kilogram in the year of its invention to 5.2 kilogram in 1913.[8] Margarine slowly superseded lard and 'mixed butter'. The victory of the new industrially produced food fat began to reach record amounts of

---

4   One Are = 100 square metres.
5   Hendricks, 1982.
6   Wollny, 1887, iv.
7   *Festschrift: Margarine aus Kleve*, 1988, 6ff.
8   Ellerbrock, 1993, 320.

production. Around 1900, 100,000 tonnes of margarine were produced yearly. The production equipment and recipes were constantly improved.

The Butter War and the Margarine Question

Artificial butter was caught in a crossfire of criticism because it irritated the consumers, who could not tell real natural butter and margarine apart, except by the shape of the margarine package, its wrapping, or the shops where it was sold. The butter dealers thought that margarine would ruin the butter market and milk production in Germany. In the beginning, many prohibited substances were added to margarine due to the greed for profit, so that strict food control became necessary.[9] Tainted eggs, forbidden colouring and preservatives, as well as animal and plant fats were being added to margarine and some consumers became ill through 'margarine-poisoning'.[10] A certificate from the Imperial health department dated 18 January 1911 shows that the margarine factory Mohr and Co. GmbH in Hamburg-Altona had added oil normally used in the production of soap to their margarine and, consequently, the Imperial German health deparment wanted to close the factory. The so-called 'butter war' broke out.[11] The artificial butter question[12] or margarine question[13] was addressed in many debates and heated discussions in the German parliament. Ironically, the dairy farmers' demands to control the production of margarine led to an improvement of the product. The associations of farmers demanded a strict control of industrially produced margarine by scientific officers. Foreign competition, falling cereal prices and the rapidly growing milk and butter market resulted in a crisis in German agriculture. The associations and lobbyists expected to be defended by the German government through legislation.[14]

Domestic Production of Margarine

From the year which saw the introduction of Bismarck's customs duty, new developments began in the German margarine industry.[15] The rise in prices in general and the limited spending power of the low-income population encouraged these changes. A conversion from arable agriculture to intensive cattle breeding became noticeable and many big dairies were opened up for the processing of

---

9   Hertkorn, 1910, 1381ff.
10   *'Amtliche Aufklärung'*, 1910.
11   Helm, 1895.
12   Wollny, 1887.
13   Burckhardt, 1895.
14   Lavalle, 1896, 258.
15   Lindemann, 1936, 112ff.

fresh milk into butter. Milk farmers started to work with dairy co-operatives. Thus, it was lucrative even for small milk farmers to produce milk and butter with the result that Germany had a huge surplus of butter which was mainly exported to England. Moreover, mixed-butter production was launched. Mixed butter was produced by adding food fats like oleomargarine, margarine, and so on, to butter. It was much cheaper than butter, but a little bit more expensive than margarine. The manager of mixed-butter production in the margarine factory in Frankfurt estimated that mixed-butter production made up 6 to 7 per cent of the whole margarine output in 1886. Because of the growth of margarine and mixed butter the farmers' co-operatives feared that it would endanger the sales of natural butter. They thought that dairy farmers would begin to mix the butter themselves in order to get better prices for mixed butter. In the face of uncertain circumstances in the food-fat market, the German government passed the first margarine law in 1887. The farmers' associations considered this law a chance to prohibit mixed butter. They also hoped to gain control of the production of margarine by way of the regulations concerning the amount of milk to be used for the production of good margarine. But the first margarine law was merely a labelling regulation. It prescribed that a poster had to be put on the wall of a shop which said that it was a place where only margarine was sold. In addition, the word 'margarine' had to be written on the container and packaging. That was not what the farmers' associations had expected. The law had no influence on the production process of margarine at all. The farmers only achieved a prohibition not to mix butter and margarine and a limitation on the addition of milk and cream, but there was no special public control of the trade in edible fats or of the ingredients of margarine. However, the aim of the farmers' associations was less to remedy an abuse than to bring the margarine production to a standstill by the new law. They thought the margarine industry was responsible for the difficulties of the butter trade. In numerous petitions, the association of German farmers [*Bund Deutscher Landwirte*] and the German council of agriculture [*Deutscher Landwirtschaftsrat*] demanded that parliament must tighten the first margarine law.

Four main demands were constantly repeated until 1894: firstly, the prohibition of mixing edible fats with milk or cream; secondly, the prohibition of colouring margarine; thirdly, the sale must take place in special shops; fourthly, the duty of declaration when margarine was used in food preparation or in bakeries.[16] The Committee of Factory Owners in the Margarine Industry [*Fabrikantenausschuss der Margarineindustrie*] defended themselves against the butter lobbyists by asking the Bavarian state ministry for an expert opinion. The food chemist, Professor Dr. Franz von Soxhlet,[17] was charged with writing a scientific report on the butter trade. He came to the conclusion that the price for high-quality butter had sunk more than the price for low-quality butter, which is to say that there were other reasons for falling butter prices than margarine. On 3 April 1894,

16   Lindemann, 1936, 117.
17   Soxhlet, 1895.

the four main demands were rejected by the German parliament. Furthermore, a dissertation on business management written by Ernst Feld showed that the rapid growth of dairy associations was the reason for the constantly falling butter prices as well as for the overproduction of butter.[18] There were also other reasons for the declining export of butter: margarine was not the reason, but rather two new major competitors. Firstly, Australian butter, which could be transported to Britain by means of the new cold-storage systems on board ship and, secondly, the big increase in Danish butter production which rose eightfold between 1870 and 1892.

The expert opinion of Dr. Soxhlet showed that the production of margarine was not responsible for the bad situation in the international butter market. A new law proposed a tax on margarine as well as colouring it from red-pink to brown which indicated its quality. This first draft of the law was rejected on 13 June 1896. A second draft came out, which made the following points: firstly, a name clearly avoiding the term 'butter' had to be used for the product and it had to be declared as margarine by its obvious name, its cube form and by a surrounding red line; secondly, the colouring of margarine was prohibited (only a latent colouring which could be made visible by way of a chemical analysis was allowed); thirdly, mixed butter was prohibited; fourthly, public health control of the imported oils and animal fats was imposed on the producers.[19] In towns, the number of retailers for butter and margarine was limited to one per 5,000 citizens. Moreover, margarine factories had to be listed and their details displayed at the local police station. In addition to this, a maximum percentage of water and salt and a mandatory minimum quality of fat were prescribed. The margarine law also expressed detailed offences and sentences.[20] It came into force on 1 October 1897 and initiated the development of margarine from a low-quality product for poorer people into a quality assured product for all.

The Kosher Margarine 'Tomor'

In 1901 Wilhelm Normann (1870–1939), an analytic chemist , developed a process to harden edible oils.[21] His German patent of 1902 and British patent of 1903 covered processes in margarine and soap production. Normann's achievement of a process for hardening plant oils marked an important point in the history of margarine. The transformation of liquid plant oils into a semi-hard, easy-to-

18   Feld, 1922, 136ff.
19   Wollny, 1887, 48.
20   Lindemann, 1936, 116ff.
21   In 1901 Wilhelm Normann was head of the laboratory at Leprince & Siveke, a fat and oil factory founded by his uncle, Wilhelm Siveke. Normann experimented with hydrogenation catalysts and successfully induced the hydrogenation of liquid fat, producing semi-solid fat. In 1908 his patent was bought by Joseph Crosfield & Sons Ltd of Warrington. In 1911 Normann became Technical Director of a Jurgens subsidiary, *Ölwerke Germania* (Germania Oil Factory) in Emmerich am Rhein.

spread edible fat enabled the development of vegetable-oil margarine. Only a few plant oils could be used for margarine production: soya-bean oil, sunflower oil, cottonseed oil, peanut oil, palm oil and rapeseed oil. The Jewish factory owner Simon Van den Bergh conceived the idea of producing a special margarine for Jewish customers. Tomor was a pure vegetable margarine, which did not contain animal fat or milk ingredients. Thus, the strict division of meat and milk, prescribed by the Jewish dietary laws, could be fulfilled. Tomor was not only kosher, but also neutral in terms of the categories of meat and milk, that is, 'parve'. Thus, Jewish people could easily prepare their meals with this margarine. To make it easier for the consumer, the manufacturers simply called it kosher. The origin of the term Tomor is not quite clear. It is presumably derived from the Yiddish term Tomor, which corresponds with the Hebrew word 'Tamar'. The latter means palm tree and refers to the ingredients of this margarine, which was produced with oil from the coconut palm like the products Palmin and Palmstolz. Almond milk was used instead of cows' milk for the production of Tomor margarine.

The production of Tomor began in 1904 by a separate company named Sana-Werk. It was located on the same grounds as Van den Bergh's main margarine factory. To guarantee the ritual purity of the product, Dr. Pinchas Wolf, a rabbi from Cologne, controlled the production. Apart from Tomor, there were two other kosher margarines: Zitomor, especially produced for bakeries, and Peri, especially produced to be exported to Palestine. A statistic of the year 1925 shows that Van den Bergh produced 1,170 tonnes of margarine every week, of which 18 tonnes was kosher margarine, that is, 1.5 per cent of the whole production. Van den Berghs spent heavily to advertise kosher products. There were colourful advertising posters and pictures which were designed by the Jewish artist Professor Moritz Oppenheim. In spite of the high advertising costs the production of kosher margarine was stopped in Kleve at the beginning of the Hitler regime. But Tomor did not disappear from the international margarine market. Kosher margarine was still produced by the Anglo-Dutch company, Unilever, to which the former Van den Bergh factory in Kleve had belonged since 1929. In 1933 or 1934, the production of kosher margarine emigrated across the German border. Thus, Tomor evaded the persecution of National Socialism. Up to 1987, Tomor continued to be sold by the British companies Van den Bergh and Jurgens Ltd. The production rights were then sold to Rakusen Foods Ltd., which still produces the kosher margarine in the Netherlands and sells it in Britain.

The History of the Family Firm Van den Bergh in Kleve from 1888

The development of the firm proceeded rapidly and within the first two years, the number of workers increased from fourteen to forty. Each week, 60 to 70 tonnes of margarine were produced. In the following five years, the production rate was raised to 200 tonnes. By 1895, the daily production rate had already reached 250 tonnes, and used 50,000 litres of milk and about 25,000 eggs. Margarine production employed 300 in the firm's administration and 1,000 workers. This rapid and positive development can be put down to the continual expansion and investments in new techniques by the production manager Johann Manger (1850–1920). He started to work for the firm in 1890 and subsequently became its managing director. His strategy was firstly to expand the factory by buying up competing firms. He changed the company's name to 'Van den Bergh GmbH' and around 1900, he launched a packaging factory, Sana GmbH and an oil refinery named Clivia Ölwerke GmbH. In 1897, Manger launched the margarine Vitello and in 1900, the margarine Sana, produced with almond milk. In 1904, the product Sanella and pure plant margarine brands like Palmkorne, Palmstolz and Tomor were sold on the margarine market. During this period, the social and economic situation of the workers was improved. There were never any strikes. The workers had their own working health insurance, a bank, a swimming pool, a medical corps, a fire brigade and free coffee. The people said it was good and safe to work 'op de botter'.

At the start of margarine production in 1887, only 15,000 tonnes of margarine as compared to 300,000 tonnes of butter were consumed annually. In 1895, margarine consumption amounted to 90,000 tonnes per year and reached 200,000 tonnes in 1913. That means statistically that three kilograms per head were used by every consumer.

In 1910, the management of the company went from Manger back to Donald Van den Bergh and later to a cousin, Leo Van den Bergh. Branches were opened in Bremen, Breslau and Cologne. The outlay on advertising was increased. Trains, lorries and house walls displayed margarine advertisements. Colourful newspapers for children like the 'Rama-Post vom kleinen Coco' and 'Vom lustigen Fips' were published in order to get children to persuade their mothers to buy margarine. Production continued to increase until the beginning of the First World War, reaching its climax in 1913 when 40,000 tonnes of margarine were sold annually.

During the war there was a crisis because of a shortage of raw materials caused by the blockades by the Allies and margarine became quite expensive. A war committee obtained and distributed the raw materials on the basis of the production output in 1913. Margarine which had already been produced was confiscated and brought to the market at fixed consumer prices. The effect was that margarine production became an industry with fixed prices for raw materials and finished goods. For this reason, only 26 of originally 145 factories in Germany existed after the end of the war. At the end of the war, Van den Bergh tried to keep up production by employing young persons or Dutch workers who came across the German border. The compulsory controlled economy ended two years after the war.

A second peak of margarine production was evident in the 1920s. As early as 1922, 480,000 tonnes of margarine were produced annually. In 1924, Van den Bergh produced a margarine with a Swan trademark called 'Blauband' which had great success even though 500 g of the margarine cost 1 Reichsmark. Van den Bergh's competitor Jurgens, in Goch, produced Rahma. The name is derived from Rahm, which means cream. In 1927, the 'h' in the word was forbidden by law because it was associated with butter. In advertisements, the word *buttergleich* [like butter] also had to be changed to *butterfein* [as soft as butter].

In 1927, the two former competitors Van den Bergh in Kleve and Jurgens in Goch, in the lower Rhine, merged to form the Margarine Union.[22] The British soap producer and food retailer, Lever Brothers joined them in 1929 to form Unilever Ltd. Both sides profited from this fusion. They needed the same raw materials: most animal fats coming from Chicago and palm oil from Nigeria in West Africa.

As a consequence of the world economic crisis in 1929, Unilever was denounced in Germany as a margarine trust under foreign control.[23] Demands for new margarine laws were raised. With Hitler's seizure of power in 1933, the National Socialists put a tax on margarine, oil and other edible fats (25 Pfenninge per 500 g margarine). The production of kosher margarine was prohibited and the Sana firm was closed. Leaflets called upon consumers to boycott margarine.[24] After 1933 rationing cards limited its consumption and the advertising of margarine was prohibited. Only half the normal production was maintained. Subsequently, an official price specification for margarine followed. In Kleve, the name Van den Bergh Margarine Gesellschaft was changed to Margarine-Werke Kleve. The factory started to produce cheese. The reprisals against the Jewish firm reached a climax when rationing cards were introduced to restrict margarine consumption. In 1939, only one official margarine was allowed to be produced in German factories, Unity margarine. On 7 October 1944, the Allies' bombs almost completely destroyed the town of Kleve and the factory. In 1945, only one kilogram of margarine per head was sold. With the end of the Second World War, the negative National Socialist propaganda against the 'Jewish Product' finally ceased. The factory was rebuilt in 1948 and production began anew.

No other industrially produced food was discussed as controversially as margarine. It was subject to a great deal of parliamentary debates, special margarine laws, arbitrary taxation and National Socialist reprisals and even periodical prohibition of production, but despite this, margarine survived as a cheap butter substitute for everybody.

References

Adelmeier, E., 1972, *Oss, die Heimat der Margarineindustrie. 100 Jahre in der Entwicklung einer berühmten Industrie* [Oss, the home of margarine production. 100 years in the development of a famous industry], o.O.

---

22 Wilson, 1954, II, ch.XVI. Both Jurgens and Van den Bergh had taken over chains of retailers in Britain to sell margarine. Jurgens controlled the Home and Colonial Stores and Van den Bergh's chain of outlets was the Meadow Dairy Company.

23 Festschrift, 1988, 22–3.

24 Stange, 1934.

Adreßbuch für die Margarine-Industrie, Talgschmelzen, Speisefett-Fabriken und Öl-Raffinerien [directory for the margarine industry, tallow melting, food fat factories and plant oil refinery], Dusseldorf,1921.

'*Amtliche Aufklärung über die Margarine-Vergiftungen*' [Official information about margarine-poisoning], in *Tägliche Rundschau*, Nr. 612, 31.12.1910.

Andés, E., 1907, *Kokosbutter und andere Kunstspeisefette* [Cocosbutter and other food fats], Wien and Leipzig.

Bartram, W., 1920, *Die Rohstoffversorgung der inländischen und ausländischen Ölmühlen-Industrie* [The raw material supply of domestic and foreign oil mills industry], Lübeck.

Blank, H., *Weltmacht Fett. Die Geschichte einer Erfindung* [The world power of fat. The history of an invention], München o.J.

Bösmann, H.G., 1969, 'Seit 100 Jahren gibt es Margarine' [There has been margarine for 100 years now], in *Unser Niederrhein* 4, S.

Burckhardt, E.H., 1895, *Der unlautere Wettbewerb im Butterhandel. Ein Beitrag zur Beurteilung der Margarinefrage* [The dishonest competition in the butter trade. A review of the margarine question], Berlin.

Der Kampf um das Margarine-Monopol. Eine Streitschrift für die Freiheit der Wirtschaft und das Wohl des deutschen Einzelhandels [The fight for the margarine monopoly. A pamphlet for the freedom of economics and for the well-being of the German retail trade], Köln 1930.

Deutsche Margarine-Zeitschrift. Offizielles Organ der Vereinigung Deutscher Margarinefabrikaten zur Wahrung der gemeinsamen Interessen G.m.b.H. [German margarine magazine. Official organ of the association of German margarine factory owners for preservation of common interests], 1. Jg. 1912–1913.

Ellerbrock, K.P., 1993, *Geschichte der deutschen Nahrungs- und Genußmittelindustrie 1750–1914*, Stuttgart.

'Entwurf eines Gesetzes, betreffend den Verkehr mit Butter, Käse, Schmalz und deren Ersatzmittel', [A draft law to control the trade with butter, cheese, lard and its substitutes] in *Stenographische Berichte über die Verhandlungen des Reichstages*, 9. Legislaturperiode, IV. Session 1895–97, Erster Anlageband, Berlin 1896.

Fahrion, W., 1920, *Die Fabrikation der Margarine, des Glyzerins und Stearins* [The production of margarine, glycerine and stearin], Berlin and Leipzig.

Feld, E., 1922, Die Deutsche Margarine-Industrie [The German margarine industry], Diss. Marburg.

Festschrift Margarine aus Kleve. 1888–1988. Ein Werk wird 100 Jahre [Festschrift: margarine from Kleve. 1888–1988. The 100th birthday of a factory], Kleve 1988.

Fitzner, R., 1919, *Die Weltwirtschaft der Fettstoffe 1. Die Ölindustrie Englands in ihren Rohstoffbezügen 1901–1918* [World economy of food fats. 1. The plant oil industry in England and its raw material sources 1901–1918], Berlin.

Franck, E., *Die Kunstbutterfrage insbesondere Entstehung, Einfhrung und wirthschaftliche Bedeutung des Margarins*, [The question of artificial butter.

The origin, introduction and economic significance of margarines] Frankfurt a.M. o.J.

Fränkel, H., 1894, *Der Kampf gegen die Margarine. Mit besonderer Berücksichtigung der Anträge des Bundes der Landwirthe* [The fight against margarine], Weimar.

Franzen, H., 1925, *Margarine* [Margarine], Leipzig.

Gesetz betr. den Verkehr mit Butter, Käse, Schmalz und deren Ersatzmittel. Vom 15. Juni 1897 [Law concerning the trade with butter, cheese, lard and its substitutes], (RGBl. 1897, S.475).

Gohren, T. von, 1877, 'Kunstbutterfabrikation' [the production of artificial butter], in *Fühlings neue landwirtschaftliche Zeitung*, 1.

Helm, W., 1895, *Der Butterkrieg und seine soziale Bedeutung* [The butter war and its social meaning], 2. Aufl. Bremen.

Hendricks, B.A., 1980, *Zur Geschichte der Margarineherstellung am Niederrhein. Die Diskussion um das Margarinegesetz von 1897* [The history of the German margarine production in the lower Rhine region. A discussion of the maragrine law of 1897], Kleve.

Hendricks, B.A., 1982, *Van den Berghs Margarinewerke und der Wunsch der Stadt Kleve nach Eingemeindung der Gemeinde Kellen* [Van den Bergh's margarine factory and the wish of the town Kleve to incorporate the community of Kellen], Kleve.

Hendricks, B.A., 1988, *Die Anfänge der Van den Bergh's Margarinegesellschaft m.b.H. Kleve* [The beginnings of the margarine factory Van den Bergh in Kleve], Eine Erinnerung zum 100 jährigen Jubiläum, Kleve.

Hepp, K., 1922, *Ernährung und Landwirtschaft* [Nutrition and agriculture] (Flugschriften der DVP, Folge 40) Berlin.

Hertkorn, J., 1910, *Über die Giftstoffe in Pflanzenbutter und Pflanzenfetten* [On toxic substances in margarine and vegetable oils], Sonderdruck Chemiker-Zeitung, Nr. 115

Hierholzer, V., '*Regulierung von Nahrungsmittelqualität in der Industrialisierung 1871–1914*' [Regulations of food quality in the time of industrialization 1871–1914], o.O. o.J., in *Kritische Studien zur Geschichtswissenschaft*, Bd. 190.

Honscha, M., 1979, *Ansätze zur Industrialisierung im 19. Jahrhundert. Die ersten Fabriken im Raum Kleve* [The beginning of industrialization in the nineteenth century. The first factories in Kleve], Kleve.

Jolles, A., 1895, *Über Margarin. Eine hygienische Studie* [About margarine], Bonn.

Knetsch, A., 1919, '*Die Rohfettwirtschaft*' [The raw material economy], in *Deutsche tierärztliche Wochenschrift*, 27.

Koch, E., 1968, *Kleve, Margarine und Van den Bergh* [Kleve, margarine and Van den Bergh], Kleve.

Koch, E., 1969, *Van den Bergh kommt nach Kleve, Die Anfänge der Margarine-Herstellung am Niederrhein* [Van den Bergh moves to Kleve. The beginnings of the margarine production in the lower Rhine], Kleve.

Krebs, W., 2002, *Tomor, Eine koschere Margarine von Niederrhein und ihre religiöse Werbung* [Tomor. A kosher margarine from the lower Rhine region and its religious advertising], Kleve.

Lang, V., 1878, *Die Fabrikation der Kunstbutter, Sparbutter und Butterine. Eine Darstellung der Bereitung der Ersatzmittel der echten Butter nach den besten Methoden* [The production of artifical butter, savings butter and butterine], Wien, Pest, Leipzig.

Lavalle, A., 1896, *Die Margarine-Gesetzgebung und ihre Entwickelung in den einzelnen Culturstaaten. Unter Berücksichtigung der dänischen Verhältnisse und der in Deutschland neuerdings gemachten Vorschläge zur Aenderung des deutschen Gesetzes* [The margarine legislation and its development in different countries], Bremen.

Limburg, H., 1980, *25 Jahre Vereinigung deutscher Margarinefabrikanten G.m.b.H.* [25 years association of German margarine factory owners], Köln.

Lindemann, W., 1936, *Die deutsche Margarineindustrie und die öffentliche Margarinepolitik bis 1935* [The German margarine industry and public margarine politics before 1935], Diss. Erlangen.

Margarine-Institut für gesunde Ernährung (hrsg.), 1980, *Ölpflanzen, Pflanzenöle, Margarine. Vom Rohstoff zum Verbraucher* [Oil plants, plant oils, margarine: from the raw material to the consumer], Hamburg.

Matenaar, F., 1954, *Die halbe Welt auf dem Abendbrottisch (Margarine)* [Half of the world on the dinner table (margarine)], Kleve.

Matenaar, F., 1979, *Von den Anfängen der Margarineproduktion in Kleve* [The beginnings of margarine production in Kleve], Kleve.

Mayer, A., 1884, *Die Kunstbutter, ihre Fabrikation, ihr Gebrauchswerth, nebst Mitteln, ihren Vertrieb in seine Grenzen zurückzuweisen* [Artifical butter, its production, value of use, and mediums to put its sale in its place], Heidelberg.

Monatsschrift für die volkswirtschaftlichen, gesetzgeberischen und kommerziellen Interessen der Margarine-Industrie [Journal of the economical, legislative and commerial interests of the margarine industry], 5.-6. Jg., 1912–1913.

Petersen, C., 1895, *Die Margarine-Frage. Referat erstattet auf der Generalversammlung des Deutschen Milchwirtschaftlichen Vereins am 18. Februar 1895 zu Berlin* [The margarine question. Paper of the general meeting of the German milk business association], Bremen.

Pollatschek, P., 1923, 'Die Fabrikation der Margarine' [The production of margarine], in: *Monographien aus dem Gebiete der Fett-Chemie*, Band IV, Stuttgart.

Rudischer, S., 1959, *Fachbuch der Margarineindustrie. Chemie, Technologie, Produktionsüberwachung, Betriebshygiene. Unter Berücksichtigung der Ölraffination und Fetthärtung* [Reference book of the margarine industry. Chemistry, technology, supervision of the production, working hygiene], Leipzig.

Schaedler, C., 1883, *Die Technologie der Fette und Oele des Pflanzen- und Thierreichs* [The technology of fats and oils from plants and animals], Berlin.

Schwitzer, M.K., 1956, *Margarine and other food fats*, London.

Sell, E., 1886, *Ueber Kunstbutter. Ihre Herstellung, sanitäre Beurtheilung und die Mittel zu ihrer Unterscheidung von Milchbutter. Beiträge zur Kenntniss der Milchbutter und der zu ihrem Ersatz in Anwendung gebrachten anderen Fette* [About artificial butter. Its production, sanitary conditions and the means of distinguishing it from milk butter], Berlin.

Soxhlet, F. Von, 1895, *Ueber Margarine. Bericht an das General-Comitdes landwirthschaftlichen Vereins in Bayern* [About margarine], München.

Stange, W., 1934, *Die Margarine-Industrie in Deutschland, der Kampf um die Vertrustung, ihre Konjunkturempfindlichkeit und die neue deutsche Fettwirtschaft* [The margarine-industry in Germany, the fight against the foreign trust, its slump and the new German fat economy], Jena.

Stuyvenberg van, J.H., 1969, *Margarine, An economic, social and scientific history 1869–1969*, Liverpool.

Van den Bergh's Margarine-Gesellschaft m.B.H. Cleve (hrsg.), 1928, *Vierzig Jahre im Dienste der Volksernährung* [Forty years on duty for national nutrition], Düsseldorf.

Van den Bergh's Margarine-Gesellschaft m.B.H. Cleve (hrsg.), *Die van den Bergh Margarinewerke in Cleve* [The Van den Bergh margarine company in Kleve], o.O. o.J., (Werbebroschüre).

Voornveld H. van, 1913, *Die Margarine ihre Herstellung, Vertrieb und volkswirtschaftliche Bedeutung, mit Würdigung der rechtlichen Gesichtspunkte* [The margarine and its production, sale and national economically importance], Trier.

Wilson, C., 1954, *The History of Unilever: A study in Economic Growth and Social Change*, 2 vols, London, Cassell.

Wollny, R., 1887, *Ueber die Kunstbutterfrage. Auf Grund eigener Beobachtungen und Erfahrungen in der holländischen Kunstbutter-Industrie und mit besonderer Berücksichtigung des Gesetzentwurfs über den Verkehr mit Kunstbutter* [About the artificial butter question], Leipzig.

Chapter 9

The Nutritional Transformation of Danish Pork, 1887–1960

Tenna Jensen

Introduction

'The pig is a very flexible animal'[1] wrote Frederik Oehlerich, one of the many experts who published production manuals aimed at Danish pig farmers around the turn of the nineteenth century. This understanding of the pig, which prevailed among all leading experts of the time, made dramatic changes possible in the Danish pork industry from 1887 onwards. Flexibility became the key to the international success of Danish pork as both the body of the pig and the system of production could be modified and quickly adjusted to changing markets and demands. The faith in flexibility as well as technological advances ensured that modifications of the pig were intensified continuously over the twentieth century. Intensive breeding programmes were set up which rapidly altered the body proportions of Danish pigs. Hence the pig of the 1960s looked significantly different from that of the 1880s. The hypothesis of this chapter is that the industrialization of Danish pork production from 1887 onwards changed not only the appearance of the pigs but also the nutritional content and composition of the meat. The aim is to investigate how the composition of pork changed between 1887 and 1960, and thus to gain new insights into the nutritional implications of the industrialization of food production in the twentieth century.

Background

Danish pork and especially bacon has been an internationally well-known food product since 1887. Even though Denmark exported a significant amount of live pigs to Germany throughout the nineteenth century it took an outbreak of swine fever to kick start the rapid industrialization of the Danish pork industry. In 1887 swine fever closed the German market to all imports of live pigs. This was a shock to the Danish pork industry as it was suddenly forced to turn its attention elsewhere. The industry quickly decided to focus on meeting the demands of the English market. The British, like the Germans, had statutory legislation in the Contagious Disease (Animals) Act which prohibited the import of live animals.

---

1 Oehlerich, 1890, 26.

As live pigs became increasingly difficult to export, the industry realized that new strategies and products were needed. Bacon proved to be the answer. Exporting bacon instead of live pigs required an entirely new system of slaughterhouses and facilities for preparation of the meat before it was shipped to British ports. Within a few years the Danish industry had constructed such a system. Co-operative slaughterhouses became an essential part of this scheme and more than 20 opened between 1887 and 1889.[2]

The rapid reorganization and industrialization of pork production brought about a rapid increase in capacity. Between 1887 and 1960 the number of pigs alive in Denmark at any time rose from 1.5 million to roughly 6 million.[3] This is equivalent to a rise in the number of slaughtered pigs per year from 2.5 million to almost 12 million.[4] Export opportunities drove the intensification of production and foreign markets soon became the main purchasers of Danish pork. Between 1900 and 1960 the percentage of meat exported rose from 48 per cent to 72 per cent.[5] In 1900, 82 per cent of that export went to Britain which continued to be the primary market until the 1960s. From the late 1960s other European markets such as Italy and Germany gained importance just as export to non-European markets escalated.[6] Danish pork was thereby not only consumed by Danes but to a large extent by Europeans. Knowledge of the nutritional changes of Danish pork thereby provides insights into the changes to a food product eaten by consumers in several European nations. The reorganization of production resulted in several visible changes to the bodies of the Danish pigs from 1887. For one, the continuously growing importance of the export market meant that an intense effort was made to standardize the pigs bred for export and domestic use alike. Experts believed that a standardization of all pigs would lead to more efficient and profitable production for all farmers. In order to ensure this, the mixture of races in the breeding of the officially recommended standard pig was continuously altered according to the latest results of the official scientific breeding and feeding programmes.[7] Alongside this genetic redesigning the requirements of the slaughterhouses became more and more specific. In a matter of years only the flesh of pigs from the right lineage could guarantee the farmer a maximum price. These developments resulted in a shift in the average body proportions from those of the 'original' randomly bred Landrace pig, which dominated in 1887, to those of the ideal export pig shown below. In 1890 this ideal was still fictional but in a few decades it had become the standard for nearly all Danish pigs.

---

2   *De første hundrede år*, 1987, 27.

3   *Landbrugsstatistik 1900–1965*, 1969, 94–5.

4   These figures are my own calculations based upon the average slaughter age and the percentage of export pigs versus pigs bred for domestic sale.

5   *Landbrugsstatistik 1900–1965*, 1969, 118–21.

6   *De første hundrede år*, 323.

7   These series can be found in *Beretninger fra den kongelige veterinær og landbrugshøjskoles Landøkonomiske Forsøgslaboratorium*.

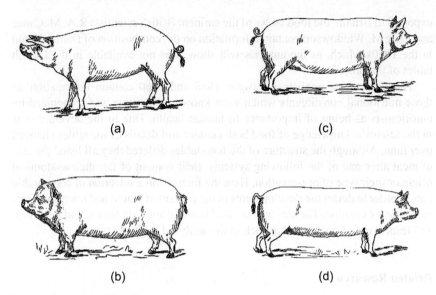

(a)   (c)

(b)   (d)

Source: Grøntvedt, 1890, 16.

Figure 9.1   Differences in the proportions of (a) Landrace, (b) Yorkshire, (c) Crossbred, and (d) The ideal export pig, 1890

The shift resulted in an 8.5 kg increase in muscle mass between 1887 and 1908, an increase which continued though less rapidly until the 1950s.[8] Increasing muscle mass meant that the weight of the individual cuts of meat grew at an equal pace. For instance average tenderloins gained 80 g between 1935 and 1958.[9] Illustrations of pigs, as Figure 9.1 above shows, clearly depict the changing body proportions. In order to investigate compositional developments of the meat it is however necessary to go beyond illustrations.

Sources and Methodology

Information on changes in the nutritional composition of pork can be found in food tables issued by nutritional scientists between 1888 and 1960. This chapter highlights those issued in two intervals, 1888 to 1910 and 1950 to 1960. These focus on the most important developments in the meat over the first half of the twentieth century. Since food tables were often published in the works of nutritional authorities, several different versions might be available to the population at the same time. This changed in the late 1960s as an official set of continuously updated food tables was issued. As the majority of the meat was

8   *10. Beretning*, 1887.
9   *312. Beretning*, 1959, 39.

exported to Britain, the food tables of the eminent British scientists R.A. McCance and Elsie M. Widdowson contain information on the composition of Danish bacon in the 1950s which, as the analysis will show, was not available in the Danish tables of the time.[10]

The food tables published between 1888 and 1960 contain information on those nutritional constituents which were known at the time and recognized by nutritionists as being of importance to human health. Due to the developments in the scientific knowledge of food both content and details of the tables changed over time. Although the structure of the food tables differed they all listed the cuts of meat after one of the following systems: their content of fat; their anatomical origin or their type of preservation. Here the focus is on a selection of comparable cuts in order to detect the developments in the content of macro and micronutrients in the meat over time. The cuts are: smoked ham, fat and lean bacon, and the fattest and leanest cut of pork listed in each of the analysed food tables.

Related Research

The Danish pork industry has been the subject of several historical studies. Most of these have told the story of one or more of the co-operative slaughterhouses which were founded in the 1880s and 1890s. These studies can be categorized as commemorative publications and as such they lack an analytical approach to the history of the slaughterhouses.[11] One publication however differs from the rest by including an analysis of the societal context as well as of the meat itself. In *Danske Slagterier, de første hundrede år 1887–1987* [the first hundred years of the Danish Slaughterhouses 1887–1987] two historians Flemming Just and Erik Helmer Petersen analyse the relationship between the slaughterhouse industry, producer and the national co-operative organization.[12] The more recent history of the Danish slaughterhouses is presented in *Konkurrence og Koncentration* by Jesper Strandskov a publication which focuses on the fusions and organizational restructurings of the sector.[13]

In *Svinets historie* [The History of the Pig] from 1984 the agronomist Hans Kloster has written a classical chronological presentation of the history of the Danish pig from ancient to present times.[14] This general way of writing the history of the pig was also predominant in the previously mentioned manuals on pig production issued to the Danish pig farmers.[15] *Grisen – en køkkenhistorie* [The pig - a story

---

10   McCance and Widdowson, 1960.

11   Complete collections of the commemorative publications can be found in the Royal Danish Library at kb.dk.

12   Just and Petersen, 1987, 313.

13   Strandskov, 2011.

14   Kloster, 1984.

15   For example, Beck, 1910.

from the kitchen] by Else Marie Boyhus concentrates instead on pork in Danish cooking. The book is an ethnological study of pork as a gastronomic subject.[16]

My perspective on the history of the pig and its meat differs from those mentioned above, as it focuses on the developments in the nutritional composition of the meat over time. These developments are also touched upon in the article *Svin kvalitet og kontrol* in which Anne Katrine Gjerløff and I focus on aspects of the changes in the perception of the health and quality of Danish pigs in the slaughterhouses around 1900.[17] Looking into the historical quality of meat sheds a new light on the consequences of the industrialization of food production in the first half of the twentieth century and shows how it has affected the nature of the food products eaten by European consumers.

The Nutritional Composition of Pork, 1888–1914

Food tables were printed in Denmark from the end of the nineteenth century. Their publication began at the same time as large statistical social surveys were initiated to uncover the consumption patterns of the working population.[18] The state of people's health had become important as the authorities increasingly perceived the undernutrition of the lower social classes as problematic. The consumption surveys thus uncovered problems of malnutrition and undernutrition and the food tables offered solutions to them. They were seen as the most efficient way of educating authorities and housewives alike on how to optimize the energy value of the diet of a working family and thus prevent deficiency diseases in both children and adults.

The first set of Danish food tables were published in 1888 by the doctor Christian Jürgensen. It was called *Grafisk Fremstilling af de menneskelige Fødemidlers og nogle spisers kemiske Sammensætning* [Graphic Presentation of Human Foods and their Chemical Composition].[19] It was reprinted eight times and remained popular for more than two decades. The first expert to challenge Jürgensen's way of presenting the composition of food was the nutritionist Mikkel Hindhede. His series of reports from the *Kontor for Ernæringsundersøgelser* [Office of nutritional research], published from 1912 to 1945, contained extensive tables on the composition of food products. Hindhede belonged to the new breed of professional nutritional scientists who carried out experiments and chemical analyses and the two scientists were often engaged in fierce debates about the

---

16 Boyhus, 1998, 8.

17 Gjerløff and Jensen, 2010.

18 The series of *Husholdningsforbrugsundersøgelser* [household budget surveys] began in 1897 and has been conducted regularly ever since. From the 1880s large surveys of specific social groups were however initiated by individual statisticians. Those of Th. Sørensen, Marcus Rubin and Poul Sveistrup especially showed how much information there was to gain from large scale statistical social surveys.

19 Jürgensen, 1888.

nature of a healthy diet.[20] As a result, the listings in the tables of the two authorities differed in many ways. They did however share one feature which affected the force of their statements; both were based on investigations of the nutritional content of pork produced outside Denmark. Jürgensen's table was based on König's analyses of German pork from the early 1880s. Hindhede's response shows their diverging understanding of good science. Hindhede stated that the primary ambition of Jürgensen must have been to present existing knowledge on food in a more comprehensible way rather than to create more accurate knowledge of the composition of Danish foods.[21]

Hindhede's information on the nutritional composition of foods was based on a variety of sources.[22] The composition of some foods were analysed in his own laboratory, some were recalculated based on other sources and finally some were copied from W.O Atwater and C.D. Woods, *The chemical composition of American food materials*.[23] Out of the five analysed cuts only one, streaky bacon, had been analysed in his own laboratory; the rest were taken from the American table.[24] This means that out of all the analysed cuts only one was directly comparable with the composition of Danish meat from around 1900. However, both Jürgensen and Hindhede must have thought that the listings were accurate enough to serve as general information to the public.

Both sets of tables emphasized that the value of any given food product was based on a combination of its energy content and its price. As the major nutritional problem of the time was undernutrition the most valuable foods were those which were both energy dense *and* cheap. These were primarily products containing large amounts of fat.[25] The two experts calculated the value of foods differently: Hindhede, by way of energy expressed as calories; Jürgensen, by way of a price quota index.[26] Just as their methods of calculating differed so did their understandings of the constituents of food. Hindhede perceived the constituents to comprise protein, carbohydrates, fat and waste. He included calories in his table which enabled experts and laymen alike to compare the value of different food products. Jürgensen also included listings of the content of protein, carbohydrates and fat. Moreover, he included the content of water in the food but unlike Hindhede he listed neither waste nor calories. Just as the constituents differed between the tables so did the listed content of the individual nutrients in the cuts (see Table 9.1).

---

20 Overgaard, 2008.
21 Hindhede, 1914, 58–64.
22 Hindhede, 1914, 7.
23 Atwater, and Woods, 1899.
24 Hindhede, 1914, 59.
25 In this context the most valuable products were fats, primarily lard and margarine as they were both (mostly) cheaper than butter.
26 The precise and rather complicated way to calculate the index is stated in Jürgensen, 1888, 11–16.

Table 9.1   The nutritional composition of Danish pork per 100 grams, 1888 and 1914

Author	Products (raw)	Description	Waste (%)	Water (%)	Protein (g)	Fat (g)	Energy value (kcal)	Energy value (kj)
Jürgensen 1888	Lean meat and game	Lean		75	21	7	143	596
	Very fat (pork)	Fat		39	10	50	490	2,050
	Fleshy bacon	Lean		39	11	44	440	1,841
	Lightly salted bacon	Fat		8	10	76	724	3,029
	Smoked ham			28	25	36	424	1,774
Hindhede 1914	Tenderloin	Lean			19	13	198	830
	Shoulder	Fat	12		12	30	326	1,365
	Streaky bacon	Lean			10	58	585	2,449
	Salted and smoked bacon, very fat	Fat			2	86.2	809	3,387
	Smoked ham		9		10	59	591	2,474

Note: Jurgensen did not provide energy values for the cuts of meat; these are my calculations.

Source: Jurgensen, 1888; Hindhede, 1914.

When comparing the data in these two sets of tables it is clear, firstly, that the content of protein was, with a single exception, higher in Jürgensen's table. The protein content ranged between 21 per cent in the leanest meat and 10 per cent in the fattest. For Hindhede the figures were 18.9 per cent in the tenderloin and a mere 1.9 per cent in the fattest bacon. Secondly, the content of fat was higher in Hindhede's table. According to Jürgensen the content of fat varied between 76 per cent in the lightly salted bacon and 6.5 per cent in the leanest meat. In Hindhede's table the fat content varied between 86.2 per cent in the salted and smoked bacon and 13 per cent in the tenderloin. The meat featuring in Hindhede's table thereby contained significantly more fat and less protein. Due to some insecurity in the origin of the leanest cut in Jürgensen's table, the differences between the content of fat and resultantly also of protein is presented most vividly in the listings of protein and fat in smoked ham. Jürgensen listed a protein content of 25 per cent and a fat content of 36 per cent. Hindhede, on the other hand, listed 9.5 per cent of protein and 59.4 per cent of fat, a quite remarkable difference.

This stemmed from the origins of the data in the tables. As mentioned previously the only cut from Danish pigs was the streaky bacon in Hindhede's table. The Danish cut had a fat and protein content which placed it between the two cuts of German bacon featured in the table of Jürgensen (see Table 9.1). The other bacon cut featuring in Hindhede's table, the American, had a much higher content of fat (86.2 per cent).

At the time pork was generally seen as a fatty food and thereby, in consequence of the desire of the time to maximize the intake of energy, as a good product. Both scientists favoured the fatty kinds of meat and Hindhede recommended that Danish housewives should spend their money on fatty not lean meat as they would then get their money's worth in calories.[27] Even if all kinds of pork were considered fatty, American meat was seen as being extremely so; '... *det amerikanske svin har en aldeles overvældende fedtmasse'*.[28] [the American pork has an utterly overwhelming amount of fat]. Even if the large fat content was seen by scientists and workers alike as pork's most valuable asset, the American cuts were still sold at a lower price due to their excessive fatty nature. As it appears that American meat was sold in Denmark but disliked, Jürgensen's table probably more accurately reflects the kind of pork eaten by the Danes around the turn of the nineteenth century than that of Hindhede. Even if the poorest parts of the population might have bought the American meat, those who in any way could afford it would pay for cuts which contained lean meat as well as fat. Even if Jürgensen's meat was remarkably leaner than Hindhede's it contained far more fat than the pork of the 1950s.

The Nutritional Composition of Danish Pork in the 1950s

In the 1950s Danish nutritional science was dominated by the two experts E. Groth Petersen and Richard Ege. Groth Petersen first published his extensive food tables in 1940. These dominated the field both during and after the Second World War. Groth Petersen's tables were based on a system of variance ranges all calculated from the values of several older food tables. In the 1950s Richard Ege became the most important expert in human nutrition. He published several series of textbooks and pamphlets on human nutrition containing food tables.

The food tables of both scientists were primarily based on foreign data. The only exception was the vitamin content which was calculated from Danish meat. Only Ege discussed the implications of the use of foreign data. Even if he was aware that it might lead to inaccurate listings he solved the problem by selecting those he found to be the most credible.[29] However, information on Danish meat can be found in the British food tables of McCance and Widdowson (see Table 9.4). As the values for the cuts are quite similar in between Ege, Groth Petersen and McCance and Widdowson it may be assumed that the Danish tables have significant values for the nutritional content of meat in the 1950s.

---

27   Hindhede, 1914, 6–7.
28   Cramer, 1886, 21.
29   Ege, 1959, 427.

Table 9.2   The nutritional composition of Danish pork per 100 grams in the 1950s from Groth Petersen, 1953

Product (raw)	Description	Protein (g)	Fat (g)	Energy value (kcal)	Energy value (kj)	Calcium (mg)	Phosphorus (mg)	Iron (mg)
Pork, lean	Lean	19	16	195	816	17	150	2.5
Pork, fat	Fat	15	36	389	1,628	17	150	1.4
Bacon, lean, fresh and smoked	Lean	15	36	447	1,870	17	150	1.4
Bacon, fat, fresh and smoked	Fat	8	66	603	2,523	17	100	1.4
Smoked Ham		15	36	389	1,628	17	150	1.4

Note: Lean bacon, fat bacon and smoked ham have a 10 per cent waste allowance.

As had been the case at the turn of century, the content of the Danish tables still differed. Groth Petersen and Ege did agree on some constituents of meat. Besides its energy value (calories), both viewed it as consisting of protein, fat, carbohydrates, calcium, phosphorus, iron and a number of vitamins. Both made an allowance for waste. The inclusion of micronutrients and vitamins showed how the scientific analysis of food had developed and how the scientific perceptions of the qualities and properties of food had changed. These findings made it more complicated to assess the beneficial effects of food. Thus both Groth Petersen and Ege found that '*Det er dermed givet, at der ikke findes et simpelt tal, der kan give et samlet udtryk for fødevarens værdi, således som man tidligere var tilbøjelig til at tro, man havde i kalorieindholdet.*'[30] [It is thus granted that there is no simple number which can express the value of a food as it was earlier believed could be found in the calorie].

As a result of the complexity of food and its effects on the human body nutritionists perceived the importance of both macronutrients and micronutrients differently. According to Ege vitamins, minerals and protein were essential components in a healthy diet. Eating enough carbohydrates was never a practical problem and to him fat was also necessary but equally unproblematic to obtain in sufficient amounts. In consequence Ege left out the content of both carbohydrate and fat in some of his tables. This shows that fat was no longer seen as the most valuable component in meat but had been replaced by protein in the hierarchy of nutrients.

---

30   Ege, 1949.

Table 9.3   The nutritional composition of Danish pork per 100 grams in the 1950s from Ege, 1959

Product (raw)	Description	Protein (g)	Fat (g)	Energy value (kcal)	Energy value (kj)	Calcium (mg)	Phosphorus (mg)	Iron (mg)
Pork, lean	Lean	20	15	220	920	9.9	175	2.75
Pork, fat	Fat	15	38	400	1,674	6.6	125	2.0
Bacon, lean, fresh and smoked	Lean	12	48	480	2,008	6.6	110	1.7
Bacon, smoked	Fat	9	63	600	2,510	6.6	75	1.25
Smoked Ham		15	30	350	1,464	9.9	150	2.5

Table 9.4   The nutritional composition of Danish pork per 100 grams in the 1950s from McCance and Widdowson, 1960

Product (raw)	Description	Protein (g)	Fat (g)	Energy value (kcal)	Energy value (kj)	Calcium (mg)	Phosphorus (mg)	Iron (mg)
Danish Wiltshire, fore end	Lean	15	32	355	1,485	14.4	138	1.1
Danish Wiltshire, middle	Fat	13	45	468	1,958	13.5	119	1.3
Danish Wiltshire, smoked ham		15	28	325	1,360	12.6	111	1.7

The values for protein and fat did not differ significantly between the tables of the two Danish scientists. The values for lean pork, for instance, only varied by 0.5 g for protein and 1 g for fat. The most significant differences between the cuts were found in lean bacon. Groth Petersen listed the protein content in lean bacon of 15 g and the fat content of 36 g, while Ege listed the content to be 12 g and 48 g respectively. Minor differences in between the nutritional composition also existed in the listings for fat bacon and smoked ham. Groth Petersen's fat bacon contained 8.1 per cent protein and 66 per cent fat while Ege's was 9 per cent protein and 63 per cent fat. Also the values for smoked ham differed with regard to fat content: Groth Petersen listed fat as 36 g and Ege only 30 g. There were however no difference between their listings of protein as both hams contained

15 g. Where differences between the food tables still existed they were no longer as prominent as they had been in between the tables of Hindhede and Jürgensen.

In Groth Petersen's table the leanest meat had a protein content of 19 g and a fat content of 16 g. The fattest meat contained 8.1 g of protein and 66 g of fat. Ege, on the other hand, gave the leanest cut containing 19.5 g of protein and 15 g of fat while the fattest contained 9 g of protein and 63 g of fat. The difference in fat content in between the fattest and the leanest cut was thus at or just below 50 g in both tables while the protein content differed by approximately 10 g between the fattest and the leanest cut. If the tables of the 1950s are compared with those from the years around 1900 it becomes evident that pork had become significantly leaner over time. In the 1950s it was, according to the tables, no longer possible to buy meat with the overwhelming fat content of the bacon listed by Jürgensen and Hindhede. As a result of the reduced fat content even the fattest of the cuts contained more protein than around 1900.

If the values for smoked ham are compared, protein and fat amounted to 61 per cent in Jürgensen's table and 68.9 per cent in Hindhede's table. Groth Petersen on the other hand listed fat and protein as 51 per cent but Ege only 45 per cent. This suggests that ham contained more water in the 1950s. All these changes in the composition of the meat show that over time Danish pork had become more homogeneous, contained a larger amount of protein and less fat.

Minerals and vitamins were included in the tables of the 1950s. These were seen by both Groth Petersen and Ege to be of importance to the human organism. Lean meat contained larger amounts of the micronutrients and fat meat thus lost the nutritional advantage it was believed to have had around 1900. The devaluation of the attributes of fat meat was underlined by the reduction in the importance of energy-dense foods. In the 1950s the Danish population was no longer suffering from systematic undernutrition and the priorities of the nutritionists had changed, undermining the nutritional value of fat meat. Whether or not this devaluation led to slimmer pigs, or whether it was the demands of the export markets which shaped the notion that lean pork was good pork, is hard to assess. Either way there is little doubt that the nutritional composition of Danish pork did change over time and that the developments were of a scale which must have influenced the way it affected the humans who ate it.

Conclusion

Analyses of food tables contain important evidence about the historical composition of food. Even if not all food products may have changed as much as pork, this study provides insights into the kinds of historical knowledge present in outdated food tables. As they show the newest and relevant scientific knowledge of their time they grant insights not only into the nutritional compositions of past foods but also into the concepts which may have influenced how these changed. Even if this study ends with the 1950s the tendency to produce ever leaner meat has continued until the present day. The cuts of today are largely fat free and even those containing fat do so in much smaller amounts than the pork of both 1900 and the 1950s. Industrialization and standardization made possible the monitoring, breeding and rearing systems which are essential to produce and develop the pork of the twentieth century. Today pork is a food product which, even if its name has remained unchanged over time, stems from animals of different varieties. The flexibility of the pig proved to have few boundaries with the result that the pork of today has a different nutritional profile from pork in the past.

References

Atwater, W.O. and Woods, C.D., 1899, *The chemical composition of American food materials*, U.S. Department of Agriculture: Office of Experiment Stations, Bull. No. 28, Washington.

Beck, N., 1910, *Svinet, Lære og Haandbog til Brug i praksis og paa Landbrugsskoler* [Pig Production Manual in practice], Odense: Andelstrykkeriet i Odense.

Boyhus, E.M., 1998, *Grisen – en køkkenhistorie* [The pig – a story from the Kitchen], Århus: Gyldendal.

Ege, R., 1949, *Vejledning i rationel kostplanlægning og kostbudgettering* [Guide to rational dietary planning and budgeting], København.

Ege, R., 1959, *Ernæringslære* [Nutritional Education] (4th edn), København: Nyt Nordisk Forlag.

Gjerløff, A.K. and Jensen, T., 2010, '*Svin – kvalitet og control*' [Pigs – Quality and Control], *kademisk Kvarter*, vol. 1.

Groth-Petersen, E., 1940, '*Grundlag for beregning af kostens næringsværdi, en Tabel*' [Basis of calculating nutritional values – a table], 1st edn, København.

Groth-Petersen, E., 1953, *Grundlag for beregning af kostens næringsværdi, en Tabel* [Basis of calculating nutritional values – a table], 2nd edn, København.

Grøntvedt, F.W., 1890, *Om opdræt og behandling af slagtesvin* [How to rear and treat a pig], Kristiania: Christiania svineslagteri.

Hindhede, M., 1914, *5te Beretning fra M. Hindhedes Kontor for Ernæringsundersøgelser*[Fifth report from M. Hindhede's Office for Nutritional Research], København.

Jensen, T., 2011, *Fødevareforbrug i Danmark i det 20. Århundrede* [Food consumption in Denmark in the Twentieth Century], København: Københavns Universitet.

Jürgensen, C., 1888, *Grafisk Fremstilling af de menneskelige Fødemidlers og nogle Spisers kemiske Sammensætning* [Graphic Presentation of Foods and their Chemical Composition], København: I.H. Schubothes Boghandel.

Just, F. and Petersen, E.H., 1987, *Danske Slagterier de første hundrede år 1887–1987* [The first hundred Years of Danish Slaughterhouses, 1887–1987], Danske Slagterier.

Kloster, H., 1984, *Svinets Historie* [The History of the Pig], København: DSR Forlag.

McCance, R.A. and Widdowson, E.M., 1960, *The Composition of Foods, MRC Special Report Series 297*, London: HMSO.

Overgaard, S.S., 2008, *Fra mad til ernæring, Mikkel Hindhedes ernæringsdiskurs og dansk madkultur 1900–1945* [From Food to Nutrition], København: Københavns Universitet.

Landbrugsstatistik 1900–1965, Bind 2, 1969 [Agricultural Statistics 1900–1965 Volume 2], København.

Strandskov, J., 2011, *Konkurrence og Koncentration. Svineslagteriernes fusionshistorie1960–2010* [Competition and Concentration. The story of the Bacon Factories 1960–2010], Odense: Syddansk Universitetsforlag.

10. Beretning fra den Kongelige Veterinær og Landbohøjskoles Laboratorium for landøkonomiske forsøg[10. Report of the Royal Veterinary and Agricultural University, Laboratory of Agronomy], 1887, København.

312. Beretning fra den Kongelige Veterinær og Landbohøjskoles Laboratorium for landøkonomiske forsøg [312. Report of the Royal Veterinary and Agricultural University, Laboratory of Agronomy], 1959, København.

Chapter 10
The Rise of the Frozen-Fish Industry in Iceland and Norway: The Case of Fish Fingers

Guðmundur Jónsson and Örn D. Jónsson

Introduction

Throughout the centuries Europeans used various methods of preserving fish, each of which was intricately linked with available resources and local custom. Before the industrial age the most common methods were salting, drying or smoking, but the late nineteenth century saw the rise of the canning industry and in the interwar period techniques of 'quick-freezing' fish were developed. It is estimated that by the middle of the twentieth century about 40 per cent of all fish consumed in Europe was fresh, the rest was processed by means of curing, that is, mainly salting or drying (26 per cent), reduction (24 per cent), freezing (6 per cent) and canning (4 per cent).[1]

The advent of freezing technology revolutionized age-old methods of processing, marketing and consumption of fish. With the quick-freezing processes developed by Clarence Birdseye, together with packaging innovations such as moisture-proof cellophane wrapping, a completely new way of fish processing opened up which allowed standardized mass production of fish with a long storage life.[2] The main products of the emerging fish-freezing industry were white fish fillets and blocks of cod and related species as well as frozen herring.

In fish-exporting countries like Iceland and Norway producers were eager to develop new products based on this new technology to meet the challenges of the economic depression of the 1930s; and in the hope of gaining new markets in

---

1   *Yearbook of Fishery Statistics* 1952, 53, 87. Reduction is a method of processing mainly pelagic fish (for example, herring) into meal and oil by way of boiling, pressing and drying. A common method was to put the herring into a boiler where it was steamboiled for ca. 10–15 minutes and then moved into a press which removed a greater part of the liquid (water and oil). The pressed cake was then moved to a hopper or grinder to grind the herring into meal, which was then moved to a drier. The oil was tapped in barrels and the meal in sacks. See Eydal, 1948, 96–9.

2   On the development of the freezing technology and frozen food, see Teuteberg, 1995, 51–65; Levenstein, 1993, 101–18; Hamilton, 2003, 33–60.

European countries such as Britain and Germany with a tradition of eating fresh fish. Eventually, the most lucrative market for frozen fish turned out to be in the United States, thanks largely to a culinary invention which was developed in the early postwar period and became a huge success: the fish finger.

The creation of the fish finger – a small strip of fish, coated with breadcrumbs and fried over – was the result of 'several forces of modernity', as Paul Josephson so lucidly explains in his study of its success: the advent of freezing technology, vessels with huge capacities for refrigeration, a distribution network stretching from the processor to the consumer, including refrigeration cars on the railways and large refrigerated trucks on the roads, as well as freezer cabinets in the fast growing supermarkets.[3] Consumer demand for frozen fish, however, remained low until the 1950s when a number of factors caused it to increase: greater affluence of Americans giving rise to suburban lifestyles, supermarket shopping, homes supplied with freezers in the kitchen, the rising popularity of 'convenience cooking' and a successful marketing strategy applied by producers.

This study examines the rise of the frozen-fish industry in two prominent fishing nations of the North Atlantic, Iceland and Norway, and how their principal food industry was transformed as a result of freezing technology. We pay special attention to the fish finger and other fish products of the new technology and seek to explain why Iceland was first of the North Atlantic fishing nations to enter the large American market. The transformation into modern industrial fishery required the producers not only to master new technology, organize production in new ways, develop new products, retrain the labour force and create an infrastructure for storing and distributing the products, but also to place themselves in a new, uncharted and very demanding market. But the rewards were also high if producers succeeded in gaining ground in the United States of America, the most developed market for frozen fish in the postwar period.

Comparison between Iceland and Norway reveals how two countries with similar physical environments, product mix, market position and in many respects industrial structure, took different development paths with the advent of modern industrial technology in fishing and fish processing. We follow the development of the frozen-fish industry in its initial phase from the 1930s to the end of the 1960s when both countries had established themselves in the US market for frozen fish. During this period the fish finger played a key role in the success of the industry but was fast losing its lead to other products due to changes in consumption habits.

The Need to Diversify: Responses to the Great Depression

Since the late eighteenth century Iceland and Norway had based their fisheries on exports to distant markets. The Atlantic cod was by far the most valuable species caught in both countries and was mainly exported dried and salted to Southern

---

3   Josephson, 2008, 41–61. In the USA the fish finger was known as the fish stick.

Europe. The principal markets for salted cod (*klipfish*) were in Spain and Portugal but Norway also sold considerable quantities in the USA, the Caribbean and South America and its markets were therefore not as concentrated as Iceland's. Norway also produced large amounts of dried fish (*stockfish*) from cod and related species which were sold mainly to Italy and West Africa. Iceland had discontinued this product in the late nineteenth century but, with the advent of trawl fishing shortly before the First World War, turned increasingly to export fresh-caught fish packed in ice to Britain.[4]

Norway's cod fishing was primarily confined to coastal waters in the North and West, carried out on smaller boats while in Iceland it was the most important type of fishing all over the country and increasingly operated by trawlers. The fisheries of the two countries had many common features: the small and dispersed units, prominence of small-scale operators, dominance of cod and herring, similar processing methods and dependence on international markets, as more than 80 per cent of the product was exported. With the rapid growth of exports during the interwar period the competition between the two countries intensified, especially in the market for dried and wet salted fish in Southern Europe.

As the fleets expanded and the gear and facilities improved, the two countries became among the leading fishing nations in Europe. By 1930, Norway had become the largest European fish producer, with a total catch exceeding 1.1 million tonnes, and Iceland was one of the fastest growing fishing economies in Europe, sharing the third place with Germany.[5] The interwar Depression was an enormous shock to the North Atlantic fisheries as international demand shrank and prices for salt cod fell by 35–40 per cent. Spain, the world's most important market for salt cod, reduced its fish imports by more than half in the 1930s, causing a major upheaval in Iceland as salt fish exports to Spain had accounted for about half of its fish exports.[6] Norway fared better because its salt-fish exports declined less and a large part of the cod catch was processed as stockfish, which suffered less contraction in demand.

In response to problems in international markets the fishing industry and government in both countries made great efforts to diversify production by developing new processing methods for cod and redfish species and encourage new types of fishing. The Icelandic government founded the Fisheries Industry Board in 1934 to enhance research and development, including the development and promotion of fish-freezing technology. The Board bought a small fish-freezing plant from a pioneer in the field, Espholin, which for many years had been using the Danish Ottesen brine-freezing technique but had lately turned to experiment with the new American technology based on Clarence Birdseye's quick-freezing process.[7] Birdseye's innovation hindered the crystallization which ruptured the cell membranes of food when it was frozen at a slower rate. The plant was renovated

---

4 Jónsson, 2009, 127–51.
5 Tande, 1957, table 3 in appendix.
6 Jónsson, 2009, 127–51.
7 Hannibalsson and Hjaltason, 1997, 20–30.

and turned into a training centre for fish producers around the country. By 1939, about 20 private freezing plants had been established, most of them using this technology. Still, frozen-fish products accounted for only 4 per cent of exports.[8]

Similar developments took place in Norway. Freezing bait-herring had been practised for decades and in 1912 Nekolai Dahl invented a new technique which was adopted by the few freezing plants in operation.[9] The Norwegian Directorate of Fisheries promoted knowledge of new fishing technology and did some experiments on its own. With legislation passed by parliament in 1932 an ambitious plan was launched to establish plants for chilling and freezing fish with financial help from the government. These plans did not materialize due to difficulties in foreign markets, cut-throat competition and widespread protectionism. Moreover, the northern fishing communities were resistant to changes that upset traditional forms of ownership and the character of fishing. By the outbreak of the Second World War only a handful of plants were in operation in Norway and their capacity was mostly confined to the freezing of herring.[10]

Divergent 'Socio-Technical' Paths

The production of frozen fish was given a boost in Iceland and Norway during the Second World War, in both cases as a consequence of foreign occupation. In Iceland, the Allies bought substantial quantities from producers that were mainly exported to Britain while in Norway the Nazi occupation force built four large freezing plants to serve the German civilian population and the army.[11]

It was only after the war that the fish-freezing sector took off, but the two countries took different paths. In Iceland, industrial fishing and processing was rapidly spreading with the expansion of the trawler fleet and establishment of large processing plants. Producers believed that future markets would lie primarily in the emerging frozen-fish market in America, as the traditional market in Britain for fish packed in ice was difficult and there were no signs of a quick recovery in the salt-fish markets in Southern Europe. The advance of the new technology was slower in Norway despite government efforts to modernize the fisheries in the North in line with its North Regional Policy. Small-boat fishery and manual processing methods continued to dominate the fisheries sector at least into the early 1960s, and production was mainly geared to traditional markets for klipfish and stockfish.

These divergent 'socio-technical' paths to modernity were shaped by complex topographical, economic and social factors.[12] The richest fishing grounds for cod

---

8   Sigurjónsson, 1945, 82–5; *Verzlunarskýrslur Íslands* 1939.

9   Hannibalsson and Hjaltason, 1997, 38.

10   Finstad, 1999, 89–105; Finstad, 2004, 27–41; Hannibalsson and Hjaltason, 1997, 38–41.

11   Finstad, 2004, 27–41.

12   Sverrisson, 2002, 227–253; Jónsson, 2009, 127–51.

in Norway were in the shallow waters off the coast, so fishermen did not have the same incentive to engage in deep-sea fishing as their Icelandic counterparts. The family household economy was more firmly rooted in Norway where fishing was conducted in fairly small boats owned mainly by the fishermen themselves who sold their catch to the processors. The fish-freezing process, however, required large quantities of fish to provide the freezing plants with sufficient raw material throughout the year. If the fisheries sector were to develop along similar lines as in Iceland, a co-ordinated sales and transport system was required, based on the economies of scale and a market-mediated information system.

The resistance to large-scale fishing was so strong that the parliament passed a law in 1936 to limit the number of trawlers to the seven or eight currently in operation in West Norway (Vestlandet).[13] The catch had to be used only for salted fish or klipfish. The ban on expansion of the trawler fleet was reaffirmed in 1939, when the limit on trawlers raised to eleven, and the law remained in effect until 1951. Another factor in delaying the rise of the fish-freezing industry was the relatively favourable market position of Norway compared to Iceland. Norway was neither as pressed as Iceland to find new outlets for its production since it retained dominance in the stockfish market, nor was the pressure as great to strive for high-efficiency in the fisheries sector since the relative size of its fisheries in the overall economy was much smaller. Given the importance of the fisheries in the overall economy of Iceland it was vital to operate them as an efficient and profitable activity. Furthermore, when designing a new fisheries policy after the war, the Norwegians were discouraged by what they saw as a competitive advantage of Icelandic producers being geographically closer to the American market.

Resistance to trawl fishing was never as strong in Iceland as Norway.[14] The trawler industry grew rapidly in the first decades of the century and led to widespread economic, social and political changes. As a large-scale, capital-intensive operation, trawl fishing was concentrated in the hands of few wealthy companies while the fishermen became wage-earners. Social and economic conditions for the rise of freezing technology were thus much more favourable than in Norway. When the market for frozen foods took off in America soon after the Second World War, Icelandic producers were in a relatively good position to seize the opportunity.

A 'Relentless pursuit of convenience': The Rise of the American Market for Frozen Fish

American food culture was increasingly leaning towards homogeneity shaped by mass production and the national advertising business. The homogenization of food consumption had been encouraged during the war with military rations and

---

13   Tande, 1957, 82–8; Christensen, 1991, 622–624; Hodne, 1983, 79–80.
14   Jónsson, 2009, 127–51.

meals designed for storage longevity and ease of preparation.[15] The 'relentless pursuit of convenience', as the *Fortune* magazine described the trend,[16] continued after the war, with processors designing strategies of mass marketing, new menus and new products that were to be nutritious and easy-to-prepare. According to the marketeers, convenience food provided the good life at low cost and emancipated housewives from the drudgery of cooking routines. Standardization and hygienic control were an integrated part of the shift towards convenience foods as exemplified by the fast-growing chain restaurants; eating out at McDonald's became good clean fun.[17]

Frozen foods were part of this new world of convenience food, but it was not until General Foods, who owned the Birds Eye trademark, introduced the fish finger in 1953, that the market for frozen fish significantly expanded. Other Massachusetts' companies, Fulham Brothers and Gorton's, entered the fish-finger business at about the same time.[18] The fish finger was a rectangle (about 7.5 cm × 2.5 cm), band-sawed from a frozen-fish block, breaded, quick-boiled or fried and then frozen, ready to be fried or heated in the oven. The greatest attribute of the new product, hailed as 'the most outstanding event' in seafood since the early 1930s, was its time-saving quality as its promoters proudly announced: 'No actual cooking is required'.[19] Manufacturers also stressed the wholesomeness and even the great taste of the product! In addition to the big users such as restaurants, hotels and schools, the most important outlet for frozen fish was the supermarket, one of the great novelties in shopping in the 1950s. It had a special frozen-food section in which individual companies had their own freezer cabinets.

The American fisheries were far from meeting the demand as the market for frozen cod and related species rapidly expanded and domestic production declined from 72 per cent of the total supply in 1948 to 7.4 per cent in 1975.[20] The American market had an enormous potential for fish importers. The response to the dramatic increase in demand for cod and other demersal fish was the development of factory freezer-trawlers in the mid-1950s, primarily operating off the coast of Newfoundland. These ships were basically floating factories which were able to process more than 500 tons a day. Britain was the first among North Atlantic fishing nations to make use of factory trawlers, soon followed by Canada and other countries. A new fishery was born, based on distant water 'fleets', with enormous production potential. In the 1950s and 1960s offshore fishing grounds east of Newfoundland were discovered, leading to a dramatic increase in annual landings; over 800,000 tons were reported by the mid-1960s, accounting for 40 per cent of the global catch.[21]

---

15   Josephson, 2008, 41–61.
16   Quotation from Levenstein, 1993, 101.
17   Hamilton, 2003, 33–60; Josephson, 2008, 41–61.
18   Josephson, 2008, 41–61.
19   Josephson, 2008, 41–61.
20   Garðarsson, 1976, 18.
21   Standal, 2008, 326–32; Cudmore, 2009, 59.

Canadian producers had a clear lead in the American frozen-fish market in the 1950s and 1960s. Iceland entered the market very early and was the second biggest importer, followed by Norway which belatedly shifted to the production of frozen products in the late 1960s.

The Success of the Frozen-Fish Industry in Iceland

The most important factor in pushing Icelandic fishing firms further into quick freezing after the war were changes in the international markets. European markets for dry salted cod were still subdued and bilateralism and protectionist policies in importing countries made it difficult for Icelanders to increase their sales significantly. Furthermore, the traditional British market for fresh fish packed in ice was closed between 1952 and 1956 as a result of an imports ban imposed on Icelandic fish because of a fishing dispute between Iceland and Great Britain over the extension of the fishery limit to 4 miles. Immediately after the war Icelandic producers made serious efforts to sell frozen fish on the Continent but markets there were fraught with difficulties, including the lack of distribution chains and storage for frozen goods.

Two potentially huge markets opened up for Icelandic frozen fish during the 1950s which were to have a lasting effect on the development of the fishing industry. One was the Russian market, with a breakthrough bilateral agreement between Iceland and the Soviet Union in 1953 entailing the sale of large quantities of frozen fillets of cod and redfish. The other was the USA, where Icelandic producers had been selling frozen fish on a small scale since 1936 though with a break during the war.[22] The American market was certainly more lucrative than the Russian one but demanded elaborate sets of labour skills, high quality standardized products and 'modern' marketing. This was foreign to Icelandic producers who were now entering a new and highly dynamic market and going much further into the retailing end of the market than they had done before.

The shift from salt fish to frozen-fish production was a major turning point in the development of Icelandic fisheries. It was certainly fraught with various, technological, organizational and political problems but it proved successful in the long term, bringing the fishing industry to a higher level of productivity with the use of advanced technology and sophisticated marketing methods. Iceland was one of the first European countries to take advantage of American freezing technology and develop it successfully. By 1960 freezing had become the most important processing method in the Icelandic fisheries and, as Table 10.1 shows, exports accounted for more than a third of total export value.

One of the factors contributing to the success of the Icelandic frozen-fish sector in America was *receptiveness to new technology*. The government, in collaboration with fish producers, had started developing quick-freezing methods already in the

---

22   Sigurjónsson, 1945, 90–93.

Table 10.1   The frozen-fish industry in Iceland, 1939–1970

	1939	1950	1960	1970
Number of processing plants	31	72	85	96
Exports of frozen demersal fish, ('000 tons)	2	19	64	81
Share of total export value (%)	4	19	35	35
Exports of frozen demersal fish to USA, ('000 tons)	0	7	18	57
Share of total export value (%)	0	8	12	26

Note: This table only includes demersal fish products. Other less valuable frozen marine products include herring and capelin, fish roe, shrimp and lobster.

Sources: Verzlunarskýrslur Íslands 1939–1970; *Ægir* XXV-LXIV (1942–1971).

mid-1930s and in the following years freezing plants were established using the new technology in an efficient way. The early adoption of the freezing technology gave Icelandic producers a head start over other potential fish importers in the USA when the market started to grow after the war. A second factor was the *cartelization of the exports of frozen fish to America* as sales were licensed by government to only two sales organizations. The bigger one, *Sölumiðstöð hraðfrystihúsanna*, comprised dozens of privately run freezing plants, and played a leading role in the American market, establishing a stockholding company in America, Coldwater Seafood Corporation, to operate the sales and fish processing plants. The other company, Iceland Products Ltd, was owned by the Federation of Co-operatives in Iceland, and operated in similar fashion as Coldwater.[23] The duopoly gave these organizations an extremely strong position in production as well as the market, ensuring a steady supply base, effectively excluding competition on the production side, and handing them strong production management control vis-à-vis the freezing plants. In the early years the two organizations rarely competed with each other in the American market, but that was to change in the 1960s.

The two companies had raw material of good quality at their disposal but the main challenge was to develop products that would meet the standards set by the most demanding consumers in the world. Big investment was put into *product development and quality control* which from early on gave the Icelandic products a reputable name. In the beginning, Icelandic freezing plants were much inferior to American ones in terms of technical sophistication and quality control. In response a two-tier system of quality control was set up after the war, on the one hand a public inspectorate and on the other a quality control system run by the sales organizations and the processing plants.[24] The head start that Icelandic importers gained in America gave them time to upgrade their products: learning occurred initially by imitating their competitors' products but increasingly in the

23   Hannibalsson and Hjaltason, 1997, 182.
24   Hannibalsson and Hjaltason, 1997, 162.

production process itself. Technological advancements were mostly restricted to the well-known technology of pan-freezing and incremental modifications of the filleting process. The learning process was focused on increasing the manual processing skills of the workforce through organizational measures as well as acquiring a better understanding of the microbiological aspects of the product's deterioration process. The main effort was placed on supplying large quantities of standardized products of acceptable quality for the retail trade and institutional buyers in America, and that required the labour-intensive process of trimming the fillets and removing bones.

The two principal products were fish blocks and fillets whose high quality enabled the sales organization to sell an increasing share of the production under their own trademarks, Coldwater using ICELANDIC BRAND (earlier ICELANDIC and FROZEN FISH) and Iceland Seafood the SAMBA trademark. As a result Icelandic fish products, especially the fillets, fetched considerably higher prices than the products of their main competitors, the Canadians.[25] In the immediate postwar period Icelandic fish producers targeted their sales primarily at the US army, selling the fish in unsophisticated packages used for the European market, that is, 7 lb fish blocks (with bones) wrapped in pergament (parchment). The next product was more advanced: ready-to-use boneless cod and haddock fillets in 1 lb colourful boxes, followed by skinned fillets in cellophane in 5 lb and 10 lb boxes. This imitated their competitors' most advanced products but with the novelty of removing all bones in the fillet, thus giving Icelandic fish an advantage: it kept for a long time. The Icelandic companies had closely followed the development of fish-finger production in America in 1952–1953 and already in February 1953 the first fish blocks aimed for the American fish-finger factories were exported from Iceland. In the following year Coldwater set up its own processing factory in Maryland to produce fish fingers and other frozen products. The fish block became the dominant product of the freezing plants in Iceland, although the sales organizations pressed them to increase the more valuable, albeit more labour-intensive, fillet production. In the 1960s fillets gradually became more prominent as fish fingers became less popular, but there was a setback in sales after 1965. This reached a critical stage in 1967 when the papal ban on eating meat on Fridays was lifted, which caused a fall in demand and in the prices of frozen fish. A sudden turn of fortune came in 1968 when fish-and-chip restaurant chains started to mushroom and Icelandic frozen fillets were well suited to the requirements of fish-and-chip shops.[26] Another outlet for frozen white fish opened with the advent of the Filet-O-Fish sandwich, first introduced at a McDonald's

---

25 Hannibalsson Hjaltason, 1997, 124; Garðarsson, 1967, 27–9.

26 Einarsson, Hannibalsson and Hjaltason, 1997, 78–9. Another, and perhaps a more plausible explanation for the slump of 1966–1967, was a price war between Danish firms trying to improve their position in the US market, cf. *Ægir,* 1968, 19–20.

hamburger restaurant in the Cincinnati area in 1962 and which became popular among the predominantly catholic clientele.[27]

Marketing and Sales Strategies

The strategies adopted by the two sales organizations proved to be effective in terms of turnover and prices after an initial stage of trial and error. Modelled on Canadian sales techniques the two companies set up a network of brokers nationwide who managed most of the sales to distributors and retailers on commission. The brokers monitored changes in taste and preferences which were reported back to the firms.[28] Fillets were sold from the Icelandic processing plants through the two companies to institutional buyers and bigger users such as hotels, restaurants and schools. Attempts to go deeper into the retail market by selling ready-made products targeting housewives gave mixed results; for example, the boiled fish with melted butter was a failure while the 12 ounce 'steak', packaged in a box of four, proved quite popular. By 1961, about 65 per cent of Coldwater's production was sold to institutional buyers and 35 per cent to smaller retailers as ready-to-use products.[29] Fish blocks were used in the companies' fish-finger plants.[30]

Political Support for the Nascent Frozen-Fish Industry

This political support was vital for its survival in America. The frozen-fish export market was celebrated as the most important growth sector of the economy and the Icelandic government was therefore ready to support it in various ways. With prices falling as fish production resumed in Europe after the war legislation was passed in the Icelandic parliament guaranteeing minimum prices for exports of frozen fish to the USA between 1946 and 1949.[31] Even more important was the US government's assistance to Icelandic fish importers. When the Russians stopped trading with Iceland in 1948, the US government, eager to maintain good political relations with Iceland because of its military-strategic interests, decided to assist exports of frozen fish from Iceland to West Germany through the Marshall Aid programme.[32] That same year American fishermen, referring to US laws, made demands on the US government to impose import duties on fish imports by 10–15 per cent from countries where the fishing industry enjoyed state support. The US government was not ready to jeopardize its political and strategic interests in

27 *USA Today,* 20 February 2007.
28 Hannibalsson and Hjaltason, 1997, 123–4.
29 Einarsson, Hannibalsson and Hjaltason, 1997, 58.
30 Hannibalsson and Hjaltason, 1997, 162.
31 Hannibalsson and Hjaltason, 1997, 123.
32 Ásgeirsson, 1955, 61–70; Landsbanki Íslands, 1948, 68.

Iceland and the case was dismissed.[33] The issue re-emerged in 1954–1956 and was only resolved after an intervention by the US president, who rejected levying import duties on 'friendly nations whose economic strength is vitally important for our continuing fight against the dangers of world communism.'[34] Thus, Iceland's strategic importance during the Cold War became a major economic asset which the Icelandic government exploited to promote Icelandic trade with both the USA and the USSR. The duty-free access of frozen fish gave Icelandic importers a significant competitive advantage over their competitors, most importantly the Canadians and the Norwegians, both of whom gave state support to their fisheries.

The Controversial Path towards Industrial Fishing in Norway

Great efforts were made in Norway after the war to modernize the economy under the guidance of the state. One of the big modernization schemes in the fisheries sector was the 'Finotro Plan' of 1948, a bold government effort to promote the freezing technology in Finnmark in North Norway by setting up big processing plants, owned and run by the state, and supplied by smaller vessels owned by the fishermen. The plan enjoyed the firm support of the fishermen in Finmark since the idea was to exclude private fish merchants and trawl fishing from the new sector so as not to upset the existing social structure in the fishery. But the plan was only partly realized: the Finotro company built only seven of the twelve proposed plants whereas a big private company, Findus, established itself in the town of Hammerfest and relied solely on supplies from trawlers. These two companies dominated the frozen-fish sector in Finnmark in the 1950s, buying about 40 per cent of all catches by 1960.

North Norway, including Finnmark, became the main area for the fish-freezing sector after the war. But for a number of reasons the large-scale, capital-intensive fishery focused on trawl fishing and frozen fish developed only slowly. Despite massive subsidies from the state the industry was marred by financial problems and Finotro turned in losses for most years during its 35 years in operation.[35] The pressure to modernize was diminished by the fact that the Norwegian fisheries retained a leading position in the international stockfish market so the fishery in the North stuck to old processing methods: more than two-thirds of cod landings were turned into stockfish in Finnmark as late as 1960. The frozen-fish industry also had supply problems as it became clear that the inshore fleet was unable to provide steady supplies of fish for fillet production.[36] Lastly, there was resistance to change within the dominant Labour Party, which exerted great influence on the operation of Finotro and fisheries policy in general. Skirmishes between the

33   Ingimundarson, 1996, 286.
34   Ingimundarson, 1996, 288; See also Hannibalsson and Hjaltason, 1997, 126–8.
35   Finstad, 2004, 27–41.
36   Finstad, 2004, 31–8.

'modernizers' and the 'traditionalists' continued throughout the 1950s and 1960s and the controversy gained a new lease of the life in the early 1970s when the entry into the EEC was debated. Still, the fisheries were gradually liberalized as indicated by the lifting of the ban on the expansion of trawl fishing in 1951. This resulted in a steep rise in the number of trawlers, an increase in fish catches and a greatly expanded capacity of the freezing industry in Norway.

A change in fisheries policy in 1960 endorsed large-scale fishing and industrial fish processing, reflecting not only changes in the political landscape but the growing importance of deep-water fishing in Norway. When the most important market for stockfish nearly collapsed with the outbreak of civil war in Nigeria in 1967, a surge in frozen-fish production occurred. Exports of frozen fillets rose from 7,000 tons in 1953 to 26,000 tons in 1960, and peaked at 126,000 tons in 1970. The 1970s and 1980s were marked by overfishing and increasing difficulties in the fisheries leading to a full-blown crisis at the end of the 1980s. The policy response was deregulation and a radical restructuring of the fishing industry.[37]

From 1946 the export of frozen fish, like other branches of fish exports, was carried out by a state sanctioned monopoly, Frionor (Norsk Frossenfisk A/L), which in the 1960s was supplemented by two competing organizations, the multinational company Nestlé in Hammerfest (under the label Findus) and the Nordic Group.[38] Frionor's exports were geographically spread, focusing its marketing on the European continent, in particular Switzerland and Holland. In 1949 the company established a sales office in the USA, under the name Norwegian Frozen Fish Ltd, but only slowly gained a foothold on the US market. In 1956 Frionor opened a fish-finger factory in the USA, taking a similar path as the Icelandic companies. In the late 1960s imports of Norwegian frozen-fish blocks and fillets soared in the US frozen-fish market, accounting for 14 per cent in the early 1970s, and only exceeded by Canada (31 per cent) and Iceland (20 per cent).[39] Norway had established itself as a major player in the US market for frozen fish.

Conclusion

The advent of the fish finger and other frozen-fish products was an important novelty in the food history of the postwar period. Although Birdseye's invention was a crucial breakthrough it was only a link in a long chain of technological, economic, social and cultural factors creating a new type of production and consumption. On the supply side the new freezing technology initiated changes in production, distribution and preservation of fish in the interwar period; whereas the socioeconomic preconditions for a comprehensive change in demand materialized only in the late 1940s and 1950s in America with the convergence of standardized

---

37   Historisk statistikk, 1978, 291, 314–18; Finstad, 2004, 27–41.
38   Tande, 1957, 238–9; Hersoug and Arbo, 1997, 121–42; Finstad, 1999, 89–105.
39   Garðarsson, 1976, 18.

industrial processing, consumerism and mass marketing. These changes were facilitated by other technological achievements symbolized most clearly by the car and the refrigerator. The introduction of quick freezing was a turning point in the development of the fisheries sectors of Iceland and Norway. In Iceland, the frozen-fish export market became the fastest growing sector of the economy in the 1950s and the 1960s, transforming production and organization and, most spectacularly, the marketing side of the industry. It did not create as much controversy as in Norway, mainly because large-scale fishing had become an acceptable mode of production when the freezing technology was introduced. In Norway, industrial fishing developed later for topographical, economic and social reasons and was mostly confined to the regions of the North. Since the traditional character of the fisheries had been better preserved, the new industrial form of fishing was much more disruptive.

Finding markets and establishing a system of distribution for frozen fish was a major challenge to Icelandic and Norwegian fish producers. Icelandic firms entered the US market remarkably early which allowed them to move relatively quickly from a stage of imitation to a more innovative phase in terms of marketing and product development. Norway was later to advance on this market but as a result of waning resistance to industrial fishing and shrinking markets for traditionally processed fish, especially stockfish, production quickly shifted to frozen fish.

References

Ásgeirsson, Þ., 1955, 'Efnahagsaðstoðin 1948–1953' [Marshall Aid, 1948–1953], Fjármálatíðindi May–June:2.
Christensen, P., 1991, '"En havenes forpester – et kjempestinkdyr". Om trålspørsmålet i Norge før 2. verdenskrig' ["The Oceans' Polluter – A Huge Skunk". On the Trawler Problem in Norway before the Second World War], in Historisk tidsskrift no. 4.
Cudmore, W.W., 2009, The Decline of Atlantic Cod. A Case Study, Salem: Northwest Center for Sustainable Resources Series, http://www.ncsr.org/Downloads/fisheriesatlanticcod.pdf
Einarsson, H., Hannibalsson, Ó. and Hjaltason, J., 1997. Sölumiðstöð hraðfrystihúsanna. Yfir lönd yfir höf. Saga dótturfyrirtækja SH erlendis 1942–1996 III [Icelandic Freezing Plants Corporation, Across Land and Sea. The History of Its Subsidiaries Abroad, 1942–1996], Reykjavík: Hið íslenska bókmenntafélag.
Eydal, Á., 1948, Silfur hafsins [Silver of the Sea], Reykjavík: Helgafell.
Finstad, B.-P., 1998, 'Modernizing the Fishing: Regional Fisheries Policy in Northern Norway, 1945–1970', in Holm, P. and Starkey, D.J., eds, North Atlantic Fisheries. Markets and Modernization, Esbjerg: Studia Atlantica, 179–90.

Finstad, B.-P., 1999, 'Freezing technology in the Norwegian Fish Processing Industry, 1930–1960', in Holm, P. and Starkey, D.J., eds, *Technological Change in the North Atlantic Fisheries* 3, Esbjerg: Studia Atlantica.

Finstad, B.-P., 2004, 'The Frozen Fillet: The Fish that Changed North Norway?', *International Journal of Maritime History*, XVI:1.

Fishery Policies in Western Europe and North America, Paris: OEEC, 1960.

Garðarsson, G.H., 1967, *'Bandaríkin eru aðalmarkaður Íslendinga fyrir frystar fiskafurðir'* [The USA is Our Principal Market], *Frjáls verzlun*, 27:1, 1.

Garðarsson, G.H., 1976, *'Ísland og bandaríski fiskmarkaðurinn'* [Iceland and the US Frozen Fish Market], *Morgunblaðið*, 18, 14.

Hagskinna. Icelandic Historical Statistics, 1997, edited by G. Jónsson and M.S. Magnússon, Reykjavík: Statistics Iceland.

Hamilton, S., 2003, 'The Economies and Conveniences of Modern-Day Living: Frozen Foods and Mass Marketing,1945–1965', *Business History Review*, 77:1.

Hannibalsson, Ó. and Hjaltason, J., 1997, *Sölumiðstöð hraðfrystihúsanna í 50 ár II. Með sprikið í sporðinum. Saga SH 1942–1996* [Icelandic Freezing Plants Corporation in 50 Years. With the Wiggle in the Tail. The History of the IFPC 1942–1996], Reykjavík: Hið íslenska bókmenntafélag.

Hersoug, B. and Arbo, P., 1997, 'The globalization of the fishing industry and the case of Finnmark', *Marine Policy*, 21:2.

Historisk statistikk 1978, 1978, *Norges offisielle statistikk XII 291*, Oslo: Statistisk sentralbyrå.

Hodne, F., 1983, *The Norwegian Economy 1920–1980*, London: Croom Helm.

Ingimundarson, V., 1960, *Í eldlínu kalda stríðsins. Samskipti Íslands og Bandaríkjanna 1945–1960* [In the Crossfire: Iceland, the United States, and the Cold War, 1945–1960], Reykjavík: Vaka–Helgafell.

Jóhannesson, G.T., 2003,'Troubled Waters. Cod War, Fishing Disputes and Britain's Fight for the Freedom of the High Seas, 1948–1964', Ph.D. thesis, Queen Mary College, University of London.

Jónsson, G., 2009, 'Fishing Nations in Crisis: The Responses of the Icelandic and Norwegian Fisheries to the Great Depression', *International Journal of Maritime History* XXI:1.

Josephson, P., 2008, 'The Ocean's Hot Dog. The Development of the Fish Stick', *Technology and Culture* 49.

Landsbanki Íslands, 1948, Ársskýrsla [National Bank of Iceland. Annual Report], Reykjavik.

Levenstein, H., 1993, *Paradox of Plenty. A Social History of Eating in Modern America*, New York, University of Califor28 Press.

Sigurjónsson, A., 1945, *Fiskimálanefnd. Skýrsla tíu ára 1934–1944* [The Fisheries Industry Board. A Decennial Report, 1934–1944], Reykjavík: Fiskimálanefnd.

Standal, D., 2008, 'The rise and fall of factory trawlers: An eclectic approach', *Marine Policy*, 32.

Sverrisson, Á., 2002, 'Small Boats and Large Ships. Social Continuity and Technical Change in the Icelandic Fisheries, 1800–1960', *Technology and Culture*, 43.

Tande, T., 1957, *Norsk fiskeripolitikk. En analyse av fiskerinæringens utvikling siden 1920* [Norwegian Fisheries Policy. An Analysis of the Fisheries Development Since 1920], Oslo, Studieselskapet samfunn og næringsliv.

Teuteberg, H.-J., 1995, 'History of Cooling and Freezing Techniques and their Impact on Nutrition in Twentieth-Century Germany', in ICREFH III: Hartog, A.P. den, ed., *Food Technology, Science and Marketing. European Diet in the Twentieth Century*, East Linton, Tuckwell Press.

USA Today, 20 February 2007: http://www.usatoday.com/money/industries/food/2007-02-20-fish2-usat_x.htm

Verzlunarskýrslur Íslands [Icelandic Trade Statistics] 1939–1971, Reykjavík, Statistics Iceland.

Yearbook of Fishery Statistics 1952–1953, 1955, IV:1, Rome, Food and Agiculture Organization of the United Nations.

Ægir [The Sea (a fisheries magazine)], 1942–1971, XXV–LXIV.

PART III
The Effect of Food Technology on Consumption Patterns

PART III

Chapter 11

Food Labelling and Packaging in the Dutch Food Industry: Persuading and Informing Consumers, 1870–1950s

Adel P. den Hartog

Introduction

The rise of modern food labelling and food packaging have been inextricably bound up with each other since 1810 when Nicolas Appert invented a method for preserving food in sealed glass jars. The initial important advance was the adaption of Appert's method to tinplated cans by Peter Durand in England. By 1814 Durand's patent was operated by the firm of Bryan Donkin and John Hall in Bermondsey, London, to supply vegetable soups and preserved meat to the Royal Navy in tinned canisters.[1] Most food was sold loose and buyers could directly see and feel what they wanted to buy. With packaged food the situation became different; buyers had to be informed in one way or another of its content. Food producers and traders started to affix labels on the packaging indicating the generic name of the product and the firm's name. Food labelling has two essential functions: the promotional function stressing how good and unique the product is, and an informative function indicating the kind of food and its ingredients.

At present in Europe fierce discussions are going on amongst consumer organizations as to what should be shown on food labels. The core of the discussion is that consumers have the right to know the precise nature of the food product and its content. The information should be indicated in such a way that it will enable consumers to make healthy food choices. In several European countries healthy choice logos were developed for this purpose, often joint efforts between producers, nutritionists and sometimes consumer organizations. In the Netherlands the Smart Choice Logo was introduced in 2006.[2]

This study examines the origins of modern food labelling, and addresses questions relating to the changing functions of food labels and the concerned interests of manufacturers, authorities and consumers. The analysis is directed at the situation in the Netherlands, but other countries are also taken into account. The focus is on the long enduring tension between what manufactures would like

---

1   Morris, 1958, 39.
2   Stasse-Wolthuis, 2009.

to state on a food label and the interests of public health. A food label is a small piece of paper or some other material with information on the food product affixed to the packaging. The food label can also be an integral part of the packaging itself. A major source used for this chapter is the popular-science weekly *Food and Hygiene*.[3]

Preindustrial Europe

In Europe before the industrial revolution foodstuffs were sold unpackaged. In towns people had to take their own containers to shops or market stalls. Labelling as such was not unknown but was confined to wholesalers' large containers such as wooden beer barrels and wine casks where the name or mark of the producers was burned onto the container. In Dutch towns after 1500, brewers were only allowed to supply beer in approved barrels provided with a town's brand mark.[4] From archaeological research on a Dutch East India Company ship which sank in 1743 near the Scilly Islands, wine bottles have been found as part of the victuals. The bottles had been sealed with a mark of the supplier.[5] Wine bottles were probably the first containers provided with a paper label (hand written) fixed upon the bottle.

Early-Modern Food Labelling and Packaging

In the first half of the nineteenth century food was sold loose in grocery shops. Customers took their own containers for products like butter and syrup. A description of a small Dutch grocery shop for low-income families in 1841 explained how the grocer mixed the sugar with some flour, and diluted Dutch gin with a little water before the arrival of customers.

The grocery was known to be inexpensive, but the rumour went round that it was due to cheating by volume and weight.[6] In the second half of the nineteenth century a new phenomenon began to enter grocery shops; packaged food products and their trade marks. Packaged food has a number of advantages when compared with selling loose products, provided an adequate food law and functioning control system is available. Packaging protects the content during transport and storage: it is more hygienic and protects the food from deterioration due to contact with air, light and heat, and may also serve as a convenient container at household level for measuring exact quantities.[7]

---

3   *Voeding en Hygiëne*, 1, 1926, 44. The journal had a close link with the Amsterdam Commodity Inspection Department.

4   Yntema, 1994, 90–93.

5   Gawronski, 1996, 263.

6   Van den Berg, 1841, 177–8.

7   Den Hartog, 1998, 249–50.

Source: Hasebroek et al, 1841.

Figure 11.1 A grocery shop in 1841

For a long time the price of materials for food packaging, such as tin plate, glass and, to a lesser extent, paper remained high and was often more costly than the food itself. The invention of lithography in 1798 by Senefelder and subsequent improvements made it possible to print coloured-paper food labels or to print labels directly on the tin can at relatively low costs.[8] Tin cans in the nineteenth century were largely confined to more luxurious products; coffee, tea and biscuits. The tin cans and boxes were beautifully decorated by lithographic printing and are now collector's items. The empty containers could be re-used at household level or returned to the grocery shop. In the second half of the nineteenth century the use of tin cans increased with the development of condensed milk, preserved meat and vegetables. Pioneering firms in condensing milk were the American New York Condensed Milk Company (1860) and the Anglo-Swiss Condensed Milk Company (1866) in Switzerland.[9] Based on the Swiss success, the Dutch firm NV Hollandia (1882) started condensing milk, mainly for export. In the 1870s the Dutch food industry began to preserve vegetables and meat in tin cans.[10]

The tin cans of less luxurious products, condensed milk, meat and vegetables were provided with paper labels and not printed on the can itself. The reason for this is not known, but printed paper labels were probably less expensive than printing labels on disposable tin cans. Only few of the disposable tin cans and their

---

8   Clark, 1977, 23.
9   Heer, 1991, 62–3.
10   Vijfvinkel, 1995, 35–7.

HOLLANDIA-VLAARDINGEN

Figure 11.2   An advertisement for tinned sterilized full-cream milk, 1930

paper labels are now to be found in industrial museums or in private collections.[11] Packaging of food products and affixing of labels was a labour-intensive process mainly done by women and girls whose labour was cheaper than that of men. According to many an employer a woman's hands were more suited to perform delicate work and women accepted monotonous work more readily than men.[12] An improvement in the beginning of the twentieth century was the filling machine. A female worker placed the empty container in the machine and by means of a handle the container was accurately filled with the required quantity. Gradually, integrated wrapping and packaging machines replaced the labour-intensive work of food labelling. Mass production of cheap glass containers became possible with the invention by M. J. Owen in the USA (1904) of a fully automatic machine for producing both jars and bottles, replacing the Ashley-semi automatic machine (1887).[13] With the rise of packaged food, opportunities for food adulteration gradually shifted from the grocery to food manufacturers and traders. Important early packaged food products were tinned vegetables, jams in glass containers, butter and margarine wrapped in paper, luxury products such as biscuits in cartons, boxes or tins, and wrapped chocolate bars. At the end of the nineteenth century coffee-roasters and tea packers gradually started to sell some of their products in paper bags provided with their brand name.[14] Beer bottling started in the 1870s but

---

11   Clark, 1977, 68; Simon Thomas and van de Weg, 2010, 142.

12   Schrover, 1993, 32.

13   Lief, 1965, 23–4; Douglas, 1978, 580–82.

14   John Horniman began to sell tea in packets in London as early as 1826, but mass-produced sales in packets date from 1884 when Mazawattee tea was introduced, followed by Lipton, Lyons and The Maypole Dairy. See Burnett, 1989, 126.

not all breweries did so. Until 1930 the Amstel Brewery had a number of agents, who bottled the beer from the barrel into swing-top bottles. Labels of the brewery with the name of the agent were affixed by hand on the bottle. Some public houses preferred bottles as they could be chilled more easily compared to the beer barrel.[15]

Paper labels remained rather expensive until the beginning of the nineteenth century. They were printed by hand with wooden presses on hand-made paper. Two inventions were a prerequisite for mass production of labels and paper wrapping: the production of cheap paper and as already mentioned, efficient printing techniques.[16] Paper was expensive, even with new paper-making techniques because it was made from rags. In 1866 the brothers Tighlman in the USA managed to make good quality paper from wood as the raw material. From then on paper-making techniques were further improved, making paper a relatively cheap material for packaging and labels.[17]

The early food labels gave scanty information: often no more than the generic name of the product such as beans, green peas or strawberry jam and the name of the manufacturer. Gradually food labels acquired a number of functions; the brand name, stating the content, instructions for use and, most importantly for the manufacturer, the label was a means to attract the consumer. The gradual acceptance of the concept of hygiene amongst consumers made hygienic packaging an important item in food advertising in the first half of the twentieth century.[18] Very specific for the development of modern packaging was the increasing emphasis on packaging and labelling as a means to sell. Some firms contracted well-known artists to design posters and, to a lesser extent, the labels of their products.

Labelling and Food Adulteration

In the absence of a National Food Law until 1919, manufacturers could put nearly any thing on their labels that they considered to be useful. The liberal ideology of the free market prevailed in the Netherlands from 1848 till the outbreak of the First World War in 1914. The buyer was considered to be the best tester and needed no governmental support. In the period before the French Revolution, food quality in the Netherlands and other European countries was controlled to some degree by the guilds and town councils. With the final dissolution of the guilds in the Netherlands in 1818, food control largely disappeared. The Penal Code of 1810, inherited from the French administration (1810–1813), forbade adulteration of food and drink. However, in practical terms, the provisions of the Code were not effective because of the absence of a food control system. The addition to the law in 1829 that adulteration with toxic or harmful substances was liable

---

15 Zwaal and de Brock, 2010, 26, 30.
16 Opie, 2001, 8–9.
17 De Wit, 1993, 214.
18 Den Hartog, 1995.

for punishment had no practical effect. In the nineteenth century the population and, in particular, the poorer classes were subject to fraud and shady dealings of unscrupulous food manufacturers and traders.[19] Neighbouring countries such as France (1851), the United Kingdom (1875), Germany and Belgium (1879) were more advanced with their food regulations. Nevertheless the nineteenth-century food laws of other European countries were far from being perfect and much had to be done to reduce food fraud.[20] The prevailing liberal ideology in the Netherlands obstructed initiatives to implement an effective food law at national level.

The city of Amsterdam started its own modest food-control system to combat food adulteration in 1858, but it failed because of the absence of a laboratory to test products. Nasty examples in the 1850s and 60s included, amongst others, sweets coloured red from vermillion or using green colorants containing arsenic.[21] The inadequacy of the Food Law of 1829 can be illustrated by the case of a fruit-juice supplier in 1881. The label on the bottle indicated 9.4 per cent of fruit extract. After laboratory testing the fruit content proved to be only 3 per cent. The food supplier was taken to court but acquitted because the extra water added was not a strange component and the fruit juice as such was not a threat to public health.[22] At the end of the nineteenth century some local authorities created municipal and provincial Commodity Inspection Departments. Of great importance was the provision of food-control laboratories in these departments. The newly established local food-control systems such as in Rotterdam became effective in combating food fraud. In 1893, 70 per cent of milk samples (43) showed that the milk was adulterated. Many other samples taken showed that products such as chocolate, fruit syrups, coffee, and redcurrant wine were often diluted with other substances. In 1902, a wine merchant sold an alcoholic drink in bottles with 'Port a Port' on the label. The product had nothing to do with port wine and the merchant was fined for fraud and promised never to do so again.[23] In the meantime, at the expense of financially weak consumers, unscrupulous firms shifted their attention to smaller towns and rural areas where food control was still absent.[24]

Consumers as well as bona fide food manufacturers were confronted with two major issues; adulteration as such and fraud with food labels and brand names. In 1860 the city council of Amsterdam advised shopkeepers to use the generic name 'flour' on their packaging. Without any mention of wheat flour or rice flour on the package the client had no juridical basis to take action in case of an inferior product. A flour mill in Utrecht aiming to prevent deception affixed enlarged labels on their packaged products, so customers could easily note it was a

19   Laan,van der, 1951, 312–17.
20   Hierholzer, 2007; Oddy, 2007; Scholliers, 2007; Teuteberg, 1994.
21   Bakker, 1992, 270.
22   Laan, van der, 1951, 317.
23   Boddaert, 1993, 4, 12–13, 32.
24   Vleesenbeek, 1995, 11.

genuine product.[25] Fraudulent manufacturers and merchants utilized already-used containers from well-known firms to package their own inferior products. Beer and wine bottles, jars, and bulk packaging such as beer and butter barrels were re-used and wrongfully provided with the original branded labels. In the 1870s some firms began to protect their good name by providing each label with their certified signature.[26] Modern dairies and model milk farms affixed labels on their bottles or paper seals on their enclosures with the firm's name and date of production. It was not always successful, as milkmen tampered with the labels by using them again on other bottles.[27] Just as in the UK, firms wanted to ensure good quality control by employing chemists, whose analytical methods were well developed.[28] Private food laboratories came into being and performed quality control tests on demand for the food industry. The food laboratory of the chemist Dr. P.F. van Hamel Roos (1850–1935) was well known. The reputation of his laboratory was so great that in 1923 the confectionery firm Tonnema was allowed to put a small portrait of Dr. Hamel Roos on its paper tube of peppermints. The buyer could see on the label the portrait of a scientist dressed in a white laboratory coat. On the label was written 'medical peppermint', suggesting a healthy buy.[29]

Butter and Margarine

The only measure the government took at national level was the enforcement of a Government Butter Label in 1904.[30] The original aim of the Government Butter Label was to protect butter exports, in particular to the UK, against fraud and not the home market. After 1870 exporting butter to Britain was gradually ruled out by high quality Danish butter and later 'colonial' Australian butter. Fraudulent traders frequently adulterated butter with water and the cheaper margarine. Probably in no other food sector was adulteration done on such a large scale as in the dairy industry by mixing butter with cheap margarine. Butter makers and later butter factories were often unaware what happened to their products. Traders, small and large, found mixing butter with margarine to be a profitable business. As long as it was confined to the national market it was a nuisance for local consumers, but as an export product it created far reaching consequences for the Dutch dairy industry. Butter was not only mixed with margarine, but swindlers utilized packaging of bona fide firms and muddled the brand names. Barrels with margarine were provided with fancy names such as 'Butter Factory Denmark' or 'Dutch Butter

---

25 Bakker, 1992, 271–2.
26 Bakker, 1992, 266–7.
27 Den Hartog, 1998, 252.
28 Horrocks, 1995, Oddy, 2007.
29 De Jager, 2010, 28–9.
30 In Dutch: *Rijksbotermerk*, Bieleman, 2008, 310.

Figure 11.3   Government certified butter label, 1905 model

Factory Amsterdam'.[31] The Butter Law of 1904 forbade mixing butter with other substances. The law was implemented by government inspectors and supported by the Government Butter Control Station with its own laboratory. The Government Butter label had to be affixed on all butter containers and packages.[32]

The quality of Dutch butter slowly regained its original good reputation, but exports to Britain continued to decline until the First World War. The loss of exports was however compensated for by increasing butter exports to Germany.[33] The protection of cheese followed in 1906 by the Government Cheese Label, a wafer which had to be affixed on the curd.[34]

At the end of the nineteenth century the margarine industry launched advertising campaigns aiming at reducing the use of butter on bread and as baking fat. In these campaigns posters suggested that margarine was a kind of dairy product, showing pictures with cows or mentioning it being 'freshly churned'. Margarine was traded in butter barrels, all in all a confusing situation.[35] During the first annual meeting of the Netherlands Association of Housewives in 1913, the issue of mixing butter with margarine was raised. Members complained that the government provided export butter with the certified Government Butter Label, but not butter destined for home market consumption. In close collaboration with the Netherlands Dairy

---

31   Bakker, 1992, 266–7.
32   Bieleman, 2008, 310.
33   Van Velden, 1943, 333.
34   Bartels, 1989, 219, 222–3.
35   Reader, 1980, 1, 15.

Association, the Housewives worked hard to prohibit butter-margarine mixtures.[36] In case prohibition was not feasible, then at least there should be a compulsory indication of the butter-margarine proportion on the label.[37] The protection of trademarks and labels became internationally regulated with the Madrid System for the International Registration of Trade Marks in 1891. The Netherlands was again late in protecting both manufacturers and buyers by legislation. In 1893 the law was enforced on the protection of factory and brand names.

Food Labelling between the Wars

During the First World War the Netherlands remained neutral. Cut off from its overseas food supply, the government was forced to set aside its liberal non-intervention policy to ensure national food security. In view of the sudden emergency, objections to a national food law and a food-control system were no longer an issue. The two basic principles of the Food Law of 1919 were the protection of public health and advancement of honesty in trade. In the mean time fundamental changes occurred in grocery shops. The Director of the important biscuit factory, Victoria, characterized the new situation of retailing in 1929:

> The old fashioned grocer selling all his products loose is rapidly disappearing.
> Before, the grocer could check and inspect all his products from the suppliers,
> but now he is passing the already packaged food to his clients. He is now largely
> saved from the laborious work of weighing food and other commodities, putting
> it into paper bags or other containers. He may lose his knowledge and expertise
> of the commodities, but on the other hand food advertising by the manufacturers
> and brand names will stimulate his trade.[38]

With the actual implementation of the Food Law in 1921, the most obvious forms of adulteration decreased quite swiftly. Some firms remained persistent in their fraudulent practices. The label on one jar stated clearly 'Table-honey' and below in small and nearly unreadable letters 'Artificial-honey'.[39] In 1937 the director of the Amsterdam Commodity Inspection Department concluded that the old unscrupulous firms now hardly dared to commit fraud because of the inspection and the risk of penalty imposed by the law. Unfortunately the Food Law had insufficient provisions concerning weight or volume, as it was not compulsory

---

36   During the depression of the 1930s, the government supported farmers on a temporary basis in 1932 by compelling margarine manufacturers to mix butter with margarine.

37   Jonker, 1987, 37.

38   *Voeding en Hygiëne*, 4, 1929, 36–7.

39   Ibid., 1, 1926, 118.

to indicate it on the label and packaging.[40] Two important issues concerning food labelling remained outstanding during the interwar years: the minimum required ingredient declaration and the weight of the product. Some firms tried to be smart and provided their labels and packaging with the text: 'the composition of the product is in accordance with the requirements of the Commodity Inspection Department' or 'In accordance with the requirements of the Food Law'. After protests from the Inspection Department, most firms discontinued these practises, but some remained very persistent in their bad behaviour. One firm stated 'Certified by the Commodity Inspection Department', but the Director made no secret of his feelings and qualified it clearly as a lie.[41]When food adulteration became more risky some firms tried to manipulate the size and weight of the packaging. Smaller bottles, bottles with an enlarged indentation (or 'kick') in the base, cardboard boxes, tin canisters and paper bags less filled than before gave the buyer the impression that he was getting the correct weight for a reasonable price.[42] For buyers and *bona fide* firms a major point of concern became the second objective of the law; honesty in trade. In essence, the quality of the product was more protected by law than its quantity.[43]

In the 1920s several organizations, the Netherlands Association of Housewives, the Netherlands Association of Wine Merchants and the Association of Wholesalers complained about fraudulent weights and volume indications or absence of any information on the labels. In 1928 the Wholesalers made a survey among their members most of whom were in favour of a regulation on weight and volume. The response of 100 questionnaires sent to food manufacturers was rather disappointing: 38 were returned of which only 20 respondents had a positive attitude towards regulation. According to the Wholesalers, of all the neighbouring countries only Germany had provisions on weight in its Food Law (*Lebensmittelgesetz*). An effort in 1923 to amend the Food Law on the weight issue failed because of opposition in Parliament. A major reason for objecting to the proposal was that food inspectors could obtain the authority to fine offenders without the intervention of a judge.[44] It seems most likely that members of parliament did not consider fraudulent weights as a serious threat to honesty in trade and public health. The Wine Merchants Association became impatient and took the initiative into their own hands. In 1926 they introduced, in co-operation with the glass industry, wine bottles with a certified volume mark in the bottle: '*NVW ¾ L*'. Bottles for fruit and lemon juices likewise became certified.[45] Small food manufacturers sometimes submitted their labels for advice to the Commodity Inspection Department.[46]

---

40   Ibid., 12, 1937, 1.
41   Ibid., 8, 1933, 47–8.
42   Ibid., 12, 1937, 1.
43   Ibid., 2, 1927, 379.
44   Ibid., 3, 1928, 134–5.
45   Ibid., 1, 1926, 123.
46   Speet, 1989, 104.

New efforts in 1931 to change the Food Law were abortive. A proposed amendment of the law to provide labels and packaging with measurement indications was rejected. Some members of parliament tried again during the revision of the Food Law in 1935. The Minister responded that because of the economic crisis, the Commodity Inspection Department could not afford an increase in its workload. Only wrong information on quantities threatening public health was liable to punishment. In response, a number of firms created the Foundation for the Promotion of Indication of Weight, Measurement and Content of Packaged Products in Amsterdam. This association was a collaborative agreement between firms with a great interest in the correct indications of measurement; wine merchants, the fruit-preserving industry, liqueur distillers, jam manufacturers and sugar factories.[47] Due to strenuous efforts of some groups of the food industry and the Netherlands Association of Housewives, Parliament accepted an amendment of the Food law to make it compulsory to indicate weight or volume on labels and packages in 1937. Text should be in Dutch, clearly visible, readable and indelible.[48] In the meantime the Measurement Law of 1935 obliged that all measurements on labels and packaging should be in metric units.[49] The metric system was introduced by law in 1820, but some traditional measurement names remained in daily use, but became metric; the old ounce became 100 grams and the pound at first 1 kilo, but later 500 grams. In colloquial Dutch, pounds and ounces are still in use today when buying unpackaged food such as meat or cheese in shops or in the market. During the occupation from 1940 to 45, the Commodity Inspection Departments managed to create some order in the rise of ersatz food products and monitored the correctness of food labelling.[50]

Years of Reconstruction: The Rise of Supermarkets and Packaging

The 1950s can be characterized as the years of reconstruction, known in Germany as the *Wirtschaftswunder*. The meagre years of the economic crisis and the Second World War were gone and people experienced a period of so far unknown increases in purchasing power. The retail sector changed completely; the traditional grocer was replaced by self-service shops and in turn by supermarkets. Chains of grocery shops existed already before the war, but retail chains began to dominate the food business. In the Netherlands the first self-service shop appeared in 1948; it was quite an event and clients had to be instructed how to take the shop basket, to walk along the shelves, to make a choice by putting the packaged product from the shelf into the basket, without the intervention of the shop assistant. One of the constraints for self-service in the beginning was that all foods were not yet

---

47   *Voeding en Hygiëne*, 12, 1937, 1–3.
48   *Voeding en Hygiëne*, 13, 1938, 37; Jonker, 1987, 37.
49   *Voeding en Hygiëne*, 8, 1934, 169–70; Verhoef, 1983.
50   Laan, van der, 1951, 325.

packaged.[51] Labels and packaging got new functions; the product on the shelf must attract the attention and persuade the consumer to take it. A new element of packaging was plastic replacing cellophane. The food industry and retailers intensified their efforts to make packaging and labelling more attractive. The food label went through a number of drastic changes; the introduction of nutrition facts on labels in the 1980s, the percentage of daily recommended intakes, the 'best before' date, ingredient declaration with E numbers and health claims (but under EU regulations only evidence based). At the turn of the twenty-first century the so-called health logos appeared.

Looking into the socio-economic history of food labelling and packaging, shows that much effort has been expended to make the food label a useful instrument informing consumers what they buy, and the impact it may have on their health. The basis was laid in the period before the Second World War. It was and still is an area of conflicting interests between food manufacturers, retailers, governments and consumers. It is a sobering thought, but surveys in the Netherlands and Germany have indicated that health logos hardly influence positive purchasing behaviour; more than half of consumers do not consult labels for their fat or sugar content.[52] Already in the early 1950s the Advisory Commission on the Food Law feared that elaborate information on food labels would be read and understood by too few consumers.[53] On the other hand governmental non-interference with food labelling is not in the interest of consumers and public health.

References

Bakker, M.S.C., 1992, *'Techniek en voeding in verandering'* [Changing technology and nutrition], in Lintsen, H.W., ed., *Geschiedenis van de techniek in Nederland. De wording van een moderne samenleving 1800–1890* [The history of technology in the Netherlands], vol. 1, Zutphen: Walburg.

Bartels, L.V., 1989, *De onmisbare koe. De koe en haar enorme invloed op de mens* [The influence of the cow on man], Bedum: Boekhandel de Haan.

Berg, S.J. van den, 1841/1963, *'De kruidenier'* [The grocer], in Hasebroek, J.P. et.al., eds, *De Nederlanden karakterschetsen, kleederdrachten, houding en voor komen van verschillende standen* [The Netherlands and its customs], s'Gravenhage: Nederlandsche Maatschappij van Schoone Kunsten, V.A. Kramers.

Bieleman, J., 2008. *Boeren in Nederland. Geschiedenis van de landbouw 1500–2000* [History of farming in the Netherlands], Amsterdam: Boom.

Boddaert, J., 1993, *Keuringsdienst van Waren Rotterdam 1893–1993* [Commodity Inspection Department Rotterdam], Rotterdam: Boddaert Produkties.

---

51   Rutte, and Koning, 1998, 41–77; van Otterloo, 2000, 274–6.
52   *Gezondheidsgids*, 2010, 6, *Der Spiegel*, 2010, 58.
53   Reith, 1956, 20.

Burnett, J., 1989, *Plenty and Want*, 3rd edn, London: Routledge.

Clark, H.M., 1977, *The tin book. The tin can as collectible art, advertising art and high art*, New York: New American Library.

Douglas, R.W., 1978, 'Glass containers', in Singer, C., Holmyard, E.J., Hall, A.R., and Williams, T.I., eds, *A history of technology*, vol. 6, 1900–1950. Part 1, Oxford: Clarendon.

Gawronski, J., 1996, *De equipage van de Hollandia en de Amsterdam. VOC-bedrijvigheid in 18e-eeuws Amsterdam* [The equipment of Amsterdam East India ships in the eighteenth century], Amsterdam: De Bataafse Leeuw.

Gezondheidsgids, 2010, '*Logo heeft weinig zin*' [Health logo makes less sense], nr. 3, 6.

Hartog, A.P. den, 1995, 'The role of nutrition in food advertisements: the case of the Netherlands', in ICREFH III: Hartog, A.P. den, ed., *Food technology, science and marketing: European diet in the twentieth century*, East Linton, Scotland: Tuckwell.

Hartog, A.P. den, 1998, 'Serving the modern consumer: the development of modern food packaging with special reference to the milk bottle', in ICREFH IV: Schärer, M.R., and Fenton, A., eds, *Food and material culture*, East Linton, Scotland: Tuckwell.

Heer, J., 1991, *Nestlé 125 years 1866–1991*, Vevey: Nestlé.

Hierzholzer, V., 2007, 'The "war against food adulteration": municipal food monitoring and citizen self-help associations in Germany', in ICREFH IX: Atkins, P.J., Lummel, P., and Oddy, D.J., eds, *Food and the city in Europe since* 1800, Aldershot: Ashgate.

Horrocks, S.M., 1995, 'Nutrition Science and the Food Industry in Britain, 1920–1990', in ICREFH III: Hartog, A.P. den, ed., *Food technology, science and marketing: European diet in the twentieth century*, East Linton, Scotland: Tuckwell.

Jager, J., 2010, *De King familie. De geschiedenis van een pepermuntje*. [The history of the King family, peppermint manufacturers], Leeuwarden: Friese Pers Boekerij.

Jonker, I., 1987, *Huisvrouw(en)vakwerk: 75 jaar Nederlandse Vereniging van Huisvrouwen* [75 years of the Netherlands Association of Housewives], Baarn: Bosch and Keuning.

Laan, F.H. van der, 1951, '*Het toezicht op de voedingsmiddelen in de loop der eeuwen* [Food control through the ages]', *Voeding*, 12.

Lief, A., 1965, *A close-up of closures. History and progress*, New York: Glass Container Manufacturers' Institute.

Morris, T.N., 1958, 'Management and preservation of food', in Singer, C., Holmyard, E.J., Hall, A.R., and Williams, T.I., eds, *A history of technology*, Oxford: Clarendon.

Oddy, D.J., 2007, 'Food quality in London and the rise of the public analyst, 1870–1939', in ICREFH IX: Atkins, P.J., Lummel, P., and Oddy, D.J., eds, *Food and the city in Europe since* 1800, Aldershot: Ashgate.

Opie, R., 2001, *The art of the label*, Edison: Chartwell Books.

Otterloo, A.H. van, 2000, '*Prelude op de consumptie maatschappij in voor- en tegenspoed 1920–1960* [Prelude on the consumer society]', in Schot, J.W., Lintsen, H.W., Rip, A., and de la Bruhèze, A.A., *Techniek in Nederland in de twintigste eeuw* [Technology in the Netherlands in the twentieth century], Zutphen: Walburg Pers. vol. 3.

Reader, W.J., 1980, *Fifty years of Unilever*, London: Heinemann.

Reith, J.F., 1956, '*Waren wet en verpakking*' [Food Law and Packaging], *Verpakkingsreeks*, nr. 6, Den Haag: Nederlands Verpakkings-Centrum.

Rutte, G. and Koning, J., 1998, *De supermarkt 50 jaar geschiedenis*. (The supermarket fifty years of history], Baarn: De Prom.

Scholliers, P., 2007, 'Fraud in the big city: Brussels' response to food anxieties in the nineteenth century', in ICREFH IX: Atkins, P.J., Lummel, P., and Oddy, D.J., eds, *Food and the city in Europe since 1800*, Aldershot: Ashgate.

Schrover, M., 1993, *Voedings- en genotmiddelen- industrie* [Food industry], Amsterdam: NEHA.

Simon Thomas, W.F. and Weg, E., van de, 2010, *Blik op blik. Design van Nederlandse verpakkingsblik* [Design of Dutch tin packaging], Deventer: Thieme Art and Historisch Museum Deventer.

Speet, B., 1989, *Keuringsdienst van Waren voor het gebied Haarlem, 1911–1986: vijfenzeventig jaar inzet voor volksgezondheid en eerlijkheid in de handel* [Seventy-five years of the Commodity Inspection Department for the Haarlem region], Haarlem: De Vrieseborch, Haarlemse Miniaturen 17.

Spiegel, Der, 2010, *Kunden ignoriren fettgehalt* [Consumers ignore fat content], 18: 58.

Stasse Wolthuis, M., 2010, '*Gezondheidsraad neemt logo's voor gezonde voeding onder de loep* [The Health Council scrutinizes health logos]', *Voedings Magazine*, 23, nr. 2.

Teuteberg, H.J., 1994, 'Food adulteration and the beginnings of uniform food legislation in the late nineteenth-century in Germany', in ICREFH II: Burnett, J. and Oddy, D.J., eds, *The origins of food policies in Europe*, London: Leicester University Press.

Velden, H. van, 1943, '*Het weidebedrijf* [Pasturelands] in Sneller, Z.W., ed., *De geschiedenis van den Nederlandschen landbouw 1795–1940* [The history of Dutch agriculture], Groningen: J.B. Wolters.

Verhoeff, J.M., 1983, *De oude Nederlandse maten en gewichten* [The old Dutch measurements and weights], Amsterdam: P.J. Meertens Instituut.

Vijfvinkel, R., 1995, '*Tieleman & Dros in verduurzaamde levensmiddelen*' [Food preservation], in Smit, C.B.A., and Tjalsma, H.D., eds, *Leids fabrikaat* [Manufactured goods in Leiden], Utrecht: Matrijs.

Vleesenbeek, V.A., 1995, *Gezien het advies: 75 jaar Adviescommissie Warenwet* [75 years Food Law Advisory Commission], Rijswijk: Adviescommissie Warenwet.

Voeding en Hygiëne, 1, 1926, *Bedrieglijke aanduiding* [Fraudulent indication].

Voeding en Hygiëne, 1, 1926, *De maathoudende flesch* [The normal bottle].

Voeding en Hygiëne, 2, 1927, *Verpakte voedingsmiddelen* [Packaged food].

Voeding en Hygiëne, 3, 1928, *De warenwet en de hoeveelheid van losse en verpakte waren* [The Food Law and the quantity of unpackaged and packaged products].

Voeding en Hygiëne, 4, 1929, *Uit en om de middenstand. Verpakte artikelen* [Groceries and packaged products].

Voeding en Hygiëne, 8,1933, *Ongewenschte reclame* [Unwanted advertising].

Voeding en Hygiëne, 8, 1934, *Warenwet en IJkwet* [Food Law and Measurement Law].

Voeding en Hygiëne, 12, 1937, *Lofwaardig streven* [laudable pursuit on weight indication].

Voeding en Hygiëne, 13, 1938, *Het nieuwste Jam- Limonade Besluit* [The latest decree on jam and lemonade].

Wit, O. de, 1993, '*Papier*' [Paper], in Lintsen, H.W., ed., *Geschiedenis van de techniek in Nederland. De wording van een moderne samenleving 1800–1890* [The history of technology in the Netherlands], vol. 2, Zutphen: Walburg Pers.

Yntema, R.J., 1994, 'A capital industry. Brewing in Holland, 1500–1800', in Kistemaker, R.E. and Vilsteren, V.T. van eds, *Beer. The story of Holland's favourite drink*, Amsterdam: De Bataafse leeuw.

Zwaal, P. and Brock, P. de, 2010, *Amstel, het verhaal van ons bier 1870-heden* [Amstel, the story of our beer], Amsterdam: Bas Lubberhuizen.

Chapter 12

Promoting Packaging and Selling Self-Service: The Rapid Modernization of the Swedish Food Retail Trade

Jenny Lee and Ulrika Torell

The transformation in Sweden from counter-service to self-service was remarkably rapid. In little more than a decade, self-service became the dominant mode in food retailing. The packaging industry, the co-operative movement, the biggest private retailer co-operative, various academics interested in distribution matters, and reform-friendly politicians formed alliances that worked in favour of self-service. The main objective was to build a modern, rational new society, and here self-service was emblematic.[1]

In Sweden, the introduction of self-service preceded the introduction of supermarkets.[2] Even small shops were converted into self-service quite quickly. By 1960, Sweden had the highest rate of self-service in Europe, well above the average number of self-service stores per 10,000 inhabitants. Depending on estimates, Sweden had between 6.4 and 7.3 self-service stores per 10,000 inhabitants compared to 1.4, which was the average for Western Europe. Norway, Switzerland and West Germany were also well above average whereas the UK was just average and France and most Southern European countries well below.[3] Sweden also differed from its inspirational source, the United States of America, in that it had a relatively low number of multiples. Instead the retail business was dominated by three retail groups, all functioning more like wholesalers than multiples: the co-operative movement KF, the retailer association ICA, and the

---

1   Nyberg, 1998; de Geer, 1978; Hermansson, 2002.

2   This adopts the definition of a supermarket as being a shop with a floor area of more than 400 square metres. The definition is of interest since it reflects the new patterns of retailing where larger stores replaced the former network of small, specialized corner shops. It also says something about city planning and how this shaped the retail landscapes. Rapid urbanization allowed for new ways of structuring the city where large modern supermarkets took on greater significance.

3   In part, the variations reflect those different national histories which have been thoroughly researched. But there are no systematic comparisons of the various national histories of retailing. See for example Lummel, 2007; Sandgren, 2009; Scarpellini, 2004; Nyberg, 1998; Oddy, 1995; Shaw et al., 2004; Lescent-Gilles, 2005.

wholesaler association ASK. All the stores who were associated with KF, ICA or ASK were independent, but they relied on their respective organization, which supplied them with goods, as well as advice and sometimes financial aid.[4]

Economists subsequently described the transition to self-service as an equally important and profound social transformation as the industrial revolution. But in Sweden it met with little discussion or protest.[5] Swedish studies in both business history and economic history have traditionally highlighted the self-service system from an innovation perspective, and often indirectly, from the wider context of food distribution and organization.[6] The general historiography has been dominated by relatively one-sided common assumptions about self-service as a success story of growth, increased consumer choice and self-realization. In recent years, however, international research with a cultural studies perspective on the restructuring of the retail trade has attracted more attention. Concerns have been raised about how the counter service was abandoned, how this affected consumption practices and consumer roles in the new commercial environment.[7]

In this chapter, our aim is to emphasize the role of the packaging industries as one of the driving forces behind the rationalization of food retailing in Sweden. We also wish to stress the role of packaging itself in shaping the new shopping environment: how standard packages engendered new commercial idioms and new cultures of consumption in the era of postwar abundance.

The Packaging Revolution

The development that would fundamentally alter the Swedish retail consumption culture was spurred by interests from outside the retail trade itself. The initiatives came mostly from economists, private packaging entrepreneurs and the food industry. Already in 1920, fellow students from the Stockholm School of Economics, Gerhard Törnqvist and Ruben Andersson (who eventually changed his name to Rausing and became the founder of Tetrapak), had travelled to

---

4   It is difficult to assess the market shares of the Swedish retail market in the 1950s and 1960s, but a rough estimate gave the co-operative movement 25 per cent, the ICA movement 25 per cent and the ASK group 14 per cent in 1955 and 1960. (See Sandgren 2009). By the early twenty-first century the Swedish retail business is highly oligopolistic in its structure and the three main groups still dominate the market with approximately 80 per cent of the total food sales. See *Dagligvaruhandeln* [Food retailing], 2002.

5   Rasmusson, 1996, 139; du Gay, 2004, 149–63. See also Andersson and Larsson, 1998, 74; Rydenfelt, 1995, 54ff; Sandgren, 2009.

6   See for example Nyberg, 1998; Kjellberg, 2001. Several studies of the organization of retailing in the Swedish context deal with self-service more or less directly; see for example Kylebäck, 2004; Aléx, 1994; Jörnmark, 1998; Gråbacke, 2002; Ossiansson, 1997; Svensson, 1998.

7   Kniazeva and Belk, 2007; Lummel and Deak, 2005; du Gay, 2004, 149–63; Cochoy, 2011; Sandgren, 2009.

America to study how the distribution of merchandise and commercial technology were increasingly organized in accordance with F.W. Taylor's ideas on scientific management.[8] They were particularly interested in cost reductions due to industrial large-scale operations, and how the Americans had begun to replace manual bulk sales in stores with standard packaged products.[9]

Törnqvist conducted a series of extensive time studies in the Swedish grocery trade, where each consumer's expedition was timed and analysed in relation to its sale value, expressed in Swedish ören per second.[10] From the results, he formulated a basic concept for how the Swedish retail trade could be rationalized: if the goods were weighed, measured and packaged by the manufacturer, the time-consuming, labour-intensive tasks could greatly be reduced. Each sales act would be faster and each assistant could turn over larger quantities of goods per hour worked. By eliminating weighing and storage less floor space would be required and further savings would be achieved.[11]

Ruben Rausing began to translate the academic ideas into practice through the development of consumer packages for the Swedish manufacturing industry. In partnership with Erik Åkerlund, he bought a printing company in 1929 in Malmö. Starting from their American experience and Törnqvist's time studies, Rausing tried to persuade the Swedish milling industry to start using standardized packaging to pre-pack flour into customer packs. This can be seen as the foundation of the modern packaging industry, since what was packaged were everyday goods that had hitherto been sold loose, and it is usually seen as a prelude to what has been called 'the distribution transformation' in Sweden. Åkerlund and Rausing would later provide the foundation for the transnational giant TetraPak.[12]

During this period, AB Åkerlund and Rausing established itself as the country's leading packaging company. In its trade journal 'Swedish Packaging' (*Svenska förpackningar*), it presented itself to the industry as 'the product packaging specialist in Sweden'. It did cost analysis, designed packaging and machinery in co-operation with the manufacturers.[13] The focus on hardware development, combined with Törnqvist's time studies, has subsequently been identified as the prerequisite for conveying the benefits of standardization to the manufacturing industry and by 1934 the company started to become profitable.[14]

---

8   Törnqvist was very much inspired by Frederick Winslow Taylor (1856–1915) and subsequently carried out a number of time and motion studies. He most certainly read both *The Principles of Scientific Management*, and *Shop Management*. Taylor, 1911a, Taylor 1911b. See Östlund, 1993; Engwall, 2001; Rasmusson, 1996.

9   See, for example, Strasser, 1989.

10   See Törnqvist, 1929, 42ff.

11   Törnqvist, in *Affärsekonomi* [Business economy] 1930, cited in Östlund, 1993.

12   Andersson and Larsson, 1998, 74.

13   *Svenska Förpackningar* [Swedish packaging] 1937–58.

14   Engwall, 2001, 128.

Source: *Svenska förpackningar*, 1938.

Figure 12.1   Propaganda from the Swedish packaging industry: brand-new flour packages and the modern equipment for the milling industry as presented in the trade journal *Svenska förpackningar*

AB Åkerlund and Rausing still had to convince everyone that to invest in industrial packaging paid off. The cost argument was the most salient when the packaging industry tried to persuade the retail trade: 'A modern flour or sugar packing machine is able to package … 3,000–6,000 kg per hour, which is 25–30 times as much as a trained clerk in retail could ever achieve.' Expenditure on bags, strings, scales, and waste was reduced. Moreover, the packages could be presented in an attractive manner in shop windows and retail spaces. Sealed pre-packaged goods could serve as a competitive tool. Åkerlund and Rausing claimed that the manufacturer could guarantee the quality of the contents and thus persuade the consumer to buy.

Hygiene and public health issues were in the front line of the arguments presented to consumers. This tallied with the overall interwar vision of modern, more hygienic living arrangements. The clean, automatically filled package was a step forward, away from the backward, 'rural and dirty' Sweden of old.[15] The former way of selling from bulk by measuring and repacking in the shop was depicted as a threat to the goods, which had arrived clean and fresh from the factory only to be soiled by human hands at the retailers.[16]

During the 1930s, more and more goods went on sale in factory-sealed bags and packages, with more-or-less elaborate trademarks visible. In Sweden, trademarks and commercial advertising was not as prominent a feature of the overall culture of consumption as in other parts of the Western world. For example, there was no commercial broadcasting until 1993, and it was not permitted to use the national public radio or television for advertising. In the social-democratic welfare state the advertising business remained a rather limited phenomenon.[17] Industrial packaging was first embraced by the food manufacturers: margarine, cream cheese, eggs, spices, crisp bread and coffee were all sold in modern, standard packages.[18] This was followed by shirts and underwear sold in cardboard boxes and household items including cutlery, glassware and porcelain.[19] Nonetheless, many food items were still sold loose: food manufacturers were not as pro-active as in the alluring American model.[20]

But problems in the shops persisted. Trade volumes increased, as did the population and the median wages. More people had access to more goods than ever before. Between 1930 and 1950 the retail sales volumes increased by 70 per cent and food sales doubled. Processed food accounted for the largest increase. At the same time, the number employed in the Swedish food trade nearly doubled, working hours were regulated and wages were raised.[21] Distribution costs for goods made up more than half the price that the customer had to pay.[22] The retail trade talked about the situation as untenable.[23] To increase the tempo and keep labour costs down was an absolutely crucial and overarching objective for the retailers. It was necessary to increase the turnover per employee.[24] The American example seemed more and more attractive.

---

15 *Svenska Förpackningar*, No. 1, 1937, 1–2; See also Andersson and Larsson, 1998, 65ff.; Palmblad and Eriksson, 1995, 25ff.

16 *Svenska Förpackningar*, No. 2, 1939, 2; see also Strasser, 1989.

17 Hermansson, 2002; Thurén, 1997, 307.

18 For a discussion of how trademarks took on an increasing importance to establish quality in food and drink, see Wilkins, 1994, and the seminal work of Penrose, 1951, 1995 [1959].

19 See Björklund, 1967, 223ff.; Engwall, 2001, 128; Rydenfelt. 1995, 44ff.; *Svenska förpackningar*. 1937–58.

20 Nyberg, 1998.

21 Bergersen and Ramström, 1956.

22 af Trolle, 1948.

23 See Larsson, 1948; af Trolle, 1948.

24 Another way to increase turnover is, of course, larger stores. But in Sweden, the discussion on the importance of the size of the shop came in the 1950s, when size was deemed crucial. See Nyberg, 1998.

Dreams of an Automatic Retail Trade

The most radical solution was to do as the Americans had done – eliminate the store 'clerks' and let customers serve themselves. During the 1930s the self-service system in the USA had attracted interest among both co-operative and Swedish traders' associations, which was primarily reflected in the trade press.[25] For the co-operative movement, the only question was how soon the Swedish consumer members could be persuaded to 'help' with servicing. The idea was really just an extension of the co-operative idea of 'exchange'. The store would be a 'big pantry' where the producers brought their goods and consumers only paid for what they took away. The assistants would be store managers who could help the 'owners' to remove such goods that were difficult to cope with on their own.[26]

The consumer co-operative movement had experimented with self-service in the war years, but the rationing system made it difficult to pursue.[27] The private retailers' organization was initially more reluctant and uncertain as to whether this would suit the Swedish character.[28] Traditional counter-service with all its attributes remained the focus of how to rationalize the retail trade. As it turned out, self-service shops were introduced very quickly and Sweden took the lead in the shift from counter-service among European countries. The start was in spring 1947 when 'Konsum quick-buy' opened in Stockholm. The store was rebuilt and designed strictly according to the latest American research. The store was modern, spectacular and at the same time strange. Now people would learn to buy food in a whole new way. Konsum's management was convinced that the Swedish housewife, like the American, would appreciate this new type of shop in Sweden.[29] From 1948 shop after shop converted to self-service and new stores were almost always self-service. In the early 1960s Sweden's conversion rate was far ahead of other European countries.[30]

Self-service was a radical change in the consumption space and presented a new way to shop. The self-service system generated a partly new commercial idiom, consisting of colour, shape, sound, characters and symbols that customers had to decipher and learn. Consumer researcher, Michael Wildt, has shown how hidden and coded references associated with the goods increased as the self-service scheme was introduced, and how demand as well as consumer satisfaction increased markedly.[31]

25   Sandgren, 2009.
26   *Vår tidning* [Our journal], no 6, 1946.
27   *Vår tidning*, no 6, 1946.
28   *Butikskultur* [Shop culture], no 2, 1946.
29   *Butikskultur*, 2, 1946.
30   For exact figures of the introduction of self-service in Sweden, see Nyberg, 1998, 112; also Gerentz and Ottosson, 1999, 314; Schulz-Klingauf, 1961, 239.
31   Wildt, 2003.

Table 12.1   Total number of self-service shops in Western European countries in 1960

Country	Self-service 1960 (number of shops)	Population 1960 ('000s)	Self-service shops (per 10,000 people)
Sweden (HUI)*	5,451	7,480	7.3
Norway	1,800	3,581	5.0
Switzerland	1,720	5,362	3.2
Germany	22,600	72,481	3.1
Netherlands	2,250	11,486	2.0
Denmark	850	4,581	1.8
United Kingdom	7,750	52,372	1.5
France	1,800	45,670	0.4
Spain	400	30,641	0.1
Italy	200	50,198	0.0
Western Europe total	45,525	323,797	1.4

Note:*HUI is the abbreviation for *Handelns utredningsinstitut*, the Swedish Retail Research Institute.
Source: Sandgren, 2009.

In addition to the very real physical change in the store itself there was a fundamental change in the mental image of the store, which focused on product presentation.[32] In the absence of personal service, the goods had to start selling themselves. Articles were exposed, organized, illustrated, decorated and displayed using visual, verbal and spatial rhetoric. Sales literature described the importance of using new visual means in the self-service stores to lead customers in the desired direction.[33] By contrast with the old service shop's ideal of order, the literature on self-service stressed instead the apparent disorder principle. The customer, who was supposed to have a developed sense of order, found it easier to pick items out of an imaginary disorder, rather than upset an arrangement of symmetrically stacked products. So-called flash signs, with goods piled up in place of the orderly rows would evoke impulse. And a moderately cluttered layout on the shelf would attract the customer, giving the impression that she was not the first to choose a particular product.[34] From now on commodities in standard packages presented

---

32   For an interesting study of the American development see Cochoy's chapter on how technical artefacts like the shopping cart and turnstile together changed the spatial expression of the sales area and how consumers shopped and acted in the store environment, Cochoy, 2011.

33   Schultz–Klingauf, 1961, 21.

34   Schultz–Klingauf, 1961, 178–83.

themselves, greeted and attracted the customer, provided information about the content, the factory owner, and manufacturing, accounted for quality, reliability, authenticity and purity – all in competition with other products on the shelves.

Customers at a Loss

'It is not easy for a consumer in our day to know how she should act', complained the School for Housewives, a popular radio show, which also resulted in a book in 1950.[35] There was uncertainty about the rapid changes of everyday life and the vast majority needed help to orient themselves in this brand-new shopping world. The self-service system called for more active participation from the customer and there were concerns that consumers were losing control over what it really was they bought in the modern supermarkets.[36] Increasingly, as the family's food was industrially produced and marketed in packages, the housewife was no longer able to assess what it contained. Prepared meals, different kinds of powdered goods, and even simple boiled potatoes were now marketed in sealed packages and it was impossible to know what hazardous chemicals the producer had used to improve taste, appearance, durability and consistency. Advertising messages and packages had replaced the knowledge housewives had previously acquired by taste, touch and contact with the shopkeeper. Now they had to learn and try to understand the meaning of the 'more or less truthful information' that greeted them verbally and visually on the store shelves. That the customer no longer could see the goods only reinforced the feeling of uncertainty.[37]

The packaging industry was very much aware of consumer uncertainty and doubt concerning goods in sealed packages. This reluctance could inhibit purchases. In the *Svenska förpackningar* theme issue 'Say it with the package' Åkerlund and Rausing presented the company's efforts to design and use aesthetics as a key marketing-technology agent in the new self-service system. Special transparent 'self-service-packaging' termed 'Sell Quick' cartons with good-sized windows were illustrated in the journal.[38] In particular, fresh foods such as fruit or meat were pre-packaged in transparent materials. Tomatoes, cucumbers, onions were displayed in modern see-through packaging for the discerning eye of the consumer.

In 1955, a public enquiry, the Packaging Standardization Committee, commissioned scientists to conduct an in-depth study of consumer opinion on food packaging.[39] A total of 300 housewives in urban regions were interviewed

---

35   *Vi går och handlar* [We go shopping], 1950.

36   Abramson, 1950.

37   Abramson, 1950, 56ff; 66–7.

38   *Svenska Förpackningar*, nos 3–5, 1951. For the use of cellophane and transparent packaging, see Cochoy, 2011.

39   af Trolle, 1959. The study was presented in *Konsumentförpackningen ur konsumentsynpunkt* [Consumer packages from a consumer's point of view].

Note: The Sell-quick packages were promoted to the food industry as a way to convince the consumer, who would be able to inspect the goods through the little transparent window without touching it, thus satisfying both the needs of hygiene on the one hand, and of curiosity and trust on the other hand.

Source: *Svenska förpackningar*, 1951.

Figure 12.2   Peepholes for the consumer

about their preferences regarding the functionality, as well as characteristics of packages. One of the most striking results from this study is that the housewives expressed the view that they could no longer control the quality or quantity of their purchases. There were plenty of critical comments about the difficulty of knowing what the packages actually contained: the information was inadequate and not entirely trustworthy; product declaration, weight and volume were often missing and the housewives requested date stamps on all packages. It was generally felt that the stores in many cases were less scrupulous with pre-packaged meat products than those sold loose by weight.[40]

Shopping Technology

Criticism of the changes in shops is harder to find, but there was initially some resistance to the self-service system. Previous research on the introduction of self-service has pointed to the arguments from both private and co-operative retailers,

---

40   af Trolle, 1959.

who worried about making large investments if they were not certain that it would pay off.[41] The apparent enthusiasm that marked the introduction of the self-service system may indicate that the transition was not as smooth as its advocates would have desired. The mere suspicion that the customers could feel disoriented, lonely or at loss in the new shopping environments was countered by descriptions of the bright, open environment where it really was easy to find one's way, with informative modern packaging and clear display of prices making shopping simple. The propaganda was massive. Retailers and customers were guided by movies, pamphlets and articles in various media.[42] However, from the mid-1950s, evaluation showed that size rather than self-service was the most decisive factor for the profitability of a store. The bigger the store, the more rational the distribution, became the conventional wisdom. Eventually this would pave the way for higher concentration in the Swedish retail sector.[43]

Time was presented as absolutely crucial in the new way to buy food. Consumers should avoid queuing and waiting time in the shop. The 'busy professional woman' was just 'rushing into Konsum quick-buy and made her purchases within minutes – without having to wait'.[44] However, the check-out counter was perceived as something of a bottleneck and certain goods, such as coffee, presented problems.[45] Still, absence of service was increasingly referred to as 'self-service', which in turn was related to higher speeds and timesaving as a positive value in itself. Thus the whole content and meaning of the concept of service changed in an age of automation, predicted mass motoring and the mechanization of housework.[46] Service was associated with speed, not with someone else's personal assistance.

But the concept of time had another equally important side. In relation to the retail trade and the manufacturing industries, the packaging industries stressed the point that the customer in a self-service store could wander around for a *long* time by herself and buy *much more* than she had first intended. Impulse purchases were presented as one of the main arguments for the new system. The specialist literature referred to American studies that showed how half the sales quantities in supermarkets were unplanned purchases. When the client met the attractive mass exposure of goods and had the opportunity to touch each item, all her desires were unleashed.[47] Åkerlund and Rausing's trade journal *Swedish packaging* let the reader follow 'Mrs Consumer' on a visit to the self-service store to illustrate how the principles of sales psychology worked (see Figure 12.3). With all her

---

41   For the packaging industries, see Rasmusson, 1996, 145; Nyberg, 1998, 99ff; and Sandgren, 2009.

42   *Tidningen Vi*, no 18; no 20, 1947; *Svenska förpackningar*, nos 3–4, 1951; *Konsum snabbköp* [Konsum quick-buy], 1947.

43   Nyberg, 1998.

44   *Tidningen Vi*, no 18, 1947.

45   Wennborg, 1955.

46   Bergman, 2003, 126f.

47   Schultz-Klingauf, 1961, 45.

Source: *Svenska förpackningar*, 1951.

Note: The sequence shows Mrs Consumer and her reaction to the mass of wonderful new packaged goods in the self-service store. It was used in an article on the benefit of allowing the customers to spend time alone with the packages.

Figure 12.3   Mrs Consumer shopping for more than she ever intended to buy

senses open to impulses and reminders, she was confronted with a sea of mouth-watering food and novelties that she did not even know existed. She intended to buy five items and ended up buying nine, the article boasts. This was the effect of a housewife confronted with enticing modern packaging.[48]

Autonomous Consumers?

The introduction of self-service fundamentally altered retail landscapes: not only the retail spaces themselves, but communications between buyers and sellers were also transformed. Ideas, meanings, and values related to the commodities were now instead mediated through the packaging rather than through the sales transaction with the shopkeeper attending the customer. Sales technology in the second half of

48   *Svenska förpackningar*, nos 3–4, 1951.

the twentieth century primarily focused on the meeting between the customer and the package: consumer competence became a question of interpreting visual codes, the shapes, colours and symbols of the new open retail landscape. The role of the customer was metamorphosed into consumer – an autonomous individual – who in solitary splendour would pick and choose among industrially filled packages.[49]

Consumers' experience of losing control over their food supply in the new self-service system was at odds with the contemporary ideal images of the autonomous consumer. Some consumers might feel that the interaction with a knowledgeable shop assistant who could demonstrate the goods and offer tasting samples would mean more freedom and power over purchases than to 'stroll around' among the standard packaged goods in the self-service store. By all accounts, it was a highly regulated freedom. In the new shopping system, the consumer was surrounded by sales technologies where an intricate arrangement of visual messages and material parameters steered her around in very specific ways.[50] Illustrative of the power of this idea is how the founder of the earliest American Piggly Wiggly stores, actually patented the design of the room itself so that the consumer would be directed around on certain courses.[51] The commercial environment carefully guided her by principles of how ideally to move around the store, directed with visual, auditory and olfactory impressions.

The new self-service system entailed a new distribution of responsibility. Earlier on, the shopkeeper had been the centre of attention: it was his personal reputation that safeguarded the customer and the producer alike. Since he dealt with goods in bulk, he put his good name at stake. The counter-service system operated according to a commercial logic founded on trust, personal accountability and honour with emphasis on the personal relationship between retailer and customer. In the self-service system the nature of this relationship was gradually redefined. With pre-packaged goods, responsibility and even agency was attributed to the package itself: it interacted with the consumer, promoted the contents and promised quality.[52] Quality itself was redefined as that which was industrially produced. The consumer had to put her faith in the word of the producer and the veracity of the promises made on the packages. The self-service system with its packaging allowed for a type of large-scale, long-distance retailing that had hitherto been impossible. The increased distance between the producer and the consumer paved the way for the placeless modern food system. The scale altered the relationship between the retailer and the consumer yet again, leaving the consumer even more alone and uncertain about whom to address and about how to make informed choices.

---

49   For a discussion of how the concept 'the consumer' turned into a super category, see Trentmann, 2006.

50   Du Gay, 2004, 149–63. See also Cochoy, 2011.

51   Savås, 2000, 66–7. Piggly-Wiggly was granted a Swedish patent in 1920.

52   Wilkins, 1994.

It seems as if postwar Sweden was particularly prone to accept and implement change. There was a readiness to embrace all that was perceived as modern and rational. The national self-image of a prosperous, effective welfare state was also endorsed outside Sweden with international commentators using the Swedish example to propagate capitalism with a human dimension.[53] The connexions between academia and the co-operative movement as well as between the private retail associations and the packaging industries provided a unique momentum for change. There was sufficient intellectual, cultural, social and commercial capital to implement changes very rapidly. In the 1920s, the co-operative movement bought a vanguard advertising agency, Svea, which then created many ultramodern advertisements for the co-operative movement and also helped them to establish their trademarks.[54] Svea also had its own architect's office from the 1920s. This office attracted talented and creative architects. They were proactive in their attitude and had visionary ideas about how to create 'a fair and just society'. This had consequences for how the co-operative stores were designed. They became the cutting edge of architecture. Very early on, they provided standardized shop fixtures, standardized interior designs which made them well suited to make the transition into self-service. What they strove for were rational, modern stores that would suit the rational, modern citizens. The private retailers felt obliged to follow suit and Hakon (later ICA) also had an architect's office from the 1930s. Their stance was perhaps more reactive to the co-operative movement and the challenges from the store culture they engendered. But even so, the result was a competition to be as attractive and modern as possible.

In the 1950s, Sweden had a comparative advantage over the rest of Europe since it had taken a neutral stance in the war and not actively participated. The economy and the industries were intact and the stimulus of the Marshall Plan had positive side effects on Sweden as well. As mentioned before, the highly successful Swedish packaging industries had a tremendous effect on the rapid transition to self-service.[55] Even if Sweden had been outside the war, the postwar era presented itself as moment of opportunity for restructuring and resuming the rationalization processes of the interwar era.[56] The retail trade collected knowledge about self-service and rational distribution from the 1920s and this process accelerated in the 1930s.[57] The economic prosperity of the postwar period created change at a rapid pace. To rationalize every aspect of society was part of the grand plan to transform Sweden into a truly modern, progressive country.[58]

---

53   See Childs, 1938; Jenkins, 1977; Popenoe, 1977; also Faramond and Glayman, 1977. For recent research on the national self-image, see Glover, 2011.
54   Jonsson, 2009.
55   Beckeman, 2006.
56   De Geer, 1978; Hermansson, 2002.
57   Sandgren, 2009.
58   See, for example, Hirdman, 1989.

With hindsight, the transition seems very smooth and the self-image of Sweden is that of harmonious consensus. The Swedish social-democrats remained in power and, with only two prime ministers during almost three decades, the political stability was spectacular. But the consensus culture was not free from friction: there were always different interests and when we look into the debates and the factors behind the rapid transition of the retail sector, we see that the pressure from the social-democrats and the threat of more state control made the representatives of retailing convert and rationalize in order to retain control.[59] This quest for rationalization of every aspect of society favoured large-scale solutions and large-scale interests. Large producer co-operatives and large wholesaling companies dominated the food sector, with political support and reforms as further leverage. In addition to this, the co-operative movement was very successful and pushed the development of the retail landscape into a uniform standardized rationality. Here the self-service concept was heralded as the most rational, the most modern and the most desirable.

The packaging industry was extremely proactive in the Swedish self-service transition. Åkerlund and Rausing's strategic marketing promised, like the pyramid game logic, great profits and increased sales to all parties. This may to some extent explain the rapidity of change. The success of the packaging industries has also been attributed to how they managed to expand outside Sweden. With international markets within reach, there was a basis for building up research and development departments. This would not have been possible with only the small national market.[60] It is also a question of a comparative geographical advantage: Åkerlund and Rausing, which eventually became Tetrapak, was located in Skåne, the most prominent agrarian region in Sweden. Skåne was close to the international markets, the soil was fertile, and early on there was a concentration of commercial agriculture and food industries. It was also geographically close to the University of Lund, which meant that there was a ready supply of well-educated chemical engineers. The story of the transformation of the package, the store and purchasing practices during the twentieth century can thus be seen as the story of how a concept was successfully sold to various parties: to the food industry which would invest in packaging technology and new distribution systems; to the retail trade that would see increased profitability of new sales ideals; and to the consumers who would be convinced that self-service would give them freedom, independence and time savings.

References

Abramson, E., 1950, '*Att köpa mat* [To buy food]' in *Vi går och handlar* [We go shopping], Stockholm: Radiotjänst.

---

59   Sandgren, 2009; Kjellberg, 2001.
60   Beckeman, 2006.

Aléx, P., 1994, *Den rationella konsumenten* [The rational consumer], Stockholm: B. Östlings bokförlag Symposion.

Andersson, P. and Larsson, T., 1998, *Tetra. Historien om dynastin Rausing* [Tetra. The history of the Rausing dynasty], Stockholm: Norstedt.

Beckeman, M., 2006, *The rise of the Swedish food sector after World War II*, Department of Design Sciences, Lund University.

Bergersen, K. and Ramström, D., 1956, '*Detaljhandelns utveckling mellan 1931–1951* [The development of retailing, 1931–1951]' in Holmqvist, E. and Alsterdal, A., eds, *Folket vid varufloden* [People and the mass of goods], Stockholm: Svenska handelsarbetareförbundet.

Bergman, B., 2003, *Handelsplats, shopping, stadsliv* [Market place, shopping, urban life], Stockholm: Symposion.

Björklund, T., 1967, *Reklamen i svensk marknad 1920–1965* [Advertising in the Swedish market 1920–1965], Stockholm: Norstedt.

Butikskultur [Shop culture], 1946, no. 2.

Childs, M.W., 1938, *Sweden, the middle way*, New Haven: Yale University Press.

Cochoy, F., 2011, 'Market-things inside: Insights from Progressive Grocer (United States, 1929–1959)', in Zwick, D. and Cayla, J., eds, *Inside Marketing*, Oxford: Oxford University Press.

Dagligvaruhandeln [Food Retailing], 2002, Stockholm: Konkurrensverket.

Engwall, L., 2001, *Från Taylor till Tetra* [From Taylor to Tetra], Uppsala: Företagsekonomiska institutionen.

Faramond, G. de, and Glayman, C., eds, 1977, *Suède: la réforme permanente*, Paris: Stock.

Gay, P. du, 2004, 'Self Service: Retail, Shopping and Personhood', in *Consumption, Markets and Culture*, vol. 7, no. 2.

Geer, H. De, 1978, *Rationaliseringsrörelsen i Sverige* [The movement for rationalizing in Sweden], Stockholm: Studieförb. Näringsliv och samhälle (SNS).

Gerentz, S. and Ottosson, J., 1999, *Handel och köpmän i Stockholm under ett sekel* [Trade and businessmen in Stockholm over a century], Stockholm: Ekerlids förlag.

Glover, N., 2011, *National relations*, Stockholm: Nordic Academic Press.

Gråbacke, C., 2002, *Möten med marknaden* [Meeting the Market], Göteborg: Ekonomisk-historiska institutionen.

Hermansson, K., 2002, *I persuadörernas verkstad. Marknadsföring i Sverige 1920–1965* [Marketing in Sweden 1920–1965], Stockholm: Ekonomisk-historiska institutionen.

Hirdman, Y., 1989, *Att lägga livet till rätta* [The desire to organize everyday life], Stockholm: Carlsson.

Jenkins, D., *Sweden – the progress machine*, London: Hale, 1969.

Jonsson, P., '*Följ de omtänksamma husmödrarnas exempel. Livsmedelsannonsering i en svensk dagstidning, 1875–1965* [Food advertising in Swedish press 1875–1965]', *Historisk tidskrift*, no. 2, 2009.

Jörnmark, J., 1998, *Innovationer och institutionell omvandling* [Innovation and institutional change], Stockholm: Ekonomisk-historisk forskning.

Kjellberg, H., 2001, *Organizing Distribution*, Stockholm: Ekonomisk-historiska institutionen.

Kniazeva, M. and Belk, R.W., 2007, 'Packaging as a Vehicle for Mythologizing the Brand', *Consumption, Markets and Culture*, vol. 10, no. 1, 51–69.

Konsum snabbköp 1947 [Konsum quick-buy 1947], 1947, KF Film archive.

Kylebäck, H., 2004, *Varuhandeln i Sverige under 1900-talet* [Retailing in Sweden during the twentieth century], Göteborg: Business Administration Studies.

Larsson, I., 1948, '*Distributionens arbetskraftsproblem* [The workforce shortage in distribution]' in *Morgondagens svenska marknad* [The Swedish Market of Tomorrow, Stockholm: Svenska Reklamförbundet.

Lescent-Giles, I., 2005, 'The rise of supermarkets in twentieth-century Britain and France', in Sarasúa, C., Scholliers, P. and Molle, L. van, eds, *Land, shops and kitchens*, Turnhout: Brepols.

Lummel, P., 2007, 'Born-in-the-city: The Supermarket in Germany', in ICREFH VIII: Atkins, P.J., Lummel, P. and Oddy, D.J., eds, *Food and the city in Europe since 1800*, Aldershot: Ashgate.

Lummel, P. and Deak, A., eds, 2005, *Einkaufen! Eine Geschichte des täglichen Bedarfs* [Grocery shopping! A history of daily demand], Berlin: Verein der Freunde der Domäne Dahlem.

Nyberg, A., 1998, *Innovation in Distribution Channels*, Stockholm: Ekonomisk-historiska institutionen.

Oddy, D.J., 1995, 'From cornershop to supermarket: The Revolution in Food Retailing in Britain, 1932–1992', in ICREFH III: Hartog, A.P. den, ed., *Food technology, science and marketing*, East Linton: Tuckwell Press.

Ossiansson, E., 1997, *Nätverk i förändring* [Changing retail networks]. Göteborg: Handelshögskolan.

Östlund, D., 1993, '*Med tidtagaruret i butiken. Gerhard Törnqvist och den rationella distributionen* [Gerhard Törnqvist and rational distribution]', in Sundin, B., ed., *Från hermetism till rationell distribution* [From Hermetism to Rational Distribution] Umeå.

Penrose, E.T., 1951, *Economics of the international patent system*, Baltimore: Johns Hopkins University Press.

Penrose, E.T., 1995 [1959], *Theory of the growth of the firm*, Oxford: Oxford University Press.

Popenoe, D., 1977, *The suburban environment*, Chicago: University of Chicago Press.

Rasmusson, E., 1996, '*Funderingar i självbetjäningsbutiken* [Reminicences in the self-service shop]', in Ahrland, K., ed., *En kreatörs tankevärld* [The world of ideas of an innovator], Stockholm: Ekerlids förlag.

Rydenfelt, S., 1995, *Sagan om Tetra pak* [The story of Tetra Pak], Stockholm: Fischer.

Sandgren, F., 2009, 'From "peculiar stores" to "a new way of thinking": Discussions on self-service in Swedish trade journals, 1935–55', *Business History*, vol. 51:5.

Savås, G., 2000, *Från handelsbod till stormarknad* [From corner shop to supermarket], Gustavsberg: G.Savås.

Scarpellini, E., 2004, 'Shopping American-Style: The Arrival of the Supermarket in Postwar Italy', *Enterprise and Society*, vol. 5 no. 4.

Schulz-Klingauf, H.-V., 1961, *Självbetjäning* [Self-Service], Stockholm: Forum.

Shaw, G., Curth, L. and Alexander, A., 2004, 'Selling Self- Service and the Supermarket: The Americanization of Food Retailing in Britain, 1945–60', *Business History*, 46:4. 568–82.

Strasser, S., 1989, *Satisfaction guaranteed*, New York: Pantheon Books.

Svenska förpackningar [Swedish Packaging], 1937–1958, Malmö: Åkerlund and Rausing.

Svensson, T., 1998, *Dagligvarudistributionens strukturomvandlin* [Restructuring retail distribution], Linköping University.

Taylor, F.W., 1911a, *The Principles of Scientific Management*, New York: Harper.

Taylor, F.W., 1911b, *Shop management*, New York: Harper.

Thurén, T., 1997, *Medier i blåsväder* [Media under fire], Värnamo: Stiftelsen etermedierna i Sverige No. 5.

Tidningen Vi [Our News], 1947, nos 18, 20.

Trentmann, F., 2006, 'Knowing consumers', in Trentmann, F., ed., *The Making of the Consumer,* New York: Berg.

Trolle, U. af, 1948, '*På vilka punkter kan distributionen ytterligare effektiviseras?* [On what grounds can distribution further be rationalized?]', in *Morgondagens svenska marknad* [The Swedish Market of Tomorrow], Stockholm: Svenska Reklamförbundet.

Trolle, U. af, 1959, *Konsumentförpackningen ur konsumentsynpunkt* [Consumer packages from a consumer perspective], Göteborg: Handelshögskolan (IDAF).

Törnqvist, G., 1929, *Kostnadsanalys och prissättning i detaljaffärer* [Cost analysis and prices in retail stores], Stockholm: P.A. Norstedt and Sons Förlag.

Vår tidning [Our journal], 1946, no.6.

Vi går och handlar [We go shopping], 1950, Stockholm: Radiotjänst.

Wennborg, E., 1955, *Ta'själv – betala i kassan* [Take it yourself – pay at the checkout counter], Stockholm: Aktiebolaget Svenska Kolonialgrossister [Swedish Colonial Wholesalers Ltd].

Wildt, M., 2003, 'Plurality and Taste. Food Consumption in West Germany during the 1950s', Clarke, D.B., Doel, M.A. and Housinaux, K.M.L. eds, *The Consumption reader*, London: Routledge.

Wilkins, M., 1994, 'When and Why Brand Names in Food and Drink?', in Morgan, N.J., and Jones, G., eds, *Adding Value: Brands and Marketing in Food and Drink,* London: Routledge.

Chapter 13

Food Preservation in Flemish Women's Magazines, 1945–1960[1]

Anneke Geyzen

Food preservation has mainly been studied as part of the development of the industrialized food chain and the mechanization of household work in the nineteenth and twentieth centuries. As a result, the invention of *appertization* (the bottling or canning of foodstuffs by means of boiling or pressure cookers) and the application of artificial cold (refrigerated storage and freezing) have captured a great deal of scholars' attention.[2] In Belgium, little research has been conducted on food preservation techniques; it has not gone further than chronologically pinpointing the main preservation practices and the introduction of innovative techniques in the nineteenth and twentieth centuries.[3]

Until the 1870s, food preservation in Belgium mainly consisted of salting, smoking, drying and fermenting. The making of jam was not popular due to high sugar prices, which turned jams into a genuine treat.[4] When sugar prices dropped around 1900, cookery books started to present more jam recipes and housewives increasingly engaged in making preserves. In the 1890s, canned foods – even though still expensive – became available, while their clear-cut breakthrough in Belgium occurred in the 1920s. At first, a limited assortment consisting of sardines, beef, peas and prunes was offered, but when large manufacturers entered the preserving business the variety of canned foods expanded significantly to include tomato paste, olives, apricots, pineapple, salmon, meat and milk.[5] After the Second World War, the Belgian government invested in a campaign to promote the mechanization of household work in order to facilitate kitchen chores. It encouraged the use of electrical kitchen appliances among which were the refrigerator and the freezer.[6] Due to a combination of the government's promotional campaign, falling prices

---

1   Special thanks are due to my supervisor Prof. Peter Scholliers and FOST colleague Olivier de Maret for their constructive comments.

2   Belasco, 2008, 1–13, 55–78; Goody, 1982, 154–74; Guillou, 1995, 291; Hardyment, 1988, 137–54.

3   Niesten, Raymaekers and Segers, 2002, 52–3; Onghena, 2006, 52–7; Scholliers, 2008a, 37–8.

4   Scholliers, 2008b, 74.

5   Van den Eeckhout and Scholliers, 2012.

6   Niesten, Raymaekers and Segers, 2002, 52–3; Scholliers, 2008a, 37.

of refrigerators, intensive advertising and rising incomes, Belgian households increasingly purchased some form of mechanized cold storage. By the end of the 1950s, 16 per cent of Belgian households owned some form of mechanized cold storage and in the 1960s, this figure had increased by 30 per cent. In 2009, 67.1 per cent of Belgian households owned a refrigerator, 46.4 per cent had a refrigerator/freezer combination and 62.4 per cent possessed a freezer.[7] Compared with the United Kingdom, where 95 per cent of households owned a refrigerator by 1985 and 87 per cent possessed a freezer by 1993, Belgium did not witness ownership saturation.[8]

By contrast to other kitchen appliances, historians have only sporadically explored the diffusion of the refrigerator and freezer in Europe.[9] This chapter takes a closer look at the period before ownership of domestic cold storage increased and its use was generally introduced to households, that is, the years between 1945 and 1960. It investigates how households were persuaded to purchase a refrigerator and/or a freezer in a period that was dominated by homemade conserves and witnessed the growing presence of canned foods. The analysis focuses on Flanders, though a comparative study of the Belgian regional ownership and use of refrigerated storage is still lacking. The question has been tackled by means of a comparative analysis of the way different preservation types were presented in two Flemish women's magazines between 1945 and 1960: a rural magazine *De Boerin/Bij de Haard* (The Farmer Woman/Around The Hearth) on the one hand, and an urban magazine *Het Rijk der Vrouw* (The Woman's Realm) on the other.

Women's Magazines and Representations of Food

The second half of the twentieth century witnessed a significant increase in food topics due to the expansion of various types of media. Besides cookery books, home economics textbooks and newspapers, a growing number of magazines have engaged in writing about food during the past.[10] These food media challenged their audiences with 'a continuous stream of conflicting information about what or what not to eat',[11] 'contrasting dissident reading material',[12] and 'a mixture of popularized information'.[13]

---

7   The total exceeds 100 per cent, implying that some households owned more than one refrigerator or freezer.

8   Oddy and Oddy, 1998, 299.

9   Important research comes from: Bruegel, 1998; Oddy and Oddy, 1998; Teuteberg, 1995.

10   Rousseau, 2012, 183–5. Television shows, websites and blogs are more recent than the period 1945-1960 under investigation.

11   Rousseau, 2012, 185.

12   Stephenson, 2007, 616.

13   Roessler, 2007, 573.

Alan Warde typifies the conflicting culinary information in the food media as 'antinomies' of taste: custom and innovation, health and indulgence, convenience and care, and economy and extravagance.[14] Although Warde's 'antinomies' present an interesting theoretical framework for interpreting culinary discourses in women's magazines, it can be argued that the idea of contradicting or conflicting information streams has to be discarded. Warde interprets traditions as nothing but ritualised and/or invented customs. It has been shown that so-called traditions are no more than distinctive forms of innovation and as a consequence, the contradiction between custom, tradition and innovation has to be reconsidered. Moreover, the early twentieth-century use of novel canned foods as a means for working-class women to cook easy yet tasty and nutritious meals invalidates the strict divide between convenience and care.[15] The supposedly conflicting information streams in women's magazines or other forms of media have to be interpreted as a *bricolage* of representations that can, but not necessarily do, conflict.

The use of women's magazines as a source for historical research proves rewarding. Magazines closely follow societal concerns that are described in the various articles, including the culinary pages and recipe sections.[16] Therefore, women's magazines form an interesting source to investigate the history of culinary mentalities (*Zeitgeist*) of certain Western societies.[17] Furthermore, media studies has shown that the cooking rubrics of women's periodicals balance the introduction of novel foods and cooking techniques on the one hand and the preservation of familiar culinary knowledge on the other.[18] Consequently, magazines constitute a valid source to investigate the representations of accustomed and innovative preservation types. Finally, it has to be pointed out that this chapter does not look at actual preserving practices. Therefore, the analysis does not focus on the actual acquisition of refrigerators and/or freezers, but on the acceptance of ideas and mentalities represented in the periodicals.[19] A rural magazine and an urban one were selected in order to find out whether or not the countryside actually did suffer from a backlog concerning the introduction of innovative preservation techniques, as scholarly research assumes.[20]

In 1909, the Belgian Farmer Women's Association (BFWA) first published its monthly magazine *De Boerin* (*The Farmer Woman*) that promoted technological novelties in order to alleviate women's work on the farm and in the household. In 1949, *De Boerin* changed its name to *Bij de Haard* (*Around the Hearth*) and instantly implemented a content shift that was characterized by a strong focus on household issues: cooking, education, interior design and fashion became central

---

14   Warde, 1994, 23; Warde, 1997.
15   Turner, 2006, 14.
16   Holmes, 2007, 517.
17   Hülsken, 2005, 4; Roessler, 2007, 566.
18   Sheridan, 2000, 323.
19   Barthes, 2008, 32; Duruz, 1999, 234; Grahame, 1994, 303; Rousseau, 2012, 196.
20   Bentley, 2012, 3.

themes. *De Boerin/Bij de Haard*'s culinary pages have appeared regularly from 1909 until today. Through these pages the BFWA wanted to offer its members advice on simple, nourishing and ready-to-use recipes. Moreover, the cookery section closely followed societal changes, as can be illustrated by the growing number of articles on the use of kitchen appliances in the 1950s and 1960s, or the increasing number of exotic recipes in the 1960s and 1970s due to the growing importance of foreign cuisines in Flanders in that period.[21]

When the urban magazine was first published in 1925 under the name *Het Modeblad* (*The Fashion Magazine*), it reached out to the urban middle classes. It mainly focused on fashion for women and girls, 'frivolous' handwork (sewing and knitting) and interior design. Furthermore, it emphasized the importance of housewives' chores in securing a happy marriage and maintaining family life. In 1931, *Het Modeblad* changed its name to *Het Rijk der Vrouw* (*The Woman's Realm*) and, while the magazine's number one focus remained fashion, the culinary pages and articles on household organization grew in importance. The cookery articles expanded as time passed and offered a combination of simple, fancy and complex recipes. The use of kitchen appliances, however, was only promoted when the technological devices fitted an urban lifestyle characterized by space constraints, time restraints (due to women's professional activities outside the house) and the employment of servants in the first couple of decades of the magazine's existence.

This chapter subjects both *De Boerin/Bij de Haard* and *Het Rijk der Vrouw*'s articles on food preservation to a quantitative and qualitative analysis, but does not include advertisements and recipes. The quantification explores how the number of articles per food preservation type evolved, and the qualification examines the concepts and metaphors that structured the magazines' representation of customary and innovative preservation techniques. For *De Boerin/Bij de Haard*, I found a total of 55 articles on food preservation for the period 1945-1960 and *Het Rijk der Vrouw* published 64 pieces on the subject. These articles were subdivided into four main categories: homemade preserves,[22] artificial cold (containing articles on refrigerators and freezers), canned foods, and a combination of two or more of these categories. It must be pointed out that although refrigerators and freezers went through different technological developments,[23] they are considered here within one category (artificial cold/mechanized cold storage), in order to distinguish them from home bottling and canned foods. The following paragraphs analyse the attention paid to the various food preservation types by the respective women's magazines and how they were represented individually and in relation to each other.

---

21   Geyzen, 2011, 279–80.

22   The terminology only refers to bottling at home, since I did not find any traces of home canning.

23   Oddy and Oddy, 1998, 299.

The Postwar Return to Normality and the Acknowledgment of Innovation

Preservation by Numbers

On 11 May 1940, the Belgian government implemented an official rationing system in order to regulate the population's food supplies and strictly control the consumption of several essential foodstuffs, such as sugar and salt. Consequently, the custom of making jam and jellies in summer – an activity that required large amounts of sugar – could not be maintained.[24] After the Second World War, however, both *De Boerin/Bij de Haard* and *Het Rijk der Vrouw* promoted the revival of prewar home bottling, but these magazines also paid attention to innovative mechanized cold storage. Consequently, the representations of preservation techniques were balanced between the discussion of the familiar and the introduction of the novel. Figure 13.1 shows the division of all articles on food preservation per category in both magazines between 1945 and 1960.

In the rural magazine, half of the articles focused on refrigerated storage, while 45 per cent touched upon homemade preserves (including sterilization, fermenting, drying and salting). Only 6 per cent combined the familiar and the novel with comparisons on the advantages and disadvantages of both categories, but not

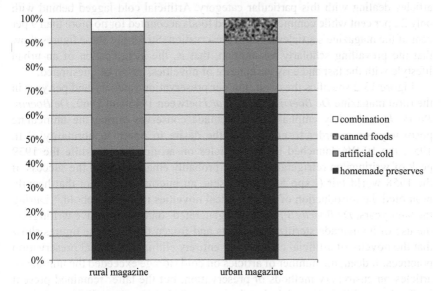

Source: Anneke Geyzen.

Figure 13.1   Articles on food preservation types in *De Boerin/Bij de Haard* and *Het Rijk der Vrouw* (1945–1960)

---

24   Geyzen, 2011, 280.

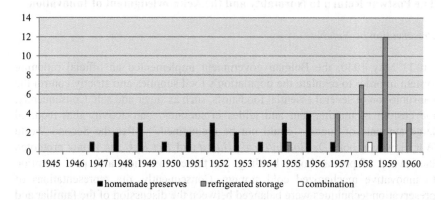

Source: Anneke Geyzen.

Figure 13.2   Evolution of food preservation types in *De Boerin/Bij de Haard* (1945–1960)

one article mentioned the use of commercial canned foods. The urban magazine emphasized the production of homemade conserves with nearly 70 per cent of the articles dealing with this particular category. Artificial cold lagged behind with only 22 per cent while commercial canned foods accounted for no more than 9 per cent of the magazine's articles on food preservation. Strikingly, these figures show that the prevailing scholarly assumption, that is, the identification of an urban lifestyle with the fast and easy acceptance of novelties, has to be questioned.

Figure 13.2 specifies the evolution per preservation category and per year in the rural magazine *De Boerin/Bij de Haard* between 1945 and 1960. *De Boerin/ Bij de Haard* solely emphasized homemade conserves during the immediate postwar years in order to encourage 'the desire to return to normality'.[25] In 1955, the BFWA launched its first articles on artificial cold, while the 1959 peak of writings on refrigerated storage probably emanated from the success of the 1958 world fair (Expo'58) in Brussels, an international event that heavily promoted the introduction of technological novelties in the household.[26] During the later years, *De Boerin/Bij de Haard* generated some comparative writings on the use of homemade sterilized products and frozen foods. These figures show that the novelty of artificial cold did not entirely eliminate habitual preservation practices. Indeed, the number of articles on cold storage exceeded the number of articles on customary methods of preservation, but the latter remained present in *De Boerin/Bij de Haard* during the years 1945–1959. A qualitative analysis of the articles explores the representation of both categories individually and in relation to each other.

---

25   Wildt, 2001, 66.
26   Van Herck and Avermaete, 2006, s.p.

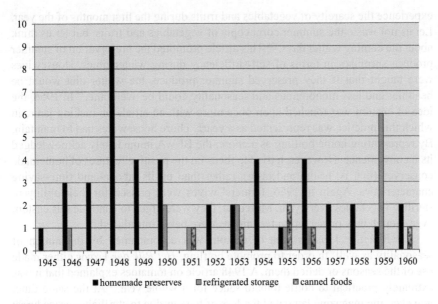

Source: Anneke Geyzen.

Figure 13.3   Evolution of food preservation types in *Het Rijk der Vrouw* (1945–1960)

Figure 13.3 shows the evolution per preservation category and per year in the urban magazine *Het Rijk der Vrouw* between 1945 and 1960. As in the rural magazine, *Het Rijk der Vrouw* was characterized by a strong postwar emphasis on homemade conserves. In 1948, the number of articles on this particular category peaked, which was most likely caused by the end of the food rationing system in the course of that year.[27] In 1946 an article on cold storage had been published already, but besides the 1959 peak, the articles in this category were few and published irregularly. Commercial canned foods appeared quite frequently in small numbers from the early 1950s onwards. Articles that compared different preservation categories, however, were never published in *Het Rijk der Vrouw*. A qualitative analysis separates the categories of the different preservation techniques.

Homemade Preserves

Both *De Boerin/Bij de Haard* and *Het Rijk der Vrouw* applied an array of intertwining concepts and notions to represent homemade bottling practices. Before anything else, homemade conserves were undeniably associated with the idea of custom and habit, and together with these concepts the notion of seasonality was regularly touched upon. In 1949, the BFWA mentioned: 'Every year we

27   Geyzen, 2011, 280.

experience the scarcity of vegetables and fruits during the first months of the year. Let us not waste the summer cornucopia of vegetables and fruits, but let us think about the coming winter days.'[28] This article promoted the preservation of summer produce surpluses in terms of self-sufficiency during winter times. Housewives were taught that if they preserved summer produce, the winter diet would be healthier and less monotonous and seasonality could be overcome.[29] In 1956, the idea of custom was touched upon once more with an article on making jams, in which this practice was represented as a yearly chore housewives had to maintain. By representing home bottling as a chore, the BFWA immediately acknowledged its inconvenience. However, it tried to focus on the positive features of homemade conserves (that is, health and taste), rather than on its labour- and time-saving characteristics. Again in 1956, farmers' wives were praised for their ability to sterilize vegetables every year. Moreover, they were urged to continue this custom even though new preservation techniques were being introduced.[30]

Het Rijk der Vrouw's idea of custom was accompanied by the notion of seasonality as well. In order to promote bottling, *Het Rijk der Vrouw* either made use of the seasons or defied them. A 1948 article on tomatoes explained that it was extremely practical to bottle tomato sauce for a whole year.[31] At the same time, however, the magazine lamented the loss of flavour due to sterilizing procedures: 'It goes without saying that preserved mushrooms have lost half of their taste. They could never compete with the aroma of fresh ones. But while waiting for April [...] they taste amazingly well.'[32] The use of bottled vegetables was promoted to get through the monotonous winter menus, but once available the consumption of fresh produce was strongly encouraged using the argument of taste.

By contrast to the rural magazine, *Het Rijk der Vrouw* mentioned convenience by emphasizing the labour-saving qualities of homemade conserves. Instead of focusing on the labour-consuming characteristics of bottling at home, the magazine mentioned the advantages of having a pantry stuffed with jars that could be quickly opened and heated after a long working day outside the home.[33] Besides representing homemade conserves as a custom, *Het Rijk der Vrouw* occasionally considered them from a nostalgic point of view and then described the custom as a tradition. In 1946, the magazine blamed the sugar shortages during the Second World War for the erosion of women's ability to make jam. The skills had been lost and the readers were instructed on this particular preservation technique in order to revive it.[34] In 1948 and 1952, *Het Rijk der Vrouw* once more lamented the loss of the jam-making knowledge and the interruption of this tradition – as the

---

28   *Bij de Haard*, August 1949, 14. All translations from Dutch are mine.
29   Ibid., August 1953, 194.
30   Ibid., July 1956, 199, 202.
31   *Het Rijk der Vrouw*, August 1948, 7.
32   Ibid., August 1950, 27.
33   Ibid., August 1947, 11.
34   Ibid., June 1946, 7.

articles explicitly called it – by wartime sugar rationing. The writings even became nostalgic when they romantically described the handing down of jam recipes from one generation to another before the Second World War. Consequently, the magazine revived these food memories in order to promote jam-making activities amongst the younger generation who lacked the skills of engaging in the preservation of fruit.[35] The association of the idea of custom with the notion of nostalgia came to the fore in an early article on refrigerated storage as well. *Het Rijk der Vrouw* stated:

> In our old Europe, that is heavily afflicted by war, the refrigerator remains a luxury item. We are forced to stick to more modest means: innocent antiseptic methods like salt, sugar, vinegar and herbs or other old procedures our grandmothers have passed on. They have survived the test of time.[36]

The magazine once more referred to a nostalgic past when grandmothers knew how to preserve foods healthily without technological devices.

Commercial Canned Foods

In articles on homemade preserves that campaigned for seasonal bottling, *De Boerin/Bij de Haard* occasionally touched upon canned foods. Even though commercial canned foods were believed to be convenient, the magazine strongly opposed their use in the kitchen. The organization did agree that the use of canned foods saved a lot of labour and time, while the making of preserves was labour- and time-consuming. The main advantage of homemade preserves over commercial cans was related to the high price of the latter. Moreover, *De Boerin/Bij de Haard* also used the aspect of taste in order to promote homemade bottled instead of canned ingredients: 'Homemade jams surpass the commercial ones in taste and low price.'[37] The BFWA's negative representations of commercial canned foods, in combination with their high price, engendered the absence of articles on this particular preservation type.

By contrast to *De Boerin/Bij de Haard*, *Het Rijk der Vrouw* embraced the labour-saving qualities of commercial canned foods and instructed women on the use of these items. In 1951, an article on the preparation of canned foods was published: on the one hand it explained the use of the can-opener and on the other it showed how canned foods could be prepared and served in order to camouflage that they had been preserved in a tin can.[38] After all, during the immediate postwar years, negative images and representations surrounded commercial canned foods, but *Het Rijk der Vrouw* saw the advantages of these particular preserves and started

---

35 Ibid., May 1948, 7; June 1952, 20.
36 Ibid., June 1946, 5.
37 *Bij de Haard*, September 1952, 252–3.
38 *Het Rijk der Vrouw*, November 1951, 14.

a campaign to promote their use in the kitchen. In order to do so, the magazine published several articles in which the industrial production of canned ingredients was explained in order to overcome consumers' prejudices and ignorance. In 1954, the chain production of canned peas was touched on[39] and in 1956, the different steps in the mechanized production of canned soups were revealed.[40] Moreover, *Het Rijk der Vrouw* explained that industrially produced canned foods were healthy in two ways: the production process was hygienic and it safeguarded the nutritional value of the ingredients.[41] However, the number of articles on this particular type of preservation was at odds with the promotional discourse the magazine developed. The high price of canned foods especially by comparison to homemade counterparts was pointed out as the main reason: canned foods were still too expensive for a typical family to consume regularly.[42]

Mechanized Cold Storage

Representations of artificial cold mainly emphasized concepts of innovation and education and also focused on homemade and labour-saving characteristics. In 1957, the BFWA described freezing as 'the preservation technique of the future'[43] and continued by explaining what a freezer was, how it had to be used correctly and how it differed from a refrigerator, about which no article appeared in *De Boerin/ Bij de Haard*. It seems that the use of both frozen and fresh foods, harvested from one's own garden might account for this void. Other pieces explained how long frozen foodstuffs could be preserved and how they could be wrapped in order to store them under hygienic conditions. Together with freezing came the activity of defrosting and again housewives were taught when foodstuffs needed to be taken out of the freezer and how they could be hygienically defrosted.[44]

Alongside the educational discourse on artificial cold, the notion of homemade frozen foods, seasonality and convenience appeared as well. The purchase of commercial frozen meats, for example, was not yet an issue in the 1950s and 1960s, since farmers' womenfolk themselves were expected to preserve all foodstuffs that ended up in the freezer. Interestingly, and by contrast to bottling practices, freezing very much focused on the preservation of meat. With the November slaughtering of pigs, women were no longer obliged to invest time in the production of sausages and *pâtés*, since they could easily wrap and freeze every part of the pig and consume it whenever they wanted.[45] A 1958 article on red

---

39   Ibid., September 1954, 20.
40   Ibid., September 1956, 14.
41   Ibid., March 1955, 34.
42   Ibid., June 1955, 36.
43   *Bij de Haard*, April 1957, 117.
44   Ibid., September 1959, 271.
45   Ibid., April 1957, 117, July 1958, 321.

fruits also described the demise of seasonal eating habits with the preservation of frozen strawberries and cherries for the Christmas menu.[46]

Finally, taste and health issues occupied a prominent place in *De Boerin/Bij de Haard*'s discourse on artificial cold. In 1957, the BFWA stated that 'the nutritional value of frozen foods equalled the nutritional value of fresh produce, as well as taste, smell and structure.'[47] The story continued in 1958: 'Does it taste good? There is no difference whatsoever from fresh meat and it is always tender.'[48] A 1959 quote immediately revealed the reason for frozen meat's popularity: 'Housewives explain that sterilized meat always turned chewy.'[49]

Het Rijk der Vrouw had already mentioned refrigerators in 1946 with an article on the use of homemade preserves and their advantages over relying on artificial cold. The magazine at that time had contrasted custom and innovation, and the breakthrough of articles on the use of a refrigerator occurred later, in the 1950s. However, in contrast to novel canned foods, *Het Rijk der Vrouw* was in doubt about the introduction of artificial cold in urban households. On the one hand, refrigerators were considered to be handy for several reasons: they reduced shopping time, since women could avoid daily grocery shopping,[50] and brought to life a sense of comfort with their ability to store food that could be taken out whenever needed.[51] On the other hand, the devices were expensive and they occupied a lot of room in urban houses and apartments that mostly did not have the required space.[52]

Het Rijk der Vrouw's hesitant attitude towards artificial cold most probably accounted for the small number of articles in the magazine on this type of preservation between 1945 and 1960. However, it is important to point out that *Het Rijk der Vrouw* did not discount the purchase of refrigerated storage as an unnecessary luxury, but as an expensive convenience. Little by little, the magazine tried to persuade its readers of the advantages of mechanized artificial cold storage by presenting to them a material world they were not yet able to afford. Media studies have shown that women's magazines often construct a fantasy world based on their articles and advertisements.[53] The same conclusion can be drawn from *Het Rijk der Vrouw*'s discourse on refrigerators. The purchase of cold storage was too expensive at the time of publication and thus *Het Rijk der Vrouw* stuck to conservative habits. Finally, it can be claimed that the magazine's longing for pre-war 'normality' also accounted for limited representations of artificial cold.

---

46   Ibid., May 1958, 151.
47   Ibid., April 1957, 117.
48   Ibid., May 1958, 151.
49   Ibid., February 1959, 50.
50   *Het Rijk der Vrouw*, February 1953, 22–3.
51   Ibid., June 1955, 36.
52   Ibid., June 1959, 54–5.
53   Stephenson, 2007, 614–15.

Conclusion

This chapter started with the question of how different types of preservation were represented in two Flemish women's magazines between 1945 and 1960. It also took a close look at how households were persuaded to purchase mechanized cold storage, by comparing refrigeration to other preservation techniques. A quantitative and qualitative analysis of a rural and an urban magazine led to several succinct answers.

As far as *De Boerin/Bij de Haard* is concerned, the quantitative analysis showed that both homemade bottling and freezing were promoted. Based on the concepts described in the qualitative analysis, it can be stated that both preservation types were used for different purposes. While fruits and vegetables remained the subject of sterilization, meat ended up in the freezer. The arguments that justified this dichotomy mainly dealt with taste: sterilized fruits and vegetables were praised for their flavour, and frozen meats by far surpassed sterilized meats in quality and taste. It can be argued that both a 'return to normality' and a desire for novelty were present in *De Boerin/Bij de Haard* depending on the purposes of the different types of preservation.

Het Rijk der Vrouw's articles on homemade conserves mainly dealt with the magazine's nostalgic desire for prewar 'normality. The urban periodical also made use of innovation, but to a much lesser extent. It promoted canned foods but in order to do so, it had to tackle the negative image that surrounded these particular preserves. However, the small number of articles on commercial canned foods (9 per cent) contrasts with *Het Rijk der Vrouw*'s positive attitude towards them. In all probability, the high price of canned foods accounted for the few articles on this preservation category, in contrast to the magazine's promotional discourse. Finally, the refrigerator did not capture *Het Rijk der Vrouw*'s full attention, since cold storage devices took up a lot of space and were costly until well into the 1960s. However, this did not prevent the magazine from representing refrigerators as a convenience that could not yet be purchased but would be sooner or later.

To conclude, *De Boerin/Bij de Haard* embraced the use of mechanized artificial cold storage, since it included all the positive features of other preservation techniques while discarding their negative characteristics. Freezers were novel and convenient and were able to conserve foodstuffs' flavour and nutritional value. Consequently, the BFWA used these concepts to promote mechanized artificial cold storage in order to persuade rural households of its use at home. In urban, middle-class dwellings, refrigerators and freezers took up a lot of space and, as a result, *Het Rijk der Vrouw* stuck to more customary preservation techniques. Housewives were persuaded of the advantages of commercial canned foods. They were convenient, tasty and healthy but their. high prices limited their popularity. It remains to be researched whether or not *Het Rijk der Vrouw*'s discourse on the convenience of refrigerated storage intensified after 1960.

References

Primary Sources

Bij de Haard. Maandblad van de Boerinnenbond, Leuven: De Boerinnenbond, 1949–1960.
De Boerin. Maandblad van de Boerinnenbond Leuven, Leuven: Uitgeverij Van Huyck, 1945–1948.
Het Rijk der Vrouw, Brussels: Het Rijk der Vrouw, 1945–1960.

Secondary Sources

Barthes, R., 2008, 'Toward a psychosociology of contemporary food consumption', in Counihan, C. and Esterik, P. Van, eds, *Food and culture. A reader*, New York and London: Routledge.
Belasco, W., 2008, *Food: the key concepts*, Oxford and New York: Berg.
Bentley, A., 2012, 'Introduction', in Bentley, A., ed., *A cultural history of food in the modern age*, London and New York: Berg.
Bruegel, M., 1998, 'From the shop floor to the home: Appertising and food preservation in households in rural France, 1810–1930', in ICREFH IV: Schärer, M.R. and Fenton, A. eds, *Food and material culture*, East Linton, Scotland: Tuckwell.
Duruz, J., 1999, 'Food as nostalgia. Eating the fifties and sixties', *Australian Historical Studies*, 113.
Geyzen, A., 2011, 'Popular discourse on nutrition, health and indulgence in Flanders, 1945–1960', *Appetite*, 56.
Goody, J., 1982, *Cooking, cuisine and class. A study in comparative sociology*, Cambridge: Cambridge University Press.
Grahame, P.J., 1994, 'Objects, texts, and practices: the refrigerator in consumer discourses between the wars', in Riggins, S.H., ed., *The solidness of things. Essays on the socio-semiotics of objects*, The Hague: Mouton de Gruyter.
Guillou, A., 1995, 'Du congélateur à la table', in Eizner, N., ed., *Voyage en alimentation*, Paris: A.R.F. Editions.
Hardyment, C., 1988, *From mangle to microwave. The mechanization of household work*, Cambridge: Polity.
Holmes, T., 2007 'Mapping the magazine. An introduction', *Journalism Studies* 8.
Hülsken, M., *'Fascinerend en veelzijdig: het vrouwentijdschrift als bron. Een leidraad voor de beginnende onderzoeker'* [Fascinating and diverse: the women's magazine as a source. Starter guidelines for the researcher], http://www.vrouwentijdschriften.nl (accessed 27 February 2012).
Niesten, E., Raymaekers, J. and Segers, Y., 2002, *Kattentongen, ezelsoren en varkenspoten. Onze keuken in de 20ste eeuw* [Cat tongues, donkey ears and pigs trotters. Our kitchen in the twentieth century], Leuven: Centrum voor Agrarische Geschiedenis.

Oddy, D.J. and Oddy, J.R., 1998, 'The iceman cometh: the effect of low-temperature technology on the British diet', in ICREFH IV: Schärer, M.R. and Fenton, A., eds, *Food and material culture*, East Linton, Scotland: Tuckwell.

Onghena, S., 2006, *Blauw bloed en confituur. Verborgen recepten van 'moderne' adellijke eetcultuur* [Blue blood and jam. Hidden recipes of 'modern' noble food culture], Alphen aan de Maas: Uitgeverij Veerhuis.

Roessler, P., 2007, 'Global players, émigrés, and Zeitgeist. Magazine design and the interrelation between the United States and Germany', *Journalism Studies*, 8.

Rousseau, S., 2012, 'Food representations', in Bentley, A., ed., *A cultural history of food in the modern age*, London and New York: Berg.

Scholliers, P., 2008a, *Food Culture in Belgium*, Westport and London: Greenwood Press.

Scholliers, P., 2008b, '*Dessert voor iedereen. Gewone mensen en hun zoetigheden in de negentiende en twintigste eeuw*' [Dessert for everyone. Ordinary people and their sweets in the nineteenth and twentieth century], in. De Vooght, D., Onghena, S. and Scholliers, P., eds, *Van Pièce Montée tot Pêche Melba: een geschiedenis van het betere nagerecht* [From Pièce Montée to Pêche Melba: a history of the better dessert], Brussels: VUB Press.

Sheridan, S., 2000, 'Eating the Other: food and cultural difference in the *Australian Women's Weekly* in the 1960s', *Journal of Intercultural Studies*, 21.

Stephenson, S., 2007, 'The changing face of women's magazines in Russia', *Journalism Studies* 8.

Teuteberg, H.J., 1995, 'History of cooling and freezing techniques and their impact on nutrition in twentieth-century Germany', in ICREFH III: Hartog, A.P. den, ed., *Food, technology, science and marketing. European diet in the twentieth century*, East Linton, Scotland: Tuckwell.

Turner, K. L., 2006, 'Buying, not cooking. Ready-to-eat food in American urban working-class neighbourhoods, 1880–1930', *Food, Culture and Society*, 9.

Van den Eeckhout, P. and Scholliers, P., 2012, 'The proliferation of brands: the case of food in Belgium, 1890–1940', *Enterprise and Society*, 13.

Van Herck, K. and Avermaete, T., 2006, *Wonen in welvaart: woningbouw en wooncultuur in Vlaanderen, 1948–1973* [Living in prosperity: housing in Flanders, 1948–1973], Rotterdam: 010 Publishers.

Warde, A., 1994, 'Changing vocabularies of taste, 1967–1992: discourses about food preparation', *British Food Journal*, 96.

Warde, A., 1997, *Consumption, food and taste. Culinary antinomies and commodity culture*, London: Sage.

Wildt, M., 2001, 'Promise of more. The rhetoric of food consumption in a society searching for itself: West Germany in the 1950s', in Scholliers, P., ed., *Food, drink and identity. Cooking, eating and drinking in Europe since the Middle Ages*, Oxford and New York: Berg.

Chapter 14
The Growth of Bread Consumption among Romanian Peasants, 1950–1980

Lucian Scrob

Introduction

This chapter focuses on the emergence and development of bakeries in the Old Kingdom of Romania (Moldavia and Wallachia) and their contribution to the dietary switch in peasants' diets from *mămăligă*, which is boiled cornmeal (maize) porridge, to bread. The study is relevant in view of the mechanism of the switch implying both a change in the ingredient of the basic foodstuff and in the technique of preparing it.

The first attempts by the state to promote consumption of bread among peasants can be traced to the set of anti-pellagra measures providing for the establishment of non-profit state-financed 'rural bakeries' after the model of the Italian *'forno rurale'* in the 1920s. However the development of industrially produced bread during the communist period was fundamental to the transformation in total consumption. The dietary change involved concerns what Sidney Mintz has termed the 'core' foods in the diets of traditional populations.[1] According to his definition, a 'core' food is characterized by high intake compared to other components of the typical diet, and is in regular consumption throughout the year. The study of pellagra in Romania became a priority during the 1950s and numerous studies of this disease were conducted by the Public Health Institute.[2] This work continued until at least the early 1970s. The incidence of pellagra underwent a gradual reduction from its high point in 1938: by 1959 the number of persons suffering from pellagra had been halved by comparison with 1938. The everyday life of the rural population in Romania during the 1960s and the 1970s was improved by two important developments at the dietary level: the nationwide increasing reliance on commercially produced foods and the regional specific process of replacing *mămăligă* with bread in the regular diet. For the rural population, baked goods bought in shops exemplified the acceptance of convenience foods, both to the extent they became part of regular meals in rural households and because of the reduction in housework. Moreover, the greater availability of bread affected standards of living since consumers in rural areas saw bread as status food. Regular consumption of industrially-produced bread was an

---

1   Mintz, 1991.

2   *Mămăligă*, when used extensively as a 'core' food may lead to pellagra, a deficiency disease from the malabsorption of the B vitamin niacin.

important factor in dietary change. An analysis of the interaction between consumers and producers within a centrally-planned economic system (functioning according to its own non-market logic) shows its limited capacity of adjustment to consumers' demands. Altogether, the degree of satisfaction of consumers' expectations, price changes, the level of bread supply and its geographical distribution determined the extent to which the state could convert one of its more successful attempts of influencing rural living standards into political capital.

Production and Economic Developments in the Baking Industry, 1950–1975

State Ownership

Complete state ownership over the means of production in the baking industry was established in 1950. The relatively less intense push for nationalization up to that date probably reflected the authorities' concerns over its detrimental effects on the production of a highly valued and still scarce commodity.[3] Statistics for bread production in the 25 years following the nationalization act show an increase in total output of industrially-produced bread from 444,400 tons[4] to 2,358,000 tons in 1975.[5] The small number of 1,017 bakeries that passed into state ownership indicates the contraction from interwar levels caused by war devastation and nationalization. These bakeries were organized by the Council of Ministers' Decree No. 1065, dated 5 October 1950, into 92 enterprises and 20 baking trusts[6] as part of the Ministry of the Food Industry.[7] Permission to produce bread as well as any other baked goods was expressly restricted to units owned by the state.[8]

From an economic perspective, Table 14.1 summarizes the developments that accompanied and enabled a 2.75 times increase in the production of bread between the nationalization of bakeries and 1975. The data support two general remarks: first, that growth originated from a combination of increases in labour and investments and from technical and organizational changes and second, that growth proceeded in stages in terms of both the magnitude of the increase between representative years and of the relative contribution of each factor.

---

3   Negreanu and Popa, 1969, 422.

4   National Archives of Romania. Central Committee of the Romanian Communist Party (C.C. al P.C.R.) *Secţia Economică*. File 119/1952, 52. All archival references are from this source unless otherwise noted.

5   Calculated from data on per capita production of bread in 1975 in *Secţ. Econ.* file 134/1976, 4 and from data on the size of the population from *Anuarul Statistic al Republicii Socialiste România pe 1976*, 1977, 9.

6   Secţ. Econ. File 119/1952, 3.

7   'Hotărârea Numărul 1065 privind înfiinţarea "Trusturilor de Panificaţie" 1950, 3–5.

8   'Hotărârea Consiliului de Miniştri privitor la o mai bună aprovizionare cu pâine' 1950, 43.

Table 14.1   Changes in bread production, value of fixed funds, number of directly productive workers and average capacity of production per unit in Romania, 1950–1975

Year	1952	1959	1965	1970	1975
Production of bread (tons)	716,400	1,110,000	1,637,000	1,820,400	1,956,000
Production of bread in equivalent black-bread units (tons)		1,296,090	2,008,610	2,640,690	3,257,500
Value of fixed funds index of growth (1950=100)	141% (1955)	199% (1960)	364% (1965)	690% (1970)	813% (1975)
Number of workers in directly productive activities	11,204	15,290			19,500
Average capacity of production per unit	3.66	6.16		10.3 (1969)	14.8 (1976)

Sources: Căliman 1969, 176; '*Pentru avântul continuu al industriei de panificație*' 1953, 5; 119/1952, 52; 77/1959, 15; 12/1966, 395, 496; 15/1966, 10; 51/1971, 41; 134/1976; Negreanu 1969, 423; Rotaru 1970, 684-686; Rotaru 1974, 31.

During the period 1950–1975, the labour force grew by nearly 75 per cent, with roughly equal increases before and after 1959. For the entire period, increases in labour input contributed 20 per cent and productivity growth 45.4 per cent of increased production. Part of the labour productivity growth resulted from qualitative changes such as superior qualifications of workers, improved payment schemes rewarding productivity and better organization of work. However, the largest part of labour productivity growth can be attributed to a sharp rise in the stock of fixed capital and, implicitly, to the flow of capital into production. The result of sustained investment in the baking industry, the rising value of basic funds reflects primarily the intensification of production through progressive mechanization and concentration in larger units rather than extensive development. During an initial phase covering the first two five-year plans, mechanization of the most demanding operations – flour sifting and dough kneading – was extended from 30 per cent[9] and 44 per cent of total production in 1952[10] to 60 per cent and 75 per cent in 1959.[11] In addition, baking in the traditional earthen ovens declined from overwhelming predominance in 1952[12] to 48 per cent of total production in 1959. This was due to the expansion of baking in ovens with indirect steam heating (47 per cent) and in mechanical ovens (5 per cent).[13] However, the loading

---

9   *Industria Alimentară* 1956, 3, 8.
10   *Secț. Econ.* File 119/1952, 23.
11   *Secț. Econ.* File 77/1959, 41 and File 23/1961, 92.
12   *Secț. Econ.* File 119/1952, 3.
13   *Secț. Econ.* File 77/1959, 42.

and unloading of bread from ovens and the mixing of raw materials continued to be performed manually while the operations of dividing, weighing and shaping the dough were only mechanized to a limited degree.[14] Several such operations were mechanized during a second phase characterized by higher levels of investment and emphasis on updated technology. Mechanical mixers of raw materials were used for 37 per cent of total production in 1975.[15] Baking in ovens with indirect heating became predominant by 1967[16] while baking in the more advanced mechanical ovens produced 29 per cent of output in 1975.[17] Sifting and kneading was completely mechanized and by 1970, 16 per cent of total bread production was mechanically loaded and unloaded from ovens. Finally, 11.4 per cent of bread production in 1975 was conducted in integrated production lines that were fully mechanized and automated. In dividing, weighing and shaping the dough however, mechanization lagged behind the other operations, a serious drawback considering their share of total labour input of 36–44 per cent if un-mechanized under the technological conditions prevailing in 1967.[18]

The application of mechanization benefited from the concentration of production in larger units. The average capacity per unit of production increased fourfold between 1952 and 1975 and reflected the marked decline of bakeries with capacities below 5 tons of bread per 24 hours, the sharp rise of bakeries with capacities of 10-20 tons of bread per 24 hours and a small but consequential rise of bakeries with capacities over 40 tons.[19] As a result, units with capacities above 10 tons in 24 hours provided 70 per cent of production in 1970, up from 29 per cent in 1950 and the rising trend to bigger bakeries continued until at least 1975 as the numbers fell but total capacity increased.

The progressive mechanization of production affected prices and capital accumulation to an extent determined by the share of the relevant factors in the cost of production. As with other branches of the food industry, the value-added component represented less than 9 per cent of production costs in 1959[20] with shares of 7.4 per cent for labour remuneration and social security expenses and 0.9 per cent for capital amortization. The saving effect of mechanization on production costs coupled with a restructuring of the output in the direction of more profitable varieties explains the state's interest in the development of an industry allowing growing accumulation rates.

---

14   *Secţ. Econ.* File 77/1959, 42.
15   *Secţ. Econ.* File 134/1976, 20.
16   *Industria Alimentară*, 1967, 1, 14.
17   *Secţ. Econ.* File 134/1976, 20.
18   *Industria Alimentară*, 1967, 1, 14.
19   Negreanu and Popa, 1969, 423.
20   The following calculations are based on *Secţ. Econ.* File 77/1959, 91–2.

Developments in the Co-Operative Sector

Concentration of production was characteristic for units administered by the Ministry of the Food Industry given their predominantly urban location. In general, however, the optimum size of baking factories was considered to be largely determined by the size of the immediate consumer population in view of the economic inefficiency of transporting large quantities of bread on a daily basis over long distances.[21] Accordingly, the construction of small-scale bakeries was proposed as a more appropriate solution to the task of promoting consumption of industrially-produced bread in villages beyond certain distances from urban localities.

With the exception of a few state-owned units, rural bakeries belonged to either Consumers or Production Co-operatives, which controlled various aspects of their production activities. Bakeries belonging to Consumers' Co-operatives engaged in bread production using state-supplied flour but also provided baking services ranging from producing bread with grains and flour provided by customers to baking home-prepared dough.[22] In calculating prices for their baking services, these bakeries followed the practice of state-owned factories and added production costs, profits and accumulation. The bakeries belonging to Production Co-operatives provided baking services to co-operative members only and charged in exchange a sum needed to maintain the bakery operations and to assure accumulation. Without the profit component, prices for baking services were 20–25 per cent lower at the Production Co-operative.[23] The possibility of payment-in-kind for baking services appealed to consumers who received part of their remuneration for work in the form of wheat not readily convertible to cash.

The proliferation of rural bakeries after 1960 expressed a new-found concern among the authorities with supplying industrially-produced bread to the rural population. Even though the task of establishing bakeries was stipulated in the 1948 model charter of the Consumers' Co-operatives,[24] bread production had barely reached 55,000 tons by 1960, giving a probable number of 230 bakeries.[25] Galvanized by state support, production doubled by 1965[26] and again by 1970[27] and finally settled at around 250,000 tons in 1975. Energetically advocated by authorities, production through baking services was introduced in 1960, but lagged

---

21   *Industria Alimentară*, 1969, 123–7 and 1968, 11, 625–7.

22   *Secţ. Econ.* File 10/1967, 57–9.

23   *Secţ. Econ.* File 10/1967, 58.

24   *Secţ. Econ.* File 56/1948, 5.

25   Calculated as the difference between marketed quantities and the quantities produced by the baking industry in 1960. Data from *Secţ. Econ.* File 11/1960, 1.

26   *Secţ. Econ.* File 15/1966, 12.

27   *Secţ. Econ.* File 51/1971, 41.

behind normal output with increases to an estimated 42,350 tons in 1965[28] and 152,450 tons in 1975.[29] In fact, Production Co-operatives had been responsible for the largest share of the growth in output throughout the period.

Quality Aspects of Bread Production

The most obvious markers of changing quality were alterations in the share of bread varieties in total bread production. The rising share of higher-grade bread in total output was the most important qualitative change. Figure 14.1 illustrates this trend, with black bread declining from overwhelming predominance (98.3 per cent of total production) in 1950 to just above one-quarter by 1976. Among the higher-grade breads, the most significant increases occurred for white and semi-white bread which by 1976 accounted for 32.3 per cent and 29.7 per cent of total production respectively. In addition, the extraction rate for flour defining each type of bread changed successively. For black bread, the level of extraction decreased from 0.90 to 0.85 in 1961,[30] increased to 0.92 in 1969[31] and decreased again to 0.88 in 1976.[32] The standard extraction rate for semi-white bread had been 0.75 between 1953 and 1969[33] but increased to 0.78 in 1969[34] and 0.81 in 1976.[35]

The choice of products had also become more varied as the number of marketed baked goods increased to 80 by 1955,[36] 112 by 1960[37] and 180 by 1967[38] with the baking sector being one of the most active branches of the food industry in introducing new products.[39] The new varieties offered differing weights or shapes but also new products in terms of ingredients. In 1976, the bread offered ranged from loaves of 4 kg to 250 g of round or elongated shapes and was complemented by baked items down to 50 g of various shapes. New ingredients such as potato paste, milk by-products, soybean, vitamins and minerals were added to the usual ingredients to enhance the nutritional value of the resulting bread while some ingredients, such as salt, were eliminated to produce special breads. Among the new ingredients introduced into bread-making, potato paste was the single most

---

28   *Secț. Econ.* File 10/1967: assuming that production co-operative and consumers' co-operative bakeries had identical average output.

29   *Secț. Econ.* File 134/1976, 4. Calculated as the difference between total production and the quantities produced by the baking industry in 1975.

30   *Industria Alimentară*, 1961, 8, 229.

31   *Secț. Econ.* File 23/1975, 2.

32   *Secț. Econ.* File 14/1977, 35.

33   *Secț. Econ.* File 77/1959, 12.

34   *Secț. Econ.* File 23/1975, 2.

35   *Secț. Econ.* File 14/1977, 35.

36   Trattner, 1956, 13, includes biscuits and other flour products.

37   *Secț. Econ.* File 11/1960, 14i.

38   *Industria Alimentară*, 1967, 4, 196.

39   1947-1972: *Un bilanț*, 655.

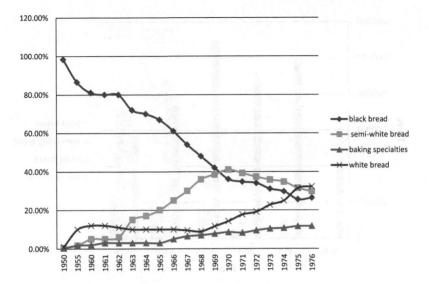

Sources: Negreanu, 1969 and C.C. al P.C.R. 14/1977, 31 (author's calculations for the 1970–1976 interval).

Figure 14.1   Percentage share of bread varieties in total bread production in Romania, 1950–1976

important addition to the established recipe as indicated by the considerable share of potato bread in total production. Amounts of potato bread were boosted to significant levels by a Council of Ministers' directive from 1963.[40] In the Dobrogea regional baking trust, production of potato bread shot up from 3 per cent of total production in 1963[41] to 75.7 per cent in 1965[42] while in the Dobrogea Milling and Baking Enterprise it rose from 8.5 per cent[43] during the fourth quarter of 1963 to 37 per cent in 1964.[44] Such high levels proved to be unsustainable in view of consumers' opposition towards the more expensive potato bread. Nonetheless, the share of potato bread in total production remained high with the black and semi-white potato bread varieties accounting for a full one-third of the planned production quantities for 1977.[45]

The rising share of higher-grade breads matched consumers' preferences in terms of taste but evidence suggests that it did not reflect their choice given the

---

40   *Direcția Județeană*, 256/1965, 65–72.
41   *Direcția Județeană*, 176/1961, 12–13; 24.
42   *Direcția Județeană*, 183/1961–66, 96–8 and 256/1965, 90.
43   *Direcția Județeană*, 34/1963, 10–11.
44   *Direcția Județeană*, 24/1965.
45   *Secț. Econ.* File 14/1977, 33, 29.

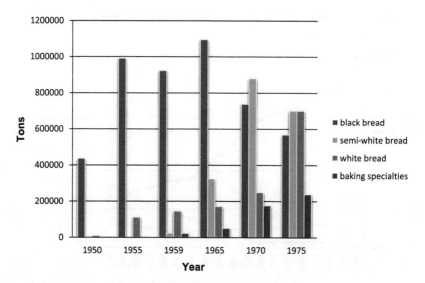

Note: Output figures for potato bread are not available.

Sources: 119/1952, 52; 79/1955, 64; 77/1959, 36; 12/1966, 41; 71/1971, 51; 134/1976, 6.

**Figure 14.2   Total output of bread varieties in Romania (tons/year), 1950–
1975**

price differentials they were required to pay. From the consumers' perspective,
the rising share of higher-grade breads in total production represented first and
foremost an additional claim on their incomes. The average price of one kilogram
of bread increased from 2 lei in 1950 to 2.44 lei in 1959 and to 3.86 lei in 1975.[46]
This reflected the combined effect of the increase of more expensive varieties and
of the decrease of cheaper varieties as illustrated in Figure 14.2.

From 1963, the relative decline of the cheaper black bread turned into an
absolute decline with marketed quantities falling from approximately 1,175,000
tons to 737,600 in 1970 and to a planned figure of 650,000 tons in 1977.[47]
Moreover, for the latter year, potato bread accounted for 58 per cent of the planned
production meaning that by that date the output of cheapest bread had declined to a
quarter of its pre-1963 level. For semi-white bread, the absolute decline had been
less marked with quantities falling from 859,200 tons in 1971 to 705,900 tons in

---

46   Calculated using prices from *Secţ. Econ.* File 13/1967, 81 and quantities from the
source listed for Figure 14.2. Except for a small drop in the price of white bread and the
abolition of subsidized prices for rationed black bread in 1955, prices remained unchanged
until the end of the 1970s.

47   *Secţ. Econ.* File 14/1977, 33.

1976.[48] Nevertheless, the rising share of potato bread from approximately 9 per cent in 1965 to 63 per cent in 1977 kept quantities of simple semi-white bread at roughly the same level, in spite of the steep rise in production during the second half of the 1960s. In exchange for this financial effort, consumers received more semi-white and white breads that had traditionally enjoyed higher prestige than black bread. The pricier potato bread offered consumers rather subtle benefits: delayed staling, better colour and enhanced fragrance.[49]

Price changes alone did not affect production, but consumers could affect production plans through formal political channels or product boycotting. As the Ministry of Internal Trade depended on the behaviour of consumers to achieve its self-assigned goals, it was expected to voice the consumer's expectations during negotiations of plans and in its contractual relations with the baking industry. Admittedly, although the scope of the Ministry's intervention was limited to preventing the production and accumulation of unsaleable goods, its activity assured a certain degree of sensitivity to consumer preferences on the part of decision-making bodies.

The limits of the system's response to consumer preferences are illustrated by the way it had managed the increasing disapproval by consumers towards the rising output of potato bread. In order to improve capital accumulation, the General Directorate of the Ministry of the Food Industry requested an increase in the share of potato bread from 27 per cent to 49.9 per cent between the first quarters of 1965 and 1966. The Ministry of Internal Trade opposed the measure on the grounds that the new quantities of potato black bread did not correspond to consumers' demand but only added to their expenses. Accordingly, the Ministry commissioned quantities of potato bread amounting to just 31.6 per cent of total production. In May 1966 in response to a drop in the value of production, the General Directorate revised the gradual pattern of growth in the share of black potato bread to an immediate significant increase (amounting to 30.3 per cent of total production for 1967 compared to 20.9 per cent the previous year). This was followed by a steady decline to slightly higher levels than originally planned.[50] Again the Ministry of Internal Trade frustrated these plans, and justified their dissent by referring to repeated consumers' complaints about the insufficient availability of ordinary black and semi-white bread.[51]

The confrontational activities of the Ministry of Internal Trade forced the General Directorate to adopt another approach to raise the value of production by combining the increased output of baking specialities (beginning with the fourth quarter of 1966[52]) and white bread with decreased extraction rates for all types of flour. This outcome illustrates the limits of the adjustment

---

48   *Secţ. Econ.* File 14/1977, 33.
49   *Industria Alimentară,* 1964, 10, 457–62.
50   *Secţ. Econ.* Files 14/1977, 33 and 18/1966, 121–3.
51   *Secţ. Econ.* File 18/1966, 33, 78, 80.
52   *Secţ. Econ.* Files 18/1966, 230–31 and 62/1966, 148.

mechanism: on the one hand the Ministry managed to reduce the share of potato bread but on the other hand it could not reverse the relative and absolute decline of black bread. Significantly, the trade-off shifted the burden of increased expenditure to higher-earning categories of people and in particular to the urban population. However, the distribution pattern favoured the rural population in the allocation of black bread and the urban population in the allocation of baking specialties and white bread. Through this trade-off, the system corrected its functioning mismatch between output mix and consumer preferences, given the rural population's option to withdraw into subsistence consumption, whether home-baked bread or *mămăligă*. In addition, the measure delayed further claims on the expenditure of low-income groups until circumstances became more favourable. In the long run, increases in the average payments for work performed in agricultural co-operatives) reduced the impact of the diminishing availability of the cheaper varieties of bread.[53] Nonetheless, inconsistencies persisted and were revealed by repeated directives to stabilize the share of higher-grade breads in total production or to increase the output of black bread that to meet requests for cheaper products and avoid undue straining of consumers' budgets.

The Distribution of Industrially-Produced Bread

The increasing availability of industrially-produced bread, rising incomes and changing work patterns meant that bread bought from markets became more important in the diets of the rural population. My estimation is that consumption of industrially-produced bread per rural resident rose from 14 kg in 1948 to 65.4 kg in 1980. This increased consumption of bought bread had a two-fold implication: first, bread gradually acquired the characteristics of a convenience food relieving housewives of one of the most arduous household tasks, and second, it promoted the transition from *mămăligă* to bread. This dietary change is important in view of the prestige attached to bread consumption in rural areas where *mămăligă* performed the function of the staple food in the diet.[54] In those areas, bread was associated with festive and ritual meals and performed the function of a social marker for the upper stratum of the peasantry. As the frequency of its consumption increased, bread underwent a transformation of status from a substitute for *mămăligă* on special occasions to that of a 'core' foodstuff on account of its regular daily consumption. As an instance of the democratization of status foods, the substitution of bread for *mămăligă* is remarkable as it became

---

53   Growth figures are for 1965–75. Changes in minimum and medium wages have been calculated using data from *Anexă lege* 263/2010 *privind sistemul unitar pentru pensii publice* and changes in the average revenue of co-operative members using data from *Secţ. Econ.* File 13/1964.

54   See Mintz 1991, 11.

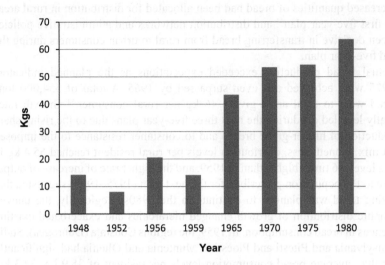

Figure 14.3   Quantity of industrially-produced bread per rural resident in Romania, (kgs/head/year) 1948–1980

the 'core' food of the diet and for the rapidity of this change, both features suggesting a noticeable impact on consumers. The quantity of bread reaching the villages was the residual quantity left after urban consumption at a certain level had been satisfied. The urban population considered here includes the residents of towns and cities and of suburban communes although in the latter localities up to one-half of the residents were occupied in agriculture.[55] Figure 14.3 presents estimates of the quantities of industrially-produced bread available to rural residents.

According to these data, between 1948 and 1959 the quantities of industrially-produced bread per rural resident declined slightly with greater urban and smaller rural population growth. Higher levels of bread consumption in urban areas absorbed the one and one-half times increase in bread production. Urban-biased rationing and distribution policies explain the 1952 and 1959 troughs in distribution of bread per rural resident and support the assumption that priority was given to satisfying the consumption requirements of the urban population. The surge in distribution during the 1960-1965 six-year plan marked a turning point in the state's policy regarding the distribution of bread to the rural population as urban consumption levels stabilized and rapid growth of production resumed. The plan for the development of the baking industry between 1960 and 1975 proposed an increase in deliveries of bread to rural residents from 40,000 tons

---

55   *Recensământul Populaţiei şi Locuinţelor din 15 martie 1966. vol. I.*

in 1960 to 250,000 in 1965 and 420,000 in 1975.[56] By comparison, no part of the increased quantities of bread had been allocated for distribution in rural areas in the first five-year plan[57] and distribution networks and administrative policies had been decisive in transferring bread from rural to urban consumers during the second five-year plan.

Actual bread production exceeded expectations as the planned indicators for 1975 were achieved and even surpassed by 1965. A total of 554,000 tons of bread went to rural areas giving 46 kg per rural consumer.[58] Growth rates gradually levelled off during the next three five-year plans due to the rising share in production of higher-grade breads and to consumer resistance to the imposed output mix. Nonetheless, distribution levels per rural resident reached 65.4 kg in 1980, a level 4.6 times higher than in 1959, and the higher rate of increase of output relative to the population prescribed for the next plan (1975–1990) suggested that the rising trend was planned to continue in the 1980s. Regionally, the uneven geographic distribution of growth changed hierarchies and exacerbated existing differences in bread consumption. In 1959, the regions Constaţa (Dobrogea), Stalin in Transylvania and Piteşti and Ploeşti in Muntenia and Oltenia had significantly higher than average bread consumption levels per resident of 35.9 kg, 32.3 kg, 25.8 kg and 26.6 kg respectively.[59] All the remaining regions except Galaţi and Bucureşti displaycd consumption levels below the national average.

Consumption changed little by 1976: the successor counties of Ploieşti and Piteşti regions, Vâlcea, Argeş, Dâmboviţa and Prahova enjoying distribution levels of 134.8 kg, 131.2 kg, 119.8 kg and 132.5 kg, per rural resident less only than Gorj (156.5 kg) at the national level.[60] One-half of the former Stalin region, Braşov County, enjoyed the sixth highest per rural resident level (100 kg), while the other half, Sibiu County, and the western portion of Ploieşti region, Buzău County, displayed respectable levels of 68.3 and 62.4 kg. Altogether, approximately one-third of the counties had distribution levels over 65 kg, one third between 40 kg and 65 kg and one-third below 35 kg.

By 1976, the rural distribution of industrially-produced bread reached 114.7 kg for the 7 counties situated on the mountainous region of the Carpathians. Dietary surveys in 1979–1980 and 1983 showed the effects of the increasing availability of bread on consumption patterns: five villages from hilly counties displayed yearly consumption averages per capita of 132.8 kg for bread and 11 kg for *mămăligă*.[61] Traditionally, however, the region displayed universally low levels of bread

---

56   *Recensământul Populaţiei*, 5, 9.

57   *Secţ. Econ.* File 27/1950, 87.

58   Data on rural and urban population taken from *Anuarul Statistic al Republicii Socialiste România pe 1968* 1969, 67.

59   *Secţ. Econ.* Files: 88–104/1959.

60   *Secţ. Econ.* File 196/1976, 21, 47–8.

61   Mincu 1993, 287–98, 325–6.

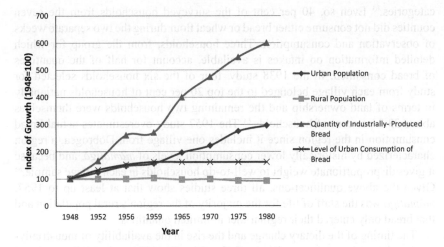

Figure 14.4   Growth indexes for urban and rural populations, urban levels of consumption and quantities of industrially-produced bread in Romania, 1948–1980

consumption as suggested by the data from the dietary surveys of 1906, 1938 and 1957 summarized in Table 14.2.[62]

Table 14.2   Changes in the consumption of *mămăligă* and bread in Romania, 1906–1983

Dietary study (year)	Households/villages studied (numbers)	Consumption of mămăligă (grams/day/adult)	Consumption of bread (grams/day/adult)
1906	25/22	1,672	132
1938	54/9	1,150	151.2
1979–1980 and 1983	350/5	44.4	402

Sources: Proca 1907; Georgescu 1940, 13–14; Ardelean 1962, 84–6; Mincu 1993, 287–98, 325–6.

When interpreting the results of these studies, there is a possibility that they overestimate actual bread consumption because of sample bias: 436 of the 496 households surveyed nationwide in 1906 belonged to the *mijlocaşi* or better-off class of peasants while the rest probably belonged equally to the rich and poor

62   Georgescu, 1940.

categories.[63] Even so, 40 per cent of the surveyed households from the seven counties did not consume either bread or wheat flour during the two separate weeks of observation and consumption. Three households, from the group for which detailed information on intakes is available, account for half of the quantities of bread consumed. In the 1938 study, four of the six households selected for study from each village belonged to the top 20 per cent of households nationally in terms of land ownership and the remaining two households were themselves above 23.3 per cent of households.[64] The 1957 study overestimates actual bread consumption in the region since it includes one village from Dobrogea, a region characterized by historically lower consumption levels of *mămăligă*, and because it gives disproportionate weight to well-to-do households in each village sample.[65] Given the above qualifications, all three studies show that at least up to 1957, *mămăligă* was the staff of life for the majority of the region's rural population and that bread only entered their regular diet in limited quantities.

The timing of the dietary change and the rise in the availability of industrially-produced bread suggests a direct relationship. By 1976 industrially-produced bought bread contributed significantly to daily consumption and accounted for 86 per cent of the 1979-1980 average consumption of 132.8 kg of bread per head. At this date, a rural resident was consuming approximately 3.6 times more bread than his prewar and interwar predecessor, of which up to 19 kg had been home-baked. Nationally, one-half of average bread consumption was provided by bakeries of every kind, but in view of the low consumption of bread in several rural regions, the share of industrially-produced bread was certainly greater.

Bread Supply and Standards of Living and Health

The greater availability and variety of the food supply enjoyed by the rural population makes an assessment of the effect of market-bought bread on standards of living more feasible, given the centrally-planned economy. Since alternatives such as home-baked bread and *mămăligă* were available, the choice of some people in the rural population to acquire industrially-baked bread reveals their preference. Consumers responded to rising incomes by opting for market-bought over home-baked bread, thus increasing the participation of women in better-paid work outside the home, and indicates a growing appreciation of leisure time. The principal reason for switching to less 'tasty' bread was the labour-saving effect of industrially-produced bread. In regions where industrially-produced bread replaced *mămăligă*, the prestige aspect of the switch has to be added to the labour-saving aspect.

63   Proca and Kirileanu, 1907.
64   Percentages calculated from Golopenția, 1941, 48–52, 268–87 and Cresin, 1945, 17.
65   Ardelean, 1962, 64

However, in 1969, out of a sample of 48,370 individuals from the Old Kingdom, 1.5 per cent were still suffering from pellagra and as late as 1972-1973 the Public Health Institute studied 75 cases from one village alone, suggesting that pockets of endemic pellagra still existed. The 1979-1980 dietary survey which included information on other metabolic diseases noted the extent to which pellagra was absent from the sample. This reflected the high levels of bread consumption and the significant rise in standards of living during the 1970s. These studies emphasized the relationship between consumption of *mămăligă* and pellagra, concluding that the deficiency disease emerged in cases where cornmeal (maize) flour supplied 65-70 per cent of nutrient needs. This linked, implicitly and explicitly, the decreasing prevalence of pellagra with the shift from *mămăligă* to bread.

If the growing availability of bread met consumer demand, changes in the assortment of bread at administratively-determined prices did not. This attempt to disguise a price increase of a basic product was only partially successful. The effect on standards of living had political repercussions for the regime, given a system of production and distribution that automatically politicized economic performance. To counter possible mismatches, adjusting mechanisms and institutions were in place but my analysis shows that while they did not pick up consumers' preferences efficiently, they were not as insensitive to them as previously thought – a conclusion of relevance for interpreting the impact of other significant changes in lifestyles occurring during those times.

References

Primary Sources

Arhivele Naționale ale României. Comitetul Central al Partidului Comunist Român. Secția Economică, 1948–1977.
Direcția Județeană Constanța a Arhivelor Naționale. Întreprinderea de morărit, panificație și produse făinoase Constanța, 1963–1965.
Direcția Județeană Constanța a Arhivelor Naționale. Trustul de Panificație Constanța, 1961–1966.

Secondary Sources

Articles in *Industria Alimentară.*[The Food Industry]
1950, 10: '*Hotărârea Numărul 1065 privind înființarea "Trusturilor de Panificație"*' [Decision Number 1065 concerning the Institution of Baking Trusts], 3–4.
1950, 11: '*Hotărârea Consiliului de Miniștri privitor la o mai bună aprovizionare cu pîine*' [Council of Ministers' Decision for improving the supply of bread], 43.
1953, 8–9: '*Pentru avântul continuu al industriei de panificație*' [The Continuing March Forward of the Baking Industry], 5–8.

1955, 7: Rotaru, V., '*Pentru reducerea continuă a preţului de cost în industria alimentară*' [For the Continuous Reduction of Production costs in the Food Industry], 3–5.

1956, 3: Mirea, I., '*Dezvoltarea Tehnică a Industriei Panificaţiei*' [Developments in Technology in the Baking Industry], 6–11.

1956, 11: Trattner, E., '*Aspecte sociale actuale ale producţiei industriei alimentare*' [Current Social Aspects of Industrial Food Production], 13–14.

1961, 8: Vegetable Products: '*Ridicarea calităţii produselor- sarcină centrală în industria alimentară*' [Raising Product Quality- A priority in the Food Industry], 229–33.

1964, 10: Spătaru, N., '*Fabricarea pîinii cu cartofi*' [The Requirements of Producing Potato Bread], 457–62.

1967, 1: Niculescu, N.I., '*Mecanizarea prelucrării aluatului, baza creşterii productivităţii muncii în industria panificaţiei*' [Mechanizing the Operation of Dough Preparation, the Basis for Raising Productivity in the Baking Industry], 14–18.

1967, 4: Zaharia, T., '*Îmbunătăţirea aprovizionării populaţiei cu pîine şi produse de panificaţie*' [Improving the Distribution of Bread and Baking Specialities to the Population], 195–6.

1967, 7: Grosu, V., and Moza, A., '*Realizarea parametrilor proiectaţi la noua fabrică de pîine din Galaţi*' [Achieving the Optimal Potential of Production at the New Baking Enterprise in Galaţi], 8–11.

1968, 11: Udrea, G., '*Limita eficienţei concentrării producţiei la fabricile de pîine*' [Limits to the Efficient Concentration of Production in the case of Baking Factories], 625–7.

1969, 3: Rotaru, V., '*Mărimea optimă a unei întreprinderi de industrie alimentară. Factorii tehnico-economici care o determină*' [The Optimum Size of a Food Processing Unit. The Determining technical and economic factors], 123–7.

1969, 4: Căliman, M., Cordăreanu, N., and Moşu, I., '*Experienţa dobîndită în elaborarea şi aplicarea normelor în cadrul noului sistem de salarizare*' [The Experience Gained in Elaborating and Applying the Norms of the New Payment System], 173–9.

1969, 8: Negreanu, A. and Popa, I.M., '*Un sfert de veac de adînci şi importante transformări în dezvoltarea industriei de panificaţie şi produse făinoase*' [A Quarter of a Century of Profound and Important Developments in the Baking and Flour Products Industries], 422–7.

1972, 12: '*1947–1972: Un bilanţ semnificativ pentru industria alimentară*' [1947–1972: An assesment of developments in the Food Industry], 655–7.

General Works

Anuarele Statistice ale Republicii Socialiste România pe 1968, 1971, 1976, 1981 [Statistical Yearbooks of the Socialist Republic of Romania for 1968], Bucharest: Direcția Centrală de Statistică.

Ardelean, I. and Sporn, A., 1962, '*Particularitățile alimentației în mediul rural din regiunile București, Argeș, Oltenia, Dobrogea și Ploiești*' [The Particulars of Rural Diets etc.,] in *Culegere de lucrări metodologice și documentare. Probleme de igienă și sănătate publică în sectorul agricol*, [Collection of Metodological and Documentary Papers. Problems of hygiene and public health in the agricultural sector], Bucharest: Ministerul Sănătății și Prevederilor Sociale Institutul de Igienă și Protecția Muncii.

Cresin, R., 1945, *Recensământul agricol al României din 1941: rezultate provizorii.* [The Agricultural Census of 1941 in Romania: Provisional results], Bucharest: Imprimeria Insitutului Central de Statistică.

Georgescu, D.C., 1940, *L'alimentation de la population rurale en Roumanie*, Bucharest: Institutul Central de Statistică.

Golopenția, A., ed., 1941, *60 Sate Românești cercetate de echipele studențești în vara 1938. Vol II: Situația economică.* [60 Romanian Villages Studied by the Student Research Teams in the Summer of 1938. Vol. 2: Economic Situation], Bucharest: Institutul de Științe Sociale al României.

Mincu, J., 1993, *Impactul Om-Alimentație: Istoria alimentației la români din cele mai vechi timpuri și până în prezent* [The Human-Nutrition Relationship: A history of Romanian diets from the earliest times until the present], Bucharest: Editura Medicală.

Mintz, S.W., 1991, *Sweetness and Power. The place of sugar in modern history*, New York: Penguin Books.

Proca, G. and Kirileanu, G. I., 1907, *Cercetări asupra hranei țăranului, de Profesori Doctori Gh. Proca și Gh. I. Kirileanu (raport)* [Inquiries into the peasants' diet], Bucharest: Imprimeria Statului.

Recensămîntul Populației și Locuințelor din 15 martie 1966. Vol. I: Rezultate Generale. Partea Întîi- Populație [The Population and Housing Census of 15 March 1966. Vol. I: General results. First Part: The Population], 1969, Bucharest: Direcția Generală de Statistică.

Rotaru, V., 1974, *Eficiența economică a investițiilor în industria alimentară și căile sporirii ei* [The Economic Efficiency of Investments in the Food Industry and Ways to improve it], Bucharest: Carus.

Chapter 15
From Roast Beef to Chicken Nuggets: How Technology changed Meat Consumption in Britain in the Twentieth Century

Derek J. Oddy

Introduction

The demand for food in Great Britain grew throughout the nineteenth century as the population expanded. Total numbers increased from 26 m at the 1871 census to 37 m in 1901 and 44.8 m in 1931. By 1901, approximately 14.75 m people lived in the extensive urbanized areas which became known as conurbations.[1] This meant a requirement for food far in excess of the output of domestic agriculture, especially as so many people were becoming reliant on shops for their food supplies. Imports became essential which in turn was a major stimulus to the development of food technology. An import trade in durable foodstuffs like grain had developed significantly during the nineteenth century but to expand the trade in perishable foodstuffs, which would give greater variety to the diet of the general population, required major changes in technology. British shipping underwent an extensive conversion from sail to steam power and from wooden to iron hulls during the second half of the nineteenth century, which reflected Britain's status as the world's leading industrial and maritime power. These changes reduced the time food cargoes spent at sea and facilitated importing meat and dairy produce from the world's newly developing agricultural lands in North America and the Southern Hemisphere, as well as fruit from tropical regions. However, to ship these perishable foods to Britain required some artificial means of preservation during the voyage to maintain appearance, texture, palatability and nutritive qualities. Lowering the temperature while foodstuffs were in store was well known as a means of slowing decay, but the availability of natural ice was limited and seasonal. The demand from Britain's food industries meant imports of natural ice from Scandinavia and North America grew annually to a peak of 0.5 m tons in 1899.[2] Beyond that point any increase in the carriage of foodstuffs by sea at

---

1 Mitchell and Deane, 1962. ch.1, Tables 2 and 6. The conurbations are: Greater London, South-east Lancashire, West Midlands, West Yorkshire, Merseyside, Tyneside and Clydeside. By 1931 they numbered 18.1 m or 40 per cent of Britain's population

2 David, 1995, 52–69. The natural ice trade had been all but eliminated by 1930.

low temperatures depended on mechanical systems of refrigeration, though requirements differed according to the commodity carried. Fresh fruit could be picked under-ripe and allowed to ripen progressively during the voyage but meat had to be carried in fully refrigerated conditions to prevent deterioration [autolysis] if it was to be landed fit for sale in urban food markets.

The Refrigerated Meat Trade 1880–1939

To ensure that meat arrived in Britain in good condition, three facilities were required: first, a freezing works at the port of loading; second, refrigeration machinery capable of maintaining cargoes at suitably low temperatures in insulated chambers on board ship; and thirdly, cold storage facilities at the point of discharge until the cargo could be sold.

Freezing plants were established successfully during the 1880s on the east coast of Australia, in New Zealand, and among the River Plate ports in South America. Cold stores developed at British ports, initially in 1877, but more generally from 1882 onwards, while hulks fitted with refrigeration machinery were used until the end of the nineteenth century to overcome seasonal shortages of capacity, even though 60 artificial ice companies were formed in London between 1880 and 1890. Refrigerated vessels might also be kept in the docks during hot weather if the rapidly growing number of ice companies could not meet demand.[3]

Before receiving on board carcasses of beef, mutton or lamb already frozen by on-shore plants, ships required an auxiliary engine to drive refrigeration compressors (or heat exchangers if an absorption-type refrigeration system was used). For the early voyages, when sail was still commonly used, as on long-distance routes like the New Zealand mutton and lamb trade, it was necessary for sailing vessels to install a small steam engine driving a reciprocating compressor. This required supplies of coal to be carried for the engine, but from 1883 onwards the New Zealand Shipping Company established a regular trade by steamships. In steamships, the main boilers provided the source of power. For early voyages a cold-air system was used as there were fears that chemical refrigerants might be dangerous if they escaped. The cold-air system, however, was inefficient and from the 1890s, the common refrigerants used were carbon dioxide (CO_2), generally referred to as carbonic anhydride, or ammonia.[4] These refrigerants were passed through evaporators in the form of steel tubes, usually suspended from

---

3   As in the hot summer of 1894, see *Meat Trades Journal*, 28 June 1894, 140. For the growth of ice companies, see David, 1994, Table 2, 55; also Leighton and Douglas, 1910, vol. II, 446–8.

4   In 1893 Turnbull, Martin and Company's *Perthshire* became the first vessel to use a chemical refrigerant instead of the less efficient compressed-air refrigerating machines. See Critchell and Raymond, 1912, 338.

Tonnage: 2,761 tons; Capacity 25,000 carcasses of frozen mutton.
Source: North Otago Museum, New Zealand, NOM509.

Figure 15.1   Steamship *Elderslie* (1884); refrigerated meat carrier

the deckhead in insulated food-storage rooms.[5] To prevent deterioration, 'frozen' meat was carried with its temperature lowered to at least −10°C. 'Chilled' food, the category used to describe much beef carried in the North Atlantic trade, was kept between −5°C and +5°C. The expansion of refrigerated capacity up to the outbreak of war in 1939 can be seen in Table 15.1.

The rapid development of the imported frozen-meat trade before 1914 is shown in Table 15.2. The figures for chilled beef from North America show how exports from the United States collapsed in the early twentieth century when the growth in domestic demand and a surge in immigration to America brought fears of meat shortages. This was offset by the doubling of beef imports from South America, where the big United States meat packers – Armour, Swift, and Morris – had acquired South American companies as their subsidiaries. By the end of the first decade of the twentieth century, cargoes reaching London were on such a scale that mechanical conveyors had been developed to assist unloading. Improvements

---

5   In 1884 Turnbull, Martin acquired the managing partnership of the first permanently insulated refrigerated steamship, *Elderslie*. She was powered by a two-cylinder compound steam engine, which gave her a speed of 9 knots. She was barque-rigged and carried sails for long ocean voyages. The whole of her 'tween decks were insulated with charcoal which gave her capacity to carry 25,000 carcasses of frozen mutton.

Table 15.1   Numbers and size of British refrigerated vessels, 1896–1939

Year	Sailing ships	Steam vessels	Largest refrigerated unit (cu.ft)	Coolant used	Vessels with Lloyd's refrigerating machinery certificate
1896	6	192	226,110	Air	
1914	nil	877	401,846	Majority CO_2	
1938–1939	nil	853	618,000	CO_2 [a]	175

Note (a): a few vessels used brine and, one or two, the newest coolant, Methyl Chloride

Source: Lloyd's Register of Shipping.

Tonnage: 9,188 tons; Capacity: 130,000 carcasses of frozen mutton.

Note: In the 20 years since the *Elderslie* was built, the size and capacity of refrigerated carriers had increased dramatically. The sailing rig has gone and *Ayrshire* has a telescopic funnel and topmasts to allow passage under the bridges over the Manchester Ship Canal; this enabled her to deliver frozen meat from New Zealand or South America to the industrial districts of northern England.

Source: Farquhar, I., 2008, 'The Shire Line, Part 2' in Clarkson, J. and Fenton R. (eds), *Ships in Focus Record 40*, 241.

Figure 15.2   Steamship *Ayrshire* (1903); refrigerated meat carrier

Table 15.2   Imports of frozen meat into the United Kingdom, 1884–1926

A   Imports of frozen and chilled beef

| Year | Frozen beef | | | | Chilled beef |
	Australia (tons)	New Zealand (tons)	South America (tons)	Total (tons)	USA[a] (tons)
1884	138		25	163	
1893	10,549	734	1,769	13,053	74,497
1903	3,883	7,992	57,611	69,485	134,696
1913	67,373	12,208	117,662	197,243	73
1922	58,330	29,017	140,758	228,105	67
1926	57,449	27,041	86,483	170,973	

Note: ([a]) US fresh beef was mostly chilled.

B   Imports of frozen and chilled mutton and lamb

| Year | Frozen mutton and lamb | | | |
	Australia (tons)	New Zealand (tons)	South America (tons)	Total (tons)
1884	3,176	12,031	2,012	17,218
1893	14,358	45,015	26,257	85,630
1903	9,063	101,772	74,289	185,124
1913	83,293	110,026	67,394	260,713
1922	49,205	150,803	85,150	285,158
1926	37,616	134,050	92,483	264,149

Sources: 1884–1913: Perren, 1978;
1922–26: Weddel, 1928.

in technology meant that much beef from South America was carried as 'chilled' rather than frozen meat, thus increasing its palatability.

When war broke out in 1914, the liner trade in frozen meat was so well established that imported cargoes made up around 45 per cent of Britain's total meat supply.[6] Frozen meat imported in British ships supplied the British army in France, Salonika and the Middle East. It was also an important source of supply

6   For a fuller treatment of the frozen-meat trade, see Oddy, 2007, 269–80; also Murphy and Oddy, 2011, 22–36.

for the other Allied armies in Europe which had never experienced such a regular supply of meat before and had not previously eaten frozen meat.[7]

The Effect of Imports on the British Market

Through most of the nineteenth century meat in Britain was supplied from locally reared animals. As towns grew in size, journeys to market became longer with cattle being rested and fattened near towns before slaughter. It was then retailed by local butchers. All this changed when retail butchers began to receive imported meat from refrigerated stores. Frozen meat required them to have refrigerators and to learn how to thaw out carcasses. Chains of retail butchers developed, the first being John Bell and Sons which began opening frozen-meat shops in 1879 and had 330 outlets when they amalgamated with Eastman's in 1889. By 1894, Eastman's had 600 shops.[8] Another large chain was Dewhurst the Master Butcher, which served as the retail outlets for the frozen meat brought into Britain by Vestey Brothers' Blue Star Line.[9] The Co-operative movement also handled large amounts of frozen meat.[10] Even in smart residential parts of London's West End, retail butchers installed refrigerators during the 1890s. The frozen-meat trade was facilitated by the Contagious Diseases (Animals) Acts (1878, 1884, and 1896) which limited the import of live animals to the United Kingdom.[11] Home agriculture could not meet the buoyant consumer demand for meat. During the 1880s annual meat consumption was 110 lbs (50 kg) per head of which almost 74 per cent was home produced; in the first decade of the twentieth century meat consumption rose to 130 lbs (59kg) per head, of which only 58 per cent was home produced. The balance was supplied by imported frozen and, later, chilled meat as the trade in live animals declined.

Despite these technological developments, meat consumption patterns in Britain changed little. Whether animals were frozen or freshly killed, butchers cut carcasses into joints for roasting and sold the offal separately, while 'trimmings' went into mincemeat or sausages. The typical weekly meat consumption by families who could afford it began with a roast joint of meat on Sunday, roast

---

7   See Dentoni, 1999, 163–5. Italy owned no refrigerated ships before 1916; France none before 1917. Neither country had any refrigerated stores before 1915.

8   See Critchell and Raymond, 1912, 24–6, 209–10; also *Meat Trades Journal*, 8 March 1894, 758 and 22 March 1894, 795.

9   Vestey Brothers commenced operating their own ships in 1909, principally for the carriage of frozen produce from South America. Their Blue Star Line was formed in 1911 with Union Cold Storage (which the Vesteys had founded in 1897) as the parent company.

10   By the 1920s the Co-operative shops were supplied by the Smithfield & Argentine Meat Company Ltd, which had its freezing plant in the province of Buenos Aires. Its cargoes were loaded into chartered meat carriers scheduled to take 22 days from the mouth of the River Plate to Liverpool.

11   See Oddy and Oddy, 1998, 289.

meat eaten cold on Monday, a meat pie (from the scraps: a 'cottage pie' if beef, or 'shepherd's pie' if lamb or mutton) on Tuesday, sausages on Wednesday, offal (liver) on Thursday – and fish on Friday. Saturday might be cold meats, pork pies, potted meats or tongue, with 'corned beef' imported from the United States or South America gaining acceptance during the interwar years. Canned meat became widely available during the 1930s and corned beef became a novelty for picnics or to make sandwiches for day excursions at holiday times.[12] Most of these new meat products were not sold by retail butchers but by 'provision merchants' – general food retailers – who already sold bacon.[13] These multiple retail chains began adding cured-meat products and sausages to the range of foods they sold.[14] The regularity of meat consumption with its narrow variety of choice was encouraged by cookery books designed for young housewives and families without servants but was also habitual amongst the working classes with sufficient income to eat meat regularly for the midday dinner. It was a pattern which changed little until 1940.

The Second World War and After

The biggest shock to the established patterns of meat consumption in Britain was the introduction of rationing in March 1940. Although rationing did not mean equality of consumption as is popularly, but incorrectly, claimed, the one shilling price limit on meat purchases meant that weekly consumption per head was restricted to around 14 ozs (c.400g).[15] The easing of the price limit to 1s. 2d. per head in 1945 made little difference, though the war did make canned meat an acceptable addition to the British diet. During the 1940s when it was not part of the meat ration, canned meat was much sought after and greatly valued. Canned meat was only available on the points-rationing scheme which was designed to share out imported foods supplied irregularly or in insufficient quantities to be placed on the basic rations. Food imported by sea, like corned beef, 'luncheon meat' and American 'Spam', was a welcome addition to relieve the monotony of everyday fare.[16]

The war also brought American airmen and soldiers to Britain in preparation for the 1944 invasion of Normandy; their taste in food in London became known

---

12   See Chapter 1, Introduction, footnote 20, for Reader, 1976, on canning. Although meat in tins had been available since the nineteenth century, its use had been limited to yachtsmen and explorers; it had few attractions for families at home

13   Provision merchants developing chains of multiple shops in towns from the late nineteenth century included Lipton's, Home and Colonial Stores, International Tea Stores, Maypole Dairies, Meadow Dairies and the Co-operative Retail Societies.

14   Sausages, strangely, were often sold by fishmongers but not by retail butchers.

15   For food rationing, see Oddy, 2003, ch.7 or Burnett, 1989, ch.13.

16   For the points-rationing scheme, see Burnett, 1989, 293–5.

through their service canteens which were the envy of British civilians. However, in postwar Britain with rationing still in force, there were few opportunities for new experiences with food. The end of Lend-Lease Aid in August 1945 removed Spam and other US imports from British consumers. Making currency available for meat imports was not a priority for Stafford Cripps, the Chancellor of the Exchequer – a vegetarian – so that in 1948, three years after the war ended, the meat ration was only 13 ozs (369 g) per head per week. By the late 1940s, consumer demand for meat had become disorganized. Choice, in many respects, was only a memory of what had been 'normal' before war was declared in 1939. However, during the final years of rationing, meat consumption began to rise rapidly in a similar manner to the '*fresswelle*' experienced across Western Europe. Final restrictions on meat consumption in Britain were removed only in 1954. The first evidence of the wartime American influence on British taste appeared when Wimpy Bars began selling hamburgers.[17] With traditional meat consumption patterns little more than a fifteen-year-old memory, the public was open to any new meat products in the shops.

The Postwar Influence of Food Technology

Developments in meat technology in the postwar years were important in widening the range of products available for consumers. Shortages most keenly felt during the war included bacon and chickens, then normal fare only at Christmas-tide. The new industrial-scale poultry farming in the 1950s led to a remarkable substitution of chicken and turkey meat for beef or lamb:

> In 1950 British households consumed only around 1 million chickens. But by
> the mid-1960s, like many other things in the country, meat-eating habits were
> transformed. Over 150 million chickens were sold for consumption in 1965,
> over 200 million by 1967. If the postwar decades of the 1950s and 1960s saw a
> transformation in British society, its revolutionaries sustained themselves with
> mouthfuls of roast chicken.[18]

Production of chickens on an industrial scale meant that from the mid-1950s innovations in the British meat market were retailer-led. To begin with, supermarkets aimed at offering chickens that were standard in size and quality. By 1963, the British poultry industry was putting 'a chicken weighing 2½ lbs (1,135 g) ready-to-eat in the shops at 7/6d to 10/-' (35–50p).[19] A later innovation was the sale of fried-chicken portions, popularized by the Kentucky Fried Chicken fast-food

---

17   Oddy, 2009, 62, Table 5.1: National Food Survey figures for consumption of meat per head per week rose from 746 g in 1945 to 955 g in 1954.

18   See Godley and Williams, 2008, 47.

19   Sykes, 1963, 47, cited by Godley and Williams from Horowitz and Belasco, 2008, 59.

chain from 1965. As retail turnover rose, the meat industry became concerned with problems of how quickly and how cheaply animals (especially poultry) could be grown to marketable size.

Meat technology enabled unpopular cuts of meat and inferior quality meat to be used in pasties, pies, sausages, sausage rolls, and ready-made dishes, many of which in the last quarter of the twentieth century began to include ethnic recipes such as birianis, samosas, curries, and meat sauces to complement pasta meals like spaghetti bolognese. The manufacture of complete meals led to a wide range of uses for meat in small portions and even unsaleable quality. From the 1970s onwards inflation and rising costs put pressure on the food industry to limit costs and to reassess how meat should be used in manufactured dishes. Although the sale of whole birds for roasting was important to production strategies, there was also the problem of how 'waste' or unused portions of the carcass could be marketed. Carcass remainders no longer sold for soup or stews as they had earlier in the twentieth century. Smaller families and reduced plate portions of meat provided an opportunity to cut up small, young chickens. A market was created for breast fillets, chicken hindquarters, thighs and drumsticks so that industrial portioning and freezing allowed supermarkets to sell carcass portions in multi-packs. Boiling the meat, before coating it with batter or breadcrumbs, led to packaged chicken portions being sold as 'ready prepared for heating up'.

As food processing became more complex, food manufacturers realized that the possibilities of contamination were increasing. This focused their attention on how to avoid bacterial infection occurring in food materials by using chemical additives, particularly in the case of cooked meat. While maintaining high standards of hygiene in the processing plant and amongst personnel working with food were fundamental, low-temperature storage became general. During the 1950s and 1960s the use of sterilizing techniques such as irradiation or 'cold sterilization' was pioneered but this aroused concern amongst consumers and health authorities alike who were alerted by news of radiation sickness and cancers following the end of the Second World War. During the 'Cold War' era there was customer sensitivity to the possibility of nuclear radiation escaping from defence establishments and power stations.[20] Irradiation was limited in Britain by the Food (Control of Irradiation) Regulations, 1967, which effectively banned this method of sterilization except for low-level dosage. Irradiation was not entirely straightforward: its early use produced changes in food quality, not only in the colour of foods treated but also distinct changes in flavour.[21] Irradiation has been used to destroy spoilage organisms in meat and poultry whether frozen or unfrozen, though some colour change may still occur. Public acceptance has remained low, coupled with the thought that the treatment might raise the price of meat.

---

20   *British Food Journal*, July/August 1984, 97-8. International regulation of irradiation was introduced in the late 1960s.

21   Pyke, 1970, 168–70.

At first the packaging of processed food into plastic containers attracted suspicion from public health authorities, as did the contact between foods and polyvinylchloride (PVC) film when this material began to be used to cover food. This apprehension gradually receded when open-top display chilled and freezer cabinets became generally used by retailers. These allowed food technologists to introduce a range of additives to stabilize the food as well as extending its life by packing it in a 'controlled atmosphere' (CO_2 and N) sealed inside a PVC cover. Traditional pickling of meats used saltpetre i.e. potassium nitrate (KNO_3) for its preservative effect by inhibiting decay-producing bacteria.[22] Other traditional preservatives were salt, sugar and vinegar. Today, a sample of a cured cooked meat on sale in a supermarket (Turkey Pastrami) may contain various phosphates (E451, E452, E450) as stabilizers[23] and a preservative like sodium nitrite ($Na SO_2$ or E250) to prevent the growth of botulism bacteria (*Clostridium botulinum*). The presence of phosphates allows the deliberate addition of water to the food product. However, some food manufacturers even claim that this is advantageous: the consumer will be told that meat has 'extra succulence' by the presence of added water! The use of a PVC film cover for food was also important for the growing practice of heating foods in microwave ovens.

Using as many parts of a carcass as possible went even further: Mechanically Recovered Meat (MRM) was introduced in food processing as ready-prepared meat dishes were developed. Meat slurry made from reconstituted or emulsified meat was developed, not for general consumption, but rather to be used as a supplement in food products made from turkey or chicken meat chopped and formed into attractive shapes.[24] Consumers in Britain avoid dark meat from poultry. It is also unpopular with food manufacturers who dislike its low plasticity, which increases the difficulty of moulding it into shapes. Processing dark meat into a slurry makes it more like white meat, easier to prepare and more attractive to consumers. After the meat has been ground and water added, the mixture is placed in a centrifuge or treated with an emulsifier to separate fats and myoglobin from the muscle.[25] It is then allowed to settle into three layers: meat, excess water, and fat. The liquefied meat is flash-frozen to retain its nutrients and flavours, and packaged for supply to food processors. Food manufacturers have copied extrusion technology from the plastics and metals industries to deliver MRM in measured portions. This enables

---

22   Pyke, 1970, 80

23   Stabilizers maintain the pH chemical balance between acidity and alkalinity.

24   Originally, meat slurry was developed from beef and lamb carcasses but scares in the 1980s about *Bovine spongiform encephalopathy* (BSE) led to it being banned in Britain. Since then poultry-meat has been the most common material from which meat slurry is made, but pork is also used.

25   Myoglobin is a pigmented chemical compound found in muscle tissue that undergoes frequent use. Because domestic poultry rarely fly, the flight muscles in the breast contain little myoglobin and appear white. Leg meat is high in myoglobin which is less useful to industry.

products such as animal shapes to be created for children's meals, like 'Turkey Dinosaurs', and, for 'easy eating', chicken nuggets, as well as fillings for sausage rolls, meat pies and ready-made cheap meat meals. Meat slurry or MRM achieved notoriety in Britain at the end of the twentieth century as the meat content of 'Turkey Twizzlers', a moulded meat product which was criticized on television for its use in school meals.

Meat consumption in Britain since the Second World War shown in Table 15.3 reveals the marked change in consumption patterns at home. Whilst rationing was

Table 15.3 Weekly household food consumption of meat in Great Britain, 1950–2000

Meat consumption in grams per person per week

Date	Beef and veal (g)	Mutton and lamb (g)	Pork (g)	Bacon and ham (g)	Poultry (g)	Sausages (g)	Total meat and meat products (g)
The era of postwar rationing							
1950	228	154	9	128	10	114	846
1954	262	170	68	173	15	96	955
Meat consumption in a free-choice market							
1955	265	186	66	172	14	99	976
1960	248	188	57	175	50	103	1,017
1965	229	167	79	179	100	106	1,066
1970	221	149	80	177	143	106	1,121
1975	238	120	78	142	160	92	1,054
1980	231	128	117	149	189	92	1,140
1985	185	93	98	137	195	84	1,042
1990	149	83	84	118	226	68	968
1995	121	54	71	115	237	63	945
2000	124	55	68	112	253	60	966

Note: Total meat and meat products include beef, veal, mutton, lamb, pork, bacon and ham, poultry and sausages.

Source: National Food Survey, 1950–2000.

still in force during the early 1950s, meat consumption edged upwards gradually as restrictions on production of pork, bacon and ham, and poultry were relaxed. Only sausages – of which everyone was tired and which symbolized wartime deprivation – saw consumption fall slightly. With restrictions removed, total meat consumption began to rise but not all kinds of meat made equal progress: beef consumption peaked earliest in 1957 at almost 300 g per head per week, followed by lamb in 1961–1962 at just over 190 g per head per week.[26] Both these principal kinds of butcher's meat then underwent a slow decline in demand as meal patterns began to change from the prewar style of midday dinners in which roast beef, roast lamb or roast pork was the principal dish. The reasons for the decline were complex. By the beginning of the 1960s as consumption of sugar increased, particularly in the form of chocolate and sugar confectionery and coupled with a decline in physical activity, there was talk of obesity as a health hazard.[27] The association between animal fats in the diet and cardiovascular disease arose from the doubling of deaths from coronary heart disease between 1948 and 1958. It became the centre of a long-running advertising campaign promoting vegetable oils and margarines.[28] The image of fat meat as dangerous to health led to the breeding of beef cattle, sheep and pigs with lower meat fat content.

As more married women began to work away from home, meal preparation on a daily basis became necessarily shorter and meals less elaborate. Meat consumption remained fairly stable in the 1960s and early 1970s when the change was relatively slow, but the decline accelerated in the 1980s once public concern was aroused over meat quality and the possible contamination of farm livestock. This was coupled with the greater availability of convenience foods and the housewife's desire to spend more time with her family viewing television than in the kitchen.[29]

Radio-active contamination (at first from strontium 90 during the 'Cold War' but later from the Chernobyl explosion in the 1990s), salmonella, and *Bovine spongiform encephalopathy* (BSE), commonly known as 'mad-cow disease' – a fatal neurodegenerative disease in cattle – reduced consumer confidence in butcher's meat. By contrast pork butchers did somewhat better, though demand rose only slowly and consumption did not peak at 117 g until 1980. Demand for bacon and ham also rose to around 175 g per head per week during the 1960s but

---

26   Mutton and veal have been included under the headings of 'beef' and 'lamb'. Very little of either was sold in Britain.

27   See Oddy, Atkins and Amilien, 2009, ch.16.

28   See *British Food Journal*, January 1962, 1-2, December 1962, 107. Coronary heart disease (CHD) rates in England rose from 1,264 per million for males and 652 per million for females in 1948 to 2,208 per million for males and 1,226 per million for females in 1958.

29   See 'Frozen Food Developments', *British Food Journal*, November/December 1982, 170, which suggests that the time families spent viewing television had risen to five hours per day.

declined thereafter, though at the end of the twentieth century it was still over 100 g per head per week during the 1990s. By the end of the twentieth century total meat consumption had declined surprisingly little: it had been just over 1 kg per head per week from 1960 to 1989 after which it fell to around 0.95 kg at the end of the century. However, this apparent stability concealed the remarkable substitution of poultry for all other kinds of meat; the consumption of chicken rose almost unchecked to over 250 g per week in the late 1990s.[30] The effect on the retail meat trade was profound and forced traditional butchers to close their shops. The biggest retail chain, Dewhurst's the Butchers, collapsed in 2007. They had operated 1,400 shops in the 1970s but only 95 remained open in 2006. Dewhurst's blamed intense competition from the supermarkets for falling sales but costs had risen significantly. Administrators were called in during March 2007 to liquidate the firm; 60 shops were closed and the administrator sold the remaining 35 stores. Consumers increasingly turned to the supermarkets to buy butchers' meat –which was already packaged in plastic wrapping – and which they no longer saw being cut up in front of them. Equally, supermarkets handled frozen or chilled ready-meal meat dishes and the versions of ethnic cuisines acceptable to British consumers which required no more culinary skills than heating up the contents of a package in a microwave oven.

The nutritional effect of these changes must be borne in mind. The first two lines of Table 15.4 indicate the effect of the long-running controversy over animal fat and heart disease on roast beef. From the interwar years to the 1970s, roast beef joints were generally from 25 to 33 per cent fat, as shown in the first line of Table 15.4. Breeding leaner animals to meet consumer demand for less fatty meat reduced the fat content of beef carcasses by the 1980s to around 20 per cent as shown in the second line of this table. The energy value of roast beef, the traditional English meat dish, has therefore been reduced. Change has been even more marked where poultry is used in meat products. Food manufacturers retain the name 'meat' for items based on chilled or frozen chicken and turkey portions but frequently the 'meat' content falls below 50 per cent of the total components of the recipe. As a result, the proportions of protein and fat are reduced and the energy value of the dish falls slightly but the non-meat components, for example, food materials consisting of carbohydrates, are increased to contribute 10–20 per cent of the energy value. The same pattern is observable in the frozen or chilled meat meals sold. The analysis of the chicken pie shown in Table 15.4 indicates that almost one-quarter of its energy is derived from carbohydrate sources rather than meat.

It is evident that the effect of contemporary food technology for food manufacturers has been to increase the water content and non-meat components of products retailed to consumers as 'meat'. Raw material costs have been reduced by diminishing the proportion of meat used. Food technology has also increased the value-added component so that the consumer is sold less of the food named on

---

30   See Oddy, 2009, Table 5.5(b).

Table 15.4   The nutritional analysis of meat and meat products in Britain in the 1990s

Code	Product	Weight (g)	H₂0 (g)	Protein (g)	Fat (g)	CHO (g)	Energy value (kcal)	(kj)
From roast beef to chicken nuggets								
366	Beef, fore rib, raw	100	48.4	22.4	28.8	0	349	1,446
18–34	Beef, fore rib, lean and fat, roast	100	49.8	29.1	20.4	0	300	1,250
19–124	Chicken nuggets, takeaway	100	47.8	18.7	13.0	19.5	265	1,111
Other chicken portions								
19–123	Chicken kiev, frozen, baked, 45–60% meat	100	51.6	18.7	16.9	11.1	268	1,119
19–116	Chicken in crumbs (stuffed*), chilled, baked, 40–53% meat	100	57.5	16.2	13.9	10.8	230	963
19–121	Chicken fingers, baked	100	56.2	12.5	9.5	18.5	205	860
Other modern meat products								
19–158	Turkey steaks in breadcrumbs, frozen, grilled, 38–49% meat	100	45.9	17.6	17.1	18.9	295	1,234
19–55	Chicken pie frozen, baked, 10.5–25% meat	100	45.6	9.0	17.7	24.6	288	1,202
19–39	Big Mac	100	n.a.	12.7	12.7	18.0	238	996
19–188	Chicken curry, chilled, reheated.	100	68.7	12.1	8.9	5.4	149	621
19–216	Cottage pie, chilled/frozen, reheated, 11.5–25% meat	100	73.1	4.5	5.4	11.9	111	467

Notes: n.a. = not available; *Stuffing = cheese and vegetables.

Sources: For Code 366, see Holland, B. et al., 1995;

For Code 18–34, see Chan, W. et al., 1995;

For Codes 19–39 to 19-216, see Chan, W. et al., 1996.

the product's packaging. Consumer satisfaction is maintained by flavouring and seasoning; colouring enhances the attractive appearance of both the product and the packaging. In effect, the systematic application of science to rearing chickens in large-scale production units and the application of food technology to the butchering, processing and retailing of poultry meat has fundamentally changed British consumers' appetite for meat in the second half of the twentieth century. Moreover, it has also changed their perception of what they eat. Consumers pay more for less because time, domestic facilities and skills devoted to food preparation on a daily basis are limited. Reheating chilled or frozen meals bought in a supermarket or convenience store in the microwave oven hardly counts as cooking – so that for many consumers in contemporary Britain, culinary skills have been taken out of the kitchen to become a subject for entertainment in cookery programmes and 'Master Chef' competitions shown on television.

References

British Food Journal (serial).

Burnett, J., 1989, *Plenty and Want*, 3rd edn, London: Routlege.

Chan, W., Brown, J., Lee, S.M. and Buss, D.H., 1995, *Meat Poultry and Game, Fifth Supplement to the Fifth Edition of McCance and Widdowson's The Composition of Foods*, Cambridge: The Royal Society of Chemistry and Ministry of Agriculture, Fisheries and Food.

Chan, W., Brown, J., Church, S.M. and Buss, D.H., 1996, *Meat Produce and Dishes, Sixth Supplement to the Fifth Edition of McCance and Widdowson's The Composition of Foods*, Cambridge: The Royal Society of Chemistry and Ministry of Agriculture, Fisheries and Food.

Critchell, J.T. and Raymond, J., 1912, *A History of the Frozen Meat Trade*, London: Constable.

David, E., 1994, *Harvest of the Cold Months*, London: Joseph.

David, R., 1995, 'The demise of the Anglo-Norwegian ice trade', *Business History*, vol. 37, 3.

Dentoni, M.C., 2003, 'Refrigeration and the Italian meat crisis during the First World War' in ICREFH VI: Hietala, M. and Vahtikari, T., eds, *The Landscape of Food*, Helsinki: Finnish Literature Society.

Godley, A. and Williams, B., 2008, 'The Chicken, the Factory Farm, and the Supermarket: The Industrialization of Poultry Farming in Britain and the United States, 1950–1980', in Horowitz, R. and Belasco, W., eds, *Food Chains: Provisioning, from Farmyard to Shopping Cart*, Philadelphia: University of Pennsylvania Press.

Holland, B., Welch, A.A., Unwin, I.D., Buss, D.H., Paul, A.A. and Southgate, D.A.T., 1995, *McCance and Widdowson's The Composition of Foods* (5th edn), Cambridge: The Royal Society of Chemistry and Ministry of Agriculture, Fisheries and Food.

Leighton, G.R. and Douglas, L.M., 1910, *The Meat Industry and Meat Inspection*, 2 vols. London: Educational Book Company.

Lloyd's Register of Shipping, London (Annual series).

Mitchell, B.R. and Deane, P., 1962, *Abstract of British Historical Statistics*, Cambridge: Cambridge University Press.

Murphy, H. and Oddy, D.J., 2011, 'The Business Interests of Sir James Caird of Glenfarquhar, Bt (1864–1954)', *The Mariner's Mirror*, 97:1.

National Food Survey, (Annual series) 1950–2000.

Oddy, D.J. and Oddy, J.R., 1998, 'The iceman cometh: the effects of low-temperature technology on the British diet' in ICREFH IV: Schärer, M.R. and Fenton, A., eds, *Food and Material Culture*, East Linton, Scotland: Tuckwell.

Oddy, D.J., 2003, *From Plain Fare to Fusion Food*, Woodbridge, Suffolk: Boydell.

Oddy, D.J., 2007, 'The Growth of Britain's Refrigerated Meat Trade, 1880–1939', *The Mariner's Mirror*, 93:3.

Oddy, D.J., 2009, 'The Stop-Go Era: Restoring Food Choice in Britain after World War II' in ICREFH X: Oddy, D.J., Atkins, P.J. and Amilien, V., eds, *The Rise of Obesity in Europe: A Twentieth Century Food History*, Farnham: Ashgate.

Perren, R., 1978, *The Meat Trade in Britain 1840–1914*, London: Routledge and Kegan Paul.

Perren, R., 1985, 'The retail and wholesale meat trade 1880–1939' in Oddy, D.J. and Miller, D.S., eds, *Diet and Health in Modern Britain*, London: Croom Helm.

Pyke, M., 1970, *Food Science and Technology*, 3rd edn, London: John Murray.

Reader, W.J., 1976, *Metal Box – a History*, London: Joseph.

Sykes, G., 1963, *Poultry – A Modern Agribusiness*, London: Lockwood.

Weddel, W. and Co., 1928, *Review of the Chilled and Frozen Meat Trade, 1927*, London: Weddel and Co.

Chapter 16
The European Food Industries in Perspective

Derek J. Oddy

In pre-industrial Europe, the uncertainty of harvests meant food supplies were unreliable. Subsistence crises were unpredictable so that people's health and even survival was very much a matter of chance. The dependence of households on their own produce and their own preservation of food declined during the nineteenth century to be supplemented and eventually replaced by external supplies and commercial processing and marketing of food. It is difficult to establish a general timescale for these changes even though they have been major themes in some earlier ICREFH symposia, notably the third in 1993 on Food Technology, Science and Marketing in the Twentieth Century, at Wageningen, in the Netherlands.[1] Discussions there took into account the concepts set out by Joseph Schumpeter in his *Theory of Economic Development*.[2] By separating invention from innovation, Schumpeter provided the logic for the early phases of the food industries. Business firms did not invent food: but by their innovations they developed raw produce into food products. This created the food chain, the lengthening of which is fundamental to the theme of this book. Perhaps nowhere was the food chain more evident than in ICREFH VIII, *The Diffusion of Food Culture in Europe from the late eighteenth century to the Present Day*.[3] However, the timing of diffusion and the degree of acceptance or resistance to innovation in connexion with foodstuffs has varied markedly: those nations on the western seaboard of Europe underwent a long progressive relationship with new and processed foods in the nineteenth century which countries in central and eastern Europe missed and for the first half of the twentieth century there was a marked development gradient from the advanced economies and consumer societies in the west of Europe which declined towards the east and south-east of Europe where mainly peasant societies did not share in these cultural changes in consumption. During the twentieth century, central as well as eastern Europe became not only the stage for major warfare as physical battlefields but also as the setting for the intolerance of rigid political systems until almost the end of the century. When these systems finally collapsed at the end of the 1980s, consumer preferences adapted rapidly to accommodate pent-up desires for previously unobtainable merchandize embellished with the trappings of packaging, branding and advertising that characterized 'products' as

---

1   Den Hartog, 1995, 1–6.
2   Schumpeter, 1951.
3   Oddy and Petráňová, 2005.

they became known when processed in the 'west' with its commercial television and food advertisements. Slovakia, for example, made this adaption in a matter of a decade, but in every case the expansion of the market for commercial food products, particularly those seen as representative of western capitalism – ice cream, processed milk products, soft drinks, confectionery and packaged frozen meals – depended upon purchasing power that was all too often absent.[4]

Until the beginning of the twentieth century there were only marginal changes in the food supplies of the countryside. For rural areas unaffected by the beginnings of industrialization, foodstuffs were limited in number and gave little choice or variety; cereals were the basis of the European diet whether as bread, pastry, pasta, dumplings or various porridge dishes. Variety depended upon vegetables, seasoning and small and often irregular items such as fats, sweeteners and pork or preserved meats; in many cases these were wrapped in heavy pastry as *pirogi* (or *piroshky*), *knedle* or *nödel* or pasties, creating a high-energy, filling diet. The food supply for towns was more complex: supplies required storing, loading and transporting with some bagging of individual items but this concerned durable produce – grains and vegetables – which were seasonally produced. The preindustrial regulation of the food supply survived in less industrial urban settlements in which the town authorities controlled markets, the weights and measures used, and assessed quality to the extent that food offered was not rotten. Food was sold mainly at market stalls but more permanent specialized outlets were developing which included chandlers, provision merchants and oilmen, though grocers, who carried on larger trades and broke bulk when importing valuable cargoes, operated on a scale beyond ordinary families' needs. As the nineteenth century progressed, urban health hazards such as cholera and fevers accentuated concerns about food and water supplies but until the beginning of modern disease theories from the 1880s onwards, the only solution was cleanliness and avoidance of contamination by waste, both human and animal. Indeed, separating humans from their animals was an important advance in domestic hygiene. In more progressive urban environments in Europe, food adulteration was recognized as a problem, though more as one of fraud than hygiene. A legislative process began to develop from the mid-nineteenth century onwards but its effectiveness was limited prior to any understanding of the aetiology of diseases. Its principal function, however, was to safeguard customers buying food and drink in local shops and markets and to provide retribution for complaining purchasers dissatisfied with the quality of goods. By 1914 food-quality legislation was in place in several west European countries. Food inspectors, independent analytical chemists and public laboratories for food analysis were increasing in number, while a series of International Congresses of Hygiene focused reformers' ideas on 'pure' food.[5] This nascent system of quality control operated by local authorities was eroded by

---

4   Dillnbergerová, 2005, 277–81.

5   For studies of this process in Brussels, London, Paris and various German cities, see Part B Food Regulation in ICREFH IX, Atkins, Lummel, and Oddy, 2007; also Paulus, 1974.

the growth of processing in the twentieth century and the geographic widening of supply and distribution systems.

During the nineteenth century industrial organization and technology had only a limited effect on food consumption patterns in Europe. For the bulk of the population, living in rural or semi-rural surroundings, only the miller and the baker might reduce the domestic labour of making bread for a family's immediate needs. Those in remote areas or without the money to buy domestic utensils in which to store and process flour or malt could obtain these items in small amounts from local traders where additional foods such as dried meats or fish might also be available.[6] For townsfolk, supplies from markets and bakers tended to supplement if not replace domestic production. Early on in its symposia, ICREFH assumed that it was possible to discuss European diet in general terms but soon realized that it did not exist as such: there were no common standards of cookery or behaviour. While richer people everywhere imitated Parisian cuisine, the commonality of food consumption in Europe lay in the low incomes of the majority of the population. Until food technology and transport developed, the food of the people was restricted to very few items beyond what gardens or smallholdings might produce. The perennial concern was to eke out supplies from one harvest to the next.

Food supplies were at best regional in source and long-distance trade in grain or north Atlantic dried fish had little impact for most European families. Some items sourced overseas – tea, coffee, cocoa and sugar – were expensive luxury goods with prices usually inflated by taxes. International imports of edible raw materials expanded as the century progressed, first, as sailing ships became larger and faster but the key to the growth of imports was the opening of the Suez Canal in 1869, which gave steamships an unmatchable advantage over sail when bringing cargoes from the Far East and Australasia. The principal source of sugar cane was its extensive cultivation in British, Dutch and French colonies in tropical areas such as Central America and the West Indies and the export of molasses to Europe led to sugar refining becoming a major industry in port towns like Amsterdam, Hamburg, Bristol and Nantes from the eighteenth century onwards. Sugar refining needed little equipment; pans to boil unrefined sugar and a simple centrifuge – initially powered by hand – to separate sugar crystals for retailing. The centrifuge was of major significance for the development of food industries since its rotative action was also of use in large scale dairies as a milk separator.

Innovation might well bring distrust of any new food product due to its strangeness and higher price. By the 1870s and 1880s, the lifestyle and diet of the industrial, urban working classes became a topic of common concern amongst reforming physicians, factory and school inspectors, military strategists and enlightened industrialists. Digestibility of foods also attracted reformers

---

6   See Stout, 1925, 40, 54, for the minimal dietary changes in the Shetland Isles to the north of Scotland. Even after the First World War, the only addition to a diet based on local cereals and potatoes with fish and some meat, was an occasional tin of corned beef or pineapple.

as dyspepsia was widely reported: it certainly provided a market for the new pharmaceutical industry and its somewhat less respectable competitors in the patent medicine industry, both of which were benefiting from the new pill or capsule production techniques in the late nineteenth century.[7]

Following from the factory legislation widely introduced in advanced European economies in the 1870s and the destabilization of bread-making by the new roller-milling technology, a market developed for 'improved' foods such as 'patent' flours. One early pioneer was Julius Maggi, a Swiss miller, whose production of cereal and pulse powders was intended to expand the range of workers' diets, improve the digestibility of their foods and limit alcoholism. Maggi developed a soup powder which interested his more affluent customers but which had little success with the workers. Maggi's product innovation in Switzerland must be compared with Dr. Klopfer's in Germany outlined in Chapter 2 prior to his business failure. Despite poor sales to begin with, Maggi's enterprise did not fail. Both entrepreneurs recognized the importance of advertising and both used slogans linked to health and wellbeing. Maggi's ultimate success was to enhance the taste of his cereal and pulse mixes by turning them into soup powders flavoured with spices and herbs.[8] The use of agricultural produce as raw materials was the starting point for a number of food industries in southern Europe, for example, the Italian tomato industry which introduced canning by the early twentieth century to become an important exporter to Britain and to Italian emigrants in the Americas.[9] Demand for food, especially novel foods, took raw materials away from earlier industrial uses. Chocolate, for example, was initially used by pharmacists but became a food when supplemented with sugar; olive oil, formerly used principally as an industrial lubricant also developed food uses by the late nineteenth century

Food Industries in the First Half of the Twentieth Century

The growth of food processing and manufacturing initially affected marketing systems in the industrializing districts of Western Europe. Traditional markets selling food as it arrived from growers, cattle dealers and fishermen began to give way to large wholesale markets in cities and bigger towns from which retail shops bought smaller amounts for their local needs. Permanent wholesale traders handled food needing transport, storage and distribution. The movement of food materials by water in ships, barges and lighters and on land the growing dependence on railways from the later part of the nineteenth century was essential to urban growth. Additionally, from early in the twentieth century the storage and transport of perishable foodstuffs depended upon refrigeration and specialized cold-storage facilities.

---

7   See Church and Tansey, 2007.

8   Schärer, 1995, 19–35.

9   Gentilcore, 2010.

Family firms developing locally-known products using brand names and easily recognizable advertising images were typical amongst food processors. Whatever production methods were used, product differentiation was of paramount importance. If this was to be achieved, brand names became essential to indicate quality.[10] The more successful achieved national markets but most brands did not travel beyond national boundaries unless within overseas empires where administrators and military personnel formed a ready market. Occasional examples of truly international brands, like Lipton's tea or Nestlé's milk products expanded beyond national frontiers. Switzerland also produced Ovaltine – a barley malt drink – which spread to Britain in 1909. However, for something like a century from, say, the 1880s to the 1970s, most food processing was specifically linked to domestic markets and economic nationalism, especially in the interwar years, limited foreign ownership of food manufacturers and raw material suppliers.[11] One novel international migrant was the breakfast cereal – a new sector of the grocery market from the end of the nineteenth century and dominated by the Kellogg and Quaker brands from the United States.

Protection of trademarks and brands became an essential marketing tool in the food industries from 1891 onwards. Attempts were made to establish the international registration of trademarks through a series of conferences.[12] Such movements collapsed in the face of increasing protectionism in the 1930s and the approach of war. One aspect that survived and grew during and after the Second World War was the influence of science and technology, as food manufacturers began to operate laboratories to control quality and to develop and introduce additives to their products. Industry was eager to embrace the developments in nutritional science when enhancement of product quality might be advantageous to sales; so that synthesizing vitamins in the interwar years led to the introduction of nutrient supplements.[13] As birth rates in interwar Europe fell, better nutrition for infants became an important consideration for parents and public health authorities alike, though nutritional enhancement of foods became more significant in the second half of the twentieth century as dietary factors became associated with coronary heart disease and sedentary ill-health.

---

10   See Penrose, 1951, 1959.

11   See Sandvik and Storli, 2013, 109–31, for Unilever's attempts to control the Scandinavian marine oil (whale, seal and fish) supplies to margarine producers.

12   The Madrid Agreement on the International Registration of Marks of 1891 was revised at Brussels in 1900, at Washington in 1911, at The Hague in 1925, and London in 1934.

13   See Horrocks, 1995, 7–18, Both Unilever and Glaxo advertised the vitamin content of their foods.

The Politics of Food in the Later Twentieth Century

The Second World War brought devastation to large areas of Europe through air attack and land warfare, which ruined many prewar businesses but marked the beginning of a new approach to food supplies, as governments of combatant nations, particularly the United Kingdom and later the United States, became major purchasers of foodstuffs internationally to feed their military personnel and, in due course, to feed people in liberated countries. Transporting food became a major problem and stimulated new techniques such as dehydration of raw produce, so that troops' ration packs might include dehydrated prepared meals. Some countries introduced fortification of foods with vitamins for their civilian populations.[14] These wartime innovations were the precursors to Accelerated Freeze Drying (AFD) techniques from which beverages like instant coffee developed in the postwar years.

European agriculture, the most productive source of food supplies in the 1930s, was decimated by the war. In anticipation of postwar food shortages, a meeting was convened at Hot Springs in the USA by President Franklin Roosevelt in 1943. This led to the formation in 1945 of the United Nations Food and Agriculture Organization (FAO) to which Sir John Orr, the eminent British nutritionist, was appointed as the first Director General.[15] Where the last campaigns of the war had been fought, civilian rations in Germany, Austria and Italy provided energy intakes varying from 1,600 kcals (6,694 kj) to 1,850 kcals (7,740 kj) per day, levels at which health and manual work were unsustainable for adult males.[16] Postwar food supplies to Europe formed part of American-led aid programmes such as the United Nations Relief and Rehabilitation Agency (UNRRA) which distributed food and farm implements to displaced persons. While such measures were seen as a political necessity to stabilize Europe before it was divided by the Iron Curtain, neither the US administration nor the British government would back the FAO plan for a World Food Board to hold stocks of food, which John Boyd Orr promoted tirelessly before his resignation from FAO in 1947.[17] The idea of stocks of food not controlled by the victorious western 'Great Powers' became politically unacceptable as fears of Euro-communism grew. In place of the World Food Board, General George Marshall, the US Secretary of State, proposed the European Recovery Programme which became popularly known as the Marshall Plan. The rising tension in Europe led America and Britain to

---

14   Fortification of foods with vitamins became government policy in Britain. See Hammond, 1951, 370.

15   Boyd Orr, 1966, 167–212.

16   Milward, 1984, 14. These are UNRRA figures for the crop year 1945–46; see also Schmidt, 2007, 69–70, for the effect of the black market on Berlin.

17   The US administration would not support an international organization holding food stocks, seeing it as an interference with a free market in food. Britain, as a major food importer, opposed the proposal as being likely to raise food prices.

oppose the USSR's blockade of access to the French, British and US zones of Berlin through the Soviet administered territory. The Berlin Blockade lasted from June 1948 to May 1949 during which time the western allies supplied their zones with food and fuel by air transports, including Sunderland flying boats using the Großer Wannsee to the south-west of Berlin to deliver salt. The Blockade grew into the Cold War and established permanent garrisons of troops from the United States, Britain and France in the western-administered zones of Germany. The Cold War also encompassed food as a strategic resource by American preferential treatment of Icelandic fisheries in return for a base in Iceland. The control of the Greenland and Denmark Straits allowed US and British navies and air forces to monitor Russian submarine movements. The presence of the American army and their families created a demand for familiar American foods and North American food-processing companies began to market in Europe and target European food producers as their subsidiaries.

Stability gradually returned to European agriculture after the uncertainties of the 1940s, especially once it became the subject of the Common Agricultural Policy (CAP) which followed the Treaty of Rome in 1957. Initially operating in the six founder members of the Common Market, the CAP aimed at raising farm incomes by a system of maintained prices and production subsidies, for example, for sugar beet. By the 1980s and early 1990s the European Commission's policies had stimulated over-production to the point that its 'food mountains' and milk and wine 'lakes' had become notorious. Limitation of production began with milk quotas from 1983 and a 'set-aside' land policy to reduce over-production of field crops. By contrast a Common Fisheries Policy (CFP) was not introduced until 1970 with the aim of modernizing the fisheries industries but the treatment of all fishing grounds as a 'common resource' distorted previous patterns of the industry and disrupted incomes in established fishing communities. The boundaries of European fishing waters were extended from 12 miles (22 km) to 200 miles (370 km) but over-fishing continued and catches declined. Increased regulation in the 1990s was widely criticized as wasteful.[18]

International regulation of the markets for the food industries was gradually re-established in the 1950s. The prewar Madrid Agreement on trademarks was revived at Nice in 1957 and reviewed in Stockholm ten years later.[19] The United States also looked favourably on the Common Agricultural Policy of the Common Market as cementing alliances in Western Europe. The recovery of European economies saw US brands of soft drinks (Coca-Cola and Pepsi) and fast-food outlets spread across Europe, not just on American bases but as stand-alone economic ventures eager to enter new markets. Beginning with Wimpy's hamburgers in the late 1940s, Kentucky Fried Chicken and Pizza Hut in the 1960s, the invasion by American

---

18   Swinbank, 1994, 249–63; European Commission, 2007.

19   Following further amendment in 1979, the Madrid system for the registration and maintenance of trademark rights has been administered by the World Intellectual Property Organization (WIPO) in Geneva, Switzerland.

fast-food chains was completed by McDonald's and Burger King in the 1970s.[20] Fast-food retailers were accompanied by large food manufacturers and multiple retailers seeking to enter the European markets. Wal-mart became the owner of Asda supermarkets in Britain, and other food and drink manufacturing companies, both North American and European, sought to profit from taking over 'national champions' in various European countries. Pillsbury, Kraft, Sara Lee, Seagram and General Mills all sought European subsidiaries while Nestlé aimed at widening its penetration of the European food market. European multiple retailers also wanted to expand internationally: Carrefour established an extensive network in Spain and Belgium, a significant presence in Bulgaria, Greece and Italy, and some outlets in Slovakia and Slovenia. Tesco expanded into Eastern Europe, notably in Hungary, but also opened numbers of outlets in the Czech Republic, Poland and Slovakia. By the end of the twentieth century European consumers were experiencing an increasing standardization of food products of similar quality grades on retailers' shelves.

The stability of the Cold War in Western Europe allowed German, French, Dutch and British food producers to expand in the second half of the twentieth century to the point that the largest European food manufacturers – Danone, Nestlé and Unilever – grew to be amongst the world's biggest companies. All three concentrated on high volume, rapid turnover, branded goods with high value-added content in fields such as dairy products, spreads, confectionery, ice cream, breakfast cereals, baby foods, bottled water, tea and coffee. By the 1990s technology transfer to Eastern Europe established a business firm, the European Food group, in Romania. Utilizing Swedish venture-capital, this company created European Drinks, European Food and Scandic Distilleries.

Developments in Technology

Developments in frozen-food technology post-Second World War made significant advances during the 1950s and early 1960s; more married women worked away from the home, more television sets were bought and branded foods began to be advertised on television. The 1970s and 1980s also saw the expansion in the range of frozen-food products for commercial cook-freeze catering by airlines and large-scale institutions such as hospitals and schools, but especially as ready-prepared meals for domestic use which became a leading line in supermarkets. By the end of the century, retailers' 'fresh food' operations were predominantly chilled or frozen foods. The growth and dispersed nature of the food market led multiple retailers to establish their own distribution systems with large regional centres often located for motorway access. The selling of frozen foods also required extensive infrastructure in the shops and cold stores, such as the development of battery-operated fork-lift trucks which could function at low temperatures for

---

20   Oddy, 2003, 194–5.

long periods. The integration of these facilities grew as the grocery market became increasingly dominated by a small number of large-scale supermarkets.

Frozen foods were initially delivered to shops in the 1960s by refrigerated 12-ton vans, but larger loads and larger vehicles with refrigerated trailers began to be used from the 1970s onwards.[21] High inflation in the 1970s led multiple retailers to question whether capital should be tied up in their own road-transport fleets. Supermarkets began to employ specialist contractors operating refrigerated-trailer units for distribution to their branches. Out-sourcing logistics became a major trend in the 1990s with specialist firms offering to store and transport foodstuffs using a wider range of temperature-controlled bands below ambient temperatures, from 'produce' to 'chilled' and 'frozen'. The growing range of products made the refrigerated-trailer units of firms such as Exel, Frigoscandia, Gist, and Christian Salvesen a familiar sight on European motorways. Other movements of foodstuffs involved transshipment of air cargoes at airports; these were generally loaded on pallets for which standard Euro-pallet trailers were introduced. However, the desire to maximize space utilization on trailers led to the development of 'composite' vehicles, capable of operating at different temperatures for different loads. During the 1990s the development of 'convenience' shops by retailers required smaller vehicles to supply city-centre stores. This was accompanied by the growth of courier firms operating refrigerated vans capable of handling loads from 200 to 300 litres as smaller refrigeration units (Hubbard, Carrier) became available.

Frozen foods became generally available for domestic use from the mid-twentieth century onwards. They removed the seasonality of vegetable and fruit supply and made variety available all year round. While frozen foods were of selected quality, their prices were higher; nevertheless the growing affluence of many households provided the purchasing power to buy home refrigerators with a small frozen-food compartment. From the late 1960s onwards domestic deep-freezers to store frozen foods became available. The increasing proportion of married women working increased household income but also reduced the time available for food preparation. This increased the utility of 'convenience foods' which needed no preparation.

Table 16.1 shows that the world trade of fresh (perishable) foodstuffs doubled from 1985 to the year 2000. At sea, refrigerated shipping expanded significantly to handle all forms of fresh food, with substantial quantities of meat, fish, dairy produce, bananas, citrus and other fruits criss-crossing the world in refrigerated ships. 'Reefer' ships are effectively large refrigerators, heavily insulated with glass fibre or similarly efficient materials.[22] Since the 1980s, specialist reefer ships have seen their cargoes increasingly taken by large container ships provided

---

21   In Britain, rigid-bodied two-axle 'reefer' vehicles up to 17 tons, frequently equipped with Thermo King refrigeration units, were used by specialist frozen-food firms up to the end of the twentieth century.

22   Below decks a reefer ship resembles a large modern warehouse, and cargo is usually carried and handled on pallets, moved about on conveyors or by electric fork-lift

Table 16.1   World trade in major perishable commodities, 1980–2000 (million tons)

Year	Bananas	Citrus fruits	Deciduous fruits	Other fruit and vegetables	Dairy products	Meat	Fish	Total Trade
1980	6.89	6.92	4.86	7.86	2.84	8.10	4.33	41.60
1981	6.92	6.76	5.38	7.98	3.02	8.86	4.50	43.41
1982	7.13	6.86	5.13	8.38	2.91	8.59	4.45	43.45
1983	6.27	6.63	5.49	7.71	2.91	8.94	5.23	43.18
1984	6.87	7.10	5.32	8.05	3.09	8.79	5.43	44.64
1985	6.74	6.81	5.36	8.54	3.09	9.07	6.22	45.82
1986	7.26	8.05	5.52	9.23	3.07	9.91	7.30	50.36
1987	7.52	7.51	5.79	10.24	3.61	10.16	7.59	52.43
1988	7.73	7.50	5.72	10.36	3.78	10.73	8.40	54.24
1989	8.21	7.45	5.71	10.91	3.46	11.30	8.58	55.61
1980	9.34	7.74	6.25	11.36	3.28	11.57	9.03	58.58
1991	10.38	7.64	6.63	12.41	3.54	12.75	9.60	62.96
1992	10.63	7.97	6.97	12.64	3.70	13.51	9.70	65.11
1993	11.12	8.56	7.77	12.56	3.83	14.03	9.84	67.72
1994	12.53	9.29	8.18	13.84	3.89	15.64	10.52	73.88
1995	13.41	9.08	8.50	13.13	3.93	16.53	10.86	75.43
1996	13.91	10.41	8.66	15.37	4.08	17.56	10.90	80.89
1997	13.99	10.72	9.28	15.39	4.31	18.60	11.23	83.72
1998	13.50	9.49	9.06	16.31	4.34	19.41	11.56	83.67
1999	14.67	10.44	9.30	16.74	4.36	20.80	11.91	88.22
2000	15.04	10.70	9.53	17.16	4.47	21.32	12.20	90.43

Note: These data are total world trade, and combine land-based and seaborne trade.
Sources: United Nations, Food and Agriculture Organization, *FAO Trade Yearbook* and *FAO Yearbook of Fishery Statistics,* Rome: various dates; *Clarkson's Reefer Register,* 2002.

with multiple refrigeration units. Cargoes can be carried frozen, chilled, cooled or increasingly at controlled temperatures that can be varied to ensure that the produce reaches the market at its optimum condition, often ripening on the voyage. With the increase in exotic food cargoes, special containers have been devised that can tailor their internal atmosphere to the precise requirement of the foodstuffs.

Customers in European supermarkets take for granted the source of the fruit and vegetables in their baskets: continual availability has destroyed any traditional seasonality. Vegetables from Africa and fruit from South America testify to the use of air transport for some items to reach the retailers' shelves. However, the scale of the food industries in the later twentieth century has required a growing refrigerated container trade by sea as well, plus the bulk cargoes handled by commodity traders like Cargill, Glencore and Yara, which include carrying agricultural produce – grains, palm oil, cocoa and soy beans – not all of which is intended for conventional human consumption as food. Some raw materials are used in food-manufacturing processes as flavourings or texturizers, but more specific other uses have included animal feedstuffs, materials to make bio-fuels, or as raw materials for the cosmetics and health products trade. Yara, the Norwegian agricultural chemical company, typifies the extension of agribusiness. Between 1978 and 1990 it acquired NSM (Netherlands), Supra (Sweden), Fisons (UK), Ruhr Sticstoff (Germany), Windmill (Netherland), and Cofaz (France). Under the name Hydro, Yara delivers plant nutrition and agronomic advice. Hydro is one of the most important suppliers of input factors to the food industry in Europe.[23] Some major European pharmaceutical companies such as BASF or Bayer have food products or nutrition divisions which supply a range of fine chemicals to beverage producers and food manufacturers including preservatives, stabilizers and vitamins to fortify food products. The Dutch company Nutreco was created from a buy-out of BP's nutrition businesses to sell animal feedstuffs and poultry meat for fresh and frozen pre-packed products in the Netherlands and for processing in Spain.[24] Another link in the food chain seldom recognized is that of the producers of the packaging materials associated with ready-prepared meals; preformed plastic containers and wooden or plastic disposable implements for the more informal methods of consuming food products.

An Overview of Change

Although Chapters 2 to 15 may seem disparate studies which are limited in their extent, together they contribute important dimensions to our understanding of the food industries. They offer case studies which illustrate technical developments

---

trucks. Large reefer ships might carry about 500,000 cubic feet of refrigerated space, and load 250 containers on deck.

23   See http://www.yara.com/

24   Nutreco website http://www.nutreco.com/

*"The wife always has dinner waiting
on the table for me"*

Source: PRIVATE EYE / S.J. Russell, issue 1285, 23.

**Figure 16.1   The value of convenience foods: you can always invite a colleague
home for a meal**

in a number of industries, show the importance of brands and trademarks to the
marketing of food and the significance of advertisements and the sales environment
in stimulating purchasing and consumption. Changes from the Second World War
onwards, as the study on retailing in Sweden in chapter 12 shows, nullified the
customer's traditional skills and knowledge of food quality. Self-service and sealed
packaging negated even the local shopkeeper's knowledge of product quality:
wholesalers, multiple retailers and even the supermarkets in the later twentieth
century concentrated on price and large-scale availability of products from their
suppliers more than on their composition.

The second half of the twentieth century has been marked by convenience
foods and kitchen implements designed to facilitate leisure in the home. This
discussion of various facets of the food industries cannot be comprehensive and
some generalizations about European food industries go beyond the content of
these chapters but the general pattern of development can be derived from them.

The 'biological *ancien régime*' broke down in the course of the nineteenth
century in areas of advanced industrial and urban economies. This progress was
uneven and large parts of Europe, where low-income subsistence agriculture and
handicraft work persisted, remained in poverty and continued to experience limited
choices of foods and restricted diets. By the beginning of the twentieth century
governments across Europe were becoming interested in the physical state of their
populations. Improvements to diets and health care, while very limited, began to
be seen, though poverty and undernutrition continued in the aftermath of the First
World War. Famine in the Volga region of Russia and acute malnutrition in Austria;

both attracted relief from the League of Nations.[25] The resumption of progress in the 1920s was terminated by the collapse of the international financial and trading system in 1931; deprivation returned to areas of Europe where unemployment was widespread and totalitarian regimes introduced *Verbrauchslenkung* (controlled consumption) in Germany and caused famine in Soviet Russia.[26] The Second World War combined privation and feeding programmes ranging from the beginning of the welfare state in Scandinavia and Britain to the '*Hongersnood*' (famine) winter of 1944-45 in the Netherlands and widespread deprivation in Germany and other territories of her former allies and dependencies. Economic recovery, which resulted in part from Cold War expenditure by the United States and other North Atlantic Treaty Organization countries, brought the return of work, incomes and a feeling of prosperity as the 'economic miracle' (*Wirtschaftswunder*) developed in Europe. It provided the basis for the '*Fresswelle*' or wave of gluttony (as it has been inappropriately termed) which would be better regarded as a 'catching-up consumption' phase when markets returned to peacetime conditions across Europe during the 1950s and early 1960s and a greater variety of foods became available for meals.

The modern European food industries expanded into their present structures during the second half of the twentieth century but for consumers the basic fact is that an ever-lengthening food chain has been built up which ranges from producers (both national and multinational) to food processors and manufacturers together with a hierarchy of ancillary contributors from machinery designers, equipment suppliers, pharmaceutical and chemical companies to printers, packaging firms, transport undertakings and including advertising agencies and public relations firms. The European food industries have created a huge variety of 'products' since the Second World War which have been presented to consumers mainly through the agency of multiple retailers. The use of the word 'product' means much more than food. A 'product' is food that has been cut, weighed, cleaned, and often pre-cooked, sealed in a stable gas atmosphere by plastic film and boxed in highly coloured and decorated cardboard or plastic trays on which appears not only the manufacturer's name and information on its nutritional composition but even recommendations on its appropriate use. Some products are advertised as 'novelties' to attract the consumer and encourage consumption. The manufacturer adds sugar, salt, texturizers and flavourings to enhance the attractiveness of the product's taste in the hope that consumers will buy more and eat more, while shops have developed attractive environments to encourage purchasing and consumption. In the last quarter of the twentieth century, new developments have concentrated on high-value-added lines like cereal and potato snack foods created by extrusion technology, milk products such as deserts and 'health' foods and sugary 'energy

---

25   Wheatcroft, 1993.

26   See Schmidt, 2009, 150. For Soviet Russia, see Davies and Wheatcroft, 2004; for Austria see Nussbaumer and Exenberger, 2009, 15–32.

drinks' containing stimulants such as caffeine.[27] Food manufacturers introduced terms like 'nutraceuticals or 'probiotic' foods which claim to lower cholesterol, provide minerals and vitamins or include 'lactobacilli'.

Not all these developments were advantageous to consumers. The length and complexity of the food chain in Europe since the Second World War has led to underlying apprehensions. Throughout the Cold War era of the 1950s and 1960s food was thought to be open to contamination by nuclear fallout, whether accidental or as a byproduct of conflict. More specifically, in the mid-1960s alarm amongst European consumers was aroused over the ethics of industrialized food by Rachel Carson's description of North American systems of food production based on the use of chemical pesticides, fungicides and herbicides.[28] Dietary phobias increased when it was reported that antibiotics and hormones were used to promote livestock growth and increase milk yields. Concern also began to be expressed about the use of dyes to colour foods lest they might have carcinogenic properties Further anxiety arose from the practice of using meat-and-bone meal (MBM) to increase the protein content of the diet of beef cattle.

During the 1980s and 1990s even more threatening food scares emerged, initially in the United Kingdom, where food manufacturing was most advanced. In 1982, a new *Escherichia* pathogen, *E. coli* O157 was identified in meat and meat products. Consumption of infected products led to acute sickness and even deaths. During the 1990s similar outbreaks were reported in Canada, the USA, Japan, Sweden, Germany and Australia. *E. coli* O157 was followed from 1986 by another zoonotic disease, Bovine Spongiform Encephalopathy (BSE), which in humans developed as variant Creutzfeldt Jakob Disease (vCJD).[29] These examples suggest that the growing complexity of the food chain in the late twentieth century was accompanied by a rising number of health hazards. One factor supporting this view is the growing internationalization of the supply chain in Europe which makes surveillance of raw food materials and processing at source difficult for manufacturers to supervise. By the end of the twentieth century the creation of a 'single market' in Europe meant some major supermarkets had become multinationals and were sourcing food materials European-wide and beyond. International control of food quality did not exist prior to the European Food Safety Act, 1990, while the ineffective European Food Safety Authority only came into existence at Parma, Italy, in 2002. No European country mounted a fully effective food quality assessment system as the twenty-first century dawned and the horsemeat scandal across Europe as this book goes to press bears testimony to these shortcomings.

---

27   These products include Benecol (Raisio, Finland), Actimel and Activia (Danone), Yakult (Yakult Honsha, Japan) and Red Bull (Austria, 1987) the most popular energy drink.

28   Carson, 1962. Consumers were alarmed by the extensive use of the insecticide dichlorodiphenyltrichloroethane (DDT).

29   Pennington, 2000, 2–9.

The European diet at the end of the twentieth century comprises foods which are increasingly energy dense and accompanied by a lifestyle that is predominantly sedentary in character. Rising body weights, larger clothing-size measurements and adverse health consequences, such as diabetes, bear out these observations. Today, the food chain has lengthened beyond the imagination of people living in the preindustrial world. The uncertainties which were ever present from season to season in the past have been reduced, at least for European consumers, to occasional empty shelves in the supermarket instead of subsistence crises.

References

Atkins, P.J., Lummel, P. and Oddy, D.J., eds, 2007, *Food and the City in Europe since 1800*, Aldershot: Ashgate.

Carson, R., 1962, 1965, *Silent Spring*, Boston: Houghton Mifflin; Harmondsworth: Penguin.

Church, R. and Tansey, E.M., 2007, *Burroughs Wellcome and Co.*, Lancaster: Crucible.

Clarkson Research Studies Ltd, 2002, *Clarkson's ship register: Clarkson's Reefer Register, 2002*, London: Clarkson Research Services, Ltd.

Davies, R.W. and Wheatcroft, S.G., 2004, *The Years of Hunger: Soviet Agriculture, 1931–1933*, Basingstoke, New York: Palgrave Macmillan.

Dillnbergerová, S., 2005, 'Industry, business and mass media as determining factors in nutrition in Slovakia', in ICREFH VIII: Oddy, D.J. and Petráňová, L., eds, 2005, *The Diffusion of Food Culture from the late eighteenth century to the present day*, Prague: Academia.

European Commission, 2007, Directorate-General for Agriculture and Rural Development, *The Common Agricultural Policy Explained*, Luxembourg, Europa.

Gentilcore, D., 2010, *Pomodoro!: a history of the tomato in Italy*, New York: Columbia.

Hammond, R.J., 1951, *History of the Second World War, Food volume I The Growth of Policy*, London: HMSO and Longmans Green.

Hartog, A.P. den, ed., 1995, *Food Technology, Science and Marketing in the Twentieth Century*, East Linton, Scotland: Tuckwell.

Horrocks, S.M., 1995, 'Nutrition science and the food industry in Britain, 1920–1990' in ICREFH III: Hartog, A.P. den, ed., *Food Technology, Science and Marketing in the Twentieth Century*, East Linton, Scotland: Tuckwell.

Milward A.S., 1984, *The Reconstruction of Western Europe 1945–51*, London: Methuen.

Nussbaumer, J. and Exenberger, A., 2009, 'Century of Hunger, Century of Plenty: How abundance arrived in Alpine valleys' in ICREFH X: Oddy, D.J., Atkins, P.J., and Amilien, V., eds, *The Rise of Obesity in Europe A Twentieth Century Food History*, Farnham: Ashgate.

Oddy, D.J., 2003, *From Plain Fare to Fusion Food*, Woodbridge, Suffolk: Boydell.

Oddy, D.J. and Petráňová, L., eds, 2005, *The Diffusion of Food Culture from the late eighteenth century to the present day*, Prague: Academia.

Orr, Lord Boyd, 1966, *As I Recall*, London: Macgibbon and Kee.

Paulus, I., 1974, *The Search for Pure Food: A Sociology of Legislation in Britain*, London: Robertson.

Pennington, T.H., 2000, 'BSE and *E coli* food crises' in ICREFH V; Fenton, A., ed., *Order and Disorder: The Health Implications of Eating and Drinking in the Nineteenth and Twentieth Centuries*, East Linton, Scotland: Tuckwell.

Penrose, E.T., 1951, *The Economics of the International Patent System*, Baltimore: Johns Hopkins.

Penrose, E.T., 1959, *The theory of the growth of the firm*, Oxford: Blackwell.

Sandvik, P.T. and Storli, E., 2013, 'Big business and small states: Unilever and Norway in the interwar years', *Econ. Hist. Rev.*, 66, 1.

Schärer, M.R., 1995, 'Analysis of nutritional status, the food industry and product innovation in the late nineteenth century, with reference to prefabricated pulse powder' in ICREFH III: Hartog, A.P. den, ed., *Food Technology, Science and Marketing in the Twentieth Century*, East Linton, Scotland: Tuckwell.

Schmidt, J., 2007, 'How to Feed Three Million Inhabitants: Berlin in the First Years after the Second World War, 1945-1948' in ICREFH IX, Atkins, P.J., Lummel, P. and Oddy, D.J., eds, *Food and the City in Europe since 1800*, Aldershot: Ashgate.

Schmidt, J., 2009, 'Diet, body types, inequality and gender: Discourses on "proper nutrition" in German magazines and newspapers (c.1930–2000)' in ICREFH X: Oddy, D.J., Atkins, P.J., and Amilien, V., eds, *The Rise of Obesity in Europe A Twentieth Century Food History*, Farnham: Ashgate.

Schumpeter, J.A., 1951, *The Theory of Economic Development*, Cambridge: Harvard.

Stout, M.B., 1925, *Cookery for Northern Wives*, Lerwick: Manson (Shetland Heritage Publications facsimile edition).

Swinbank, A., 1994, 'The EC's policies and its food' in ICREFH II: Burnett, J. and Oddy, D.J., eds, *The Origins and Development of Food Policies in Europe*, London, Leicester University Press.

United Nations, Food and Agriculture Organization, *FAO Trade Yearbook* and *FAO Yearbook of Fishery Statistics*, Rome: various dates.

Wee, H. van der, 1986, *Prosperity and upheaval: the world economy 1945–1980*, London: Viking.

Wheatcroft, S.G., 1993, 'Famine and food consumption records in early Soviet history, 1917–25', in Geissler, C. and Oddy, D.J., eds, *Food, Diet and Economic Change Past and Present*, Leicester: Leicester University Press.

Index

adulteration 45, 119, 168–71, 173–4, 248
advertising 33–4, 43, 75, 102–3, 107, 109,
    111n, 112, 115n, 116, 125–7, 151,
    169, 172–3, 185, 188, 193, 200,
    242, 247, 250–51, 259
agriculture 1, 2, 5, 21, 23, 31, 49, 52, 65n,
    76n, 122–3, 194, 223, 231, 236,
    252–3, 258
Amsterdam 19, 166n, 170, 172–3, 175, 249
Appert, Nicolas 7, 91n, 165, 199

beer 18, 20, 108–10, 112, 114, 166, 168–9,
    171
    brewing 3–4, 17, 108
Belgium 3, 8n, 25, 121, 170, 199,
    200–202, 254
    Flemish women's magazines 11, 199,
        200, 210
    food rationing 1940–48 203, 205, 207
    preserves 199, 202–3, 205, 207, 209
Birdseye, Clarence 11, 147, 149

canned foods 11, 199–202, 204–5, 207–10
    can openers 7, 207
    sterilization (sterilizing) 7–8, 91, 203,
        206, 210, 239
Chaptal, J.A. 60, 64, 91n
cheese 2n, 9, 10, 41, 47, 55–68, 172, 175,
    185, 244
    cheese industry 55–6, 59, 63
    Roquefort cheese 55–66
chocolate 6, 9–10, 22–3, 65, 91–3, 95, 97,
    99, 101–4
coffee 9, 19, 22, 24, 33, 126, 167–8, 170,
    185, 190, 249, 252, 254
convenience foods 17, 24, 152, 213, 242,
    255, 258
Czech lands, later Czechoslovakia, then
    Czech Republic 10, 107–117, 254

Anniversary Land Exhibition, 1891
    107–9, 112, 116
    beer 108–10, 112, 114
    chocolate 107, 111–16
    Turkish Delight 110–12

dairies 60, 64, 122, 171, 237n, 249
Denmark 3, 6, 11, 133–4, 137,138, 140, 187
drinks 6, 248, 253–4, 260
    energy drinks 259–60
    instant coffee 252

Europe
    advanced economies 12, 247
        development gradient 247
    agriculture 1–2, 5, 21, 23, 31, 49, 52,
        122–3, 194, 223, 231, 236, 252–3,
        258
    food supplies 1, 3–4, 203, 231, 247–9,
        251–2
    demography, 1, 4, 223, 231, 249, 252,
        258; *see also* population
    urbanization xiii, 4, 23, 30, 44, 64,
        119, 181n, 231

famine 1, 258–9
fishing 8, 96, 148–53, 156–9, 253
    demersal fish 152, 154
        factory freezer-trawlers 152
        trawl-fishing, trawlers 149, 151–2,
            157–8
    fish fingers 147, 155
    pelagic fish 147n
    salted cod (klipfish) 149–51
    stockfish (dried cod) 3, 149–51, 157–9
food brand names and trademarks 4, 9,
    166, 170–71, 173, 251
    Madrid System (1891) 173, 251n, 253
food industries 1, 5, 7–10, 12, 17, 26, 60,
    194, 231, 247, 249–51, 253, 257–9

flour 2–3, 5–6, 18, 26, 29, 31–2, 34,
        47, 52, 92, 110, 166, 170, 183–4,
        215, 217–18, 221, 226–7, 249, 250
palatability of products 7, 43, 231, 235
food labelling and packaging 165–76, 188
food manufacturers 10, 157–8, 168, 170,
        174, 176, 185, 239–40, 243, 251,
        254, 257, 260
    jam and marmalade makers 42, 47,
        48n, 50, 51
    sauce and pickle makers 42–51
        Crosse and Blackwell 42, 44–8,
            50–51
        Lazenby 42–3, 51
food retailers 4, 34, 237, 254
    butchers 8, 107, 236–7, 242–3
    grocers and provision merchants 43,
        46, 103, 237, 248
    supermarkets 12, 148, 175, 181, 188,
        190, 238–9, 243, 254–5, 257–8, 260
food quality 5, 9, 11, 20, 29, 31, 33, 41,
        43, 45–6, 52, 57, 64, 72, 75–6,
        78, 80, 93, 99n, 112, 123–4, 137,
        152–5, 169, 171–2, 174, 184–5n,
        188–9, 192, 210, 238–9, 242, 248,
        251, 254–5, 258, 260; *see also*
        adulteration
food trade 5, 185
    bio-fuels 257
    commodity traders 10, 257
    North America 5, 8, 10, 231, 233,
        253–4, 260
    Southern Hemisphere 8, 12, 231
    Suez Canal 249
    transatlantic telegraph cables 10
France
    chocolate (Menier company) 91–3, 95,
        97, 99, 101–4
    industrial organization – *societé*
        anonyme 60–63, 66, 93n
    Parisian cuisine 249
    Saulnier, Jules, architect, 94–5n, 97,
        99, 100n
    Tellier, Charles 65, 99
    World Fairs (1889, 1900) 103

Germany 3–4, 10, 17–18, 20–25, 27–9,
        32, 103n, 104n, 108–9, 119, 121–3,

        125, 126–7, 133–4, 148–9, 156,
        170, 172, 174–6, 181, 187, 250,
        252–3, 257, 259–260
    beet sugar 17–23n
    health foods 17–18
    Wirtschaftswunder 175
Great Britain 1, 4–6, 8–12, 25, 41, 47n, 52,
        104, 124–5, 127n 134, 136, 148–50,
        152–3, 171–2, 231–2, 235–42,
        244–5, 250–54, 255n, 259–60
    fishing industry 8, 152–3
    food manufacturing 260
        extrusion technology 240, 259
    industrial poultry production 12,
        238–43, 245
    irradiation 239
    London 7, 10, 42–7, 49–51, 91, 165,
        168n, 231–3, 236–7, 248n, 251n
        food manufacturing districts 7, 42,
            44–6, 48n, 50–51, 165
    meat 2–3, 7–9, 11–12, 42–4, 46, 52,
        134, 231–45, 248–9, 255–7, 260
        Bovine spongiform encephalopathy
            (BSE) 240n, 242, 260
        mechanically recovered meat (MRM)
            240–41
Great Depression (1874–1896) 63, (1930s)
        148
    falling cereal prices 122

hygiene and public health 11, 31, 34, 98,
        100, 103, 120, 124, 166, 169–70,
        173–6, 184, 189, 213, 227, 239–40,
        248, 251

Iceland 8, 31, 147–51, 153–9, 253
    Icelandic companies in the USA 154
industrialization xiii, 2, 4–5, 12, 17–18,
        23, 55, 59–61, 63–4, 119, 133–4,
        137, 144, 248
intellectual property 66, 253n
    patents 6, 67
Italy xiii, 2, 4, 8, 71–2n, 73n, 75n, 76–85,
        134, 149, 187, 236n, 252, 254, 260

machinery (food) and equipment 8n, 71–3,
        75–6, 78, 84, 99, 108n, 110, 183,
        232, 234

centrifuge 7, 31, 240, 249
Maggi, Julius 28–9, 250
margarine 6–7, 9–10, 48, 119–27, 138n,
    168, 171–3, 185, 242, 251n
    Dutch production in Kleve 119, 121,
        125, 127
    kosher margarine 124–5
    Mège, Hippolyte (Mège-Mouriès) 6, 120
    'mixed butter' (adulterated fats) 119,
        121, 123–4
    import duty imposed by Bismarck
        121–2
Marshall, Alfred 55
Marshall Plan, *see* Wars, Cold War
meat products and processed meat 2–3, 7,
        8–9, 11–12, 27, 29, 33, 44, 46, 52,
        165, 167, 189, 199, 208–9, 236–7,
        239–45, 248–9, 257, 260
microwave ovens 240, 243, 245
milk (including processed milk) 5–7, 9,
        55–7, 62–4, 95, 104, 116, 120,
        122–3, 125, 167–8, 170–71, 199,
        218, 248–9, 251, 253, 259–60
Mintz, Sidney 24n, 213

Netherlands 3, 6, 8n, 11, 19, 21–2,
        119–21, 125, 165, 169–70, 172–6,
        187, 247, 257, 259
    condensed milk 6, 167
    Housewives, Association of 172–5
Norway 3, 8, 147–151, 153, 157–9, 181,
        187, 257
    Finnmark 157
    Frionor 158
    Yara 257
nutrition 9, 11, 18–19, 24, 28–9, 31–2,
        35–6, 52, 119, 133–44, 165, 176,
        208–10, 218, 243–4, 251–2, 257–9
    nutritionists 136, 141, 145, 165
    vitamins 9, 140–41, 143, 218, 251–2,
        257, 260

olive-oil industry 71, 76–7, 81, 83–4
    edible olive oil 72, 74–5, 78–80,
        83–4
    industrial lubrication 4, 72, 74
    olive pomace 75

packaging
    Åkerlund and Rausing
        Rausing (formerly Anderrson), R.
            182–4, 188, 190, 194
        Törnqvist, G. 182–3
population 1–5, 11, 23, 34, 64, 100, 108–
        9, 119, 122, 135, 137, 140, 143,
        150, 170, 185, 187, 203, 213–14n,
        217, 222–6, 231, 249, 252, 258
preservation of food
    cellophane 147, 155, 176, 188n
    glass jars and bottles 7, 41, 44, 46, 51,
        115, 166, 168–71, 174
    Owen, M.J. 168
    pergament 155
    polyvinylchloride (PVC) 240
    pottery vessels 41, 47,
    sugar 6–7, 41, 206–7, 240
    vinegar 41, 44–5, 50–51, 207, 240

rationalization 23, 28, 30, 48n, 91, 97–8,
        182, 193–4
refrigeration 8, 65, 67, 91, 99, 148, 210,
        232, 250, 255, 257
    commercial refrigeration 8, 65, 67, 91,
        99, 148, 232, 255
        cold storage 8, 124. 232, 236, 250,
            255
    domestic cold storage
        freezers 11, 148, 201–2, 210, 255
        refrigerators 11, 201–3, 210
    marine refrigeration, *see* shipping
restaurants 100, 109n, 152, 156
Romania
    baked goods as convenience foods 213
    European Food Group 254
    mămăligă 2, 213, 222, 224–7
    pellagra 2n, 11–12, 213, 227
Russia (and USSR) 1, 3, 112n–113n, 153,
        156, 253, 258–9

scientific research 63, 67, 96–7, 138, 245,
        248, 251
    Hamel Roos, Dr P.F. van, 171
shipping 98, 231–4, 250, 255, 257
    refrigerated ships 236, 255, 257
Spain 10, 58, 71–2n, 75–85, 149, 187,
        254, 257

sugar
    beet sugar 7, 18, 20, 22, 23, 253
    sugar cane 7, 18–21, 101, 249
    sugar refining 20, 249
Sweden 11, 181–3, 185–7, 193–4, 257–8,
    260
    Packaging Standardization research 188
       housewives' reaction 188–9
    Self service 186–94
    'Sell Quick' cartons 188–9

tea 9, 19, 22, 33, 42, 48, 167–8, 237n, 249,
    251, 254
television 185, 241–2, 245, 248, 254

United Nations
    Food and Agriculture Organization
       (FAO) 252
    Relief and Rehabilitation Agency
       (UNRRA) 252
United States of America (USA) 6, 11,
    148–9, 153–4, 156–8, 168–9,181,
    186, 252, 260
    Roosevelt, President Franklin D. 252
    Hot Springs conference, 1943 252

Van den Bergh 119–21, 125–7
    Brands (Tomor, Vitello, Sana,
       Blauband) 125–6
    formed Margarine Union and later
       Unilever 127

wars
    Cold War 157, 239, 242, 253–4,
       259–60
       Marshall Aid 156
    Napoleonic wars 1–2
    World War I 6, 81, 114, 169
    World War II 8, 11, 151, 176
       American Lend-Lease Aid 238
       spam 237–8
weights and measures 9, 19n, 21n, 174,
    189, 218, 248, 261
women
    food preparation and shopping 209
       household income 255
       leisure 226, 242
       work 11, 24, 50, 60, 67, 168, 201, 202,
       208, 226, 242, 255

For Product Safety Concerns and Information please contact our
EU representative GPSR@taylorandfrancis.com / Taylor & Francis
Verlag GmbH, Kaufingerstraße 24, 80331 München, Germany